T0214479

Lecture Notes in Computer Science   11348

Commenced Publication in 1973
Founding and Former Series Editors:
Gerhard Goos, Juris Hartmanis, and Jan van Leeuwen

More information about this series at http://www.springer.com/series/7410

Anupam Chattopadhyay · Chester Rebeiro
Yuval Yarom (Eds.)

Security, Privacy, and Applied Cryptography Engineering

8th International Conference, SPACE 2018
Kanpur, India, December 15–19, 2018
Proceedings

 Springer

Editors
Anupam Chattopadhyay 🆔
School of Computer Science and
Engineering
Nanyang Technological University
Singapore, Singapore

Yuval Yarom 🆔
University of Adelaide
Adelaide, Australia

Chester Rebeiro 🆔
Indian Institute of Technology Madras
Chennai, India

ISSN 0302-9743 ISSN 1611-3349 (electronic)
Lecture Notes in Computer Science
ISBN 978-3-030-05071-9 ISBN 978-3-030-05072-6 (eBook)
https://doi.org/10.1007/978-3-030-05072-6

Library of Congress Control Number: 2018962545

LNCS Sublibrary: SL4 – Security and Cryptology

This Springer imprint is published by the registered company Springer Nature Switzerland AG
The registered company address is: Gewerbestrasse 11, 6330 Cham, Switzerland

Preface

The Conference on Security, Privacy, and Applied Cryptography Engineering 2018 (SPACE 2018), was held during December 15–19, 2018, at the Indian Institute of Technology Kanpur, India. This annual event is devoted to various aspects of security, privacy, applied cryptography, and cryptographic engineering. This is a challenging field, requiring expertise from diverse domains, ranging from mathematics to solid-state circuit design.

This year we received 34 submissions from 11 different countries. The submissions were evaluated based on their significance, novelty, technical quality, and relevance to the SPACE conference. The submissions were reviewed in a double-blind mode by at least three members of the 36-member Program Committee. The Program Committee was aided by 22 additional reviewers. The Program Committee meetings were held electronically, with intensive discussions. After an extensive review process, 12 papers were accepted for presentation at the conference, for an acceptance rate of 35.29%.

The program also included six invited talks and five tutorials on several aspects of applied cryptology, delivered by world-renowned researchers: Nasour Bagheri, Shivam Bhasin, Jo Van Bulck, Shay Gueron, Avi Mendelson, Mridul Nandi, Abhik Roychoudhury, Sandeep Shukla, Vanessa Teague, and Eran Toch. We sincerely thank the invited speakers for accepting our invitations in spite of their busy schedules. Like its previous editions, SPACE 2018 was organized in co-operation with the International Association for Cryptologic Research (IACR). We are thankful to the Indian Institute of Technology Kanpur for being the gracious host of SPACE 2018.

There is a long list of volunteers who invested their time and energy to put together the conference, and who deserve accolades for their efforts. We are grateful to all the members of the Program Committee and the additional reviewers for all their hard work in the evaluation of the submitted papers. We thank Cool Press Ltd., owner of the EasyChair conference management system, for allowing us to use it for SPACE 2018, which was a great help. We thank our publisher Springer for agreeing to continue to publish the SPACE proceedings as a volume in the *Lecture Notes in Computer Science* (LNCS) series. We are grateful to the local Organizing Committee, especially to the organizing chair, Sandeep Shukla, who invested a lot of effort for the conference to run smoothly. Our sincere gratitude to Debdeep Mukhopadhyay, Veezhinathan Kamakoti, and Sanjay Burman for being constantly involved in SPACE since its very inception and responsible for SPACE reaching its current status.

Last, but certainly not least, our sincere thanks go to all the authors who submitted papers to SPACE 2018, and to all the attendees. The conference is made possible by you, and it is dedicated to you. We sincerely hope you find the proceedings stimulating and inspiring.

October 2018

Anupam Chattopadhyay
Chester Rebeiro
Yuval Yarom

Organization

General Co-chairs

Sandeep Shukla	Indian Institute of Technology Kanpur, India
Manindra Agrawal	Indian Institute of Technology Kanpur, India

Program Co-chairs

Anupam Chattopadhyay	Nanyang Technological University, Singapore
Chester Rebeiro	Indian Institute of Technology Madras, India
Yuval Yarom	The University of Adelaide, Australia

Local Organizing Committee

Biswabandan Panda	Indian Institute of Technology Kanpur, India
Pramod Subramanyan	Indian Institute of Technology Kanpur, India
Shashank Singh	Indian Institute of Technology Kanpur, India

Young Researcher's Forum

Santanu Sarkar	Indian Institute of Technology Madras, India
Vishal Saraswat	Indian Institute of Technology Jammu, India

Web and Publicity

Sourav Sen Gupta	Nanyang Technological University, Singapore

Program Committee

Divesh Aggarwal	Ecole Polytechnique Fédérale de Lausanne, France
Reza Azarderakhsh	Florida Atlantic University, USA
Lejla Batina	Radboud University, The Netherlands
Shivam Bhasin	Temasek Labs, Singapore
Swarup Bhunia	University of Florida, USA
Billy Brumley	Tampere University of Technology, Finland
Arun Balaji Buduru	Indraprastha Institute of Information Technology Delhi, India
Claude Carlet	University of Paris 8, France
Rajat Subhra Chakraborty	Indian Institute of Technology Kharagpur, India
Anupam Chattopadhyay	Nanyang Technological University, Singapore
Jean-Luc Danger	Institut Télécom/Télécom ParisTech, CNRS/LTCI, France

Thomas De Cnudde	K.U. Leuven, Belgium
Junfeng Fan	Open Security Research, China
Daniel Gruss	Graz University of Technology, Austria
Sylvain Guilley	Institut Télécom/Télécom ParisTech, CNRS/LTCI, France
Jian Guo	Nanyang Technological University, Singapore
Naofumi Homma	Tohoku University, Japan
Kwok Yan Lam	Nanyang Technological University, Singapore
Yang Liu	Nanyang Technological University, Singapore
Subhamoy Maitra	Indian Statistical Institute Kolkata, India
Mitsuru Matsui	Mitsubishi Electric, Japan
Philippe Maurine	LIRMM, France
Bodhisatwa Mazumdar	Indian Institute of Technology Indore, India
Pratyay Mukherjee	Visa Research, USA
Debdeep Mukhopadhyay	Indian Institute of Technology Kharagpur, India
Chester Rebeiro	Indian Institute of Technology Madras, India
Bimal Roy	Indian Statistical Institute, Kolkata, India
Somitra Sanadhya	Indian Institute of Technology Ropar, India
Vishal Saraswat	Indian Institute of Technology Jammu, India
Santanu Sarkar	Indian Institute of Technology Madras, India
Sourav Sengupta	Nanyang Technological University, Singapore
Sandeep Shukla	Indian Institute of Technology Kanpur, India
Sujoy Sinha Roy	KU Leuven, Belgium
Mostafa Taha	Western University, Canada
Yuval Yarom	The University of Adelaide, Australia
Amr Youssef	Concordia University, Canada

Additional Reviewers

Cabrera Aldaya, Alejandro
Carre, Sebastien
Chattopadhyay, Nandish
Chauhan, Amit Kumar
Datta, Nilanjan
Guilley, Sylvain
Hou, Xiaolu
Jap, Dirmanto
Jha, Sonu
Jhawar, Mahavir
Kairallah, Mustafa

Marion, Damien
Massolino, Pedro Maat
Mozaffari Kermani, Mehran
Méaux, Pierrick
Patranabis, Sikhar
Poll, Erik
Raikwar, Mayank
Roy, Debapriya Basu
Saarinen, Markku-Juhani Olavi
Saha, Sayandeep

Keynote Talks/Tutorials Talks

Symbolic Execution vs. Search for Software Vulnerability Detection and Patching

Abhik Roychoudhury

School of Computing, National University of Singapore
abhik@comp.nus.edu.sg

Abstract. Many of the problems of software security involve search in a large domain, for which biased random searches have been traditionally employed. In the past decade, symbolic execution via systematic program analysis has emerged as a viable alternative to solve these problems, albeit with higher overheads of constraint accumulation and back-end constraint solving. We take a look at how some of the systematic aspect of symbolic execution can be imparted into biased-random searches. Furthermore, we also study how symbolic execution can be useful for purposes other than guided search, such as extracting the intended behavior of a buggy/vulnerable application. Extracting the intended program behavior, enables software security tasks such as automated program patching, since the intended program behavior can provide the correctness criterion for guiding automated program repair.

Keywords: Fuzz testing · Grey-box fuzzing · Automated program repair

1 Introduction

Software security typically involves a host of problems ranging from vulnerability detection, exploit generation, reaching nooks and corners of software for greater coverage, program hardening and program patching. Many of these problems can be envisioned as huge search problems, for example the problem of vulnerability detection can be seen as a search for problematic inputs in the input space. Similarly the problem of repairing or healing programs automatically can be seen as searching in the (huge) space of candidate patches or mutations. For these reasons, biased random searches have been used for many search problems in software security. In these settings, a more-or-less random search is conducted over a domain with the search being guided or biased by an objective function. The migration from one part of the space to another is aided by some mutation operators. A common embodiment of such biased random searches is the genetic search inherent in popular grey-box fuzzers like American Fuzzy Lop or AFL [1] which try to find inputs to crash a given program.

In the past decade symbolic or concolic execution has emerged as a viable alternative for guiding huge search problems in software security. Roughly speaking, symbolic execution works in one of two modes. Either the program is executed with a symbolic or unknown input and an execution tree is constructed. Then, the constraint along each root-to-leaf path in the tree is solved to generate sample inputs or tests.

Alternatively, in concolic execution, a random input i is generated and the constraint capturing its execution path is constructed to capture all inputs which follow the same path as i. Subsequently, the constraint captured from i's path is systematically mutated and the mutated constraints are solved to find inputs traversing other paths in the program. The aim is to enhance the path coverage for the set of inputs generated. The path constraint for a program path π, denoted $pc(\pi)$ captures the set of inputs which trace the path π.

An overview of symbolic execution for vulnerability detection and test generation appears in [2].

2 Symbolic Analysis Inspired Search

Let us consider the general problem of software vulnerability detection. Symbolic execution and search techniques both have their pros and cons. For this reason, software vulnerability detection or fuzz testing considers three flavors. The goal here is to generate program inputs which will expose program vulnerabilities. Thus, it involves a search over the domain of program inputs.

- Black-box fuzzing considers the input domain and performs mutations on program inputs, without any view of the program.
- Grey-box fuzzing has a limited view of the program such as transitions between basic blocks via compile-time instrumentation. The instrumentation helps us predict during run-time about the coverage achieved by existing set of tests, and accordingly mutations can be employed on selected tests to enhance coverage.
- White-box fuzzing has a full view of the program, which is analyzed via symbolic execution. Symbolic execution along a path produces a logical formula in the form of a path constraint. The path constraint is mutated, and the mutated logical formula is solved to (repeatedly) generate tests traversing other program paths.

Symbolic execution is clearly more systematic than grey-box/black-box fuzzing, and it is geared to traverse a new program path, when a new test input is generated. At the same time, it comes with the overheads of constraint solving and program analysis. In recent work, we have studied how ideas inspired from symbolic execution can augment the underlying genetic search in a grey-box fuzzer, such as AFL. In our recent work on AFLFast [3], we have suggested a prioritization mechanism for mutating inputs. In conventional AFL, any input selected for mutation is treated "similarly", that is, any selected input may be mutated a fixed number of times to examine the "neighbourhood" of the input. Instead, given an input, we seek to predict whether the input traces a "rare" path, a path that is frequented by few inputs. For these predicted rare paths, we subject them to enhanced examination by mutating such inputs more number of times. The amount of mutation done for a test input is governed by a so-called *power schedule*.

Another use of symbolic execution lies in reachability analysis. Specifically it is useful for finding the constraints under which a location can be reached. If paths π_1 and π_2 reach a control location L in the program, then inputs reaching L can be obtained by solving $pc(\pi_1) \lor pc(\pi_2)$ where $pc(\pi_i)$ is the path constraint for path π_i. We can incorporate this kind of reachability analysis into the genetic search inherent in grey-box fuzz testing tools like AFL. In a recent work, we have developed AFLGo [4], a directed greybox fuzzer built on top of AFL [1]. Given one or more target locations to reach, at the compile time, we instrument each basic block with approximate values of distance to the target location(s). The distance is then used in the power schedule. At the initial stages of a fuzzing session, thus the distance is not used and the search is primarily geared towards exploration. At a certain point of time, the search moves from exploration to exploitation and tries to devote more time mutating inputs whose paths are deemed to be close to the target location(s). Such an enhancement of grey-box fuzzing is an example of how the systematic nature of symbolic analysis can be imparted into search-based software security tasks.

3   Symbolic Reasoning for Program Repair

Of late, we have also explored how symbolic reasoning can be used for purposes other than guiding search or reaching locations in a program. In particular, we observe that symbolic execution can be used to extract a specification of the intended behavior of a program, directly by analyzing a buggy program. This, indeed, is a key issue, since formal specifications of intended behavior are often not available. As a result, we can envision using symbolic execution for completely new purposes, such as automated program repair or self-healing software.

The problem of automated program repair can be formally stated as follows. Given a buggy program P and a correctness criterion given as a set of tests T, how do we construct P', the minimal modification of P which passes the test-suite T.

Once again, the problem of program repair can be seen as a huge search problem in itself, it involves searching in the huge space of candidate patches of P. For this purpose, genetic search has been employed as evidenced in the GenProg tool [5]. Such a tool is based on a generate and validate approach, patches are generated, often by copying/mutating code from elsewhere in the program or from earlier program versions, and these generated patches are checked against the given tests T. Genetic search has also been used for program transplantation, a problem related to program repair, where key functionality is transplanted from one program to another [6].

Given certain weak specifications of correctness, such as a given test-suite T, we can instead try to extract a glimpse of the specification about intended program behavior, using symbolic execution. Such specifications can act as a *repair constraint*, a constraint that needs to be satisfied for the program to pass T. Subsequently, program synthesis technology can be used to synthesize patches meeting the repair constraint. Such an approach has been suggested by the SemFix work [7] and subsequently made more scalable via the Angelix tool [8] which performs multi-line program repair. Furthermore, such general purpose program repair tools have been shown to be useful for automatically generating patches for well-known security vulnerabilities such as the Heartbleed vulnerability.

There also exist opportunities for generating patches systematically from earlier program versions if one is available. If an earlier program version is available, one can repair for absence of regressions via the simultaneous symbolic analysis of the earlier and current program versions [9]. Such a technique leads to *provably correct repairs*, which can greatly help in making automated program repair an useful tool in building trustworthy systems.

Acknowledgments. This research is supported in part by the National Research Foundation, Prime Ministers Office, Singapore under its National Cybersecurity R&D Program (Award No. NRF2014NCR-NCR001-21) and administered by the National Cybersecurity R&D Directorate.

References

1. Zalewski, M.: American fuzzy lop (2018). http://lcamtuf.coredump.cx/afl/
2. Cadar, C., Sen, K.: Symbolic execution for software testing: three decades later. Commun. ACM **56**(2), 82–90 (2013)
3. Böhme, M., Van Pham, T., Roychoudhury, A.: Coverage based greybox fuzzing as a markov chain. In: 23rd ACM Conference on Computer and Communications Security (CCS) (2016)
4. Böhme, M., Pham, V.-T., Nguyen, M.-D., Roychoudhury, A.: Directed greybox fuzzing. In: Proceedings of the ACM SIGSAC Conference on Computer and Communications Security (CCS) (2017)
5. Weimer, W., Nguyen, T.V., Le Goues, C., Forrest, S.: Automatically finding patches using genetic programming. In: ACM/IEEE International Conference on Software Engineering (ICSE) (2009)
6. Barr, E.T., Brun, Y., Devanbu, P., Harman, M., Sarro, F.: The plastic surgery hypothesis. In: Proceedings of the 22nd ACM SIGSOFT International Symposium on Foundations of Software Engineering (FSE) (2014)
7. Nguyen, H.D.T., Qi, D., Roychoudhury, A., Chandra, S.: SemFix: program repair via semantic analysis. In: ACM/IEEE International Conference on Software Engineering (ICSE) (2013)
8. Mechtaev, S., Yi, J., Roychoudhury, A.: Angelix: scalable multiline program patch synthesis via symbolic analysis. In: ACM/IEEE International Conference on Software Engineering (ICSE) (2016)
9. Mechtaev, S., Nguyen, M.-D., Noller, Y., Lars, G., Roychoudhury, A.: Semantic program repair using a reference implementation. In: ACM/IEEE International Conference on Software Engineering (ICSE) (2018)

Persistence Wears down Resistance: Persistent Fault Analysis on Unprotected and Protected Block Cipher Implementations (Extended Abstract)

Shivam Bhasin[1], Jingyu Pan[1,2], and Fan Zhang[2]

[1] Temasek Laboratories, Nanyang Technological University, Singapore
sbhasin@ntu.edu.sg
[2] Zhejiang University, China
joeypan,fanzhangg@zju.edu.cn

Abstract. This works gives an overview of persistent fault attacks on block ciphers, a recently introduced fault analysis technique based on persistent faults. The fault typically targets stored constant of cryptographic algorithms over several encryption calls with a single injection. The underlying analysis technique statistically recovers the secret key and is capable of defeating several popular countermeasures by design.

Keywords: Fault attacks · Modular redundancy · Persistent fault

1 Introduction

Fault attacks [1, 2] are active physical attacks that use external means to disturb normal operations of a target device leading to security vulnerability. These attacks have been widely used for key recovery from widely used standard cryptographic schemes, such as AES, RSA, ECC etc.

Several types of faults can be exploited to mount such attacks. Commonly known fault types are *transient* and *permanent*. A transient fault, which is most commonly used, generally affects only one instance of the target function call (eg. one encryption). On the other hand, a permanent fault, normally owing to device defects, affects all calls to the target function. Based on these two fault types, several analysis techniques have been developed. The most common are differential in nature, which require a correct and faulty computation with same inputs, to exploit the difference of final correct and faulty output pair for key recovery. Common examples of such techniques are differential fault analysis (DFA) [2], algebraic fault analysis (AFA) [4], etc. Some analyses are also based on statistical methods which can exploit faulty ciphertexts only like statistical fault analysis (SFA) [5] and fault sensitivity analysis (FSA) [6].

Recently, a new fault analysis technique was proposed [8] with a *persistent* fault model. Persistent fault lies between transient and permanent faults. Unlike transient fault, it affects several calls of the target function, however, persistent fault is not permanent, and disappears with a device reset/reboot. The corresponding analysis technique is called *Persistent Fault Analysis (PFA)* [8].

2   Persistent Fault Analysis (PFA)

PFA [8] is based on persistent fault model. In the following, the fault is assumed to alter a stored constant (like one or more entries in Sbox look-up) in the target algorithm, typically stored in a ROM. The attacker observes multiple ciphertext outputs with varying plaintext (not known). The modus operandi of PFA is explained with the following example. Let us take PRESENT cipher which uses a 4×4 Sbox i.e. 16 elements of 4-bits each, where each element has an equal expectation $\mathbb{E}$ of $\frac{1}{16}$. A persistent fault alters value of element x in Sbox to another element x', it makes $\mathbb{E}(x) = 0, \mathbb{E}(x') = \frac{2}{16}$, while all other elements still have the expectation $\frac{1}{16}$. The output ciphertext is still correct if faulty element x is never accessed during the encryption else the output is faulty. This difference can be statistically observed in the final ciphertext where some values will be missing (related to x) and some occuring more often than others (due to x'), which leaks information on the key k. This is illustrated in Fig. 1 (top) with $x = 10, x' = 8$. The key can be recovered even if x, x' are not known by simple brute-forcing. The strategy for key recovery can be one of the following:

1. t_{min}: find the missing value in Sbox table. Then $k = t_{min} \oplus x$;
2. $t \neq t_{min}$: find other values t where $t \neq t_{min}$ and eliminate candidates for k;
3. t_{max}: find the value with maximal probability $k = t_{max} \oplus x'$.

The distribution of t_{min} or t_{max} can be statistically distinguished from the rest. The minimum number of ciphertexts N follows the classical coupon collector's problem [3] where it needs $N = (2^b - 1) \times (\sum_{i=1}^{(2^b-1)} \frac{1}{i})$, where b is the bit width of x. In PRESENT $(b = 4)$ $N \approx 50$, as shown in Fig. 1 (bottom).

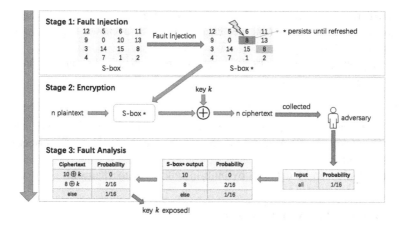

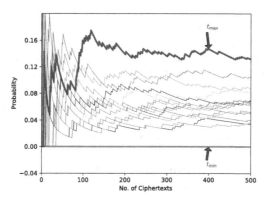

Fig. 1. Overview of Persistent Fault Attack (top), distribution of t_{min} and t_{max} against no. of ciphertexts for PRESENT leading to key recovery (bottom)

2.1 PFA vs Other Fault Analysis

Here we list the key merits and demerits of PFA against other fault analysis.

Merits

– The main advantage of PFA is that it needs only one fault injection, which reduces the injection effort to minimum. Fault targets a constant in memory which persists over several following encryptions. This also reduces the injection effort in terms of timing precision within an injection. Moreover, live detection by sensors can be bypassed by injecting before the sensitive computation starts and sensors become active.

– The attack is statistical on ciphertexts only, and thus unlike differential attacks, needs no control over plaintexts.

- The fault model remains relaxed compared to other statistical attacks which may require multiple injections (one per encryption) with a known bias or additional side-channel information.
- Unlike any other known attacks, PFA can also be applied in the multiple fault (in a single encryption) setting.

Demerits

- Being statistical in nature, it needs a higher number of ciphertexts as compared to DFA. Some known DFA can lead to key recovery with 1 or 2 correct/faulty ciphertext pair.
- Persistent faults can be detected by built-in self check mechanism.

2.2 Application of PFA on Countermeasures

PFA has natural properties which make several countermeasures vulnerable. The details on analysis of the countermeasure remain out of scope of this extended abstract due to limited space and interested readers are encouraged to refer [8]. Dual modular redundancy (DMR) is a popular fault countermeasure. The most common DMR proposes to compute twice and compare outputs. This countermeasure is naturally vulnerable to PFA if shared memories for constants are used, which is often the case due to resource constraint environments. Other proposals use separate memories or compute forward followed by compute inverse and compare inputs. All these countermeasures output a correct ciphertext when no fault is injected. For a detected fault, the faulty output can be suppressed by no ciphertext output (NCO), zero value output (ZVO), or random ciphertext output (RCO) [8]. As PFA leaves certain probability for correct ciphertext output despite the persistent fault, it leads to key recovery using statistical method. However, more ciphertexts would be required in the analysis as some information is suppressed by the DMR countermeasure. Masking [7] on the other hand is a side channel countermeasure which is widely studied. As a persistent fault injects a bias in the underlying computation due to a biased constant, the bias can also affect the masking leading to key recovery.

3 Conclusion

Persistent fault analysis is a powerful attack technique which can make several cryptographic schemes vulnerable. With as low as one fault injection and simple statistical analysis on ciphertexts, PFA can perform key recovery. The introduced vulnerability also extends to protected implementations. We briefly discussed the impact of PFA on modular redundancy and masking based countermeasures. Existing countermeasures and other cryptographic schemes including public key cryptography must be analyzed to check their resistance against PFA. This further motivates research for dedicated countermeasures to prevent PFA.

References

1. Bar-El, H., Choukri, H., Naccache, D., Tunstall, M., Whelan, C.: The sorcerer's apprentice guide to fault attacks. Proc. IEEE **94**(2), 370–382 (2006)
2. Biham, E., Shamir, A.: Differential cryptanalysis of the data encryption standard. Cryst. Res. Technol. **17**(1), 79–89 (2006)
3. Blom, G., Holst, L., Sandell, D.: Problems and Snapshots from the World of Probability. Springer, Heidelberg (2012)
4. Courtois, N.T., Jackson, K., Ware, D.: Fault-algebraic attacks on inner rounds of DES. In: e-Smart'10 Proceedings: The Future of Digital Security Technologies. Strategies Telecom and Multimedia (2010)
5. Fuhr, T., Jaulmes, E., Lomne, V., Thillard, A.: Fault attacks on AES with faulty ciphertexts only. In: The Workshop on Fault Diagnosis & Tolerance in Cryptography, pp. 108–118 (2013)
6. Li, Y., Sakiyama, K., Gomisawa, S., Fukunaga, T., Takahashi, J., Ohta, K.: Fault sensitivity analysis. In: Mangard, S., Standaert, F.-X. (eds.) CHES 2010. LNCS, vol. 6225, pp. 320–334. Springer, Heidelberg (2010)
7. Rivain, M., Prouff, E.: Provably secure higher-order masking of AES. CHES **2010**, 413–427 (2010)
8. Zhang, F., Lou, X., Zhao, X., Shivam, B., He, W., Ding, R., Qureshi, S., Ren, K.: Persistent fault analysis on block ciphers. IACR Trans. Cryptogr. Hardw. Embed. Syst. **2018**(3), 150–172 (2018)

Tutorial: Uncovering and Mitigating Side-Channel Leakage in Intel SGX Enclaves

Jo Van Bulck and Frank Piessens

imec-DistriNet, KU Leuven, Celestijnenlaan 200A, B-3001 Belgium
{jo.vanbulck,frank.piessens}@cs.kuleuven.be

Abstract. The inclusion of the Software Guard eXtensions (SGX) in recent Intel processors has been broadly acclaimed for bringing strong hardware-enforced trusted computing guarantees to mass consumer devices, and for protecting end user data in an untrusted cloud environment. While SGX assumes a very strong attacker model and indeed even safeguards enclave secrets against a compromised operating system, recent research has demonstrated that considerable private data (e.g., full text and images, complete cryptographic keys) may still be reconstructed by monitoring subtle side-effects of the enclaved execution. We argue that a systematic understanding of such side-channel leakage sources is essential for writing intrinsically secure enclave applications, and will be instrumental to the success of this new trusted execution technology. This tutorial and write-up therefore aims to bring a better understanding of current state-of-the-art side-channel attacks and defenses on Intel SGX platforms. Participants will learn how to extract data from elementary example applications, thereby recognizing how to avoid common pitfalls and information leakage sources in enclave development.

Keywords: Side-channel · Enclave · SGX · Tutorial

1 Introduction

Trusted Execution Environments (TEEs), including Intel SGX, are a promising new technology supporting secure isolated execution of critical code in dedicated *enclaves* that are directly protected and measured by the processor itself. By excluding vast operating system and hypervisor code from the trusted computing base, TEEs establish a minimalist hardware root-of-trust where application developers solely rely on the correctness of the CPU and the implementation of their own enclaves. Enclaved execution hence holds the promise of enforcing strong security and privacy requirements for local and remote computations.

Modern processors unintendedly leak information about (enclaved) software running on top, however, and such traces in the microarchitectural CPU state can be abused to reconstruct application secrets through side-channel analysis. These attacks have received growing attention from the research community and significant understanding has been built up over the past decade. While information leakage from side-channels is generally limited to specific code or data access patterns, recent work

[4, 5, 8–11] has demonstrated significant side-channel amplification for enclaved execution. Ultimately, the disruptive real-world impact of side-channels became apparent when they were used as building blocks for the high-impact Meltdown, Spectre, and Foreshadow speculation attacks (where the latter completely erodes trust on unpatched Intel SGX platforms [7]).

Intel explicitly considers side-channels out of scope, clarifying that "it is the enclave developer's responsibility to address side-channel attack concerns" [2]. Unfortunately, we will show that adequately preventing side-channel leakage is particularly difficult — to the extent where even Intel's own vetted enclave entry code suffered from subtle yet dangerous side-channel vulnerabilities [3]. As such, we argue that side-channels cannot merely be considered out of scope for enclaved execution, but rather necessitate widespread developer education so as to establish a systematic understanding and awareness of different leakage sources. To support this cause, this tutorial and write-up present a brief systematization of current state-of-the-art attacks and general guidelines for secure enclave development.

All presentation material and source code for this tutorial will be made publicly available at https://github.com/jovanbulck/sgx-tutorial-space18.

2   Software Side-Channel Attacks on Enclaved Execution

We consider a powerful class of software-only attacks that require only code execution on the machine executing the victim enclave. Depending on the adversary's goals and capabilities, the malicious code can either be executing interleaved with the victim enclave (interrupt-driven attacks [4, 8–11]), or launched concurrently from a co-resident logical CPU core (HyperThreading-based resource contention attacks [5]). In the following, we overview known side-channels.

Memory Accesses. Even before the official launch of Intel SGX, researchers showed the existence of a dangerous side-channel [11] within the processor's virtual-to-physical address translation logic. By revoking access rights on selected enclave memory pages, and observing the associated page fault patterns, adversaries controlling the operating system can deterministically establish enclaved code and data accesses at a 4 KiB granularity. This attack technique has been proven highly practical and effective, extracting full enclave secrets in a single run and without noise. Following the classic cat-and-mouse game, subsequent proposals to hide enclave page faults from the adversary led to an improved class of stealthy attack variants [10] that extract page table access patterns without provoking page faults. It has furthermore been demonstrated [8] that privileged adversaries can mount such interrupt-driven attacks at a very precise instruction-level granularity, which allows to accurately monitor enclave memory access patterns in the time domain so as to defeat naive spatial page alignment defense techniques [2, 8].

A complementary line of SGX-based Prime+Probe cache attacks exploit information leakage at an improved 64-byte cache line granularity [6]. Adversaries first load carefully selected memory locations into the shared CPU cache, and afterwards measure the time to reload these addresses to establish code and data evictions by the victim enclave. As with the paging channel above, these attacks commonly exploit the adversary's control over untrusted system software to frequently interrupt the victim enclave and gather side-channel information at a maximum temporal resolution [8]. This is not a strict requirement, however, as it has been demonstrated that even unprivileged attacker processes can concurrently monitor enclave cache access patterns in real-time [6].

In summary, the above research results show that enclave code and data accesses on SGX platforms can be accurately reconstructed, both in space (at a 4 KiB or 64-byte granularity) as well as in time (after every single instruction).

Instruction-Level Leakage. It has furthermore been shown that enclave-private control flow leaks through the CPU's internal Branch Target Buffer [4]. These attacks essentially follow the general principle of the above Prime+Probe attacks by first forcing the BTB cache in a known state. After interrupting the enclave, the adversary measures a dedicated shadow branch to establish whether the secret-dependent victim branch was executed or not. Importantly, unlike the above memory access side-channels, such branch shadowing attacks leak control flow at the level of individual branch instructions (i.e., basic blocks).

Apart from amplifying conventional side-channels, enclaved execution attack research has also revealed new and unexpected sub-cache level leakage sources. One recent work presented the Nemesis [9] attack that measures individual enclaved instruction timings through interrupt latency, allowing to partially reconstruct a.o., instruction type, operand values, address translation, and cache hits/misses. MemJam [5] furthermore exploits selective instruction timing penalties from false dependencies induced by an attacker-controlled spy thread to reconstruct enclave-private memory access patterns *within* a 64-byte cache line.

Speculative Execution. In the aftermath of recent x86 speculation vulnerabilities, researchers have successfully demonstrated Spectre-type speculative code gadget abuse against SGX enclaves [1]. Recent work furthermore presented Foreshadow [7] which allows for arbitrary in-enclave reads and completely dismantles isolation and attestation guarantees in the SGX ecosystem. Intel has since revoked the compromised attestation keys, and released microcode patches to address Foreshadow and Spectre threats at the hardware level.

3   Enclave Development Guidelines and Caveats

Existing SGX side-channel mitigation approaches generally fall down in two categories. One line of work attempts to harden enclave programs through a combination of compile time code rewriting and run time randomization or checks, so as to obfuscate the attacker's view or detect side-effects of an ongoing attack. Unfortunately, as these heuristic proposals do not block the root information leakage in itself, they often fall victim to improved and more versatile attack variants [5, 8, 10]. A complementary line of work therefore advocates the more comprehensive constant time approach known from the cryptography community: eliminate secret-dependent code and data paths altogether. While this approach is relatively well-understood for small applications, in practice even vetted crypto implementations exhibit non-constant time behavior [5, 6, 10]. In the context of SGX, it has furthermore been shown [9, 11] that enclave secrets are typically not limited to well-defined private keys, but are instead scattered throughout the code and hence much harder to manipulate in constant time.

We conclude that side-channels pose a real threat to enclaved execution, while no silver bullet exists to eliminate them at the compiler or system level. Depending on the enclave's size and security objectives, it may be desirable to strive for intricate constant time solutions, or instead rely on heuristic hardening measures. However, further research and raising developer awareness are imperative to make such informed decisions and adequately employ TEE technology.

Acknowledgments. This research is partially funded by the Research Fund KU Leuven. Jo Van Bulck is supported by the Research Foundation – Flanders (FWO).

References

1. Chen, G., Chen, S., Xiao, Y., Zhang, Y., Lin, Z., Lai, T.H.: SgxPectre attacks: Leaking enclave secrets via speculative execution arXiv:1802.09085 (2018)
2. Intel: Software guard extensions developer guide: Protection from side-channel attacks (2017). https://software.intel.com/en-us/node/703016
3. Intel: Intel Software Guard Extensions (SGX) SW Development Guidance for Potential Edger8r Generated Code Side Channel Exploits (2018)
4. Lee, S., Shih, M.W., Gera, P., Kim, T., Kim, H., Peinado, M.: Inferring fine-grained control flow inside SGX enclaves with branch shadowing. In: Proceedings of the 26th USENIX Security Symposium, Vancouver, Canada (2017)
5. Moghimi, A., Eisenbarth, T., Sunar, B.: Memjam: a false dependency attack against constant-time crypto implementations in SGX. In: Smart, N.P. (ed.) Cryptographers' Track at the RSA Conference, LNCS, vol 10808, pp. 21–44. Springer, Cham (2018)
6. Schwarz, M., Weiser, S., Gruss, D., Maurice, C., Mangard, S.: Malware guard extension: using SGX to conceal cache attacks. In: Polychronakis M., Meier M. (eds.) Detection of Intrusions and Malware, and Vulnerability Assessment. DIMVA 2017. LNCS, vol 10327, pp. 3–24. Springer, Cham (2017)
7. Van Bulck, J., et al.: Foreshadow: extracting the keys to the Intel SGX kingdom with transient out-of-order execution. In: Proceedings of the 27th USENIX Security Symposium. USENIX Association (2018)
8. Van Bulck, J., Piessens, F., Strackx, R.: SGX-Step: a practical attack framework for precise enclave execution control. In: Proceedings of the 2nd Workshop on System Software for Trusted Execution, SysTEX'17, pp. 4:1–4:6. ACM (2017)
9. Van Bulck, J., Piessens, F., Strackx, R.: Nemesis: studying microarchitectural timing leaks in rudimentary CPU interrupt logic. In: Proceedings of the 25th ACM Conference on Computer and Communications Security, CCS'18 (2018)

10. Van Bulck, J., Weichbrodt, N., Kapitza, R., Piessens, F., Strackx, R.: Telling your secrets without page faults: stealthy page table-based attacks on enclaved execution. In: Proceedings of the 26th USENIX Security Symposium, USENIX (2017)
11. Xu, Y., Cui, W., Peinado, M.: Controlled-channel attacks: deterministic side channels for untrusted operating systems. In: 2015 IEEE Symposium on Security and Privacy, pp. 640–656. IEEE (2015)

A Composition Result for Constructing BBB Secure PRF

Nilanjan Datta[1], Avijit Dutta[2], Mridul Nandi[2], Goutam Paul[2]

[1] Indian Institute of Technology, Kharagpur
[2] Indian Statistical Institute, Kolkata
nilanjan_isi_jrf@yahoo.com,
avirocks.dutta13@gmail.com, mridul.nandi@gmail.com,
goutam.paul@isical.ac.in

Abstract. In this paper, we propose **Double-block Hash-then-Sum** (DbHtS), a generic design paradigm to construct a BBB secure pseudo random function. DbHtS computes a *double block hash* function on the message and then *sum* the encrypted outputs of the two hash blocks. Our result renders that if the underlying hash function meets certain security requirements (namely cover-free and block-wise universal advantage is low), DbHtS construction provides $2n/3$-bit security. We demonstrate the applicability of our result by instantiating all the existing beyond birthday secure deterministic MACs (e.g., SUM-ECBC, PMAC_Plus, 3kf9, LightMAC_Plus) as well as their reduced-key variants.

1 Introduction

Pseudo Random Function (PRF) plays an important role in symmetric key cryptography to authenticate or encrypt any arbitrary length message. Over the years, there have numerous candidates of PRFs (e.g., CBC-MAC [BKR00] and many others). These PRFs give security only upto *birthday bound*, i.e., the mode is secure only when the total number of blocks that the mode can process does not exceed $2^{n/2}$, where n is the block size of the underlying primitive (e.g., block cipher). Birthday bound secure constructions are acceptable in practice with a moderately large block size. However, the mode becomes vulnerable if instantiated with some smaller block size primitive. In this line of research, SUM-ECBC [Yas10] is the first beyond the birthday bound (BBB) secure rate-1 / 2 PRF with $2n/3$-bit security. Followed by this work, many BBB secure PRFs e.g., PMAC_Plus [Yas11], 3kf9 [ZWSW12], LightMAC_Plus [Nai17], 1K-PMAC_Plus [DDN+17] etc. have been proposed and all of them gives roughly $2n/3$-bit security. Interestingly, all these constructions possess a common structural design which is the composition of (i) a double block hash (DbH) function that outputs a $2n$-bit hash value of the input message and (ii) a finalization phase that generates the final tag by xor-ing the encryption of two n-bit hash values. However, all these PRFs follow a different way to bound the security. This observation motivates us to come up with a generic design guideline to construct BBB secure PRFs and hence brings all the existing BBB secure PRFs under one common roof and enables us to give a unified security proof for all of them.

Our Contributions. We introduce **Double-block Hash-then-Sum** (DbHtS) a generic design of BBB secure PRF by xor-ing the encryption of the outputs of a DbH function. Based on the usage of the keys, we call the DbHtS construction three-keyed (resp. two-keyed), if two block cipher keys are (resp. a single block cipher key is) used in the finalization phase along with the hash key. We show that if the cover-free and the block-wise universal advantage of the underlying DbH function is sufficiently low, then the two-keyed DbHtS is secure beyond the birthday bound. We show the applicability of this result by instantiating existing beyond birthday secure deterministic MACs (i.e., SUM-ECBC, PMAC_Plus, 3kf9, LightMAC_Plus) and their two-keyed variants and showing their beyond birthday bound security.

2 DbHtS : A BBB Secure PRF Paradigm

Double-block Hash-then-Sum (DbHtS) is a paradigm to build a BBB secure VIL PRF where the Double-block Hash (DbH) function is used with a very simple and efficient single-keyed or two-keyed sum function:

- SINGLE-KEYED SUM FUNCTION: $Sum_K(x, y) = E_K(x) \oplus E_K(y)$,
- TWO-KEYED SUM FUNCTION: $Sum_{K_1,K_2}(x, y) = E_{K_1}(x) \oplus E_{K_2}(y)$.

Given a DbH function and the sum function over two blocks, we apply the composition of the DbH function and the sum function to realize the DbHtS construction. Based on the types of sum function i.e., single-keyed or (resp. two-keyed) used in the composition, we have three keyed or (resp. two-keyed) DbHtS construction.

2.1 Security Definitions for DbH Function

Let $\mathcal{K}_b$ be a set of bad hash keys. A DbH function is said to be **(weak) cover-free** if for any triplet of messages out of any q distinct messages, the joint probability, over a random draw of the hash key, that the values taken by the two halves of the hash outputs of a message also appears in the (corresponding) either halves of the hash outputs of two other messages of the triplet, and the sampled hash key falls to the set $\mathcal{K}_b$, is low. A DbH function is said to be **(weak) block-wise universal** if for any pair of messages out of any q distinct messages, the joint probability, over a random draw of the hash key, that any half of the hash output for a message collides with (the same) any half of the hash output for the other message of the pair, and the sampled hash key falls to the set $\mathcal{K}_b$, is low. Finally, a DbH function is said to be **colliding** if for any messages out of any q distinct messages, the joint probability, over a random draw of the hash key, that any half of the hash output of the message collides with other halves of the output, and the sampled hash key falls to the set $\mathcal{K}_b$, is low.

2.2 Security Result of DbHtS

Let q denotes the maximum number of queries by any adversary and ℓ denotes the maximum number of message blocks among all q queried messages.

Theorem 1
(i) If H is a ϵ_{cf}-cover-free, ϵ_{univ}-block-wise universal and ϵ_{coll}-colliding hash function for a fixed set of bad hash keys $\mathcal{K}_b$, then the distinguishing advantage of two-keyed DbHtS from the random function is bounded by

$$\epsilon_{bh} + q\epsilon_{coll} + \frac{q^3}{6}\epsilon_{cf} + \frac{3q^3}{2^n}\epsilon_{univ} + \frac{6q^3}{2^{2n}} + \frac{q}{2^n},$$

where ϵ_{bh} is the upper bound on the probability of a sampled hash key falls to $\mathcal{K}_b$.
(ii) If H is a ϵ_{wcf}-weak cover-free and ϵ_{wuniv}-weak block-wise universal hash function for a fixed set of bad hash keys $\mathcal{K}_b$, then the distinguishing advantage of three-keyed DbHtS from the random function is bounded by

$$\epsilon_{bh} + \frac{q^3}{6}\epsilon_{wcf} + \frac{3q^3}{2^n}\epsilon_{wuniv} + \frac{2q^3}{2^{2n}},$$

where ϵ_{bh} is the upper bound on the probability of a sampled hash key falls to $\mathcal{K}_b$.

Instantiations of DbHtS

In this section, we revisit two BBB secure parallel mode PRF PMAC_Plus, LightMAC_Plus and two BBB secure parallel mode PRF SUM-ECBC, 3kf9. We also consider simple two-key variants of these constructions. All the specifications are given in Fig. 1. Applying Theorem 1 on these constructions, we obtain the following bounds:

Constructions	Security Bound	Constructions	Security Bound
2K-PMAC_Plus	$q^3\ell/2^{2n} + q^2\ell^2/2^{2n}$	2K-SUM-ECBC	$2q\ell^2/2^n + q^3\ell^2/2^{2n}$
2K-LightMAC_Plus	$q^3/2^{2n} + q/2^n$	2Kf9	$q^3\ell^4/2^{2n}$
PMAC_Plus	$q^3\ell/2^{2n} + q^2\ell^2/2^{2n}$	SUM-ECBC	$q\ell^2/2^n + q^3/2^{2n}$
LightMAC_Plus	$q^3/2^{2n}$	3kf9	$q^3\ell^4/2^{2n}$

Open Problems. Here we list down some possible future research works:

(i) One may try to extend this work to analyze the security of the single-keyed DbHtS, where the hash key would be same as the block cipher key used in the sum function.

(ii) Leurent et al [LNS18] have shown attacks on SUM-ECBC, PMAC_Plus, 3kf9 and LightMAC_Plus with query complexity of $O(2^{3n/4})$. Establishing the tightness of the bound is an interesting open problem.

Algorithm $\boxed{\text{2K}}$-PMAC_Plus(M)

1. $\Delta_0 \leftarrow E_K(0^n); \ \Delta_1 \leftarrow E_K(0^{n-1}1)$
2. **for** $j = 1$ **to** l
3. $\quad X_j = M_j \oplus 2^j \Delta_0 \oplus 2^{2j} \Delta_1$
4. $\quad Y_j = E_K(X_j)$
5. $\Sigma' = \oplus_{i=1}^l Y_i; \Lambda' = \oplus_{i=1}^l 2^{l-i} \cdot Y_i$
6. $\boxed{\Sigma = \mathsf{fix0}(\Sigma'); \ \Lambda = \mathsf{fix1}(2\Lambda')}$
7. **return** $E_{K_1}(\Sigma') \oplus E_{K_2}(\Lambda')$
8. **return** $\boxed{E_K(\Sigma) \oplus E_K(\Lambda)}$

Algorithm $\boxed{\text{2K}}$-LightMAC_Plus(M)

1. **for** $j = 1$ **to** l
2. $\quad X_j = \langle j \rangle_s \| M_j$
3. $\quad Y_j = E_K(X_j)$
4. $\Sigma' = \oplus_{i=1}^l Y_i; \Lambda' = \oplus_{i=1}^l 2^{l-i} \cdot Y_i$
5. $\boxed{\Sigma = \mathsf{fix0}(\Sigma'); \ \Lambda = \mathsf{fix1}(2\Lambda')}$
6. **return** $E_{K_1}(\Sigma') \oplus E_{K_2}(\Lambda')$
7. **return** $\boxed{E_K(\Sigma) \oplus E_K(\Lambda)}$

Algorithm $\boxed{\text{2K}}$-SUM-ECBC(M)

1. $(Y, Y') \leftarrow (0^n, 0^n)$
2. **for** $j = 1$ **to** l
3. $\quad X = M_j \oplus Y; X' = M_j \oplus Y'$
4. $\quad (Y, Y') \leftarrow (E_K(X), E_{K_*}(X'))$
5. $(\Sigma' \Lambda') \leftarrow (Y, Y')$
6. $\boxed{\Sigma \leftarrow \mathsf{fix0}(\Sigma'); \Lambda \leftarrow \mathsf{fix1}(\Theta')}$
7. **return** $E_{K_1}(\Sigma') \oplus E_{K_2}(\Lambda')$
8. **return** $\boxed{E_K(\Sigma) \oplus E_K(\Lambda')}$

Algorithm $\boxed{\text{2Kf9}}$3kf9(M)

1. $(Y, Y') \leftarrow (0^n, 0^n)$
2. **for** $j = 1$ **to** l
3. $\quad X = M_j \oplus Y; Y \leftarrow E_K(X)$
4. $\quad Y' \leftarrow Y \oplus Y'$
5. $(\Sigma', \Lambda') = (Y, Y')$
6. **return** $E_{K_1}(\Sigma') \oplus E_{K_2}(\Lambda')$
7. **return** $\boxed{E_K(\Sigma') \oplus E_K(\Lambda')}$

Fig. 1. Specification of existing MACs with BBB Security and their two-key variants. Here $\langle j \rangle_s$ denotes the s-bit binary representation of integer j and fixb function takes an n-bit integer and returns the integer with its least significant bit set to bit b.

References

[BKR00] Bellare, M., Kilian, J., Rogaway, P.: The security of the cipher block chaining message authentication code. J. Comput. Syst. Sci. **61**(3), 362–399 (2000)

[DDN+17] Datta, N., Dutta, A., Nandi, M., Paul, G., Zhang, L.: Single key variant of pmac_plus. IACR Trans. Symmetric Cryptol. **2017**(4), 268–305 (2017)

[LNS18] Leurent, G., Nandi, M., Sibleyras, F.: Generic attacks against beyond-birthday-bound macs, vol. 2018, p. 541 (2018)

[Nai17] Naito, Y.: Blockcipher-based macs: beyond the birthday bound without message length. Cryptology ePrint Archive, Report 2017/852 (2017)

[Yas10] Yasuda, K.: The sum of CBC macs is a secure PRF. CT-RSA **2010**, 366–381 (2010)

[Yas11] Yasuda, K.: A new variant of PMAC: beyond the birthday bound. In: Rogaway, P. (ed.) CRYPTO 2011. LNCS, vol. 6841, pp. 596–609. Springer, Heidelberg (2011)

[ZWSW12] Zhang, L., Wu, W., Sui, H., Wang, P.: 3kf9: enhancing 3GPP-MAC beyond the birthday bound. In: Wang, X., Sako, K. (eds.) ASIACRYPT 2012. LNCS, vol. 7658, pp. 296–312. Springer, Heidelberg (2012)

Contents

An Observation of Non-randomness in the Grain Family of Stream Ciphers with Reduced Initialization Round

Deepak Kumar Dalai$^{(\boxtimes)}$ and Dibyendu Roy

School of Mathematical Science, National Institute of Science Education and Research (HBNI), Bhubaneswar 752 050, Odisha, India
{deepak,dibyendu}@niser.ac.in

Abstract. The key scheduling algorithm (KSA) of the Grain family of stream ciphers expands the uniformly chosen key (K) and initialization vector (IV) to a larger uniform looking state. The existence of non-randomness in KSA results a non-randomness in final keystream. In this paper, we observe a non-randomness in the KSA of Grain-v1 and Grain-128a stream ciphers of reduced round R. However, we could not exploit the non-randomness into an attack. It can be claimed that if the KSA generates pseudorandom state, then the probability of generating a valid state T (i.e., in the range set of KSA function) of Grain-v1, Grain-128a must be $2^{-\delta}$, where δ is the length of padding bits. In case of Grain-v1 and Grain-128a, $\delta = 16, 32$ respectively. We show that a new valid state can be constructed by flipping 3 and 19 bits of a given state in Grain-v1 and Grain-128a respectively with a probability higher than $2^{-\delta}$. We show that the non-randomness happens for $R \leq 129$ and $R \leq 208$ rounds of KSA of Grain-v1 and Grain-128a respectively. Further, in the case of Grain-v1, we also found non-randomness in some key, IV bits from the experiment.

Keywords: Stream cipher · Cryptanalysis · Grain-v1 · Grain-128a KSA · Non-randomness

1 Introduction

In 2008, eSTREAM [1] finalized Grain-v1 [11] designed by Hell et al. as a candidate for stream ciphers in the hardware category. The cipher is based on an NFSR and an LFSR of length 80 bits each and a nonlinear filter function. Grain-v1 runs in two phases. In the first phase, the state of cipher is initialized by a secret key and an initialization vector of length 80 bits and 64 bits respectively. This phase is known as key scheduling phase and the method is known as Key Scheduling Algorithm (KSA). The KSA is followed by Pseudo-Random Generation Algorithm (PRGA) to generate the keystream bits. The design specification of Grain-v1 is described in Sect. 3.

© Springer Nature Switzerland AG 2018
A. Chattopadhyay et al. (Eds.): SPACE 2018, LNCS 11348, pp. 1–20, 2018.
https://doi.org/10.1007/978-3-030-05072-6_1

In 2006, the design specification of Grain-128 [10] was introduced by Hell et al. Later in 2011, Ågren et al. proposed a modified design of Grain-128 with authentication, which is known as Grain-128a [2]. Grain-128a is based on an NFSR and an LFSR of length 128 bits each and a nonlinear filter function. Grain-128a also runs in two phases. In the key scheduling phase, the cipher is initialized by one 128-bit secret key and 96-bit initialization vector. Finally, the cipher generates the output bits for encryption and authentication purpose. The design specification of Grain-128a is presented in Subsect. 5.1.

In last few years, Grain family of stream ciphers received serious attention among the cryptanalysts. In 2009, Aumasson et al. [3] found some non random-ness in Grain-v1 of 81 round and Grain-128 of 215 round. A distinguisher up to 97 and 104 round of Grain-v1 was observed by Knellwolf et al. [12] in 2010. Later, in 2014 Banik [5] has improved the result and a proposed conditional dif-ferential attack on 105 round of Grain-v1. Sarkar [15] has found a distinguisher of Grain-v1 at 106 rounds. In 2016, Ma et al. [14] proposed an improved condi-tional differential attack on 110 round of Grain-v1. In the same year, Watanabe et al. [16] proposed a conditional differential attack on 114 round of Grain-v1 in related key/weak key setup. In 2012, Lehmann and Meier [13] found non-randomness at the 189-th round of Grain-128a. Few more cryptanalytic results on this family have been proposed in [4,6–9].

OUR CONTRIBUTION: In this paper, we observe a non-randomness in the KSA of Grain-v1 and Grain-128a. We spotted some fact which should not be expected in a pseudo-random bit generator. However, we could not exploit the non-randomness to propose any kind of attack on Grain-v1 and Grain-128a. The purpose of KSA in Grain family of stream ciphers is to generate a random look-ing state of n bits from a secret key of m bits and a known initialization vector of l bits. Further, the pseudo-random keystream bits are generated from the random looking state. Therefore, if the randomness of the generated state gets compromised then it affects the randomness in the keystream. The KSA function is a mapping from the set of strings of $(m + l)$ bits to the set of strings of n bits where $n > m + l$. We say a state (i.e., a string of n bits) is a valid state if the state is in the range set of KSA function (i.e., the state can be generated from a key and an IV). An n bit string chosen uniformly in random can be a valid state with probability $2^{-\delta}$, where $\delta = n - (m + l)$. In our work, we can generate a valid state with probability higher than the uniform probability $2^{-\delta}$ from a given valid state S. The KSA in Grain-v1 and Grain-128a constitutes a process for 160 and 256 rounds respectively. Here, we consider the KSA of reduced rounds R and found the non-randomness exists till $R = 129, 208$ for Grain-v1 and Grain-128a respectively. The results are explained in Sect. 4 and Subsect. 5.2.

ORGANIZATION: The rest of the article is organized as follows. In Sect. 2, the notations and definitions are listed. In this section, we have also defined the pseudorandom state generator in a general set up of Grain like ciphers. The design specification of Grain-v1 and inverse of its KSA is described in Sect. 3 and Subsect. 3.2 respectively. The design specification of Grain-128a is described in Subsect. 5.1. A non-randomness in the KSA of Grain-v1 is presented in Sect. 4.

A bias between the key of given valid state and the key of the generated valid state is observed in Subsect. 4.1. Non-randomness in the KSA of Grain-128a is described in Sect. 5.2. Finally, the article is concluded in Sect. 6.

2 Preliminary

In this section, we provide notations, general setup and some definitions, which are followed in the article.

2.1 Notations

The notations used in the paper are listed as following.

- V_n: The vector space $\mathbb{F}_2^n$ over the two elements field $\mathbb{F}_2$.
- K, IV: The secret key and the initialization vector respectively.
- K^*, IV^*: The modified secret key and modified initialization vector respectively.
- k_i, k_i^*, iv_i, iv_i^*: The i-th bit of the key K, K^* and initialization vectors IV, IV^* respectively.
- l, m, n: The length (in bits) of the initialization vector, the secret key and the state in the cipher respectively, where $n > m + l$. In the case of Grain-v1, $l = 64, m = 80, n = 160$ and in the case of Grain-128a, $l = 96, m = 128, n = 256$.
- δ: The difference between the length of state and the length of the secret key and initialization vector i.e., $\delta = n - (m + l)$ (i.e., the length of padding bits). In the case of Grain-v1 and Grain-128a, $\delta = 16, 32$ respectively.
- F: The function of the KSA, $F : V_m \times V_l \mapsto V_n$.
- R_F: The range set of the function F, which is a subset of V_n.
- l_i, n_i: The i-th state bit in LFSR and NFSR respectively. In case of Grain-v1 and Grain-128a, the range of index i is $0 \leq i \leq 79$ and $0 \leq i \leq 127$ respectively.
- $S(l_i), S(n_i)$: The value of state bits l_i and n_i in a state S respectively.
- R: The number of state update rounds involved in the KSA. In the case of Grain-v1 and Grain-128a, the actual value of R is 160 and 256 respectively. For this work, we consider the reduced values of R.
- S: A valid state output by the KSA i.e., $S \in R_F$.
- T: A generated state after flipping few bits in S.
- $\Delta(S, T)$: The set of state bits where S and T differ, i.e., $\Delta(S, T) = \{l_i : S(l_i) \neq T(l_i)\} \cup \{n_i : S(n_i) \neq T(n_i)\}$.
- $S_i, 0 \leq i \leq R$: The state after the i-th round of state update in the KSA. Here, $S_R = S$.
- $T_{R-i}, 0 \leq i \leq R$: The state after the i-th round of inverse state update from the state $T_R = T$.
- $K(S_R), IV(S_R)$: The secret key and the initialization vector used to generate a valid state S_R after R rounds of clocking respectively. That is, $K(S_R) = (S_0(n_0), S_0(n_1), \cdots, S_0(n_{m-1}))$ and $IV(S_R) = (S_0(l_0), S_0(l_1), \cdots, S_0(l_{l-1}))$.

2.2   General Setup of Grain Like Ciphers

In this section, we define a necessary condition for the pseudo-randomness in a general set up of a family of stream ciphers. The ciphers follow the key scheduling phase and pseudorandom bit stream generation phase to produce the keystream bits. The idea of key scheduling algorithm (KSA) is to generate a uniformly random looking state from a pair of shorter uniformly chosen key (K) and initialization vector (IV). Further, the pseudorandom generation algorithm (PRGA) generates the keystream of some length α from the random looking state. In another way, we can say, the cipher transforms a short uniformly random pair K and IV into a longer keystream in two-step processes. That is, the KSA expands the uniformly selected K of length m and IV of length l to a uniformly random looking state of larger length $(n > m+l)$ and the PRGA further, expands the uniformly random looking state of length n to a pseudorandom keystream of length α. If the uniformity is compromised in the output of KSA, the non-randomness is transmitted to the keystream generated from PRGA. Similarly, if uniformity is compromised in the output of PRGA, the non-randomness occurs in the keystream. Therefore, a necessary condition for the keystream to be pseudorandom is that the distribution of output state from KSA and output keystream from PRGA to be pseudorandom.

Let $F : V_m \times V_l \mapsto V_n$ be the KSA function which converts a key of length m bits and an initialization vector of length l bits to a state of length n bits. That is, $S = F(K, IV) \in V_n$ be the state generated by the KSA function F with the input key $K \in V_m$ and initialization vector $IV \in V_l$. Further, let $G : V_n \mapsto V_n \times V_1$ be the PRGA function which generates a new state in V_n and a keystream bit from the input of a state.

In this paper, we study a non-randomness behavior of the KSA function F. Let denote D_F be the distribution on n-bit string generated from F by choosing a uniform m bit key and l bit initialization vector. Now we define pseudorandom state generator as follows.

Definition 1. *The function F is a pseudorandom state generator if and only if the distribution D_F is pseudorandom.*

Therefore, we say F is a pseudorandom state generator if no efficient distinguisher can detect whether given a string $S \in V_n$ is a valid state (i.e., $S \in R_F$) or chosen uniformly in random from V_n. Now we define the pseudorandom state generator in a formal way.

Definition 2. *Let $F : V_m \times V_l \mapsto V_n$ be a polynomial time computable function and $n > m + l$. F is said to be a pseudorandom state generator if, for any probabilistic polynomial time algorithm D, there is a negligible function ngl such that $|Pr[D(F(K, IV)) = 1] - Pr[D(S) = 1]| \leq ngl(m + l)$, where K, IV and S are chosen uniformly in random from V_m, V_l and V_n respectively.*

In practice, the computation of F^{-1} can be done very efficiently, so one can efficiently perform $F^{-1}(S)$ to check whether $S \in R_F$ or $S \notin R_F$. However, for any random $S \in V_n$ one can find whether $S \in R_F$ or $S \notin R_F$ without applying F^{-1} on S with some probability.

Let consider $\delta = n - (m + l)$. The cardinality of the set R_F is 2^{m+l}, with the assumption that F is one to one. If F is a pseudorandom state generator then given a uniformly chosen S from V_n, any efficient distinguisher D can distinguish with probability $Pr[D(S) = 1] = 2^{-\delta} \pm ngl(m+l)$. Therefore, without computing F or F^{-1}, no adversary can be able to pick a valid state S from V_n (i.e., $S \in R_F$) with probability significantly higher than $2^{-\delta}$. For a stronger security notion, we can consider more freedom to the adversary, like querying the value of $F(K, IV)$ for some pairs $(K, IV) \in V_m \times V_l$ and querying whether $S^* \in R_F$ for some $S^* \in V_n \setminus \{S\}$. Let denote this indistinguishability experiment using such chosen queries be as "chosen query indistinguishability experiment".

If F is pseudorandom state generator then any polynomial time adversary should not be able to distinguish with significant probability in any chosen query indistinguishability experiment. Now denoting the distinguisher as D^c, which can query whether $S^* \in R_F$ for any $S^* \in V_n \setminus \{S\}$. Now we define the pseudorandom state generator in stronger notion as following.

Definition 3. *Let $F : V_m \times V_l \mapsto V_n$ be a polynomial time computable function and $n > m + l$. F is a pseudorandom state generator if for any probabilistic polynomial time algorithm D^c, there is a negligible function ngl such that $|Pr[D^c(F(K, IV)) = 1] - Pr[D^c(S) = 1]| \le ngl(m+l)$, where K, IV and S are chosen uniformly from V_m, V_l and V_n respectively.*

In the light of this stronger definition, if F is a pseudorandom state generator then no adversary can distinguish a uniformly chosen string $S \in V_n$ from a string in R_F even after querying on the value of F^{-1} on some chosen strings $S^* \in V_n \setminus \{S\}$.

3 Design Specification of Grain-V1 Stream Cipher

The stream cipher Grain-v1 [11] is based on one 80-bit LFSR, one 80-bit NFSR and one nonlinear filter function of 5 variables. The state bits of LFSR and NFSR are denoted by $l_i, i = 0, 1, \cdots, 79$ and $n_j, j = 0, 1, \cdots, 79$ respectively. The state bits l_i and n_i for $0 \le i \le 79$ are updated in each clock. At the t-th clock, $t \ge 0$, the value of state bits $l_i, n_i, 0 \le i \le 79$ are denoted as l_{t+i}, n_{t+i} respectively. The updates at the t-th clock are done as $l_{t+i} = l_{(t-1)+(i+1)}$ and $n_{t+i} = n_{(t-1)+(i+1)}$ for $0 \le i \le 79$. The state bits l_{t+80}, n_{t+80} are computed as the relations specified in Eqs. (1) and (2) respectively. The linear feedback relation of the LFSR is

$$l_{t+80} = l_{t+62} + l_{t+51} + l_{t+38} + l_{t+23} + l_{t+13} + l_t, \text{ for } t \ge 0. \tag{1}$$

The nonlinear feedback relation of the NFSR is

$$
\begin{aligned}
n_{t+80} = {} & l_t + n_{t+62} + n_{t+60} + n_{t+52} + n_{t+45} + n_{t+37} + n_{t+33} + n_{t+28} + n_{t+21} \\
& + n_{t+14} + n_{t+9} + n_t + n_{t+63}n_{t+60} + n_{t+37}n_{t+33} + n_{t+15}n_{t+9} \\
& + n_{t+60}n_{t+52}n_{t+45} + n_{t+33}n_{t+28}n_{t+21} + n_{t+63}n_{t+45}n_{t+28}n_{t+9} \\
& + n_{t+60}n_{t+52}n_{t+37}n_{t+33} + n_{t+63}n_{t+60}n_{t+21}n_{t+15} \\
& + n_{t+63}n_{t+60}n_{t+52}n_{t+45}n_{t+37} + n_{t+33}n_{t+28}n_{t+21}n_{t+15}n_{t+9} \\
& + n_{t+52}n_{t+45}n_{t+37}n_{t+33}n_{t+28}n_{t+21}, \text{ for } t \geq 0.
\end{aligned}
\tag{2}
$$

The nonlinear filter function is a 5 variable 1-resilient Boolean function of non-linearity 12. The algebraic normal form is given below.

$$
\begin{aligned}
h(x) = {} & x_1 + x_4 + x_0x_3 + x_2x_3 + x_3x_4 + x_0x_1x_2 + x_0x_2x_3 + x_0x_2x_4 \\
& + x_1x_2x_4 + x_2x_3x_4.
\end{aligned}
$$

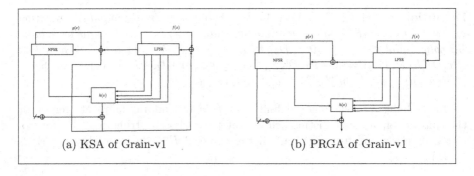

(a) KSA of Grain-v1   (b) PRGA of Grain-v1

Fig. 1. Design specification of Grain-v1

At the t-th clock, the variables $x_0, x_1, \cdots, x_4$ correspond to the state bits $l_{t+3}, l_{t+25}, l_{t+46}, l_{t+64}, n_{t+63}$ respectively. In each clock, the keystream bit z_t is computed by masking few state bits from NFSR with the function h and computed as

$$
z_t = \sum_{k \in A} n_{t+k} + h(l_{t+3}, l_{t+25}, l_{t+46}, l_{t+64}, n_{t+63}),
\tag{3}
$$

where $A = \{1, 2, 4, 10, 31, 43, 56\}$ and $t \geq 0$. The graphical representation of Grain-v1 is provided in Fig. 1.

3.1   KSA of Grain-V1

The cipher is initialized by an 80-bit long secret key (K) and a 64-bit long initialization vector (IV). Let the bits of the secret key K and the initialization vector IV be $k_i, 0 \leq i \leq 79$ and $iv_i, 0 \leq i \leq 63$ respectively. The cipher is initialized to convert the partially random state (i.e., a randomly chosen K) to a full pseudorandom state by spreading the unknown uniform secret key over the whole state. The procedure of this conversion is known as key scheduling algorithm (KSA), which is described as following:

– The NFSR state is loaded by the secret key K as $n_i = k_i, 0 \leq i \leq 79$.
– The LFSR state is loaded by the initialization vector IV and 16 bit long all 1 string (called padding bits) as $l_i = iv_i, 0 \leq i \leq 63$ and $l_i = 1, 64 \leq i \leq 79$.

Then the cipher is clocked for R rounds without generating any keystream bit as output. In each round, the keystream bit (i.e., the output of the masked filter function h) is added to the feedback bits of the LFSR and NFSR. The description of KSA is presented in Algorithm 1 and Fig. 1a. In the case of Grain-v1, the actual number of round R is 160.

Algorithm 1. KSA of Grain-v1
_____

Input : $K = (k_0, k_1, \cdots, k_{79}), IV = (iv_0, iv_1, \cdots, iv_{63})$.
Output: State $S = (n_0, \cdots, n_{79}, l_0, \cdots, l_{79})$ of Grain-v1 after key scheduling
        process.

1 Assign $n_i = k_i$ for $i = 1, \cdots, 79$; $l_i = iv_i$ for $i = 0, \cdots, 63$; $l_i = 1$ for
    $i = 64, \cdots, 79$;

2 **for** R *rounds* **do**

3   Compute $z = \sum_{k \in \mathcal{A}} n_k + h(l_3, l_{25}, l_{46}, l_{64}, n_{63})$, for
       $\mathcal{A} = \{1, 2, 4, 10, 31, 43, 56\}$;

4       $t_1 = z + l_{62} + l_{51} + l_{38} + l_{23} + l_{13} + l_0$;

5       $t_2 = z + n_{80}$ where n_{80} is computed as Equation (2) putting $t = 0$;

6       $n_i = n_{i+1}$ and $l_i = l_{i+1}$ for $i = 0, 1, \cdots, 78$;

7       $l_{79} = t_1$ and $n_{79} = t_2$;

8 **end**

9 **return** $S = (n_0, n_1, \cdots, n_{79}, l_0, l_1, \cdots, l_{79})$;
_____

As defined in Sect. 2.2, the computation of KSA function F consists of both the key loading process and the operations in R rounds of clocking on $m = 80$ bit key and $l = 64$-bit initialization vector. Here we provide the definition of valid padding bits of Grain-v1,

Definition 4. *The last 16 bits of the initial state of the LFSR of key scheduling phase of Grain-v1 (i.e., $(S_0(l_{64}), S_0(l_{65}), \cdots, S_0(l_{79})))$ is known as padding bits of Grain-v1. The padding bits is valid if $S_0(l_{64}) = S_0(l_{65}) = \cdots = S_0(l_{79}) = 1$.*

3.2 Inverse of KSA of Grain-V1

The KSA function F is invertible. Let $S_R = (n_0, \cdots, n_{79}, l_0, \cdots, l_{79}) \in V_{160}$ be an 160 bit string which needs to be inverted to find the corresponding state S_0. Algorithm 2 presents the inverse process of KSA of Grain-v1.

Algorithm 2. Inverse algorithm of KSA of Grain-v1

Input : $S_R = (n_0, n_1, \cdots, n_{79}, l_0, l_1, \cdots, l_{79})$.
Output: Initial state S_0 of KSA i.e., K, IV and the 16 padding bits.
1 **for** R *rounds* **do**
2 $\quad$ $t_1 = n_{79}$ and $t_2 = l_{79}$;
3 $\quad$ $n_i = n_{i-1}$ and $l_i = l_{i-1}$ for $i = 1, 2, \cdots, 79$;
4 $\quad$ Compute $z = \sum_{k \in \mathcal{A}} n_k + h(l_3, l_{25}, l_{46}, l_{64}, n_{63})$, for
   $\quad$ $\mathcal{A} = \{1, 2, 4, 10, 31, 43, 56\}$;
5 $\quad$ $l_0 = z + t_2 + l_{62} + l_{51} + l_{38} + l_{23} + l_{13}$;
6 $\quad$ $n_0 = z + t_1 + l_0 + B(n_1, \cdots, n_{79})$;
7 **end**
8 **return** $S_0 = (n_0, n_1, \cdots, n_{79}, l_0, l_1, \cdots, l_{79})$;

The function B used in Algorithm 2 can be defined from Eq. (2) as $B(n_1, \cdots, n_{79}) = n_{80} + n_0 + l_0$. If the padding bits of the output S_0 is valid then $S_R \in R_F$ and $F^{-1}(S_R)$ returns $K(S_R) = (S_0(n_0), \cdots, S_0(n_{79}))$ and $IV(S_R) = (S_0(l_0), S_0(l_1), \cdots, S_0(l_{63}))$. A random string $S \in V_{160}$ belongs to R_F if Algorithm 2 returns a state S_0 with the valid padding bits. We define a valid state as following.

Definition 5. *A state $S \in V_{160}$ is said to be a valid state of Grain-v1 after KSA (or, simply a valid state), if $S \in R_F$ i.e., the inverse KSA with input S generates a state with the valid padding bits.*

As the KSA of Grain-v1 is one to one (i.e., it is invertible), $|R_F| = 2^{80+64} = 2^{144}$. Therefore, the probability of a uniformly chosen state from V_{160} is a valid state is 2^{-16}. That is, $Pr[S \in R_F | S$ is chosen uniformly from $V_{160}] = 2^{-16}$. This observation is presented in Theorem 1.

Theorem 1. *Any random state $S \in V_{160}$ is a valid state of Grain-v1 after KSA with probability 2^{-16}.*

Therefore, a question is raised as "can one choose a valid state from V_n with probability greater than 2^{-16}?". We define the problem in a more formal way as follows.

Problem 1. Consider we are having a set $\Gamma \subset R_F$ where the size of Γ is as small as possible. Without knowing the computation of F^{-1}, is it possible to choose a S from V_{160} such that S belongs to $R_F \setminus \Gamma$ with probability significantly greater than 2^{-16} ?

Considering the number of rounds $R \leq 129$ in KSA, we show that it is possible to choose an element from R_F with probability significantly greater than 2^{-16}.

4   A Non-randomness of KSA of Grain-V1

Let consider the number of rounds used in Grain-v1 is R. In the actual description of Grain-v1, the value of R is 160. In this section, we prove the existence of a non-randomness in the KSA of Grain-v1 where $R \leq 129$. Given a valid state $S \in V_{160}$, we are able to construct another valid state T with a probability higher than 2^{-16}. Moreover, the distance between the valid states S and T is small. As a result, the initial part of keystream bits generated from both the valid states S and T are very close. Since the KSA function is invertible, one can get two pairs of secret key and initialization vector which generate equal keystream bits with high probability. Therefore, the non-randomness in KSA is transmitted into the keystream from the non-randomness in KSA of Grain-v1.

Our aim is to generate a valid state $T \in V_{160}$ from a given valid state $S \in V_{160}$ for R as large as possible and the distance of S and T is as close as possible. For that purpose, we generate T by flipping few bits in S. For $R = 64$, the values of $S_0(l_{64}), S_0(l_{65}), \cdots, S_0(l_{79})$ are just shifted to $S_{64}(l_0), S_{64}(l_1), \cdots, S_{64}(l_{15})$. Therefore, the first 16 bits of state S_R are 1 (i.e., $S_{64}(l_0) = S_{64}(l_1) = \cdots = S_{64}(l_{15}) = 1$). Then flipping any other bits, one will always get a valid state as the inverse of KSA generates a state with the valid padding bits.

Lemma 1. *Let the number of round in KSA is $R = 64$ and $S \in V_{160}$ is a valid state (i.e., $S \in R_F$). Then the new state $T \in V_{160}$ generated from S by flipping any subset of bits from $\{l_{16}, \cdots, l_{79}, n_0, \cdots, n_{79}\}$ is a valid state (i.e., $T \in R_F$) with probability 1.*

Let consider $R > 64$ and after performing $(R - 64)$ inverse round operations on a valid state $S = S_R$, we have a new state with S_{64} with $l_0 = l_1 = \cdots = l_{15} = 1$. Note that we do not want to flip the bits in the states of NFSR as the feedback function and masking contains many tap points from NFSR which makes the relation complicated. Therefore, our aim is to generate a state T_R by flipping few LFSR bits in the valid state S_R such that after performing $(R - 64)$ inverse rounds on T_R we have $T_{64}(l_0) = \cdots = T_{64}(l_{15}) = 1$ with probability higher than 2^{-16}.

Lemma 2. *Let the number of rounds in KSA is $R > 64$ and $S_R \in V_{160}$ is a valid state (i.e., $S_R \in R_F$). Let a state $T_R \in V_{160}$ is generated from S_R by flipping the state bits in $\Delta(S_R, T_R) \subset \{l_0, l_1, \cdots, l_{79}\}$. After performing $(R - 64)$ inverse rounds of KSA, if we have $T_{64}(l_0) = T_{64}(l_1) = \cdots = T_{64}(l_{15}) = 1$, then T_R is a valid state (i.e., $T_R \in R_F$).*

Let consider $R > 64$. Since S_R is a valid state, then $S_{64}(l_0) = S_{64}(l_1) = \cdots = S_{64}(l_{15}) = 1$ happens with probability 1. However, the probability of $T_{64}(l_0) = T_{64}(l_1) = \cdots = T_{64}(l_{15}) = 1$ is reduced because of the involvement of the flipped bits in the filter function h and the feedback relation in the inverse rounds in KSA (see Algorithm 2). Therefore, our aim is to choose the state bits $\Delta(S_R, T_R) \subset \{l_0, l_1, \cdots, l_{79}\}$ such that flipping those state bits, the involvement of flipped bits in filter function h and the linear feedback relation in Eq. (1)

are minimized or canceling each other. Now we will explore few situations to understand it more a clearly.

Observation 1. Let $\Delta(S_R, T_R) = \{l_{79}\}$ for $R = 65$. As l_{79} is involved in the computation of l_0 in the inverse round computation, the probability of $T_{64}(l_0) = S_{64}(l_0)$ (i.e., $T_{64}(l_0) = 1$) is 0. Same thing happens if the flipping bit is from $\{l_{79}, l_{61}, l_{50}, l_{37}, l_{22}, l_{12}\}$. More generally, if the subset $\Delta(S_R, T_R)$ contains any odd number of state bits from $\{l_{79}, l_{61}, l_{50}, l_{37}, l_{22}, l_{12}\}$, then the probability of $T_{64}(l_0) = 1$ is 0. Hence, T can not be a valid state.

Observation 2. Let $\Delta(S_R, T_R) = \{l_{61}, l_{79}\}$ for $R = 65$. As both l_{62} and l_{79} are involved in the computation of l_0 in the inverse round computation, the probability of $T_{64}(l_0) = S_{64}(l_0)$ (i.e., $T_{64}(l_0) = 1$) is 1. More generally, if the subset $\Delta(S_R, T_R)$ contains any even number of state bits from $\{l_{79}, l_{61}, l_{50}, l_{37}, l_{22}, l_{12}\}$, then the probability of $T_{64}(l_0) = 1$ is 1. Hence, T is always a valid state.

Observation 3. Consider $\Delta(S_R, T_R) = \{l_{24}\}$ for $R = 65$. Here, l_{24} is involved in the computation of l_0 as being an input of the filter function h in the inverse round computation. Therefore, $Pr[T_{64}(l_0) = 1] = Pr[T_{64}(l_0) = S_{64}(l_0)]$ is same as $p = Pr[h(x_1, x_2, x_3, x_4, x_5) = h(x_1, 1 + x_2, x_3, x_4, x_5)]$. The involvement of the flipped bits in the filter function h changes the probability. Hence, T is a valid state with probability p. In more general way, the probability is being changed when a subset of flipped bits are from $\{l_2, l_{24}, l_{45}, l_{63}\}$.

From Observation 2, it is clear that if an even number of flipped bits are involved in the linear feedback relation then no new flipped bit is generated as they cancel each other. Therefore, to reduce the number of new flipped bit generation, we need to choose the bits such that an even number of flipped bits are very often involved in the inverse rounds.

We see that $l_3, l_{13}, l_{23}, l_{25}, l_{38}, l_{46}, l_{51}, l_{62}, l_{64}, l_{80}$ are the LFSR state bits (in increased order of their index) which are involved in the feedback function and the filter functions during each inverse round of KSA. The difference between the indices of the pair of states l_{46} and l_{62} (i.e., 16) is same as the difference between the indices of the pair of states l_{64} and l_{80}. This equality helps to move the flips at l_{46} and l_{64} to l_{61} and l_{79} respectively, in 15 inverse rounds. But in between when l_{46} reaches at l_{51} after 5 inverse rounds, it faces a tab point in feedback function. To cancel the difference we consider a flip at l_{75}. So, at the 5-th inverse round, the flips are given at l_{46} and l_{75} reaches as l_{51} and l_{80} respectively. They cancel each other and the flipped bit l_{80} goes out. At the 16-th inverse round, the flips are given at l_{46} and l_{64} reach as flips at l_{62} and l_{80} respectively and no extra flip is generated. Hence only one flip at l_{62} remains as l_{80} goes out. Table 1 summarizes the execution of 17 inverse rounds of KSA on the state which is flipped at l_{46}, l_{64}, l_{75}. Let denote $\Delta(S_r, T_r) = \{l_i : S_r(l_i) \neq T_r(l_i)\} \cup \{n_i : S_r(n_i) \neq T_r(n_i)\}$.

At the 18-th inverse KSA round, the LFSR state bit l_{64} is used in the filter function h as the variable x_3.

The function h has a property that $Pr[h(x_0, x_1, x_2, x_3, x_4) = h(x_0, x_1, x_2, 1 + x_3, x_4)] = \frac{1}{4}$. $Pr[\Delta(S_{R-18}, T_{R-18}) = \{l_{64}\}] = \frac{1}{4}$ and $Pr[\Delta(S_{R-18}, T_{R-18}) =$

Table 1. Movement of flips in the execution of inverse rounds with certainty

Round No.(r)	$\Delta(S_r, T_r)$
R	$\{l_{46}, l_{64}, l_{75}\}$
$R - 1$	$\{l_{47}, l_{65}, l_{76}\}$
$R - 4$	$\{l_{50}, l_{68}, l_{79}\}$
$R - 5$	$\{l_{51}, l_{69}\}$
$R - 15$	$\{l_{61}, l_{79}\}$
$R - 16$	$\{l_{62}\}$
$R - 17$	$\{l_{63}\}$

$\{l_{64}, l_0\}] = \frac{3}{4}$. Hence, two different paths are created with different probabilities. Now we consider the simpler situation where $\Delta(S_{R-18}, T_{R-18}) = \{l_{64}\}$. Note that the other situation too adds some more probability for the happening of T_r be a valid state. Table 2 summarizes the execution of 20 more inverse rounds of KSA from the $(R - 17)$-th inverse round.

Table 2. Movement of flips in the execution of inverse rounds with partial probability

Round No.(r)	$\Delta(S_r, T_r)$
$R - 18$	$\{l_{64}\}$ with probability $\frac{1}{4}$
$R - 19$	$\{l_{65}\}$ with probability $\frac{1}{4}$
$R - 32$	$\{l_{78}\}$ with probability $\frac{1}{4}$
$R - 33$	$\{l_{79}\}$ with probability $\frac{1}{4}$
$R - 34$	$\{l_0, b_0\}$ with probability $\frac{1}{4}$
$R - 35$	$\{l_0, l_1, b_1\}$ with probability $\frac{1}{4}$
$R - 36$	$\{l_0, l_1, l_2, b_2\}$ with probability $\frac{1}{4}$
$R - 37$	$\{l_1, l_2, l_3, b_3\}$ with probability $\frac{1}{8}$ $\{l_0, l_1, l_2, l_3, b_3\}$ with probability $\frac{1}{8}$

In the 37-th round, l_3 is involved in h as the variable x_0 and $Pr[h(x_0, x_1, \cdots, x_4) = h(1 + x_0, x_1, x_2, x_3, x_4)] = \frac{1}{2}$. Hence, $Pr[\Delta(S_{R-37}, T_{R-37}) = \{l_1, l_2, l_3, b_3\}] = \frac{1}{2}$ and $Pr[\Delta(S_{R-37}, T_{R-37}) = \{l_0, l_1, l_2, l_3, b_3\}] = \frac{1}{2}$. As a result, two more different paths are created with probability $\frac{1}{2}$.

Let consider $R = 97$ and T_R is generated from a valid state S_R by flipping the values at l_{46}, l_{64}, l_{75}. Then after executing 33 inverse rounds, the valid state S_{64} and the state T_{64} are different only at l_{79} with probability at least $\frac{1}{4}$. The state values of S_{64} and T_{64} at $l_0, l_1, \cdots, l_{15}$ remains same with value 1. Therefore, the chance of T_R is being a valid state is at least $\frac{1}{4}$.

However, if we would consider $R = 98$, then T_R is generated from a valid state S_R by flipping the values at l_{46}, l_{64}, l_{75}. Then after executing 34 inverse rounds, the valid state S_{64} and the state T_{64} are different at l_0 and b_0 with probability at least $\frac{1}{4}$. As the state values of S_{64} and T_{64} at l_0 are different, the chance of T_R is not being a valid state is at least $\frac{1}{4}$. From these two situations, we claim Theorem 2 and Corollary 1.

Theorem 2. *Consider $R > 64$ and a new state $T_R \in V_{160}$ is generated from a valid state $S_R \in V_{160}$ by flipping the value of the state bits at $\Delta(S_R, T_R) \subseteq \{l_0, l_1, \cdots, l_{79}\}$. If $\Delta(S_{64}, T_{64}) \cap \{l_0, l_1, \cdots, l_{15}\} = \emptyset$ with probability p then the probability of T_R is a valid state is p.*

Corollary 1. *A state $T_R \in V_{160}$ is generated from a valid state $S_R \in V_{160}$ by flipping the value of the state bits at $\Delta(S_R, T_R) = \{l_{46}, l_{64}, l_{75}\}$.*

1. *If $65 \le R \le 81$ then T_R is always a valid state.*
2. *If $82 \le R \le 97$ then T_R is a valid state with probability $\frac{1}{4}$.*
3. *For some positive integer t, T_R is a valid state with probability 0 where $98 \le R \le 98 + t$.*

Proof. 1. If $65 \le R \le 81$ then $\Delta(S_{64}, T_{64})$ never contains a state value from $l_0, l_1, \cdots, l_{15}$ (see Table 1). Hence, T_R always yields a valid state.
2. If $R \ge 82$ it is clear from Table 2 that at the 18-th inverse round, $\Delta(S_{R-18}, T_{R-18})$ forks into $\Delta_1 = \{l_{64}\}$ with probability $\frac{1}{4}$ and $\Delta_2 = \{l_{64}, l_0\}$ with probability $\frac{3}{4}$. In the direction of the second fork, as Δ_2 contains l_0 for $82 \le R \le 97$, $\Delta(S_{64}, T_{64})$ always contains a state value from $l_0, l_1, \cdots, l_{15}$. Hence, T_R never yields a valid state in the second fork which happens with probability $\frac{3}{4}$. However, in the direction of first fork (which happens with probability $\frac{1}{4}$), $\Delta(S_{64}, T_{64})$ never contains a state value from $l_0, l_1, \cdots, l_{15}$. Hence, T_R always yields a valid state with probability $\frac{1}{4}$.
3. In the direction of first fork, it is clear from $(R - 34)$-th inverse round in Table 2 that $\Delta(S_{64}, T_{64})$ always contains a state value from $l_0, l_1, \cdots, l_{15}$ for some $R \ge 98$. Similarly, in the direction of the second fork, it can be checked that $\Delta(S_{64}, T_{64})$ always contains a state value from $l_0, l_1, \cdots, l_{15}$ for some $R \ge 98$. Hence, for $98 \le R \le 98 + t$, T_R can not be a valid state for some values of $t \ge 0$.

We performed experiments on random data size of 2^{26} key $K \in V_{80}$ and initialization vector $IV \in V_{64}$ pairs. We generate $S_R \in V_{160}$ for each pair of $(K, IV) \in V_{144}$ and corresponding $T_R \in V_{160}$ by flipping the state values at l_{46}, l_{64}, l_{75}. Our experiments for each $R, (65 \le R \le 160)$ and the probability of T_R being a valid state are presented in Table 3. The experiment results support the facts presented in Corollary 1.

The experimental results show that we can answer Problem 1 for $R \le 129$. It is possible to construct a valid state from a given valid state with probability different than 2^{-16}. However, it is observed that for $R = 124, 125$ the bias is significant than the uniformity.

Table 3. Experimental result of probability of T_R being a valid state

Round no. (R)	Probability	Round no. (R)	Probability
$65 \leq R \leq 81$	$=1$	$82 \leq R \leq 97$	$=\frac{1}{4}$
$98 \leq R \leq 117$	$=0$	$R = 118$	$\approx 4.17 \times 2^{-16}$
$R = 119$	$\approx 3.13 \times 2^{-16}$	$R = 120$	$\approx 2.30 \times 2^{-16}$
$R = 121$	$\approx 2.78 \times 2^{-16}$	$R = 122$	$\approx 1.91 \times 2^{-16}$
$R = 123$	$\approx 1.26 \times 2^{-16}$	$R = 124$	$\approx 4.10 \times 2^{-16}$
$R = 125$	$\approx 3.80 \times 2^{-16}$	$R = 126$	$\approx 1.94 \times 2^{-16}$
$R = 127$	$\approx 1.98 \times 2^{-16}$	$R = 128$	$\approx 1.51 \times 2^{-16}$
$R = 129$	$\approx 1.16 \times 2^{-16}$	$130 \leq R \leq 160$	$\approx 1 \times 2^{-16}$

4.1 Non-randomness in the Key, IV Bits

From a valid state $S = S_R$ ($R \leq 129$), we can generate another valid state $T = T_R$ with probability greater than 2^{-16}. Let the key and initialization vector pair corresponding to the valid state S and the generated valid state T be (K, IV) and (K^*, IV^*) respectively. The next natural question raised as, what is the relation between these two key, initialization vector pairs. We observed experimentally that there are significant biases in the secret key bits. The Table 5 summarizes the significant biases in key bits as $p_i = Pr(k_i = k_i^*), 0 \leq i \leq 79$ where k_i and k_i^* are i-th key bits of K and K^* respectively.

There are also biases in IV bits. We observed that for $R = 118, 125$, the bias $Pr[iv_{63} = iv_{63}^*] = 0, 0.43$ respectively. Let construct a key $\tilde{K}$ from K^* as the i-th bit $\tilde{k}_i = k_i^*$ where $p_i \geq 0.5$ else $\tilde{k}_i = 1 + k_i^*$. Let denote $\epsilon_i = p_i$ if $p_i \geq 0.5$ else $\epsilon_i = 1 - 0.5$. Therefore, the original key K will match with the new key $\tilde{K}$ with probability $P = \prod_{i=0}^{79} \epsilon_i$. A necessary condition for randomness in KSA would be that the keys K and K^* are not having any bias i.e., $P = \prod_{i=0}^{79} \epsilon_i = 2^{-80}$. From the observation presented in Table 5, it is clear that the keys are related. However, we present the value of $\prod_{i=0}^{79} \epsilon_i$ for rounds R in Table 4.

Table 4. Biases in the secret key for different rounds R

Round (R)	Biases $P = \prod_{i=0}^{79} \epsilon_i$	Round (R)	Biases $P = \prod_{i=0}^{79} \epsilon_i$
118	$\approx \frac{2^{17}}{2^{80}}$	119	$\approx \frac{2^{17}}{2^{80}}$
120	$\approx \frac{2^{15}}{2^{80}}$	121	$\approx \frac{2^{10}}{2^{80}}$
122	$\approx \frac{2^{7}}{2^{80}}$	123	$\approx \frac{2^{7}}{2^{80}}$
124	$\approx \frac{2^{13}}{2^{80}}$	125	$\approx \frac{2^{12}}{2^{80}}$
126	$\approx \frac{2^{10}}{2^{80}}$	127	$\approx \frac{2^{8}}{2^{80}}$
128	$\approx \frac{2^{6}}{2^{80}}$	129	$\approx \frac{2^{5}}{2^{80}}$

Table 5. Biases into the secret key bits for different rounds R

Round (R)	Indices of key bits (i)	Biases $p_i = Pr[k_i = k_i^*]$
118	$59, 64 \leq i \leq 79$	$0.38, 1, 0, 0, 0, 1, 0, 0, 0, 1, 1, 0, 0, 1, 0, 0, 1$
119	$51, 57, 65 \leq i \leq 79$	$0.66, 0.67, 0.97, 1, 0, 0.034, 0.034, 0, 0, 0.97,$ $0.34, 1, 0.034, 0.034, 1, 0, 0.034$
120	$52, 58, 59, 65 \leq i \leq 79$	$0.59, 0.62, 0.39, 0.25, 0.99, 1, 0.3, 0.009, 0.31, 0,$ $0, 0.7, 0.31, 1, 0.009, 0.009, 1, 0$
121	$54, 63 \leq i \leq 66,$ $68 \leq i \leq 79$	$0.41, 0.61, 0.41, 0.6, 0.38, 0.78, 0.38, 0.24, 0.38,$ $0.29, 0.21, 0.6, 0.2, 1, 0.35, 0.35, 1$
122	$64, 65, 69, 71, 73, 74,$ $76 \leq i \leq 79$	$0.6, 0.38, 0.6, 0.28, 0.38, 0.3, 0.16, 1, 0.33, 0.42$
123	$66, 70, 72, 74, 75,$ $77 \leq i \leq 79$	$0.38, 0.62, 0.32, 0.36, 0.3, 0.18, 1, 0.37$
124	$63, 66 \leq i \leq 79$	$0.83, 0.69, 0.84, 0.85, 0.15, 0.15, 0.87, 0.86,$ $0.11, 0.15, 0.11, 0.8, 0.16, 0.79, 1$
125	$61, 62, 64 \leq i \leq 79$	$0.43, 0.69, 0.84, 0.6, 0.32, 0.71, 0.85, 0.85, 0.39,$ $0.46, 0.78, 0.87, 0.11, 0.39, 0.34, 0.84, 0.16, 0.82$
126	$56, 63, 65 \leq i \leq 71,$ $73 \leq i \leq 79$	$0.6, 0.68, 0.81, 0.43, 0.4, 0.65, 0.8, 0.8, 0.36, 0.7,$ $0.8, 0.15, 0.37, 0.31, 0.8, 0.18$
127	$59, 66, 72 \leq i \leq 79$	$0.61, 0.82, 0.25, 0.28, 0.8, 0.8, 0.17, 0.26, 0.2, 0.81$
128	$67, 73 \leq i \leq 79$	$0.68, 0.33, 0.35, 0.73, 0.71, 0.22, 0.35, 0.3$
129	$74 \leq i \leq 79$	$0.38, 0.36, 0.67, 0.64, 0.31, 0.41$

5   Non-randomness in KSA of Grain-128a Stream Cipher

Grain-128a is a longer state version stream cipher in Grain family. Using similar technique as in Grain-v1, we too found a non-randomness in KSA of Grain-128a. In this section, we briefly present the result of the non-randomness in KSA of Grain-128a.

5.1   Design Specification of Grain-128a Stream Cipher

In 2011, Ågren et al. [2] modified the Grain-128 stream cipher [10] and introduced Grain-128a with authentication mode. Grain-128a is based on one 128-bit NFSR, one 128-bit LFSR and a nonlinear filter function. The state bits of the NFSR is denoted by n_i, $0 \leq i \leq 127$ and LFSR state bits are denoted by l_i, $0 \leq i \leq 127$. In each clock, the state bits of LFSR and NFSR are shifted by usual method and feedback bits are computed as in Eqs. (4) and (5) respectively.

$$l_{t+128} = l_t + l_{t+7} + l_{t+38} + l_{t+70} + l_{t+81} + l_{t+96}, \text{ for } t \geq 0. \tag{4}$$

$$n_{t+128} = s_t + n_t + n_{t+26} + n_{t+56} + n_{t+91} + n_{t+96} + n_{t+3}n_{t+67} + n_{t+11}n_{t+13}$$
$$+ n_{t+17}n_{t+18} + n_{t+27}n_{t+59} + n_{t+40}n_{t+48} + n_{t+61}n_{t+65} + n_{t+68}n_{t+84}$$
$$+ n_{t+88}n_{t+92}n_{t+93}n_{t+95} + n_{t+22}n_{t+24}n_{t+25}$$
$$+ n_{t+70}n_{t+78}n_{t+82}, \text{ for } t \geq 0. \tag{5}$$

The nonlinear filter function (h) is a Boolean function involving 9 variables. These 9 variables correspond to 7 state bits of LFSR and 2 state bits of NFSR. The algebraic normal form of the nonlinear filter function is

$$h(x) = x_0 x_1 + x_2 x_3 + x_4 x_5 + x_6 x_7 + x_0 x_4 x_8, \tag{6}$$

where $x_0, x_1, \cdots, x_8$ correspond to $n_{t+12}, l_{t+8}, l_{t+13}, l_{t+20}, n_{t+95}, l_{t+42}, l_{t+60}, l_{t+79}, l_{t+94}$ respectively.

In each clocking (t), the keystream bit y_t is computed by masking 7 state bits of NFSR, one state bit from LFSR with the output of the nonlinear filter function h as

$$y_t = h(x) + l_{t+93} + \sum_{j \in A} n_{t+j}, \tag{7}$$

where $A = \{2, 15, 36, 45, 64, 73, 89\}$. Grain-128a is presented graphically in Fig. 2a,

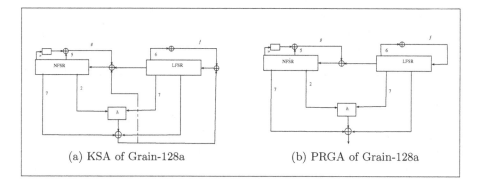

(a) KSA of Grain-128a   (b) PRGA of Grain-128a

Fig. 2. Design specification of Grain-128a

In the key scheduling phase, the cipher is initialized by one 128-bit secret key (K) and one 96-bit initialization vector (IV). The secret key bits are denoted by $k_i, 0 \leq i \leq 127$ and IV bits are denoted by $iv_i, 0 \leq i \leq 95$. The state is loaded with key bits, initialization vector bits and padding bits as follows.

- The secret key bits are loaded into the NFSR as $n_i = k_i$ for $0 \leq i \leq 127$.
- IV bits are loaded into the LFSR as $l_i = iv_i$ for $0 \leq i \leq 95$.
- Remaining 32 positions of LFSR are filled by the padding bits as $l_i = 1$ for $96 \leq i \leq 126$ and $l_{127} = 0$.

Then the cipher is clocked for R rounds, without producing any output bits, rather in each clocking the output bit (y_t) is added to the feedback bits of the NFSR and LFSR (see Fig. 2b). In case of full round Grain-128a the number of rounds $R = 256$. The KSA of Grain-128a is presented in Algorithm 3.

Algorithm 3. KSA of Grain-128a

Input : $K = (k_0, k_1, \cdots, k_{127}), IV = (iv_0, iv_1, \cdots, iv_{95})$.
Output: State $S = (n_0, \cdots, n_{127}, l_0, \cdots, l_{127})$ of Grain-v1 after key scheduling
process.

1 Assign $n_i = k_i$ for $0 \le i \le 127$; $l_i = iv_i$ for $0 \le i \le 95$; $l_i = 1$ for $96 \le i \le 126$,
$l_{127} = 0$;

2 **for** R *rounds* **do**

3 $\quad$ Compute $z = \sum_{k \in \mathcal{A}} n_k + l_{93} + h(n_{12}, l_8, l_{13}, l_{20}, n_{95}, l_{42}, l_{60}, l_{79}, l_{94})$ for
$\quad$ $\mathcal{A} = \{2, 15, 36, 45, 64, 73, 89\}$;

4 $\quad$ $t_1 = z + l_0 + l_7 + l_{38} + l_{70} + l_{81} + l_{96}$;

5 $\quad$ $t_2 = z + n_{128}$ where n_{128} is computed as Equation (5) ;

6 $\quad$ $n_i = n_{i+1}$ and $l_i = l_{i+1}$ for $i = 0, 1, \cdots, 126$;

7 $\quad$ $l_{127} = t_1$ and $n_{127} = t_2$;

8 **end**

9 **return** $S = (n_0, n_1, \cdots, n_{127}, l_0, l_1, \cdots, l_{127})$;

Definition 6. *The last 32 bits of the initial state of the LFSR of key scheduling phase of Grain-128a is known as padding bits. The padding bits is valid if first 31 bits are 1 and last bit is 0.*

The KSA function F of Grain-128a is invertible. The inversion algorithm on the input $S_R = (n_0, n_1, \cdots, n_{127}, l_0, l_1, \cdots, l_{127}) \in V_{256}$ to get the initial state S_0 is presented in Algorithm 4.

The function G used in Algorithm 4 can be defined from Eq. (5). If the output of the Algorithm 4 i.e., the state S_0, contains the valid padding bits then $S_R \in R_F$ and F^{-1} returns $K(S_R) = (S_0(n_0), S_0(n_1), \cdots, S_0(n_{127}))$ and $IV(S_R) = (S_0(l_0), S_0(l_1), \cdots, S_0(l_{95}))$.

Definition 7. *A state S after KSA of Grain-128a is said to be a valid state if the inverse KSA of Grain-128a returns a state S_0 with a valid padding on the input S.*

As $|R_F| = 2^{128+96} = 2^{224}$, the probability of a uniformly chosen state from V_{256} is a valid state is 2^{-32}. i.e., $Pr[S \in R_F|\ S$ is chosen uniformly from $V_{256}] = 2^{-32}$. This observation is presented in Theorem 3.

Theorem 3. *Any random state $S \in V_{256}$ is a valid state of Grain-128a after KSA with a probability 2^{-32}.*

Therefore, in the following subsection, we will generate a valid state with probability higher than 2^{-32} to prove the existence of non-randomness in the KSA of Grain-128a.

Algorithm 4. Inverse KSA of Grain-128a

   Input : $S_R = (n_0, n_1, \cdots, n_{127}, l_0, l_1, \cdots, l_{127})$.
   Output: Initial state of KSA of Grain-128a.
1 **for** R *clockings* **do**
2 | $t_1 = n_{127}$ and $t_2 = l_{127}$;
3 | $n_i = n_{i-1}$ and $l_i = l_{i-1}$ for $i = 1, 2, \cdots, 127$;
4 | Compute $y = l_{93} + h(n_{12}, \cdots, l_{94}) + \sum_{k \in \mathcal{A}} n_k$, $\mathcal{A} = \{2, 15, 36, 45, 64, 73, 89\}$;
5 | $l_0 = y + t_2 + l_7 + l_{38} + l_{70} + l_{81} + l_{96}$;
6 | $n_0 = y + t_1 + l_0 + G(n_1, \cdots, n_{127})$;
7 **end**
8 **return** $S_0 = (n_0, n_1, \cdots, n_{127}, l_0, l_1, \cdots, l_{127})$;

5.2   Non-randomness of KSA of Grain-128a

In this section, we prove a non-randomness in the KSA of Grain-128a for a reduced round $R \leq 208$, whereas $R = 256$ in the proposed one. Like the case of Grain-v1 in Sect. 4, we could generate a valid state T after flipping some state bits in a given valid state with a probability higher than 2^{-32}.

The goal is to generate a valid state T_R from a valid state $S_R \in V_{256}$ of Grain-128a for R as large as possible. To maintain a small distance between T_R and S_R, we construct T_R by flipping few bits of S_R. It can be observed that at $R = 96$, the values of $S_0(l_{96}), S_0(l_{97}), \cdots, S_0(l_{127})$ are shifted to $S_{96}(l_0), S_{96}(l_1)$, $\cdots, S_{96}(l_{31})$. Since $S_{96}(l_0) = S_{96}(l_1) = \cdots = S_{96}(l_{30}) = 1$ and $S_{96}(l_{31}) = 0$, another valid state T_R can be generated by flipping any other bits of S_{96}.

Lemma 3. *Let the number of round in KSA is $R = 96$ and $S_R \in V_{256}$ is a valid state (i.e., $S_R \in R_F$). Then $T_R \in V_{256}$, which is generated from S_R by flipping any subset of bits of $\{l_{32}, \cdots, l_{127}, n_0, \cdots, n_{127}\}$, is a valid state (i.e., $T_R \in R_F$) with probability 1.*

Now we consider the case when $R > 96$. If we perform $(R - 96)$ inverse KSA rounds from a valid state S_R then we will have a state S_{96} with $l_0 = l_1 = \cdots = l_{30} = 1, l_{31} = 0$. Hence, we should flip few bits of S_R to generate T_R such that after performing $(R - 96)$ inverse rounds on T_R, we will get $T_{96}(l_0) = T_{96}(l_1) = \cdots = T_{96}(l_{30}) = 1, T_{96}(l_{31}) = 0$ with a probability greater than 2^{-32}.

Lemma 4. *Let the number of rounds in KSA be $R > 96$ and $S_R \in V_{256}$ is a valid state (i.e., $S_R \in R_F$). A state $T_R \in V_{256}$ is generated from S_R by flipping the state bits in $\Delta(S_R, T_R) \subset \{n_0, \cdots, n_{127}, l_0, \cdots, l_{127}\}$. After performing $(R - 96)$ inverse rounds of KSA, if $T_{96}(l_0) = T_{96}(l_1) = \cdots = T_{96}(l_{30}) = 1, T_{96}(l_{31}) = 0$, then T_R is a valid state (i.e., $T_R \in R_F$).*

Now from the valid state S_R for $R > 96$, we construct another state T_R by flipping the bits l_{35} and l_{93}. We perform the inverse algorithm of Grain-128a Algorithm 4 for $R = 141$ rounds on the state T_R. We observed that the padding bits of T_0 is valid with a probability much greater than $\frac{1}{2^{32}}$. For this experiment, we have randomly chosen 2^{30} random key, IV pairs. If the feedback bits of j-th inverse KSA round where $j = 45, 44, \cdots, 13$ on S_R and T_R remain same, then the last 32 bits of S_0 and T_0 will be same. Therefore, we need to select the flipping positions in such a way that the number of times the happening of the event $S_{R-t}(l_0) = 1 + T_{R-t}(l_0)$ (i.e., the LFSR feedback bit during the t-th inverse KSA round) is minimized for $0 \leq t \leq 96$. Looking into this fact, we have chosen the l_{35} and l_{93} as the flipping bits and experimentally observed that one can construct another valid state from a valid state of Grain-128a of 141 round with a probability much greater than $\frac{1}{2^{32}}$.

Our next task is to extend this non-randomness to the higher rounds. Hence, we start the KSA of Grain-128a from the round 141 with two states S_{141} and T_{141}. These two states are exactly same except at the two positions (i.e., at the 35-th and 93-rd positions) where they are flipped. That is, $\Delta(S_{141}, T_{141}) = \{l_{35}, l_{93}\}$. Now we run the KSA on the states S_{141} and T_{141}. Since l_{93} is involved in the keystream bit z as a part of the mask bits, the feedback bits of LFSR and NFSR are flipped in the next clock i.e., $S_{142}(l_{127}) = 1 + T_{142}(l_{127})$ and $S_{142}(n_{127}) = 1 + T_{142}(n_{127})$. Hence, we have $\Delta(S_{142}, T_{142}) = \{n_{127}, l_{34}, l_{92}, l_{127}\}$.

Now, we continue the KSA for more rounds and update the set $\Delta(S_R, T_R)$. We include more flipping positions in $\Delta(S_R, T_R)$ when the feedback bits directly flips as in the case of $R = 142$. We continue this process for 67 rounds and we have $\Delta(S_{208}, T_{208})$ as

$$\Delta(S_{208}, T_{208}) = \{n_{57}, n_{89}, n_{94}, n_{96}, n_{104}, n_{112}, l_{22}, l_{57}, l_{69}, l_{80}, l_{85}, l_{89}, l_{96}, l_{101},$$
$$l_{112}, l_{116}, l_{117}, l_{120}, l_{124}\}.$$

Therefore, for a given S_{208}, we generate T_{208} with flipping the bits at $\Delta(S_{208}, T_{208})$. Then after 67 inverse KSA rounds, we will get a state T_{141} where $\Delta(S_{141}, T_{141}) = \{l_{35}, l_{93}\}$ with some probability, say q_1. Further, running the 141 inverse KSA rounds from T_{141} we will have a valid state T_0 with some probability q_2 which will be lesser than q_1. However, our aim is to check whether the q_2 is significantly greater than the uniform probability $\frac{1}{2^{32}}$. To verify this fact, we performed the experiment for 2^{30} random key and IV pairs and we found that $Pr[T_{208}$ is a valid state$] \approx \frac{9}{2^{30}} > \frac{1}{2^{32}}$.

As a conclusion of this section, we state that from a valid state S_{208} at the 208-th round of KSA of Grain-128a one can generate another valid state T_{208} with probability greater than $\frac{1}{2^{32}}$ by flipping the bits mentioned in $\Delta(S_{208}, T_{208})$.

6   Conclusion

In this paper, we have presented a non-randomness criterion in KSA of Grain family of stream ciphers. We have shown that it is possible to construct a valid state by flipping few bits of a valid state at R-th round of KSA of Grain-v1 and Grain-128a with probability significantly different than the uniform probability 2^{-16} and 2^{-32} respectively. We have shown the existence of the non-randomness up to 129 and 208 KSA round of Grain-v1 and Grain-128a respectively. Although we could not exploit the non-randomness into an attack, the existence of such non-randomness should not be expected in any pseudorandom keystream generator. As the states are very close, the initial keystream bits generated from these two states will be same with very high probability. We further, observed the bias among the secret keys of the two valid states in Grain-v1. As some lightweight ciphers such as Lizard, Plantlet share a very similar type of design as Grain family of stream ciphers, a similar kind of analysis can possibly be implemented on them.

References

1. eSTREAM: Stream cipher project for Ecrypt (2005)
2. Ågren, M., Hell, M., Johansson, T., Meier, W.: A new version of Grain-128 with authentication. In: Symmetric Key Encryption Workshop (2011)
3. Aumasson, J.P., Dinur, I., Henzen, L., Meier, W., Shamir, A.: Efficient FPGA implementations of high-dimensional cube testers on the stream cipher Grain-128. SHARCS 2009 Special-Purpose Hardware for Attacking Cryptographic Systems, p. 147 (2009)
4. Banik, S.: Some insights into differential cryptanalysis of Grain v1. In: Susilo, W., Mu, Y. (eds.) ACISP 2014. LNCS, vol. 8544, pp. 34–49. Springer, Cham (2014). https://doi.org/10.1007/978-3-319-08344-5_3
5. Banik, S.: Conditional differential cryptanalysis of 105 round Grain v1. Crypt. Commun. **8**(1), 113–137 (2016)
6. Banik, S., Maitra, S., Sarkar, S.: A differential fault attack on the grain family of stream ciphers. In: Prouff, E., Schaumont, P. (eds.) CHES 2012. LNCS, vol. 7428, pp. 122–139. Springer, Heidelberg (2012). https://doi.org/10.1007/978-3-642-33027-8_8
7. Banik, S., Maitra, S., Sarkar, S.: A differential fault attack on the grain family under reasonable assumptions. In: Galbraith, S., Nandi, M. (eds.) INDOCRYPT 2012. LNCS, vol. 7668, pp. 191–208. Springer, Heidelberg (2012). https://doi.org/10.1007/978-3-642-34931-7_12
8. Dinur, I., Shamir, A.: Breaking Grain-128 with dynamic cube attacks. In: Joux, A. (ed.) FSE 2011. LNCS, vol. 6733, pp. 167–187. Springer, Heidelberg (2011). https://doi.org/10.1007/978-3-642-21702-9_10
9. Fischer, S., Khazaei, S., Meier, W.: Chosen IV statistical analysis for key recovery attacks on stream ciphers. In: Vaudenay, S. (ed.) AFRICACRYPT 2008. LNCS, vol. 5023, pp. 236–245. Springer, Heidelberg (2008). https://doi.org/10.1007/978-3-540-68164-9_16
10. Hell, M., Johansson, T., Maximov, A., Meier, W.: A stream cipher proposal: Grain-128. In: IEEE International Symposium on Information Theory (ISIT 2006). Citeseer (2006)
11. Hell, M., Johansson, T., Meier, W.: Grain: a stream cipher for constrained environments. Int. J. Wirel. Mob. Comput. **2**(1), 86–93 (2007)
12. Knellwolf, S., Meier, W., Naya-Plasencia, M.: Conditional differential cryptanalysis of NLFSR-based cryptosystems. In: Abe, M. (ed.) ASIACRYPT 2010. LNCS, vol. 6477, pp. 130–145. Springer, Heidelberg (2010). https://doi.org/10.1007/978-3-642-17373-8_8

13. Lehmann, M., Meier, W.: Conditional differential cryptanalysis of Grain-128a. In: Pieprzyk, J., Sadeghi, A.-R., Manulis, M. (eds.) CANS 2012. LNCS, vol. 7712, pp. 1–11. Springer, Heidelberg (2012). https://doi.org/10.1007/978-3-642-35404-5_1

14. Ma, Z., Tian, T., Qi, W.F.: Improved conditional differential attacks on Grain v1. IET Inf. Secur. **11**(1), 46–53 (2016)

15. Sarkar, S.: A new distinguisher on Grain v1 for 106 rounds. In: Jajodia, S., Mazumdar, C. (eds.) ICISS 2015. LNCS, vol. 9478, pp. 334–344. Springer, Cham (2015). https://doi.org/10.1007/978-3-319-26961-0_20

16. Watanabe, Y., Todo, Y., Morii, M.: New conditional differential cryptanalysis for NLFSR-based stream ciphers and application to Grain v1. In: 2016 11th Asia Joint Conference on Information Security (AsiaJCIS), pp. 115–123. IEEE (2016)

Template-Based Fault Injection Analysis of Block Ciphers

Ashrujit Ghoshal$^{(\boxtimes)}$, Sikhar Patranabis , and Debdeep Mukhopadhyay

Indian Institute of Technology Kharagpur, Kharagpur, India
{ashrujitg,sikhar.patranabis}@iitkgp.ac.in,
debdeep@cse.iitkgp.ac.in

Abstract. We present the first template-based fault injection analysis of FPGA-based block cipher implementations. While template attacks have been a popular form of side-channel analysis in the cryptographic literature, the use of templates in the context of fault attacks has not yet been explored to the best of our knowledge. Our approach involves two phases. The first phase is a profiling phase where we build templates of the fault behavior of a cryptographic device for different secret key segments under different fault injection intensities. This is followed by a matching phase where we match the observed fault behavior of an identical but black-box device with the pre-built templates to retrieve the secret key. We present a generic treatment of our template-based fault attack approach for SPN block ciphers, and illustrate the same with case studies on a Xilinx Spartan-6 FPGA-based implementation of AES-128.

Keywords: Template attacks · Fault injection · Fault intensity

1 Introduction

The advent of implementation-level attacks has challenged the security of a number of mathematically robust cryptosystems, including symmetric-key cryptographic primitives such as block ciphers and stream ciphers, as well as public-key encryption schemes. Implementation attacks come in two major flavors - side-channel analysis (SCA) and fault injection analysis (FIA). SCA techniques typically monitor the leakage of a cryptographic implementation from various channels, such as timing/power/EM radiations, and attempt to infer the secret-key from these leakages [14,16]. FIA techniques, on the other hand, actively perturb the correct execution of a cryptographic implementation via voltage/clock glitches [1,2,23], EM pulses [8] or precise laser beams [4,5]. With the growing number of physically accessible embedded devices processing sensitive data in today's world, implementation level attacks assume significance. In particular, a thorough exploration of the best possible attacks on any cryptographic implementation is the need of the hour.

© Springer Nature Switzerland AG 2018
A. Chattopadhyay et al. (Eds.): SPACE 2018, LNCS 11348, pp. 21–36, 2018.
https://doi.org/10.1007/978-3-030-05072-6_2

1.1 Fault Models for Fault Injection Analysis

Nearly all FIA techniques in the existing literature assume a given *fault model* (such as random faults [8] and/or stuck-at-faults [21]) in a given location of the cipher state. Some of these techniques, such as differential fault analysis (DFA) [18,20,24] and differential fault intensity analysis (DFIA) [10,11] are found to be more efficient in the presence of highly localized faults, such as single bit flips, or faults restricted to a given byte of the cipher state. While DFA attacks are possible using multiple byte faults, e.g. diagonal faults [22], the fault pattern impacts the complexity of key-recovery. In particular, with respect to AES-128, faults restricted to a single diagonal allow more efficient key-recovery as compared to faults spread across multiple diagonals. Similarly, DFIA typically exploits the bias of fault distribution at various fault intensities, under the assumption that the fault is restricted to a single byte/nibble of the cipher state [11]. Other techniques such as fault sensitivity analysis (FSA) [15,17] require the knowledge of the critical fault intensity at which the onset of faulty behavior is observed. This critical value is then correlated with the secret-key dependent cipher state value. Finally, FIA techniques such as safe-error analysis (SEA) [3] and differential behavioral analysis (DBA) [21] require highly restrictive fault models such as stuck-at faults, where a specific target bit of the cipher state is set to either 0 or 1. In recent literature, microcontroller-based implementation of cryptographic algorithms have been subjected to instruction-skip attacks [7,12], where the adversary uses precise injection techniques to transform the opcode for specific instructions into that for NOP (no-operation).

Similarity Between FIA and SCA. The above discussion clearly reveals that existing FIA techniques are *inherently dependent* on the ability of an adversary to replicate a *specific fault model on an actual target device*. Fault precision and fault localization contribute to the efficiency of the attack, while the occurrence of random faults outside the target model generate *noisy ciphertexts*, thereby degrading the attack efficiency. Observe that this is conceptually similar to the effect of noise on the efficiency of traditional SCA techniques such as simple power analysis (SPA) and differential power analysis (DPA). In particular, the success rate for these techniques is directly proportional to the signal-to-noise ratio (SNR) of an implementation.

Our Motivation. In this paper, we aim to devise a generalized FIA strategy that overcomes the dependency of existing techniques on specific fault models. Rather than analyzing the behavior of the target implementation under a given set of faults, our approach would *learn* the behavior of the device-under-test (DUT) under an unrestricted set of fault injection parameters, irrespective of the fault nature. Such an attack strategy would allow a larger exploitable fault space, making it more powerful than all reported FIA techniques. As discussed next, an equivalent of the same approach in the context of SCA is well-studied in the literature.

1.2   Template Attacks: Maximizing the Power of SCA

Template attacks (TA) were proposed in [6] as the strongest form of SCA in an information-theoretic setting. Unlike other popular SCA techniques such as DPA, TA does not view the noise inherent to any cryptographic implementation as a hindrance to the success rate of the attack. Rather, it models precisely the noise pattern of the target device, and extracts the maximum possible information from any available leakage sample. This makes TA a threat to implementations otherwise secure based on the assumption that an adversary has access to only a limited number of side-channel samples. On the flip side, TA assumes that the adversary has full programming capability on a cryptographic device identical to the target black-box device.

1.3   Our Contribution: Templates for Fault Injection Analysis

The existing literature on TA is limited principally to SCA, exploiting passive leakages from a target cryptographic device for key recovery. In this paper, we aim to extend the scope of TA to active FIA attacks. Figure 1 summarizes our template-based FIA technique. Our approach is broadly divided into two main phases:

- The first phase of the attack is a *profiling phase*, where the adversary is assumed to have programming access to a device identical to the black-box target device. The adversary uses this phase to characterize the *fault behavior of the device* under varying fault injection intensities. We refer to such characterizations as the *fault template* for the device. We choose the *statistical distribution of faulty ciphertext values* under different fault injection intensities as the basis of our characterization. The templates are typically built on small-segments of the overall secret-key, which makes a divide-and-conquer key recovery strategy practically achievable. Note that the matching phase does not require the correct ciphertext value corresponding to a given encryption operation.
- The second phase of the attack is the *matching phase*, where the adversary obtains the fault behavior of the target black-box device (with an embedded non-programmable secret-key K) under a set of fault injection intensities, and matches them with the templates obtained in the profiling phase to try and recover K. The idea is to use a maximum likelihood estimator-like distinguisher to identify the key hypothesis for which the template exhibits the maximum similarity with the experimentally obtained fault behavior of the target device.

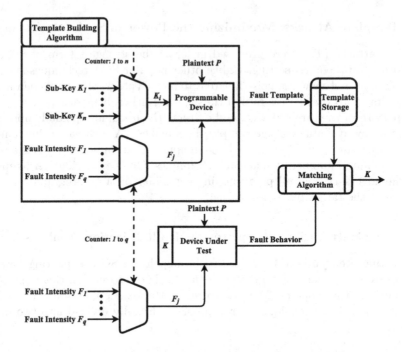

Fig. 1. Template-based fault injection analysis: an overview

1.4   Comparison with Existing FIA Techniques

In this section, we briefly recall existing FIA techniques, and explain their differences with our proposed template-based FIA approach. As already mentioned, our technique has two phases, and assumes that the adversary has programmable access to a device identical to the device under test. At the same time, it allows modeling the behavior of the device independent of specific fault models, as is done in most state-of-the-art FIA techniques. We explicitly enumerate these differences below.

Differential Fault Analysis (DFA): In DFA [9,13,20,24], the adversary injects a fault under a specific fault model in target location of the cipher state, and analyzes the fault propagation characteristics using the knowledge of the fault-free and faulty ciphertexts. Our template-based FIA does not trace the propagation of the fault; rather it simply creates a template of the faulty ciphertext distribution under different fault injection intensities. This makes our approach independent of any specific fault model.

Differential Fault Intensity Analysis (DFIA): DFIA [11,19] exploits the underlying bias of any practically achieved fault distribution on the target device, once again under a chosen fault model. It is similar in principle to DPA in the sense that it chooses the most likely secret-key value based upon a statistical analysis of the faulty intermediate state of the block cipher, derived from the faulty ciphertext values only. Our template-based FIA can be viewed as a generalization of DFIA with less stringent fault model requirements. Similar to DFIA, our approach also does not require the correct ciphertext values. However, our approach does not statistically analyze the faulty intermediate state based upon several key hypotheses. Rather, it pre-constructs separate templates of the *faulty ciphertext distribution* for each possible key value, and matches them with the experimentally obtained faulty ciphertext distribution from the black-box target device. Rather than focusing on specific fault models, the templates are built for varying fault injection intensities.

Fault Sensitivity Analysis (FSA): FSA [15, 17] exploits the knowledge of the critical fault intensity under which a device under test starts exhibiting faulty output behavior. The critical intensity is typically data-dependent, which allows secret-key recovery. FSA does not use the values of either the correct or the faulty ciphertexts. However, it requires a precise modeling of the onset of faults on the target device. Our methodology, on the other hand, uses the faulty ciphertext values, and is free of such precise critical fault intensity modeling requirements.

Safe Error Analysis (SEA): In SEA [3, 21], the adversary injects a fault into a precise location of the cipher state, and observes the corresponding effect on the cipher behavior. A popular fault model used in such attacks is the stuck-at fault model. The adversary injects a fault to set/reset a bit of the cipher state, and infers from the nature of the output if the corresponding bit was flipped as a result of the fault injection. Quite clearly, this fault model is highly restrictive. Our approach, on the other hand, allows random fault injections under varying fault intensities, which makes easier to reproduce in practice on real-world target devices.

2   Template-Based FIA: Detailed Approach

In this section, we present the details of our proposed template-based FIA. Given a target device containing a block cipher implementation, let $\mathcal{F}$ be the space of all possible fault intensities under which an adversary can inject a fault on this device. Now, assume that a random fault is injected in a given-segment S_k of the cipher state under a fault intensity $F_j \in \mathcal{F}$. Also assume that this state segment has value $P_{i'} \in \mathcal{P}$, and subsequently combines with a key segment $K_i \in \mathcal{K}$, where $\mathcal{P}$ and $\mathcal{K}$ are the space of all possible intermediate state values and key segment values respectively, resulting in a faulty ciphertext segment $C_{i,i',j,k}$. The granularity of fault intensity values depends on the injection equipment used - precise injection techniques such as laser pulses are expected to offer higher granularity levels than simpler injection techniques such as clock/voltage glitches. Note that we do not restrict the nature of the faults resulting from such injections to any specific model, such as single bit/single byte/stuck-at faults. With these assumptions in place, we now describe the two phases - the template building phase and the template matching phase - of our approach.

2.1 Template Building Phase

In this phase, the adversary has programmable access to a device identical to the device under test. By programmable access, we mean the following:

- The adversary can feed a plaintext P and master secret-key K of his choice to the device.
- Upon fault injection under a fault intensity $F_j \in \mathcal{F}$, the adversary can detect the target location S_k in the cipher state where the fault is induced.
- The adversary has the knowledge of the corresponding key segment $K_i \in \mathcal{K}$ and the intermediate state segment $P_{i'} \in \mathcal{P}$. The key segment combines with the faulty state segment to produce the faulty ciphertext segment $C_{i,i',j,k}$.

Algorithm 1. Template Building Phase

Require: Programmable target device
Require: Target block cipher description
Ensure: Fault template T for the target device
1: Fix the set $\mathcal{S}$ of fault locations to be covered for successful key recovery depending on the block cipher description
2: Fix the space $\mathcal{F}$ of fault injection intensities depending on the device characteristics
3: Fix the number of fault injections N for each fault intensity
4: $T \leftarrow \phi$
5: **for each** fault location $S_k \in \mathcal{S}$ **do**
6:     **for each** corresponding intermediate state segment and key segment $(P_{i'}, K_i) \in \mathcal{P} \times \mathcal{K}$ **do**
7:         **for each** fault injection intensity $F_j \in \mathcal{F}$ **do**
8:             **for each** $l \in [1, N]$ **do**
9:                 Run an encryption with plaintext segment $P_{i'}$ and the target key segment K_i simultaneously
10:                 Inject a fault under intensity F_j in the target location S_k
11:                 Let $C_{i,i',j,k}^l$ be the faulty ciphertext segment
12:             **end for**
13:             $T_{i,i',j,k} \leftarrow \left(C_{i,i',j,k}^1, \cdots, C_{i,i',j,k}^N \right)$
14:             $T \leftarrow T \cup T_{i,i',j,k}$
15:         **end for**
16:     **end for**
17: **end for**
18: **return** T

Let $C_{i,i',j,k}^1, \cdots, C_{i,i',j,k}^N$ be the faulty ciphertext outputs upon N independent fault injections in the target location S_k under fault injection intensity F_j, corresponding to the intermediate state segment $P_{i'}$ and key segment K_i. We refer to the tuple $T_{i,i',j,k} = \left(C_{i,i',j,k}^1, \cdots, C_{i,i',j,k}^N \right)$ as a *fault template instance*. This template instance is prepared and stored for possible tuples $(K_i, P_{i'}, F_j, S_k) \in \mathcal{K} \times \mathcal{P} \times \mathcal{F} \times \mathcal{S}$, where $\mathcal{S}$ is the set of all fault locations in the cipher state that need to be covered for full key-recovery. The set of all such template instances constitutes the *fault template* for the target device. Algorithm 1 summarizes the main steps of the template building phase as described above.

Note: The number of fault injections N required per fault intensity during the template building phase may be determined empirically, based upon the desired success rate of key recovery in the subsequent template matching phase. Quite evidently, increasing N improves the success rate of key recovery.

2.2 Template Matching Phase

In this phase, the adversary has black-box access to the target device. Under the purview of black-box access, we assume the following:

– The adversary can feed a plaintext P of his choice to the device and run the encryption algorithm multiple times on this plaintext.
– Upon fault injection under a fault intensity $F_j \in \mathcal{F}$, the adversary can deduce the target location S_k in the cipher state where the fault is induced, by observing the corresponding faulty ciphertext $C'_{j,k}$.
– The adversary has no idea about the intermediate state segment $P_{i'}$ where the fault is injected, or the key segment K_i that subsequently combines with the faulty state segment to produce the ciphertext.

The adversary again performs N independent fault injections under each fault injection intensity F_j in a target location S_k, and obtains the corresponding faulty ciphertexts $C'^1_{j,k}, \cdots, C'^N_{j,k}$. All fault injections are performed during encryption operations using the same plaintext P as in the template building phase. These faulty ciphertexts are then given as input to a distinguisher $\mathcal{D}$. The distinguisher ranks the key-hypotheses $K_1, \cdots, K_n \in \mathcal{K}$, where the rank of K_i is estimated based upon the closeness of the experimentally obtained ciphertext distribution with the template instance $T_{i,i',j,k}$, for all possible intermediate state segments $P_{i'}$. The closeness is estimated using a statistical measure $\mathcal{M}$. The distinguisher finally outputs the key hypothesis K_i that is ranked consistently highly across all rank-lists corresponding to different fault injection intensities. Algorithm 2 summarizes our proposed template matching phase.

2.3 The Statistical Measure M

An important aspect of the template matching phase is choosing the statistical measure M to measure the closeness of the experimentally observed faulty ciphertext segment distribution, with that corresponding to each template instance. We propose using a correlation-based matching approach for this purpose. The first step in this approach is to build a frequency-distribution table of each possible ciphertext segment value in each of the two distributions. Let the possible ciphertext segment values be in the range $[0, 2^{x-1}]$ where x is the number of bits in the ciphertext segment(for example, $[0, 255]$ for a byte, or $[0, 15]$ in case of a nibble). Also, let $f(y)$ and $f'(y)$ denote the frequency with which a given

---

Algorithm 2. Template Matching Phase

Require: Fault template T corresponding to plaintext P
Ensure: The secret-key
 1: **for each** fault location $S_k \in \mathcal{S}$ **do**
 2:     **for each** fault injection intensity $F_j \in \mathcal{F}$ **do**
 3:         **for each** $l \in [1, N]$ **do**
 4:             Inject a fault under intensity F_j in location S_k
 5:             Let $C''^l_{j,k}$ be the faulty ciphertext segment
 6:         **end for**
 7:         $E_{j,k} \leftarrow \left(C'^1_{j,k}, \cdots, C'^N_{j,k} \right)$
 8:     **end for**
 9: **end for**
10: **for each** fault location $S_k \in \mathcal{S}$ **do**
11:     **for each** fault injection intensity $F_j \in \mathcal{F}$ **do**
12:         **for each** possible key hypothesis $K_i \in \mathcal{K}$ and intermediate state segment $P_{i'} \in \mathcal{P}$ **do**
13:             $\rho_{i,i',j,k} \leftarrow \mathcal{M}\left(E_{j,k}, T_{i,i',j,k} \right)$
14:         **end for**
15:     **end for**
16:     Store the pair $(K_i, P_{i'})$ pair such that $\sum_{F_j \in \mathcal{F}} \rho_{i,i'j,k}$ is maximum for the given fault location S_k.
17: **end for**
18: **return** the stored key hypothesis corresponding to each unique key segment location.

---

ciphertext segment value $y \in [0, 2^{x-1}]$ occurs in the template and the experimentally obtained distribution, respectively. Since there are exactly N sample points in each distribution, we have $\sum_{y \in [0, 2^{x-1}]} f(y) = \sum_{y \in [0, 2^{x-1}]} f'(y) = N$.

The next step is to compute the Pearson's correlation coefficient between the two distributions as:

$$\rho = \frac{\sum\limits_{y \in [0, 2^{x-1}]} \left(f(y) - \frac{N}{2^x} \right) \cdot \left(f'(y) - \frac{N}{2^x} \right)}{\sqrt{\sum\limits_{y \in [0, 2^{x-1}]} \left(f(y) - \frac{N}{2^x} \right)^2} \sqrt{\sum\limits_{y \in [0, 2^{x-1}]} \left(f'(y) - \frac{N}{2^x} \right)^2}}$$

The Pearson's correlation coefficient is used as the measure M. The choice of statistic is based on the rationale that, for the correct key segment hypothesis, the template would have a similar frequency distribution of ciphertext segment values as the experimentally obtained set of faulty ciphertexts, while for a wrong key segment hypothesis, the distribution of ciphertext segment values in the template and the experimentally obtained ciphertexts would be uncorrelated.

An advantage of the aforementioned statistical approach is that it can be extended to relaxed fault models such as multi-byte faults, that are typically not exploited in traditional FIA techniques. In general, if a given fault injection affects multiple locations in the block cipher state, the correlation analysis is simply repeated separately for each fault location. This is similar to the divide-and-conquer approach used in SCA-based key-recovery techniques.

3   Case Study: Template-Based FIA on AES-128

In this section, we present a concrete case study of the proposed template-based FIA strategy on AES-128. As is well-known, AES has a plaintext and key size of 128 bits each, and a total of 10 rounds. Each round except the last one comprises of a non-linear S-Box layer (16 S-Boxes in parallel), a linear byte-wise ShiftRow operation, and a linear MixColumn operation, followed by XOR-ing with the round key. The last round does not have a MixColumn operation. This in turn implies that if a fault was injected in one or more bytes of the cipher state after the 9th round MixColumn operation, the faulty state byte (or bytes) combines with only a specific byte (or bytes) of the 10th round key. For example, if a fault was injected in the first byte of the cipher state, the faulty byte would pass through the S-Box and ShiftRow operation, and combine with the first byte of the 10th round key to produce the first byte of the faulty ciphertext. The exact relation between the fault injection location and the corresponding key segment depends solely on the ShiftRow operation, and is hence deterministic. This matches precisely the assumptions made in our attack description in the previous section. Consequently, this case study assumes that all faults are injected in the cipher state between the 9th round MixColumn operation and the 10th round S-Box operations. The aim of the fault attack is to recover byte-wise the whole 10th round key of AES-128, which in turn deterministically reveals the entire secret-key. We note that fault injection in an earlier round will lead to extremely large templates, making the attack impractical.

3.1   The Fault Injection Setup

The fault injection setup (described in Fig. 2) uses a Spartan 6 FPGA mounted on a Sakura-G evaluation board, a PC and an external arbitrary function generator (Tektronix AFG3252). The FPGA has a Device Under Test (DUT) block, which is an implementation of the block cipher AES-128. Faults are injected using clock glitches. The device operates normally under the external clock signal clk_{ext}. The glitch signal, referred to as clk_{fast}, is derived from the clk_{ext} via a Xilinx Digital Clock Manager (DCM) module. The fault injection intensity in our experiments is essentially the glitch frequency, and is varied using a combination of the DCM configuration, and the external function generator settings. In the template building phase, the intermediate cipher state $P_{i'}$ and the intermediate round key K_i are monitored using a ChipScope Pro analyzer, while in the template matching phase, the DUT is a black box with no input handles or internal monitoring capabilities. Table 1 summarizes the glitch frequency ranges at which these fault models were observed on the target device.

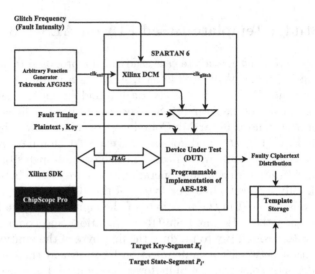

(a) Template Building Phase

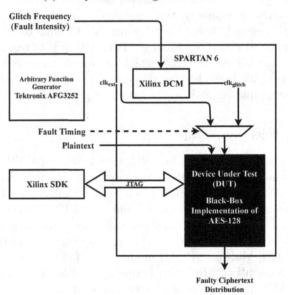

(b) Template Matching Phase

Fig. 2. Experimental set-up

Table 1. Glitch frequencies for different fault models

Glitch frequency (MHz)	Faulty bytes	Bit flips per byte
125.3–125.5	1	1
125.6–125.7	1	2
125.8–126.0	1	3
126.1–126.2	2–3	1–3
>126.2	>3	>5

3.2 Templates for Single Byte Faults

In this section, we present examples of fault templates obtained from the device under test, for glitch frequencies that result in single byte fault injections in the AES-128 module. Since only a single byte is affected between the 9th round Mix-Column operation and the 10th round S-Box operations, we are interested in the distribution of the corresponding faulty byte in the ciphertext. Figure 3 presents fault templates containing ciphertext byte distributions for three categories of faults - single bit faults, two-bit faults, and three-bit faults. The templates cor-

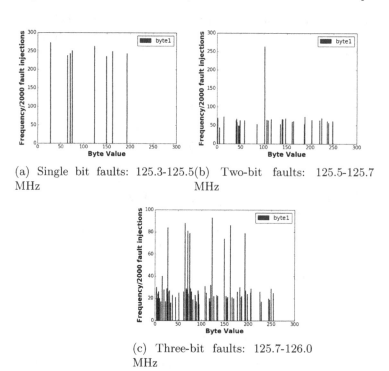

(a) Single bit faults: 125.3-125.5 (b) Two-bit faults: 125.5-125.7
MHz   MHz

(c) Three-bit faults: 125.7-126.0
MHz

Fig. 3. Templates for single byte faults: distribution of faulty ciphertext byte for different fault injection intensities

respond to the same pair of intermediate state byte and last round key byte
for an AES-128 encryption. Quite evidently, the ciphertext distribution for each
template reflects the granularity of the corresponding fault model. In particular,
for a single bit fault, most of the faulty ciphertext bytes assume one of 8 possible
values, while for three-bit faults, the ciphertext bytes assume more than 50 different values across all fault injections. In all cases, however, the distribution of
ciphertext values is non-uniform, which provides good scope for characterizing
the fault behavior of the device in the template building phase.

3.3   Templates for Multi-byte Faults

In this section, we present examples of fault templates constructed for glitch
frequencies that result in multi-byte fault injections. Figure 4 shows the distribution of different bytes injected with different faults. It is interesting to observe
that at the onset of multi-byte faults, the distribution of faulty ciphertext bytes
is *not uniformly random*; indeed, it is possible to characterize the fault behavior
of the device in terms of templates under such fault models. Given the absence
of MixColumn operation in the last round of AES, each faulty intermediate state
byte combines independently with a random last round key byte. This allows a
divide-and-conquer template matching approach, where the statistical analysis
may be applied to each faulty ciphertext byte independently. This is a particularly useful mode of attack, since it can be launched even without precise fault
injection techniques that allow targeting a single byte of the cipher state.

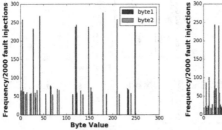
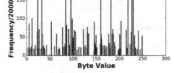

(a) 1-bit, 2-bit fault in 2 bytes: (b) 1-bit, 2-bit, 3-bit fault across 3
126.1 MHz   bytes: 126.2 MHz

Fig. 4. Templates for multi-byte faults: distribution of multiple faulty ciphertext byte
values

3.4   Variation with Key Byte Values

The success of our template matching procedure with respect to AES-128 relies
on the hypothesis that for different key byte values, the ciphertext distribution corresponding to the same fault location is different. Otherwise, the key
recovery would be ambiguous. We validated this hypothesis by examining the

ciphertext distribution upon injecting a single bit fault in the first byte of the cipher state, corresponding to different key byte values. We illustrate this with a small example in Fig. 5. Figures 5a, b, c and d represent the frequency distributions for faulty ciphertext byte corresponding to the same intermediate byte value of 0x00, and key byte values 0x00, 0x01, 0x02 and 0x03, respectively. Quite evidently, the three frequency distributions are unique and mutually non-overlapping. The same trend is observed across all 256 possible key byte values; exhaustive results for the same could not be provided due to space constraints.

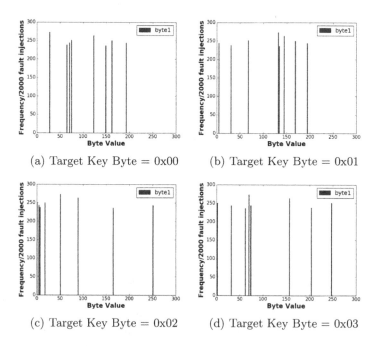

(a) Target Key Byte = 0x00   (b) Target Key Byte = 0x01

(c) Target Key Byte = 0x02   (d) Target Key Byte = 0x03

Fig. 5. Frequency distributions for faulty ciphertext byte: same intermediate state byte but different key byte values

3.5   Template Matching for Key-Recovery

In this section, we present results for recovering a single key-byte for AES-128 under various fault granularities. As demonstrated in Fig. 6, the correlation for the correct key hypothesis exceeds the average correlation over all wrong key hypotheses, across the three fault models - single bit faults, two-bit faults and three-bit faults. As is expected, precise single-bits faults within a given byte enable distinguishing the correct key hypothesis using very few number of fault injections (50–100); for less granular faults such as three-bit faults, more number of fault injections (200–500) are necessary. Finally, the same results also hold for multi-byte fault models, where each affected byte encounters a certain number of bit-flips. Since the key-recovery is performed byte-wise, the adversary can use the same fault instances to recover multiple key bytes in parallel.

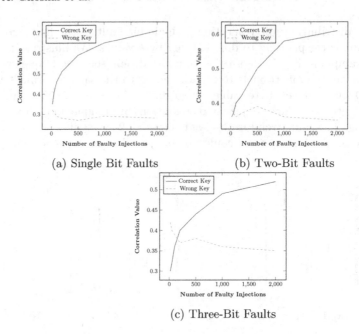

(a) Single Bit Faults   (b) Two-Bit Faults

(c) Three-Bit Faults

Fig. 6. Correlation between template and observed ciphertext distribution: correct key hypothesis v/s wrong key hypothesis

4   Conclusion

We presented the first template based fault injection analysis of block ciphers. We presented a generic algorithm comprising of a template building and a template matching phase, that can be easily instantiated for any target block cipher. The templates are built on pairs of internal state segment and key segment values at different fault intensities, while the number of fault instances per template depends on the statistical methodology used in the matching phase. In this paper, we advocated the use of the Pearson correlation coefficient in the matching phase; exploring alternative techniques in this regard is an interesting future work. In order to substantiate the effectiveness of our methodology, we presented a case-study targeting a hardware implementation of AES-128 on a Spartan-6 FPGA. Interestingly, our attack allowed exploiting even low-granularity faults such as multi-byte faults, that do not require high precision fault injection equipment. It may be emphasized that the attack is devoid of the exact knowledge of the underlying fault model. Such fault models also allowed parallel recovery of multiple key-bytes, thus providing a trade-off between the number of fault injections, and the number of recovered key-bytes. An interesting extension of this work would be apply template-based analysis against implementations with fault attack countermeasures such as spatial/temporal/information redundancy.

Acknowledgements. We would like to thank the anonymous reviewers for providing constructive and valuable comments. Debdeep would also like to thank his DST Swarnajayanti fellowship (2015–16) for partial support. He would also like to thank DRDO, India for funding the project, "Secure Resource - constrained communication Framework for Tactical Networks using Physically Unclonable Functions (SeRFPUF)" for partially supporting the research. He would also like to thank Information Security Education Awareness (ISEA), DIT, India for encouraging research in the area of computer security. Sikhar would like to thank Qualcomm India Innovation Fellowship 2017–18.

References

1. Agoyan, M., Dutertre, J.-M., Naccache, D., Robisson, B., Tria, A.: When clocks fail: on critical paths and clock faults. In: Gollmann, D., Lanet, J.-L., Iguchi-Cartigny, J. (eds.) CARDIS 2010. LNCS, vol. 6035, pp. 182–193. Springer, Heidelberg (2010). https://doi.org/10.1007/978-3-642-12510-2_13

2. Barenghi, A., Bertoni, G.M., Breveglieri, L., Pelosi, G.: A fault induction technique based on voltage underfeeding with application to attacks against AES and RSA. J. Syst. Softw. **86**(7), 1864–1878 (2013)

3. Blömer, J., Seifert, J.-P.: Fault based cryptanalysis of the advanced encryption standard (AES). In: Wright, R.N. (ed.) FC 2003. LNCS, vol. 2742, pp. 162–181. Springer, Heidelberg (2003). https://doi.org/10.1007/978-3-540-45126-6_12

4. Canivet, G., Clédière, J., Ferron, J.B., Valette, F., Renaudin, M., Leveugle, R.: Detailed analyses of single laser shot effects in the configuration of a virtex-ii FPGA. In: 14th IEEE International On-Line Testing Symposium, IOLTS 2008, pp. 289–294. IEEE (2008)

5. Canivet, G., Maistri, P., Leveugle, R., Clédière, J., Valette, F., Renaudin, M.: Glitch and laser fault attacks onto a secure AES implementation on a SRAM-based FPGA. J. Cryptol. **24**(2), 247–268 (2011)

6. Chari, S., Rao, J.R., Rohatgi, P.: Template attacks. In: Kaliski, B.S., Koç, K., Paar, C. (eds.) CHES 2002. LNCS, vol. 2523, pp. 13–28. Springer, Heidelberg (2003). https://doi.org/10.1007/3-540-36400-5_3

7. Choukri, H., Tunstall, M.: Round reduction using faults. FDTC **5**, 13–24 (2005)

8. Dehbaoui, A., Dutertre, J.M., Robisson, B., Tria, A.: Electromagnetic transient faults injection on a hardware and a software implementations of AES. In: 2012 Workshop on Fault Diagnosis and Tolerance in Cryptography (FDTC), pp. 7–15. IEEE (2012)

9. Dusart, P., Letourneux, G., Vivolo, O.: Differential fault analysis on A.E.S. In: Zhou, J., Yung, M., Han, Y. (eds.) ACNS 2003. LNCS, vol. 2846, pp. 293–306. Springer, Heidelberg (2003). https://doi.org/10.1007/978-3-540-45203-4_23

10. Fuhr, T., Jaulmes, E., Lomné, V., Thillard, A.: Fault attacks on AES with faulty ciphertexts only. In: 2013 Workshop on Fault Diagnosis and Tolerance in Cryptography (FDTC), pp. 108–118. IEEE (2013)

11. Ghalaty, N.F., Yuce, B., Taha, M., Schaumont, P.: Differential fault intensity analysis. In: 2014 Workshop on Fault Diagnosis and Tolerance in Cryptography (FDTC), pp. 49–58. IEEE (2014)

12. Heydemann, K., Moro, N., Encrenaz, E., Robisson, B.: Formal verification of a software countermeasure against instruction skip attacks. In: PROOFS 2013 (2013)

13. Kim, C.H.: Differential fault analysis against AES-192 and AES-256 with minimal faults. In: 2010 Workshop on Fault Diagnosis and Tolerance in Cryptography (FDTC), pp. 3–9. IEEE (2010)
14. Kocher, P., Jaffe, J., Jun, B.: Differential power analysis. In: Wiener, M. (ed.) CRYPTO 1999. LNCS, vol. 1666, pp. 388–397. Springer, Heidelberg (1999). https://doi.org/10.1007/3-540-48405-1_25
15. Li, Y., Sakiyama, K., Gomisawa, S., Fukunaga, T., Takahashi, J., Ohta, K.: Fault sensitivity analysis. In: Mangard, S., Standaert, F.-X. (eds.) CHES 2010. LNCS, vol. 6225, pp. 320–334. Springer, Heidelberg (2010). https://doi.org/10.1007/978-3-642-15031-9_22
16. Mangard, S., Oswald, E., Popp, T.: Power Analysis Attacks: Revealing the Secrets of Smart Cards, vol. 31. Springer, Boston (2007). https://doi.org/10.1007/978-0-387-38162-6
17. Mischke, O., Moradi, A., Güneysu, T.: Fault sensitivity analysis meets zero-value attack. In: 2014 Workshop on Fault Diagnosis and Tolerance in Cryptography, FDTC 2014, Busan, South Korea, 23 September 2014, pp. 59–67 (2014). https://doi.org/10.1109/FDTC.2014.16
18. Mukhopadhyay, D.: An improved fault based attack of the advanced encryption standard. In: Preneel, B. (ed.) AFRICACRYPT 2009. LNCS, vol. 5580, pp. 421–434. Springer, Heidelberg (2009). https://doi.org/10.1007/978-3-642-02384-2_26
19. Patranabis, S., Chakraborty, A., Nguyen, P.H., Mukhopadhyay, D.: A biased fault attack on the time redundancy countermeasure for AES. In: Mangard, S., Poschmann, A.Y. (eds.) COSADE 2014. LNCS, vol. 9064, pp. 189–203. Springer, Cham (2015). https://doi.org/10.1007/978-3-319-21476-4_13
20. Piret, G., Quisquater, J.-J.: A differential fault attack technique against SPN structures, with application to the AES and KHAZAD. In: Walter, C.D., Koç, Ç.K., Paar, C. (eds.) CHES 2003. LNCS, vol. 2779, pp. 77–88. Springer, Heidelberg (2003). https://doi.org/10.1007/978-3-540-45238-6_7
21. Robisson, B., Manet, P.: Differential behavioral analysis. In: Paillier, P., Verbauwhede, I. (eds.) CHES 2007. LNCS, vol. 4727, pp. 413–426. Springer, Heidelberg (2007). https://doi.org/10.1007/978-3-540-74735-2_28
22. Saha, D., Mukhopadhyay, D., Chowdhury, D.R.: A diagonal fault attack on the advanced encryption standard. IACR Cryptology ePrint Archive 2009/581 (2009)
23. Selmane, N., Guilley, S., Danger, J.L.: Practical setup time violation attacks on AES. In: Seventh European Dependable Computing Conference, EDCC 2008, pp. 91–96. IEEE (2008)
24. Tunstall, M., Mukhopadhyay, D., Ali, S.: Differential fault analysis of the advanced encryption standard using a single fault. In: Ardagna, C.A., Zhou, J. (eds.) WISTP 2011. LNCS, vol. 6633, pp. 224–233. Springer, Heidelberg (2011). https://doi.org/10.1007/978-3-642-21040-2_15

NEON SIKE: Supersingular Isogeny Key Encapsulation on ARMv7

Amir Jalali[1]([✉]), Reza Azarderakhsh[1], and Mehran Mozaffari Kermani[2]

[1] Department of Computer and Electrical Engineering and Computer Science,
Florida Atlantic University, Boca Raton, FL, USA
{ajalali2016,razarderakhsh}@fau.edu
[2] Department of Computer Science and Engineering, University of South Florida,
Tampa, FL, USA
mehran2@usf.edu

Abstract. We present a highly-optimized implementation of Supersingular Isogeny Key Encapsulation (SIKE) mechanism on ARMv7 family of processors. We exploit the state-of-the-art implementation techniques and processor capabilities to efficiently develop post-quantum key encapsulation scheme on 32-bit ARMv7 Cortex-A processors. We benchmark our results on two popular ARMv7-powered cores. Our benchmark results show significant performance improvement of the key encapsulation mechanism in comparison with the portable implementation. In particular, we achieve almost 7.5 times performance improvement of the entire protocol over the SIKE 503-bit prime field on a Cortex-A8 core.

Keywords: ARM assembly · Embedded device · Key encapsulation
Post-quantum cryptography
Supersingular isogeny-based cryptosystem

1 Introduction

The first post-quantum cryptography (PQC) standardization workshop by National Institute of Standards and Technology (NIST) started a process to evaluate and standardize the practical and secure post-quantum cryptography candidates for the quantum era. Considering the rapid growth in the design and development of practical quantum computers, there is a critical mission to design and develop post-quantum cryptography primitives, the cryptography schemes which are assumed to be resistant against quantum adversaries. The standardization process takes into account different aspects of the candidates such as the security proofs as well as their performance benchmark on a variety of platforms. Therefore, it is necessary to evaluate and possibly improve the efficiency of the approved proposals[1] on different processors.

---

[1] Available at: https://csrc.nist.gov/Projects/Post-Quantum-Cryptography/Round-1-Submissions (accessed in June 2018).

© Springer Nature Switzerland AG 2018
A. Chattopadhyay et al. (Eds.): SPACE 2018, LNCS 11348, pp. 37–51, 2018.
https://doi.org/10.1007/978-3-030-05072-6_3

Different PQC candidates are constructed on hard mathematical problems which are assumed to be impossible to solve even for large-scale quantum computers. We can categorize these problems into five main categories: code-based cryptography, lattice-based cryptography, hash-based cryptography, multivariate cryprography, and supersingular isogeny-based cryptography, see, for instance [5,19,25,26]. In this work, we focus on the efficient implementation of the supersingular isogeny key encapsulation (SIKE) mechanism on ARMv7 family of processors.

Although the new generation of ARM processors, i.e., ARMv8 is designed to take advantage of 64-bit wide general registers and provide fast performance benchmark, the 32-bit ARMv7 processors are still used inside many embedded devices. In particular, many IoT devices are designed and manufactured based on ARMv7 processors which require low-power consumption and efficiency. Therefore, further optimization of PQC on embedded devices is essential.

Moreover, NIST calls for the efficient implementation of PQC candidates on different platforms to be able to evaluate the efficiency and performance of PQC candidates accordingly. In particular, the public announcement by NIST regarding more platform-specific optimizations[2] is the main motivation behind this work. Furthermore, supersingular isogeny-based cryptography is assumed to be one of the promising candidates in quantum era because of its small key-size and the possibility of designing different schemes such as digital signatures [16, 33], identification protocols [16], and multiparty non-interactive key-exchange [7] with reasonable performance and parameter size.

Since the isogeny-based cryptography includes a large number of operations to compute the large-degree isogeny maps, the constructed protocols on this primitive still suffer from an extensive number of curve arithmetic compared to other PQC primitives. To address this, optimized implementations of the underlying Diffie-Hellman key-exchange protocol have been presented both on hardware [23] and software [13,14,18,24], taking advantage of state-of-the-art engineering techniques to reduce the overall timing of the protocol. Moreover, new optimization techniques for field arithmetic implementation of SIDH-friendly primes have been recently proposed by Bos et al. [8,9] and Karmakar et al. [22]. However, these works are based on the parameters which are not in compliance with the SIKE reference proposal.

The SIKE reference implementation provides optimized implementations of this protocol on both Intel and ARMv8 processors [19]; however, the optimized implementation of this mechanism on ARMv7 cores is still unsettled. Early attempt by Azarderakhsh et al. [4] and later by Koziel et al. [24] is focused on the implementation of the supersingular isogeny Diffie-Hellman (SIDH) key-exchange on ARMv7 processors which is based on affine coordinates. The proposed implementations suffered from the extensive number of field inversions and they are not assumed to be resistant against simple power analysis attacks due to the lack of constant-time implementation.

---

[2] Available at: https://groups.google.com/a/list.nist.gov/forum/#!topic/pqc-forum/nteDiyV66U8 (accessed in June 2018).

In this work, we address all these shortcomings. We design constant-time SIKE protocol using ARMv7 NEON hand-crafted assembly efficiently and benchmark our libraries on the two most popular ARMv7 cores, i.e., Cortex-A8 and Cortex-A15. Our optimized implementation significantly outperforms the portable implementation of SIKE and make it practical for use inside ARMv7-powered devices with high efficiency. We outline our contributions in the following:

- We implement optimized and compact field arithmetic libraries using ARMv7 NEON assembly, taking advantage of multiplication and reduction algorithms which are most suitable for our target platforms and finite field size. The proposed libraries are integrated inside SIKE software and improve the performance and power-consumption of this protocol on the target platforms.
- We analyze the use of different implementations of Montgomery reduction algorithm on ARMv7 NEON associated with the SIKE-friendly primes. The previous optimized implementations on ARMv7 mostly used generic approaches which is not optimal. Our proposed method, on the other hand, is designed and optimized for the SIKE-friendly primes, taking advantage of their special forms.
- The proposed library significantly improves the SIKE performance on ARMv7-A processors. On power-efficient cores such as Cortex-A8, the portable version benchmark results are extremely slow and almost impractical to use in the real settings. Our optimizations decrease the overall process time remarkably and make SIKE as one of the possible candidates for PQC on IoT devices.

Organization. In Sect. 2, we briefly recall the supersingular isogeny key encapsulation protocol from [19], and [20]. In Sects. 3 and 4, we discuss our implementation parameters and the target platform capabilities. We also propose our highly-optimized method to efficiently implement the finite field arithmetic on ARMv7-A processors. In Sect. 5, we show the SIKE performance benchmark on our target processors and analyze the performance improvement over the portable version. We conclude the paper in Sect. 6.

2   Background

This section includes a presentation of SIKE mechanism in a nutshell. The main protocol is designed on top of the SIDH protocol which was proposed by Jao and De Feo [20] and further presented more effciently by Costello et al. [13] using projective coordinates and compact arithmetic algorithms. To simply understand the whole key encapsulation mechanism, we explain the combination of prior works including all the protocol optimizations which are designed inside the SIKE protocol in this section.

2.1 Isogenies of Supersingular Elliptic Curves

Let p be a prime of the form $p = \ell_A^{e_A} \ell_B^{e_B} - 1$, and let E be a supersingular elliptic curve defined over a field of characteristic p. E can be also defined over $\mathbb{F}_{p^2}$ up to its isomorphism.

An isogeny $\phi : E \to E'$ is a rational map from E to E' which translates the identity into the identity that is defined by its degree and kernel. The degree of an isogeny is its degree as morphism. An ℓ-isogeny is an isogeny with degree ℓ.

A subgroup of points G on a supersingular elliptic curve which contains $\ell + 1$ cyclic subgroups of order ℓ is the torsion subgroup $E[\ell]$. Each element of this group is associated to an isogeny of degree ℓ.

The small degree isogeny can be computed using Vélu's formula [32] which is the main property of computations in the supersingular isogeny cryptography.

The isogeny map is denoted as $\phi : E \to E'/\langle G \rangle$. Since Vélu's formula can only compute the isogeny of small degrees, in order to compute large degree isogenies, we need to define a set of optimal walks inside an isogeny graph. These walks contain point multiplication and small isogeny evaluation. Jao and De Feo [20] introduced this optimal strategy of computing large-degree isogeny by representing the isogenous points inside a full binary tree and retrieving the optimal computations using dynamic algorithms. This strategy is still considered as the most efficient way of computing large degree isogeny and it is adopted inside all the efficient implementations of isogeny-based protocols to date, as well as PQC SIKE proposal [19] reference implementation.

One of the main properties of supersingular elliptic curves is their j-invariant. This value is the same for the curves of a isogeny class and therefore it is used inside the key-exchange protocol as the computed shared key between two parties [20]. Two parties compute two isomorphic curves of the same class, and the shared secret is computed as the j-invariant value of the resulting isomorphic curves.

Theoretically, the supersingular isogeny-based cryptography can be constructed over supersingular curves with the property $\#E(\mathbb{F}_{p^2}) = (p+1)^2$. However, Costello et al. [13] showed that the use of Montgomery curves and Montgomery arithmetic can speed up the entire key-exchange procedure notably. Following by their work, in the SIKE proposal, the starting curve $E_0/\mathbb{F}_{p^2} : y^2 = x^3 + x$ is an instance of Montgomery curves that has implementation properties because of its special form.

Moreover, all the curve arithmetic are computed using Montgomery group and field operations, taking advantage of their fast and compact algorithm while the computed isomorphic curves are all still in the Montgomery form. This leads to x-coordinate only efficient formulae for group operations such as computing isogeny, ladder algorithm, point addition and multiplication as well as field operations such as Montgomery reduction.

Another benefit of Montgomery curves in the context of isogeny-based cryptography is that to find the j-invariant value, we only need to compute the curve coefficient A. Furthermore, one can compute curve coefficient A only by using the x-abscissas of two points x_P and x_Q and their difference x_R using

$$A = \frac{(1 - x_P x_Q - x_P x_R - x_Q x_R)^2}{4 x_P x_Q x_R} - x_P - x_Q - x_R, \tag{1}$$

where $x_R = x_P - x_Q$ is also a point on E. This leads to a significant performance improvement of SIDH since at the beginnig of the second round of key-exchange, each party can efficiently retrieve other party's public key.

We observe that the curve coefficient computation from (1) can be also computed projectively to eliminate the expensive field inversion. However, since this value needs to be evaluated in the second round of the protocol from exchanged public values, the Z-coordinates are also required to be encapsulated inside the public parameters which increases the public-key size. Therefore, it is not reasonable to sacrifice the most important benefit of isogeny-based cryptography, i.e., small key size, to a negligible performance improvement.

2.2 Supersingular Isogeny Key Encapsulation (SIKE) Mechanism

Public Parameters. SIKE protocol [19], similar to other PQC schemes, is defined over a set of public and secret set of parameters. The public parameters of the key encapsulation mechanism are listed as follows:

1. A prime p of the form $p = \ell_A^{e_A} \ell_B^{e_B} - 1$, where e_A, e_B are two positive integers. The corresponding finite field is defined over $\mathbb{F}_{p^2}$. Note that the form of the prime which is proposed in the SIKE definition is sligtly different from the one which was originally proposed by Jao and De Feo. This slight difference is for the efficiency reason; this form enables the implementation to adopt a tailored version of Montgomery reduction [13], while it does not affect the security level of the protocol at the same bit-length. In this work, we take advantage of this special form inside the reduction implementation.
   Moreover, the form of the prime contains two small integers ℓ_A and ℓ_B which define the order of torsion subgroups for isogeny computations. In particular, the isogeny computations using Vélu's formula need to be constructed over these torsion subgroups, i.e., $E[\ell_A^{e_A}]$ and $E[\ell_B^{e_B}]$ of points on the curve for each party.
2. A starting supersingular Montgomery curve $E_0 : y^2 = x^3 + x$ defined over $\mathbb{F}_{p^2}$.
3. Two sets of generators which contain 3-tuple x-coordinates from $E_0[\ell_A^{e_A}]$ and $E_0[\ell_B^{e_B}]$. For the efficiency reasons, the 3-tuple contains two distinct points and their difference represented in x-coordinates to encode these bases, i.e., $x_{R_A} = x_{P_A} - x_{Q_A}$ and $x_{R_B} = x_{P_B} - x_{Q_B}$.

The key encapsulation mechanism is a protocol between two parties which generates a shared-secret between the communication entities using public parameters. In this section, we describe the SIKE protocol. We refer the readers to [19, 20] for more details.

Key Generation. The key generation randomly chooses a secret-key from keyspace $\mathcal{K}_B$ and computes the corresponding public-key, i.e., a 3-tuple x-coordinates $\mathbf{pk}_B$ by evaluating $\ell_B^{e_B}$-degree isogeny from starting curve E_0 to E_B. Moreover, an n-bit secret random message $s \in \{0,1\}^n$ is generated and concatenated to $\mathbf{sk}_B$ and $\mathbf{pk}_B$ to construct the SIKE secret-key $\mathbf{sk}_B$. The generated $\mathbf{pk}_B$ and $\mathbf{sk}_B$ are the output of this procedure [19]:

$$E_0 \to E_B/\langle x_{P_B} + [\mathbf{sk}_B]x_{Q_B}\rangle \to \mathbf{sk}_B : (s, \mathbf{sk}_B, \mathbf{pk}_B). \tag{2}$$

Key Encapsulation. This algorithm gets the generated public-key $\mathbf{pk}_B$ from the key-generation procedure as the input. First, an n-bit random string $m \in \{0,1\}^n$ is generated and concatenated with the public-key $\mathbf{pk}_B$. Further, the result is hashed using the hash function (cSHAKE256) G. This produced hash value is the *ephermeral secret-key* r which is used to compute the SIKE ciphertext. The hash function H inside the encryptor is also a cSHAKE256 function. The generated ciphertexts are further concatenated with m and hashed to generate the SIKE shared-key K [19]:

Bob	**Alice**
KeyGen:	
$\mathbf{pk}_B = [E_B, \phi_B(x_{P_A}), \phi_B(x_{Q_A})]$	
$s \in_R \{0,1\}^\ell$	
	Encapsulation:
	$m \in_R \{0,1\}^\ell$
	$r = G(\mathbf{pk}_B, m)$
	$\mathbf{pk}_A(r) = [E_A, \phi_A(x_{P_B}), \phi_A(x_{Q_B})]$
	$j_{\mathbf{inv}} = j(E_{AB})$
	$\mathbf{Enc}(\mathbf{pk}_B, m, r) \to (c_0, c_1)$
	$(c_0, c_1) = (\mathbf{pk}_A(r), G(j_{inv}) \oplus m)$
	$K = H(m \parallel (c_0, c_1))$

$$\xleftarrow{\quad (c_0, c_1) \quad}$$

Decapsulation:
$j_{\mathbf{inv}} = j(E_{BA})$
$m' = c_1 \oplus G(j_{\mathbf{inv}})$
$r' = G(\mathbf{pk}_B, m')$
$\mathbf{pk}_A(r') = c_0 \to K = H(m' \parallel (c_0, c_1))$
$\mathbf{pk}_A(r') \neq c_0 \to K = H(s \parallel (c_0, c_1))$

Fig. 1. SIKE protocol using isogenies on supersingular curves.

$$\mathbf{Enc}(\mathbf{pk}_B, m, G(m \parallel \mathbf{pk}_B)) \to (c_0, c_1) \tag{3}$$

$$H(m \parallel (c_0, c_1)) \to K.$$

Key Decapsulation. Computes the shared-key K from the outputs of equations (2) and (3). First, 2-tuple ciphertext is decrypted using secret-key sk_B and hashed to retrieve m'. Further, m' is concatenated with public-key pk_B and hashed using the G function to retrieve an ephemeral secret-key r' [19].

$$\mathsf{Dec}(\mathsf{sk}_B, (c_0, c_1)) \to m'$$

$$G(m' \parallel \mathsf{pk}_B) \to r'.$$

Next, c'_0 is computed by evaluating $\ell_A^{e_A}$-isogeny of starting curve E_0 using the kernel $\langle x_{P_A} + [r']x_{Q_A} \rangle$:

$$E_0 \to E_A/\langle x_{P_A} + [r']x_{Q_A} \rangle \to c'_0.$$

The final correction defines the exact value of the shared-key as follows: if the c_0 value and c'_0 are equal, the shared-key K is computed as $K = H(m' \parallel (c_0, c_1))$ which is the correct shared key, otherwise the provided ciphertext is not correct and the shared key should be randomly generated as $K = H(s \parallel (c_0, c_1))$ to be IND-CCA secure [19].

The whole key encapsulation mechanism is illustrated in Fig. 1.

In the next section, we describe SIKE parameters and a brief discussion on the security of supersingular isogeny-based problem.

3   SIKE Parameters and Security

The first proposal on constructing public-key cryptography schemes from the isogenies of regular elliptic curves was introduced by Rostovtsev and Stolbunov [27] in 2006. Later, Charles-Lauter-Goren [11] presented a set of cryptography hash functions constructed from Ramanujan graphs, i.e., the set of supersingular elliptic curves over $\mathbb{F}_{p^2}$ with ℓ-isogenies. Inspired by their work, Jao and De Feo introduced the first post-quantum cryptography protocol based on the hardness of computing isogenies [20] which has exponential complexity against classical and quantum attacks such as Childs et al. [12] quantum attack. In 2016, Galbraith et al. [15] proposed a set of new attacks on the security of SIDH which proved the security vulnerabilities inside the protocol when Alice and Bob reuse static keys. To address this problem, SIKE scheme implements an actively secure key encapsulation (IND-CCA KEM) which resolves the static key issue. Currently, the best known quantum attack against the Computational Supersingular Isogeny (CSSI) problem is based on claw-finding algorithm using quantum walks [31], which theoretically can find the isogeny between two curves in $O(\sqrt[3]{\ell^{e_\ell}})$, where ℓ^{e_ℓ} is the size of the isogeny kernel; accordingly, the provided quantum security level for SIKE is inherited by the minimum bit-length of each isogeny kernel, i.e., $\min(\sqrt[3]{\ell_A^{e_A}}, \sqrt[3]{\ell_B^{e_B}})$. This definition can be scaled up for different isogeny-based protocols such as undeniable signature [17,21] which is constructed on three of such torsion subgroups. In this case, the quantum security level of the protocol can be defined as $\min(\sqrt[3]{\ell_A^{e_A}}, \sqrt[3]{\ell_B^{e_B}}, \sqrt[3]{\ell_C^{e_C}})$.

Recent work by Adj et al. [1] provides a set of realistic models of quantum computation on solving CSSI problem. Based on their analysis, the Oorschot-Wiener golden collision search is the most powerful attack on the CSSI problem [1]; accordingly, both classical and quantum security level for SIKE and SIDH protocols are increased significantly for the proposed parameters set [19]. In particular, they claimed that 434- and 610-bit primes can meet NIST's category 2 and 4 requirements, respectively [1]. However, in this work, we still focus on the implementation of the conservative parameter sets which are proposed in [19] to illustrate the efficiency of our library even over relatively large finite fields.

The proposed implementation targets three different levels of security in compliance with SIKE parameter sets, i.e., SIKEp503, SIKEp751, and SIKEp964 providing 83-, 124-, and 159-bit *conservative* quantum security. We discuss the details of our implementation in the next section.

4   Optimized Implementation on ARMv7-A Processors

Supersingular isogeny-based cryptography provides the smallest key size compared to other PQC candidates. This feature is favorable for the applications such as IoT device communication with a central hub with limited bandwidth for each client. However, as already mentioned, large degree isogeny computations require a large amount of finite filed arithmetic operations on elliptic curves. This is in contrast with IoT protocol requirements where the communications should be reasonably efficient in terms of power and time. To address this problem, since the invention the isogeny-based cryptography, efficient implementations of this primitive have been proposed on a variety of platform. In this section, we describe a highly-optimized implementation of key encapsulation mechanism on ARMv7-A platforms which are equipped with NEON technology; we need to describe our target platforms and introduce their capabilities first, and then discuss the methodology we used which leads to remarkable performance improvement of the library.

4.1   Target Platform

Our implementation is optimized for the 32-bit ARMv7 Cortex-A with a focus on two cores, i.e., A8 and A15. Note that the proposed library can be run on other ARMv7-A cores which support NEON technology. We describe the target platform capabilities in the following:

Cortex-A8. Similar to other ARM processors, this core performs operations through a pipeline with different stages. First, the instruction fetch unit loads the fetched instructions from L1 cache and stores them into a buffer. Next, the decode unit decodes the instructions and passes them to the execute unit where all the arithmetic operations are performed inside a pipeline. This family of processors takes advantage of a separate 10-stage NEON pipeline in which all the NEON instructions are decoded and executed [3]. Since Cortex-A8 is a power-efficient processor, the execution pipeline performs in-order execution of the instructions, and all the instructions are queued in the pipeline. This leads to a remarkable performance degradation, while reduces the power consumption.

Cortex-A15. This high-performance core benefits from an advanced microcontroller bus architecture as well as fully out-of-order pipeline. This core consists of one to four processing units inside a single MPCore device providing fast L1 and L2 cache subsystems [2]. The main advantage of this processor over the other ARMv7-A cores is its *out-of-order* variable-length pipeline which enhances the instructions operation significantly. We benchmark our library on this processor to show the efficiency of our design when it runs on the high-performance cores. We state that, this family of processors is often used in the applications where the power-consumption is not crucial.

Both Cortex-A8 and Cortex-A15 processors feature 32 NEON vectors which are 128-bit wide and can be accessed using d and q notations which provide 64-bit or 128-bit overview of data, respectively. The main performance improvement of hand-crafted assembly implementation comes from this feature since we take advantage of these wide vectors and SIMD arithmetic unit to boost up the field arithmetic operations. Moreover, the wide vectors reduce the number of expensive memory-register transitions by loading and storing multiple vectors at once using ldmia and stmia instructions. In the following section, we describe our method in details.

4.2   Arithmetic Optimization

Finite field arithmetic are the fundamental operations inside any public-key cryptography scheme. Isogeny-based cryptography, at the lowest level, requires hundred thousands of field arithmetic operations to compute the large-degree isogenies. Moreover, since the supersingular curve is constructed over an extension field $\mathbb{F}_{p^2}$, different optimization techniques such as lazy reduction are adopted to boost the overall performance further. Recent work by Faz-Hernández et al. [14] shows that using some innovative optimization techniques such as precomputed look-up tables to improve the performance of group operation (three-point ladder) can enhance the overall performance of the SIDH protocol; however, the improvements are not significant compared to optimizations in the base field arithmetic. Therefore, in this work, we concentrate on the lowest level of implementation hierarchy and optimize the expensive multiplication/reduction as well as large modular additions and subtractions functions. Note that we follow the strategy which is used in the SIKE reference implementation [19], and separate the multiplication and the Montgomery reduction methods to be able to adopt lazy reduction technique inside extension field implementation.

Addition and Subtraction. Although field addition and subtraction are not very expensive operations, they can cause noticeable pipeline stalls over the large field sizes. In particular, taking advantage of lazy reduction inside extension field requires to have out of field addition. This means over a b-bit prime p, we also need to implement $2b$-bit addition and subtraction. On the constrained devices with 32-bit architecture, this results in multiple load and store operations due to the lack of enough number of registers. To address this problem, specifically in the case of SIKEp964 which requires the implementation of 2048-bit addition and subtraction, we take advantage of NEON vectorization.

The idea is simple and straightforward. Since the NEON parallel addition and subtraction do not support any carry/borrow propagation, we use vector transpose operation VTRN and zero vectors to divide a full 128-bit vector into two vectors of 64-bit data and use the 64-bit space for carry/borrow propagation. This technique is inspired by the optimized NEON operand-scanning Montgomery multiplication in [28]. This helps us to eliminate redundant load and store operations in A32 instructions and load multiple wide vectors at the same time. We observed notable performance improvement in addition and subtraction methods by adopting this technique.

Multiplication. Since the release of ARMv7-A series of processors equipped with NEON technology, different optimized implementations of field arithmetic have been proposed to exploit this capability. First attempts to implement cryptography multiplication and reduction over pseudo-Mersenne prime using NEON by Bernestein et al. [6] followed by the vectorized Montgomery multiplication implementation by Bos et al. [10] showed that vectorization can improve the efficiency of public-key cryptography protocols significantly. Subsequently, Seo et al. [28] introduced an operand-scanning Montgomery multiplication over generic form of primes with better performance results. Their implementation is highly-optimized and takes advantage of parallel NEON addition. We believe their proposed method is the most efficient way of implementing the Montgomery multiplication; however, in this work we need to implement the multiplication and the Montgomery reduction separately. Therefore, we follow the same implementation technique to vectorize multi-precision multiplication for the three different finite fields, i.e., 503-, 751-, and 964-bit primes. We refer the reader to [28] for further details. Note that, in case of 964-bit multiplication, we adopted one-level Karatsuba multiplication to increase the availability of vector registers and reduce the pipeline stalls. We found this method to be very effective for the relatively large fields.

Tailored Montgomery Reduction. SIKE implementation parameters benefit from a set of optimized reduction algorithms because of their special form. In particular, all the proposed parameters are Montgomery-friendly primes. This reduces the complexity of Montgomery reduction from $\mathcal{O}(n^2 + n)$ to $\mathcal{O}(n^2)$, where n is the number of platform words to allocate the finite field elements. Furthermore, Costello et al. [13] improved this complexity for the prime of the form $p = 2^{e_A} . \ell_B^{e_B} - 1$ by computing the Montgomery reduction regarding to $\hat{p} = p + 1$ and ignoring multiple multiplications with "0" words. Their proposed method is implemented using the product-scanning (Comba) multiplication and the optimized implementation on Intel and ARMv8 processors are provided in the SIKE submission [19].

Since the optimized multiplication on ARMv7-A platforms is designed based on operand-scanning method, in this work, we design a tailored operand-scanning Montgomery multiplication which benefits from all the SIKE-friendly prime fea-

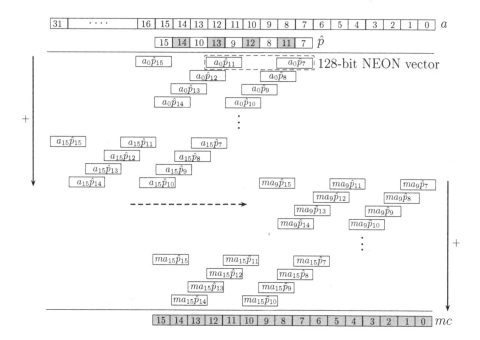

Fig. 2. SIKEp503 Montgomery reduction using NEON instruction set.

tures. We only describe the implementation of SIKEp503 in this section; however, the same strategy is scaled up for the larger parameters. We illustrate our method in the Fig. 2. The 503-bit value of $\hat{p} = p_{503} + 1$ has 9 non-zero elements which can be allocated inside three 128-bit vector registers. Note that the third vector is only occupied with 32 bits and we can use the rest of it as per requirement. After loading $\hat{p}$ into vector registers, we shuffle it in a new order as it is highlighted in Fig. 2. We load the first 16×32-bit (least significant half) of the multiplication results into 4 vectors. We continuously update data inside these vectors until the end of the algorithm where the final reduction result is stored back to the memory.

As it is illustrated in Fig. 2, our implementation is based on the operand-scanning method, in contrast to the efficient implementations of SIKE submission which are all based on Comba method. At the beginning of the algorithm, we transpose the values inside $\hat{p}$ in a special order to be able to use the NEON parallel multiplication. In the middle of the algorithm, we need to compute the ma array which is computed by multiplication and addition of the input operand with $\hat{p}$. The proposed method reduces the total number of multiplication inside the Montgomery reduction algorithm notably and provides the optimal timing results. Similar to [28], we take advantage of VMLAL instruction inside our code which computes the multiplication and addition with previous values inside a vector at once. This instruction eliminates hundreds of addition instructions inside the code, while it requires the exact same number of clock cycles as VMULL to execute the arithmetic. Considering other possible implementations of tailored Montgomery reduction, we believe the above method is the most efficient way of implementing this algorithm on ARMv7-A processors to date. We justify our claim by the significant performance improvement which we obtain in this work in the following section.

5   Performance Result and Discussion

In this section, we provide the performance results of the SIKE protocol on the target platforms for different security levels. Moreover, we benchmarked the portable C implementation of the protocol and include it to show the enhancement we obtain by using NEON instructions and our proposed optimized implementation.

We benchmark our library on two ARMv7-powered devices:

– A BeagleBone development board equipped with a low-power Cortex-A8 running at 1.0 GHz.
– An NVIDIA Jetson-TK1 board with a Cortex-A15 core running at 2.3 GHz.

Table 1. Performance results (presented in millions of clock cycles) of the proposed softwares in comparison with reference implementation on ARMv7-A platforms (benchmarks were obtained on 1.0 GHz Cortex-A8 and 2.3 GHz Cortex-A15 cores running Linux)

Scheme	Operation	NEON ASM		Optimized C [19]	
		Cortex-A8	Cortex-A15	Cortex-A8	Cortex-A15
SIKEp503	KeyGen.	99	68	813	577
	Encap.	162	112	1,339	910
	Decap.	174	121	1,424	955
	Total	**435**	**301**	3,576	2,442
SIKEp751	KeyGen.	364	280	2,842	2,089
	Encap.	589	439	4,598	3,331
	Decap.	618	491	4,944	3,531
	Total	**1,571**	**1,210**	12,384	8,951
SIKEp964	KeyGen.	870	635	6,037	4,409
	Encap.	1,504	1,098	10,376	7,678
	Decap.	1,598	1,176	10,835	7,963
	Total	**3,972**	**2,909**	27,248	20,050

The binaries are natively compiled with gcc 4.7.3 using -O3 -fomit-frame-pointer -mfloat-abi=softfp -mfpu=neon flags. In case of SIKEp964 on Cortex-A8, we cross-compiled the library using arm-linux-gnueabi-gcc 7.3.0 due to memory limitations on BeagleBone development board.

We benchmarked the executables using taskset command to ensure that the code is benchmarked only on a single core. Table 1 shows the performance of our library in comparison with the portable version on each target platform.

Based on the benchmark results, our arithmetic libraries improve the performance of the portable version roughly 7.5 times on both platforms. This significant improvement is obtained from the parallelism and wide vectorization by adopting NEON assembly instruction set.

We state that even two-level Karatsuba multiplication can be beneficial for the large parameter sets on some platforms; however, we believe 512-bit multiplication using NEON can be implemented optimally on ARMv7-A processors and further division of the computation may not provide any performance improvement.

Since the Cortex-A8 is working at 1.0 GHz frequency, the obtained clock cycles are also representing the actual time in milliseconds. Therefore, the entire key encapsulation mechanism takes 1.5 and 3.9 s for SIKEp751 and SIKEp964, respectively using NEON assembly optimizations. While these timings are smaller than portable implementation results, they still can result in latency challenges on low-power embedded devices.

6 Conclusion

In this work, we presented a set of highly-optimized ARMv7-A arithmetic library integrated into the SIKE reference implementation. We benchmarked our library on two popular ARMv7-A cores and compared the performance with optimized portable version. The proposed libraries improve the performance of the key encapsulation protocol significantly; accordingly, the total number of clock cycles as well as power consumption is decreased notably. This makes it possible for the SIKE scheme to be used on low-power IoT devices which are equipped with ARMv7 core such as Cortex-A8. We engineered the filed multiplication and reduction so that they are fit for the SIKE parameters over different quantum security levels. In particular, we suggested using the operand-scanning method instead of product-scanning method for modular multiplication and reduction on NEON technology. The main motivation behind this work was to evaluate the optimized target-specific codes for SIKE protocol. Moreover, we believe supersingular isogeny cryptography deserves more investigation by scientists and engineers because of its advantages such as small key size. We hope this work be a motivation for the further investigation into the efficiency of the SIKE protocol on embedded devices.

The recent optimized implementation of SIDH protocol on ARMv7-A platforms by Seo et al. [29] was not publicly available at the time of the submission of this work. We state that the proposed optimization techniques in this work differs from [29]. Moreover, this work presents the efficient implementation of SIKE protocol, while authors of [29] target SIDH key-exchange on ARMv7-A platforms.

Acknowledgment. The authors would like to thank the reviewers for their comments. This work is supported in parts by grants from NIST-60NANB16D246 and ARO W911NF-17-1-0311.

References

1. Adj, G., Cervantes-Vázquez, D., Chi-Domínguez, J., Menezes, A., Rodríguez-Henríquez, F.: On the cost of computing isogenies between supersingular elliptic curves. IACR Cryptology ePrint Archive 2018, 313 (2018). https://eprint.iacr.org/2018/313
2. ARM Limited: Cortex-A15 Technical Reference Manual (2010). http://infocenter.arm.com/help/topic/com.arm.doc.ddi0438c/DDI0438C_cortex_a15_r2p0_trm.pdf. Accessed June 2018
3. ARM Limited: Cortex-A8 Technical Reference Manual (2010). http://infocenter.arm.com/help/topic/com.arm.doc.ddi0344k/DDI0344K_cortex_a8_r3p2_trm.pdf. Accessed June 2018
4. Azarderakhsh, R., Fishbein, D., Jao, D.: Efficient implementations of a quantum-resistant key-exchange protocol on embedded systems. Technical report (2014). http://cacr.uwaterloo.ca/techreports/2014/cacr2014-20.pdf
5. Bernstein, D.J., et al.: Classic McEliece: conservative code-based cryptography. NIST submissions (2017)
6. Bernstein, D.J., Schwabe, P.: NEON crypto. In: Prouff, E., Schaumont, P. (eds.) CHES 2012. LNCS, vol. 7428, pp. 320–339. Springer, Heidelberg (2012). https://doi.org/10.1007/978-3-642-33027-8_19
7. Boneh, D., et al.: Multiparty non-interactive key exchange and more from isogenies on elliptic curves. arXiv preprint arXiv:1807.03038 (2018)
8. Bos, J.W., Friedberger, S.: Fast arithmetic modulo $2^x p^y \pm 1$. In: 24th IEEE Symposium on Computer Arithmetic, ARITH 2017, London, United Kingdom, pp. 148–155 (2017)
9. Bos, J.W., Friedberger, S.: Arithmetic considerations for isogeny based cryptography. IEEE Trans. Comput. (2018)
10. Bos, J.W., Montgomery, P.L., Shumow, D., Zaverucha, G.M.: Montgomery multiplication using vector instructions. In: Lange, T., Lauter, K., Lisoněk, P. (eds.) SAC 2013. LNCS, vol. 8282, pp. 471–489. Springer, Heidelberg (2014). https://doi.org/10.1007/978-3-662-43414-7_24
11. Charles, D.X., Lauter, K.E., Goren, E.Z.: Cryptographic hash functions from expander graphs. J. Cryptol. 22(1), 93–113 (2009)
12. Childs, A.M., Jao, D., Soukharev, V.: Constructing elliptic curve isogenies in quantum subexponential time. J. Math. Cryptol. 8(1), 1–29 (2014)
13. Costello, C., Longa, P., Naehrig, M.: Efficient algorithms for supersingular isogeny Diffie-Hellman. In: Robshaw, M., Katz, J. (eds.) CRYPTO 2016. LNCS, vol. 9814, pp. 572–601. Springer, Heidelberg (2016). https://doi.org/10.1007/978-3-662-53018-4_21
14. Faz-Hernández, A., López, J., Ochoa-Jiménez, E., Rodríguez-Henríquez, F.: A faster software implementation of the supersingular isogeny diffie-hellman key exchange protocol. IEEE Trans. Comput. (2017)
15. Galbraith, S.D., Petit, C., Shani, B., Ti, Y.B.: On the security of supersingular isogeny cryptosystems. In: Cheon, J.H., Takagi, T. (eds.) ASIACRYPT 2016. LNCS, vol. 10031, pp. 63–91. Springer, Heidelberg (2016). https://doi.org/10.1007/978-3-662-53887-6_3
16. Galbraith, S.D., Petit, C., Silva, J.: Identification protocols and signature schemes based on supersingular isogeny problems. In: Takagi, T., Peyrin, T. (eds.) ASIACRYPT 2017. LNCS, vol. 10624, pp. 3–33. Springer, Cham (2017). https://doi.org/10.1007/978-3-319-70694-8_1

17. Jalali, A., Azarderakhsh, R., Mozaffari-Kermani, M.: Efficient post-quantum unde-niable signature on 64-Bit ARM. In: Adams, C., Camenisch, J. (eds.) SAC 2017. LNCS, vol. 10719, pp. 281–298. Springer, Cham (2018). https://doi.org/10.1007/978-3-319-72565-9_14
18. Jalali, A., Azarderakhsh, R., Kermani, M.M., Jao, D.: Supersingular isogeny Diffie-Hellman key exchange on 64-bit arm. IEEE Trans. Dependable Secure Comput. (2017)
19. Jao, D., et al.: Supersingular isogeny key encapsulation. Submission to the NIST Post-Quantum Standardization project (2017). https://csrc.nist.gov/Projects/Post-Quantum-Cryptography/Round-1-Submissions
20. Jao, D., De Feo, L.: Towards quantum-resistant cryptosystems from supersingular elliptic curve isogenies. In: Yang, B.-Y. (ed.) PQCrypto 2011. LNCS, vol. 7071, pp. 19–34. Springer, Heidelberg (2011). https://doi.org/10.1007/978-3-642-25405-5_2
21. Jao, D., Soukharev, V.: Isogeny-based quantum-resistant undeniable signatures. In: Mosca, M. (ed.) PQCrypto 2014. LNCS, vol. 8772, pp. 160–179. Springer, Cham (2014). https://doi.org/10.1007/978-3-319-11659-4_10
22. Karmakar, A., Roy, S.S., Vercauteren, F., Verbauwhede, I.: Efficient finite field multiplication for isogeny based post quantum cryptography. In: Duquesne, S., Petkova-Nikova, S. (eds.) WAIFI 2016. LNCS, vol. 10064, pp. 193–207. Springer, Cham (2016). https://doi.org/10.1007/978-3-319-55227-9_14
23. Koziel, B., Azarderakhsh, R., Kermani, M.M., Jao, D.: Post-quantum cryptography on FPGA based on isogenies on elliptic curves. IEEE Trans. Circuits Syst. **64–I**(1), 86–99 (2017)
24. Koziel, B., Jalali, A., Azarderakhsh, R., Jao, D., Mozaffari-Kermani, M.: NEON-SIDH: efficient implementation of supersingular isogeny Diffie-Hellman key exchange protocol on ARM. In: Foresti, S., Persiano, G. (eds.) CANS 2016. LNCS, vol. 10052, pp. 88–103. Springer, Cham (2016). https://doi.org/10.1007/978-3-319-48965-0_6
25. Naehrig, M., et al.: FrodoKEM: practical quantum-secure key encapsulation from generic lattices. NIST submissions (2017)
26. Poppelmann, T., et al.: Newhope. NIST submissions (2017)
27. Rostovtsev, A., Stolbunov, A.: Public-key cryptosystem based on isogenies. IACR Cryptology ePrint Archive 2006, 145 (2006)
28. Seo, H., Liu, Z., Großschädl, J., Choi, J., Kim, H.: Montgomery modular multi-plication on ARM-NEON revisited. In: Lee, J., Kim, J. (eds.) ICISC 2014. LNCS, vol. 8949, pp. 328–342. Springer, Cham (2015). https://doi.org/10.1007/978-3-319-15943-0_20
29. Seo, H., Liu, Z., Longa, P., Hu, Z.: SIDH on ARM: faster modular multiplications for faster post-quantum supersingular isogeny key exchange. IACR Cryptology ePrint Archive 2018, 700 (2018)
30. Silverman, J.H.: The Arithmetic of Elliptic Curves. GTM, vol. 106. Springer, New York (2009). https://doi.org/10.1007/978-0-387-09494-6
31. Tani, S.: Claw finding algorithms using quantum walk. Theor. Comput. Sci. **410**(50), 5285–5297 (2009)
32. Vélu, J.: Isogénies entre courbes elliptiques. CR Acad. Sci. Paris Sér. AB **273**, A238–A241 (1971)
33. Yoo, Y., Azarderakhsh, R., Jalali, A., Jao, D., Soukharev, V.: A post-quantum digital signature scheme based on supersingular isogenies. In: Kiayias, A. (ed.) FC 2017. LNCS, vol. 10322, pp. 163–181. Springer, Cham (2017). https://doi.org/10.1007/978-3-319-70972-7_9

A Machine Vision Attack Model on Image Based CAPTCHAs Challenge: Large Scale Evaluation

Ajeet Singh[✉], Vikas Tiwari[✉], and Appala Naidu Tentu[✉]

C.R. Rao Advanced Institute of Mathematics, Statistics, and Computer Science,
University of Hyderabad Campus, Hyderabad 500046, India
ajeetcs@uohyd.ac.in, vikas.tiwari2403@gmail.com, naidunit@gmail.com

Abstract. Over the past decade, several public web services made an attempt to prevent automated scripts and exploitation by bots by interrogating a user to solve a Turing-test challenge (commonly known as a CAPTCHA) before using the service. A CAPTCHA is a cryptographic protocol whose underlying hardness assumption is based on an artificial intelligence problem. CAPTCHAs challenges rely on the problem of distinguishing images of living or non-living objects (a task that is easy for humans). User studies proves, it can be solved by humans 99.7% of the time in under 30 s while this task is difficult for machines. The security of image based CAPTCHAs challenge is based on the presumed difficulty of classifying CAPTCHAs database images automatically.

In this paper, we proposed a classification model which is 95.2% accurate in telling apart the images used in the CAPTCHA database. Our method utilizes layered features *optimal tuning* with an improved *VGG16 architecture* of *Convolutional Neural Networks*. Experimental simulation is performed using *Caffe* deep learning framework. Later, we compared our experimental results with significant state-of-the-art approaches in this domain.

Keywords: Computing and information systems · CAPTCHA
Botnets · Security · Machine learning · Advanced neural networks
Supervised learning

1 Introduction

A CAPTCHA (Completely Automated Public Turing test to tell Computers and Humans Apart) can be considered as a test $\mathbb{V}$, on which majority of humans have success probability almost close to 1, whereas its hard to write a computer program that has high success rate on test $\mathbb{V}$. *If any program exists that has high success over $\mathbb{V}$ can be utilized to solve a hard AI problem* [10]. The important characteristics of a CAPTCHA are: (A) Easy for a user to solve. (B) Difficult for a program/automated script or a computer to solve. Mainly CAPTCHA's challenge are of two types - text based CAPTCHA and image based CAPTCHA.

© Springer Nature Switzerland AG 2018
A. Chattopadhyay et al. (Eds.): SPACE 2018, LNCS 11348, pp. 52–64, 2018.
https://doi.org/10.1007/978-3-030-05072-6_4

While the security of text based CAPTCHAs rely on hardness of distinguishing distorted text through machines, image based CAPTCHAs rely on the problem of distinguishing images of object A and B. It possesses many practical security oriented applications, i.e. -

- **Search Engine Bots:** Some websites want to prevent themselves to be indexed by various search engines but the specific html tag which prevent search engine bots [1] fron reading web pages, doesn't guarantee that those bots will never read the pages. So, CAPTCHAs are needed to make sure that bots are not entering into targeted web site.
- **Free E-mail Services:** "Bots" is a specific type of attack, with which companies like Microsoft, Indiatimes, Yahoo! etc. suffer shall be need to face while offering free e-mail services. "Bots" can do sign up for millions of e-mail accounts per minute. This drastic situation can be avoided by asking user to prove that they are human before they process. Some of the examples of CAPTCHAs challenge are given in Fig. 1.
- **Online Elections(e-voting:)** Online polls are also proven to be highly vulnerable through bots. In 1999, *slashdot.com* released an online poll asking - which was the best graduate school in computer science (a dangerous question to ask over the web!). As is the case with most online polls, IP addresses of voters were recorded in order to prevent single users from voting more than once. However, students at Carnegie Mellon found a way to stuff the ballots by using programs that voted for CMU thousands of times. CMU's score started growing rapidly. The next day, students at MIT wrote their own voting program and the poll became a contest between voting bots. MIT finished with 21,156 votes, Carnegie Mellon with 21,032 and every other school with less than 1,000. So, can we trust the result of any online poll?

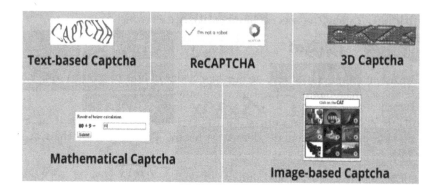

Fig. 1. CAPTCHA solving services

1.1 Motivation and Our Contribution

In the case of conventional cryptography, for an instance, one assumption taken is that - in a reasonable amount of time, an adversary can't factor 2048-bit integer. In the same way, CAPTCHA model functions on an assumption that the adversary can't solve an AI (Artificial Intelligence) problem with higher accuracy than what is currently known among the AI community. If the considered AI problem is useful, CAPTCHA implies a win-win situation - either its hard to break CAPTCHA and there exist a way to differentiate humans from machines, or a CAPTCHA is broken and an appropriate AI problem can be solved successfully. The main contributions of our paper are as follows -

- We have given an extensive state-of-the-art review.
- We propose an attack model for image based CAPTCHAs challenge and performed experiments on high end *Tesla K80* GPU accelerator up to *8.73 teraflops single-precision* performance. We also compare our proposed technique with earlier techniques described in literature.

1.2 Preliminaries: Definitions and Notation

Here we present some definitions and notations. Consider γ be a PDF (probability distribution function), $[\gamma]$: denote the support of γ. If P(.) denotes - probabilistic program, then we denote $P_r(.)$ as the deterministic program.

Let, (P, V) is a pair of probabilistic interacting programs, then denote the output of V after interaction between P and V with random coins u_1 & u_2, (here assume, this interaction will terminate by $< P_{u_1}, V_{u_2} >$).

Test: A program V is called a test if $\forall$ P and u_1, u_2, the interaction between P_{u_1} & V_{u_2} terminates and $< P_{u_1}, V_{u_2} > \in \{Accept, Reject\}$. We termed V as tester (verifier) and any P which interacts with V the prover.

Definition 1. Define the success of an entity A over a test V by -

$$Success_A^V = P_{r_{(r,r')}}[< A_r, V_{r'} >= Accept]$$

Here, we assume that A can have precise knowledge of how program V functions; A can't know - (the factor r', internal randomness of V).

Definition 2. A test V is said to be (α, β) - human executable if at least an α portion of object (human) density is having success greater than β over tester (V).

Note: The success of various groups of humans may depend on several biological/non-biological factors, their origin language, sensory disabilities etc. For an instance, partial color-blind individual might posses comparatively lesser success rate on tests.

Definition 3. A triple $\phi = $ (S, D, f) represents an AI problem, where S: a set of problem instances, D: a probability distribution over the problem set S, and f: S → $\{0, 1\}^*$ answers the instances. Let, $\delta \in (0, 1]$. For an $\alpha > 0$ fraction of humans H,

$$P_{r_{x \leftarrow D}}[H(x) = f(x)] > \delta$$

Definition 4. An AI problem will be considered to be (δ, τ) - solved if $\exists$ a program A, running in time at most τ on any input from S, such that,

$$P_{r_{x \leftarrow D, r}}[A_r(x) = f(x)] \geq \delta$$

Definition 5. An (α, β, η) - CAPTCHA is a test V i.e. its (α, β) - human executable with success and posses following property -

$\exists$ (δ, τ) - hard AI problem ϕ and a program A, such that if B has success more than η over test V, then A^B is a (δ, τ) solution to ϕ.

Overfitting and Underfitting: Overfitting generally occurs when a model learns the noise in the training data to the scope that it impacts the performance of the model on new data in negative way. The meaning is that the noise or random fluctuations in the training data is picked up and learned as concepts by the model. Overfitting is more likely with nonparametric and nonlinear models that have more flexibility when learning a target function.

Underfitting all to a model that can neither model the training data nor generalize to the new unseen data. An underfit machine learning prototype is not a suitable model and will be self-evident as it will have performance deficiency on the training data. An illustration is shown in Fig. 2.

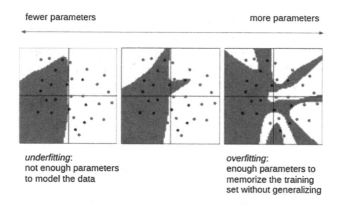

Fig. 2. Overfitting and underfitting

1.3 Organization of the Paper

The organization of this paper is as follows. In Sect. 2, we review related work briefly. A brief discussion about threat possibilities in form of attacks is discussed in Sect. 3. In Sect. 4, our proposed attack model is described. An extensive experimental analysis is given in Sect. 5. Conclusive summary is given in Sect. 6.

2   Related Work

Firstly, the idea for "Automated Turing Tests" appeared in an unpublished manuscript by Naor [5], but it didn't contain any practical proposal. For preventing"bots" from automatically registering web pages, first practical example of an Automated Turing Test was developed by [6]. The challenge was based on the hardness of - reading and recognizing slightly distorted english characters. Similar systems were developed by Coates et al. [7], Xu et al. [8] and Ahn et al. [9]. Simard et al. showed that Optical Character Recognition can achieve human-like accuracy, even in the case, when letters are distorted, as long as the image can be reliably segmented into its constituent letters [11]. Mori et al. [12] demonstrated that von Ahn's original CAPTCHA can be solved automatically 92% of the time. Chellapilla et al. [2] given the model design for human interaction proofs. Chew et al. [3] describe method using labelled photographs to generate a CAPTCHA. The authors Elson et al. [14] conjecture that "based on a survey of machine vision literature and vision experts at Microsoft Research, classification accuracy of better than 60% will be difficult without a significant advance [15,16] in the state of the art".

Object recognition algorithms [17] were used in very successful breaks of the text-based Gimpy and EZ-Gimpy CAPTCHAs. Attacks have been reported in the popular press against the CAPTCHAs used by Yahoo! [18] and Google [19]. Yan et al. [20] gives a detailed description of character segmentation attacks against Microsoft and Yahoo! CAPTCHAs. Chow et al. [21] given an attack approach for clickable CAPTCHAs. Recently, Google used convolutional neural network [22] for detecting home addresses in society images. Use of Recurrent Neural Networks achieved good results recently, as shown by the [23] paper by Google, where they generate a caption (variable length) for a given image. Kwon et al. in [13] proposed an approach with inclusion of uncertainty content in image-based CAPTCHAs. Althamary et al. given a provably secure scheme [26] for CAPTCHA-based authentication in cloud environment. Tang et al. [27] proposed a generic and fast attack on text CAPTCHAs.

3   Threat Possibilities

Before going into the discussion of the security of image based CAPTCHAs [3], here we review the threat model. CAPTCHA challange models are an unusual area of security where one can't guarantee to completely prevent attacks, only an attempt can be made practically to slow down attackers. From a mechanistic (orthodox) view, there exist no method to prove that a program cannot pass a test which a human can pass, since there is a program - the human brain - which passes the test.

3.1   Machine Vision Attacks

Based on the state-of-the-art study and according to vision of experts, the classification accuracy of better than 89% will be hard to achieve without significant advances in methodologies to deal with uncertain boundary region conditions. Some attacks of these types are adopted in literature which utilize color histogram analysis but are more theoretical and impractical upto significant extent.

3.2 Brute Force Attack

The simplest and classical attack on image based CAPTCHAs is - brute force attack i.e. provide random solution to the CAPTCHA challenges until final success. A token bucket scheme is discussed in [14]. In summary, the scheme castigates IP addresses that usually obtain many successive incorrect answers by asking them to answer two challenges in correct manner within the three attempts prior to gaining a ticket. In each 5.6 million guesses, attackers can expect only one service ticket.

3.3 Database Attacks

One possible way to induce attack on image based CAPTCHAs is to partially construct the underlying database. Every challenge, when it is displayed, reveals some portion of database but the question here is - "Is it economically feasible to rebuild the database?" This task may be easy for image database containing less number of images, but for a database which consists millions of images, this approach is unfeasible unless the financial incentives are available.

3.4 Implementation Attacks

Weak implementations are vulnerability factors sometimes for CAPTCHAs. Consider, the case if same session id, in which the authorization is performed, is reused in repeated manner to gain access. In a statefull implementation scenario, user sessions and forms of stateful can be tracked while an stateless service may act as a solution to get rid of this scenario.

4   CAPTCHAs Challenge: Proposed Attack Model

Web services are often protected with a challenge that's supposed to be easy for people to solve, but difficult for computers. Such a challenge is often called a CAPTCHA or HIP (Human Interactive Proof) [2]. HIPs are used for many purposes, such as to reduce email and blog spam and prevent brute-force attacks on web site passwords. In present scenario, *GPUs, Deep Neural Networks and Big Data* help us to solve some of the computationally hard problems that were previously seemed to be impossible. Deep learning frameworks and libraries removed the limitation that any computer researcher can only solve those problems whose solutions are expressible as stepwise instructions. In this section, we show that using *Deep Convolutional Neural Network*, our model can learn the mapping between huge amount of 256×256 input color images to an output stipulating the likelihood that each CAPTCHA image belonged to an specific class - either

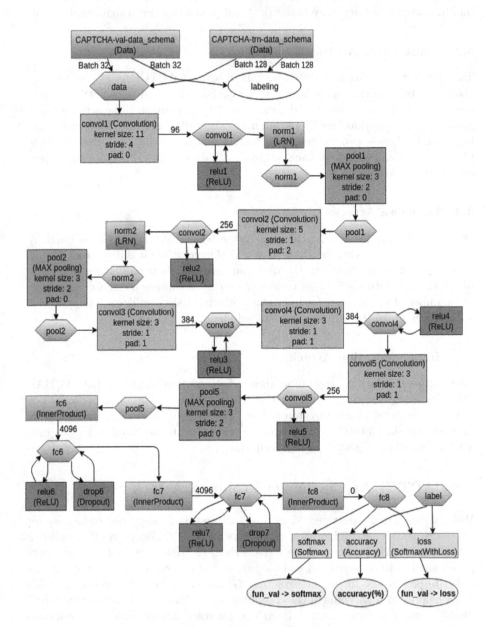

Fig. 3. Proposed classification based attack model

class 'A' or class 'B' with better accuracy. The detailed component-wise diagram for our adopted attack model is represented as Fig. 3.

Algorithm 1. Proposed Classification based Attack Model Steps -

1: Begin procedure
   Input: Large sized CAPTCHA images database

2: Use *.flow_from_directory()* to generate Batches of image data (and their labels) directly from our jpgs in their respective folders.

3: Augment training section via several random transformations. This will prevent images' collision while pre-computation, as well as prevents model overfitting.

4: Deploy *Convolutional Neural Network (convnet)* with *VGG16* architecture.

5: Modulate the entropic capacity by opting one of available choice i.e. choice of parameters count in model (count of layers along with each layer size) or choice of employing weight regularization (e.g. L_1 or L_2 regularization).

6: A layer is prevented from pattern matching redundantly by reduction in overfitting through Dropout.

7: Choose appropriate number of convolution layers along with corresponding *LRN (Local Response Normalization)* layer, *ReLU (Rectified Linear Unit)* and followed by *MAX-Pooling* layers.

8: Model is end-up with *ReLU7* and *Dropout7* functional layers. It seems to be perfect for binary classification based attack model.

9: Model is trained using Batch generators upto optimal epochs. More computational efficacy is achieved by storing the features offline instead of adding fully connected model directly on top of a frozen convolutional base.

10: Fine-tune the model using steps 11-16.

11: Adopt instantiation of the *VGG16* convolutional base and load weights (layers parameters).

12: Add fully-connected model (defined previously) on the top, and load its weights (very small weight updates).

13: Perform freezing the layers of *VGG16* model till last convolutional block.

14: Adopt comparatively more contentious data augmentation and dropout.

15: Fine-tune an extended convolutional block beside higher regularization.

16: Steps 11-15 must be done preferably with a very slow learning rate.

17: End procedure

---

5   Experimental Analysis and Discussion of Results

This section presents the experimental setup, description of utilized CAPTCHA database, our results and finally the comparison of obtained results with state-of-the-art approaches.

5.1 Experimental Set-up

In our experiments the software and hardware specifications are as follows -

We utilized NGC (NVIDIA GPU Cloud). The high end *Tesla K80* GPU accelerator consists of 4992 NVIDIA CUDA cores with a dual-GPU design, 8.73 teraflops single-precision performance, 24 GB of GDDR5 RAM, 480 GB/s aggregate memory bandwidth. Experimental model simulation is performed using *Caffe* [4] deep learning framework.

5.2 Dataset Description

For experimentation, Asirra database [24] is utilized. Asirra (Animal Species Image Recognition for Restricting Access) is a HIP (Human Interactive Proof) that works by asking users to identify photographs of cats and dogs. It is a security challenge which protects websites from bot attacks. The archive contains 25,000 images of dogs and cats. Asirra is unique because of its partnership with *Petfinder.com*, the world's largest site devoted to finding homes for homeless pets. They have provided Microsoft Research with over three million images of cats and dogs, manually classified by people at thousands of animal shelters across the United States.

The motivation behind choosing the cats and dogs as image CAPTCHA's object categories is - Google images have about 262 million cat and 169 million dog images indexed. About 67% of United States household have pets (approx 39 million households have cats, approx 48 million households have dogs). Difficulty in automatic classification of cats and dogs images was exploited to build a security system for web services.

5.3 Procedure and Results

The CAPTCHA images database obtained from Asirra are 256×256 pixels. Next, we have the collection of 25,000 images. First we performed manual categorization followed by manual verification, in this process 331 misclassified images (which is 1.3% of the total archive) were identified and further moved into correct category. After this verification procedure, we obtained 12,340 images of object category A (cats), 12,353 images of object category B (dogs) and 307 images placed in *other* category. *Other* category contained images which has either no well recognizable object (animal) or it contained both object A and B. Now the *other* category image instances are simply discared from experiment and rest of the images of object category A and object category B are kept.

We adopted our procedure (given in Sect. 4). Each color feature vector consist of the statistical values named: {Minima, Maxima, Skewness, Mean, Standard deviation}; all these feature vectors are combined to form feature space. Next, we build the deep classifier model for attacking Asirra. We used 75% : 25% split procedure for entire database archive, where 75% partition (18,520 images) are used for training [DB-train] and 25% partition (6173 images) utilized for validation [DB-val]. The total number of epochs used in the experiment is 26, with that we achieved an optimal predictive power and performance without overfitting.

Fig. 4. Features representation at head portion pixels - (i) at left: object B(dog) (ii) at right: object A(cat)

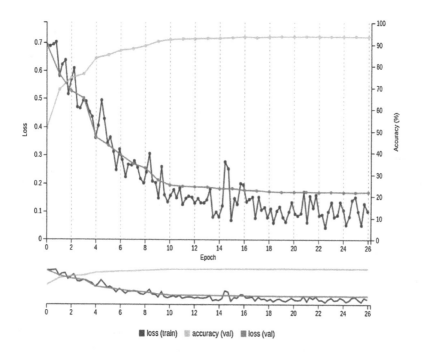

Fig. 5. Performance graph

In Fig. 4, one can observe that head portion of the object's body is the dominating part (better discrimination for categorization) in features representation and processing in our scenario. It gives an extra edge for better performance in our CAPTCHA attack task. The performance parameters are clearly visible in Fig. 5. Our trained machine achieved 95.2% accuracy (val), the entire simulation time was 2,113 s. Loss at validation is also represented in the same graph. Graph representation for Epoch vs Learning Rate is shown in Fig. 6. Image-based

Asirra CAPTCHA challenge contains a set of 12 images of objects A (Cats) and B (Dogs) at a time. For solving the challenge, one must be able to correctly diagnose the subset of dog images.

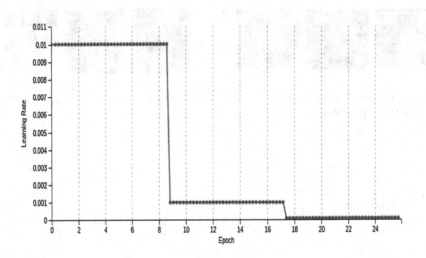

Fig. 6. Epoch vs learning rate fluctuation

A machine classifier possessing a success probability $0 < p < 1$ of accurately categorizing a single Asirra archive image succeeds in interpreting a 12-image challenge with probability p^{12}. *VGG16* is chosen as base pre-trained model over other models as it performed comparatively well due to its simple architecture and the flexibility it provides in terms of choosing the number of network layers based on use case. As our experimental simulation resulted 95.2% accuracy, implies that Asirra image CAPTCHA challenge can completely automatically be solved with higher probability.

5.4   Comparison with State-of-the-Art

This section presents the comparison of our adopted procedure with significant state-of-the-art CAPTCHA attack models/approaches in this domain. The comparative analysis is given in Table 1. In the table, almost all the methodologies i.e. Elson et al. [14], Golle et al. [25], SVM (Polynomial Kernel) and SVM (Radial Basis Function Kernel) which have been taken here into consideration for comparison point of view, were applied on the same dataset.

The experimental simulation adopting our proposed procedure resulted 95.2% accuracy, which implies that Asirra image CAPTCHA challenge can completely automatically solved with higher probability. The comparative summary presented in Table 1 proves the novelty of our adopted procedure. Results shows that our procedure outperforms over other existing models/approaches.

Table 1. Comparative summary

Method/Reference	Data archive size in experiment	CAPTCHA type	Accuracy(%)
Elson et al. [14]	13,000 Training images	Image based	56.9%
Mori et al. [12]	362 Instances	Text based	92%
Golle et al. [25]	13,000 Training images	Image based	82.7%
SVM (Poly Kernel)	25,000 Images	Image based	81.3%
SVM (RBF Kernel)	25,000 Images	Image based	79.5%
Proposed procedure	25,000 Images	Image based	95.2%

6   Summary and Conclusions

The domains of cryptography and AI have a lot to bestow to one another. In literature, we investigated several attacks on text and image based CAPTCHAs. We described a machine vision based attack model (classifier) which is 95.2% accurate in detecting apart the images in binary object categories in Asirra. The optimal possible obstacle against our machine vision based attack are strict Internet Protocol (IP) tracking schemes. These schemes can inhibit an adversary to request and attempt to solve exceeding number of CAPTCHA challenges. Another approach to enhance security is - web services should increase the number of images that are employed in challenges. Further work needs to be done to construct CAPTCHAs based on other hard AI problems.

Acknowledgments. We would like to thank P.V. Ananda Mohan, Ashutosh Saxena for their valuable suggestions, insights and observations. We would also like to thank the anonymous reviewers whose comments helped improve this paper.

References

1. BotBarrier.com. On the web. http://www.botbarrier.com/
2. Chellapilla, K., Larson, K., Simard, P., Czerwinski, M.: Designing human friendly human interaction proofs (HIPs). In: Proceedings of ACM CHI 2005 Conference on Human Factors in Computing Systems. Email and Security, pp. 711–720 (2005)
3. Chew, M., Tygar, J.D.: Image recognition CAPTCHAs. In: Zhang, K., Zheng, Y. (eds.) ISC 2004. LNCS, vol. 3225, pp. 268–279. Springer, Heidelberg (2004). https://doi.org/10.1007/978-3-540-30144-8_23
4. http://caffe.berkeleyvision.org/
5. Naor, M.: Verification of a human in the loop or Identification via the Turing Test. Unpublished Manuscript (1997). Electronically: www.wisdom.weizmann.ac.il/~naor/PAPERS/human.ps
6. Lillibridge, M.D., Adabi, M., Bharat, K., Broder, A.: Method for selectively restricting access to computer systems. Technical report, US Patent 6,195,698, Applied April 1998 and Approved February 2001
7. Coates, A.L., Baird, H.S., Fateman, R.J.: Pessimal print: a reverse turing test. In: Proceedings of the International Conference on Document Analysis and Recognition (ICDAR 2001), Seattle WA, pp. 1154–1159 (2001)

8. Xu, J., Lipton, R., Essa, I.: Hello, are you human. Technical Report GIT-CC-00-28, Georgia Institute of Technology, November 2000
9. von Ahn, L., Blum, M., Hopper, N.J., Langford, J.: The CAPTCHA (2000). http://www.captcha.net
10. von Ahn, L., Blum, M., Langford, J.: Telling humans and computers apart (Automatically) or how lazy cryptographers do AI. Commun. ACM (2002, to appear)
11. Simard, P., Steinkraus, D., Platt, J.C.: Best practices for convolutional neural networks applied to visual document analysis. In: International Conference on Document Analysis and Recognition, pp. 958–962. IEEE Computer Society (2003)
12. Mori, G., Malik, J.: Recognizing objects in adversarial clutter: breaking a visual CAPTCHA. In: Conference on Computer Vision and Pattern Recognition (CVPR 2003), pp. 134–144. IEEE Computer Society (2003)
13. Kwon, S., Cha, S.: A paradigm shift for the CAPTCHA race: adding uncertainty to the process. IEEE Softw. **33**(6), 80–85 (2016)
14. Elson, J., Douceur, J., Howell, J., Saul, J.: Asirra: a CAPTCHA that exploits interest-aligned manual image categorization. In: Proceedings of ACM CCS 2007, pp. 366–374 (2007)
15. Azakami, T., Shibata, C., Uda, R.: Challenge to impede deep learning against CAPTCHA with ergonomic design. In: IEEE 41st Annual Computer Software and Applications Conference, Italy (2017)
16. Golle, P., Wagner, D.: Cryptanalysis of a cognitive authentication scheme. In: Proceedings of the 2007 IEEE Symposium on Security and Privacy, pp. 66–70. IEEE Computer Society (2007)
17. Mori, G., Malik, J.: Recognizing objects in adversarial clutter: breaking a visual CAPTCHA. In: Proceedings of the 2003 Conference on Computer Vision and Pattern Recognition, pp. 134–144. IEEE Computer Society (2003)
18. SlashDot. Yahoo CAPTCHA Hacked. http://it.slashdot.org/it/08/01/30/0037254.shtml. Accessed 29 Jan 2008
19. Websense Blog: Google's CAPTCHA busted in recent spammer tactics, 22 February 2008. http://securitylabs.websense.com/content/Blogs/2919.aspx
20. Yan, J., El Ahmad, A.: A low-cost attack on a Microsoft CAPTCHA. In: Proceedings of ACM CCS (2008, to appear)
21. Chow, R., Golle, P., Jakobsson, M., Wang, X., Wang, L.: Making CAPTCHAs clickable. In: Proceedings of HotMobile (2008)
22. Goodfellow, I.J., Bulatov, Y., Ibarz, J., Arnoud, S., Shet, V.: Multi-digit number recognition from street view imagery using deep convolutional neural networks. In: Proceedings of ICLR, April 2014
23. Vinyals, O., Toshev, A., Bengio, S., Erhan, D.: Show and tell: a neural image caption generator. arXiv:1411.4555 [cs.CV], 20 April 2015
24. www.microsoft.com/en-us/download/details.aspx?id=54765
25. Golle, P.: Machine learning attacks against the Asirra CAPTCHA. In: CCS 2008, Virginia, USA, 27–31 October 2008
26. Althamary, I.A., El-Alfy, E.M.: A more secure scheme for CAPTCHA-based authentication in cloud environment. In: 8th International Conference on Information Technology (ICIT), Jordan, May 2017
27. Tang, M., Gao, H., Zhang, Y.: Research on deep learning techniques in breaking text-based CAPTCHAs and designing image-based CAPTCHA. IEEE Trans. Inf. Forensics Secur. **13**(10), 2522–2537 (2018)

Addressing Side-Channel Vulnerabilities in the Discrete Ziggurat Sampler

Séamus Brannigan[✉], Máire O'Neill, Ayesha Khalid, and Ciara Rafferty

Centre for Secure Information Technologies (CSIT), Queen's University Belfast, Belfast, UK
sbrannigan11@qub.ac.uk

Abstract. Post-quantum cryptography with lattices typically requires high precision sampling of vectors with discrete Gaussian distributions. Lattice signatures require large values of the standard deviation parameter, which poses difficult problems in finding a suitable trade-off between throughput performance and memory resources on constrained devices. In this paper, we propose modifications to the Ziggurat method, known to be advantageous with respect to these issues, but problematic due to its inherent rejection-based timing profile. We improve upon information leakage through timing channels significantly and require: only 64-bit unsigned integers, no floating-point arithmetic, no division and no external libraries. Also proposed is a constant-time Gaussian function, possessing all aforementioned advantageous properties. The measures taken to secure the sampler completely close side-channel vulnerabilities through direct timing of operations and these have no negative implications on its applicability to lattice-based signatures. We demonstrate the improved method with a 128-bit reference implementation, showing that we retain the sampler's efficiency and decrease memory consumption by a factor of 100. We show that this amounts to memory savings by a factor of almost 5,000, in comparison to an optimised, state-of-the-art implementation of another popular sampling method, based on cumulative distribution tables.

1 Introduction

Lattice-based Cryptography (LBC) has become popular in the field of post-quantum public-key primitives and aids research into more advanced cryptographic schemes such as fully-homomorphic, identity-based and attribute-based encryption. For a thorough review on applications and background of LBC, see [1]. This attention is partly due to the low precision arithmetic required to implement a lattice scheme, which rarely extends beyond common standard machine word lengths. The algorithmic complexities are based on vector operations over the integers.

There is one, increasingly contentious, component which requires extra precision: Gaussian sampling. By cryptographic standards, this extra precision is low and begins and ends in the sampling phase. First introduced theoretically to

© Springer Nature Switzerland AG 2018
A. Chattopadhyay et al. (Eds.): SPACE 2018, LNCS 11348, pp. 65–84, 2018.
https://doi.org/10.1007/978-3-030-05072-6_5

LBC in [2], Gaussian sampling has been shown to reduce the required key sizes of lattice schemes, but also to be prone to side channel attacks. As an example of this, an attack [3] on the sampler in the lattice-based signature scheme, BLISS [4], has been demonstrated using timing differences due to cache misses.

Regardless of the push toward other solutions for cryptographic primitives, Gaussian sampling is prevalent in LBC. It appears in the proofs of security of the fundamental problems [2] and the more advanced applications, especially those using lattice trapdoors [5], rely on it. Each of these applications will be expected to adapt to constrained devices in an increasingly connected world. The NIST call for post-quantum cryptographic standards [6] has resulted in a large number of lattice-based schemes being submitted, of which a significant proportion use Gaussian sampling [7–9].

Issues around the timing side channel exposed by the Gaussian sampling phase would ideally be dealt with by implementing outright constant-time sampling routines. However, popular candidates for LBC include the CDT [10] and Knuth/Yao [11] samplers, based on cumulative distribution tables and random tree traversals, respectively. The impact of ensuring constant-time sampling with these methods is a reduction in their performance.

1.1 Related Work

The large inherent memory growth of these samplers with increasing precision and standard deviation, combined with constant-time constraints, prompted the work of Micciancio and Walter [12]. An arbitrary base sampler was used to sample with low standard deviation, keeping the memory and time profile low, then convolutions on the Gaussian random variables were used to produce samples from a Gaussian distribution with higher standard deviation. The result was a significant reduction in the memory required to sample the same distribution with just the base sampler, with no additional performance cost. Importantly, given a constant-time base sampler operating at smaller standard deviation, the aggregate method for large standard deviation is constant-time.

The Micciancio-Walter paper boasts a time-memory trade off similar to that of Buchmann et al.'s Ziggurat sampler [13]. The former outperforms the latter as an efficient sampler, but the latter has a memory profile better suited to constrained devices. It can be seen in the results of [12] that the convolution method's lowest memory usage is at a point where the Ziggurat has already maximised its increasing performance. The potential performance of the Ziggurat method exceeds that of the CDT, for high sigma, the latter being commonly used as a benchmark. We ported the former to ANSI C using only native 64-bit `double` types, we compared their performances and memory profiles, finding the Ziggurat to be favourable for time and space efficiency, for increasing size of inputs and parameters. See Fig. 1 for throughput performance and Table 1 for memory consumption. This comparison is the first of its kind, where Buchmann's Ziggurat has been implemented in ANSI C, free from the overhead of the NTL library and higher-level C++ constructs, as the CDT and others have been.

The problem with the Ziggurat method is that it is not easy to contain timing leakage from rejection sampling. The alternative is to calculate the exponential function every time. But it is the exponential function, in fact, which causes the most difficulty. Both the NTL [14], used in [13], and glibc [15], used in Fig. 1, exponential functions are prone to leakage, the former from early exit of a Taylor series and the latter from proximity to a table lookup value.

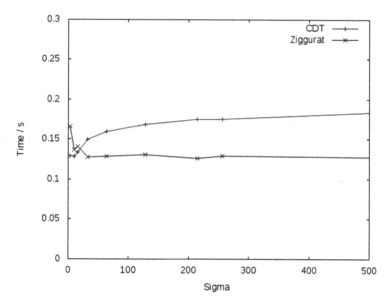

Fig. 1. Time taken for preliminary Ziggurat and CDT samplers to sample 1 million Gaussian numbers. These early experiments were done to 64 bit precision using floating point arithmetic on one processor of an Intel(R) Core(TM) i7-6700HQ CPU @ 2.60 GHz

Table 1. Memory usage of the 64-bit CDT and Ziggurat samplers at $\sigma = 215$. Value for Ziggurat is for 64 rectangles, where its performance peaks.

Sampler	Memory usage (bytes)
CDT	32,778
Ziggurat	1,068

1.2 Our Contribution

We build on the work of Buchmann et al. [13] by securing the Ziggurat sampler with respect to information leakage through the timing side channel. The algorithms proposed in this paper target schemes which use a large standard deviation on constrained devices.

- We highlight side-channel vulnerabilities in the Ziggurat method, not mentioned in the literature, and propose solutions for their mitigation.
- The Ziggurat algorithm is redesigned to prevent leakage of information through the timing of operations.
- We propose a novel algorithm for evaluating the Gaussian function in constant time. To the best of our knowledge, this is the first such constant-time algorithm.
- The Gaussian function, and the overall Ziggurat sampler, is a fixed-point algorithm built from 64-bit integers, using no division or floating point arithmetic, written in ANSI C.
- The reference implementation achieves similar performance to the original sampler by Buchmann et al. and, as it is optimised for functionality over efficiency, we expect the performance can be further improved upon.
- The amount of memory saved by using our algorithm is significantly greater than the advantage seen, already, in the original sampler.
- We argue that the proposed sampler now has sufficient resilience to physical timing attacks to be considered for constrained devices (such as microcontrollers) and hardware implementations not making use of a caching system.

The paper is organised as follows. After a preliminary discussion in Sect. 2, Gaussian sampling via the Ziggurat method of [13] is outlined in Sect. 3. The new fixed-point Ziggurat algorithm is described in Sect. 4, as is the new fixed-point, constant-time Gaussian function, in Sect. 4.2. We discuss the results of the sampler and the security surrounding the timing of operations in Sect. 5.

2   Preliminaries

Notation. We use the shorthand $\{x_i\}_{i=a}^n \overset{def}{=} \{x_i | i \in \mathbb{Z}, a \leq i \leq n\}$. When dealing with fixed-point representations of a number x, we refer to the fractional part as $x_\mathbb{Q}$ and the integer part as $x_\mathbb{Z}$. The same treatment is given to the results of expressions of mixed numbers, where the expression is enclosed in parentheses and subscripted accordingly. The approximate representation of a number y is denoted $\bar{y}$.

Discrete Gaussian Sampling. A *discrete Gaussian distribution* $\mathcal{D}_{\mathbb{Z},\sigma}$ over $\mathbb{Z}$, having 0 mean and a standard deviation denoted by σ, is defined as $\rho_\sigma(x) = \exp(-x^2/2\sigma^2)$ for all integers $x \in \mathbb{Z}$. the support, β, of $\mathcal{D}_{\mathbb{Z},\sigma}$ is the (possibly infinite) set of all x which can be sampled from it. The support can be superscripted with a $+$ or $-$ to indicate only the positive or negatives subsets of β and a zero subscripted to either of these to indicate the inclusion of 0.

Considering $S_\sigma = \rho_\sigma(\mathbb{Z}) = \sum_{k=-\infty}^{\infty} \rho_\sigma(k) \approx \sqrt{2\pi}\sigma$, the sampling probability for $x \in \mathbb{Z}$ from the Gaussian distribution $\mathcal{D}_{\mathbb{Z},\sigma}$ is calculated as $\rho_\sigma(x)/S_\sigma$. For the LBC constructions undertaken in this research, σ is assumed to be fixed and known, hence it suffices to sample from $\mathbb{Z}^+$ proportional to $\rho(x)$ for all $x > 0$

and to set $\rho(0)/2$ for $x = 0$, where a sign bit is uniformly sampled to output values over $\mathbb{Z}$.

Other than the standard deviation, σ, and the mean, $c = 0$ for brevity, there are two critical parameters used to describe a finitely computed discrete Gaussian distribution. The first is the precision parameter, λ, which governs the statistical distance between the finitely represented probabilities of the sampled distribution and the theoretical Gaussian distribution with probabilities in $\mathbb{R}^+$.

The second is the tail-cut parameter, τ, which defines how much of the Gaussian distribution's infinite tail can be truncated, for practical considerations. This factor multiplies the σ parameter to give the maximum value which can be sampled, such that $\beta_0^+ = \{x \mid 0 \le x \le \lceil \tau\sigma \rceil\}$. The choice of λ and τ affects the security of LBC schemes, the proofs of which are often based on the theoretical Gaussian distribution. The schemes come with recommendations for these, for a given security level.

The parameters λ and τ are not independent of each other. Sampling to λ-bit precision corresponds to sampling from a distribution whose probabilities differ by, at most, $2^{-\lambda}$. The tail is usually cut off so as not to include those elements with combined probability mass below $2^{-\lambda}$. By the definition of the Gaussian function, this element occurs at the same factor, τ, of σ. For 128-bit precision, $\tau = 13$, and for 64-bit precision, $\tau = 9.2$.

Taylor Series Approximation. The exponential function, e^x, expands as a Taylor series evaluated at zero like such, $e^x = \sum_{i=0}^{\infty} x^i/i!$. When the term to be summed is $<2^{-\lambda}$, the function has been approximated to λ bits.

3   Discrete Ziggurat Sampling

The Ziggurat sampling technique of Marsaglia and Tsang [16], is a rectangle-wedge approach to rejection sampling originally proposed for both normal and exponential distributions. The basic method of 'rejection' sampling a distribution is to uniformly sample two numbers, x and y. If $y \le \rho_\sigma(x)$, then x is returned as the sampled variable. In other words, x is rejected with probability determined by the distribution $\mathcal{D}_\sigma$. The computational expense in calculating $\rho_\sigma(x)$, or, the alternative, storing all the information in the distribution, motivated the development of the Ziggurat method.

The distribution is enclosed by a set of m rectangles, $\{\mathcal{R}_i\}_{i=1}^n$, such that the bottom-right corner of each rectangle is a point on the distribution. Figure 1 shows the first few and the mth rectangles of such a set. Each $\mathcal{R}_i$, in the continuous case, is the area given by $x_i(y_{i-1} - y_i)$ and $\mathcal{R}_0$ is simply the x_0 co-ordinate. A continuous description is given here and then adapted for the discrete case.

For each $\mathcal{R}_{i \ne 1}$, there is a continuous set of $x_j \le x_{i-1}$ such that every y_j within $\mathcal{R}_i$ is completely under the distribution and such that every rectangle contains the same 2-dimensional sample space. In the continuous case, this corresponds to rectangles of equal area. It is therefore possible to uniformly sample an $\mathcal{R}_i$ and accept the majority of x_js without having to compute $f(x) = \rho_\sigma(x)$. Increasing

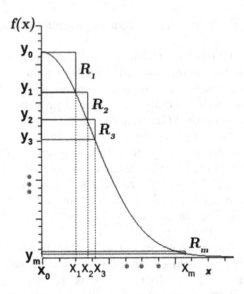

Fig. 2. The Ziggurat setup. Rectangles of equal area enclose a Gaussian distribution.

the number of rectangles covering the distribution decreases the probability of x being in the 'rejection zone' and improves the efficiency of the algorithm. However, more rectangles require more storage and a balance must be found between time and space. With the Ziggurat method, $f(x)$ need only be computed in a relatively low number of instances; when the number to be sampled is in the rejection zone. Also, the second co-ordinate, y, need only be generated in these instances. Generating a random integer within the range of the number of rectangles is more efficient than generating a number to the required precision of the sampled distribution (Fig. 2).

The discrete Gaussian distribution, and the Ziggurat method for sampling from it, are similar to their continuous counterparts. The intuitive difference is that the distribution now takes the form of a histogram. The x value which multiplies the y value to give the common area, as opposed to being the horizontal distance from zero to x_i, is now the number of integer values on the x-axis contained within the rectangle. This will be the value $\lfloor x \rfloor + 1$, to account for zero.

The discrete Ziggurat of [13] is summarised in Algorithm 1, although note that we have omitted the sLine() phase, for simplicity, as we do not use it in our algorithm. For now, we wish to simplify and merge the paths through the sampler, so we restrict the algorithm to its minimally essential form.

In Algorithm 1, the 2-dimensional sample space is uniformly sampled in y, i.e. an $\mathcal{R}_i$ is chosen, then uniformly sampled in x over $\{\lfloor x_i \rfloor\}_{i=1}^m$. These samples are mostly accepted. In some cases, when x is higher than x_{i-1}, sampling to finer precision is needed in y. Then, the vertical space of the rectangle is discretised into 2^λ elements and uniformly sampled. Should this point lie within the vertical

---

Algorithm 1. ZIG_NTL_SAMPLE$(m, \sigma, \lambda, \{\lfloor x_i \rfloor\}_{i=1}^m, \{\bar{y}_i\}_{i=0}^m)$

1: **while** *true* **do**
2:     $r \xleftarrow{\$} \{i\}_{i=1}^m, s \xleftarrow{\$} \{-1,1\}, x \xleftarrow{\$} \{i\}_{i=0}^{x_r}$
3:     **if** $0 < x \leq x_{i-1}$ **then**
4:        **return** sx
5:     **else**
6:        **if** $x = 0$ **then**
7:           $b \xleftarrow{\$} \{0,1\}$
8:           **if** $b = 0$ **then**
9:              **return** sx
10:          **else**
11:              **continue**
12:        **else**
13:           $y' \xleftarrow{\$} \{i\}_{i=0}^{2^\lambda-1}, \bar{y} = y' \cdot (\bar{y}_{i-1} - \bar{y}_i)$
14:           **if** $\bar{y} \leq \bar{\rho}_\sigma(x) - \bar{y}_i$ **then**
15:              **return** sx
16:           **else**
17:              **continue**

---

region covered by the distribution, it is accepted. Rejection of a sample causes the process to begin again, until the function outputs a sample.

4 Fixed-Point Ziggurat Method with Time Considerations

Here, we describe and analyse how the proposed sampler operates. Specifically, this section details the novel contribution of this work. Section 4.1 provides an overview of how the Ziggurat method has been adapted to consider the timing side-channel and suitability for constrained devices at parameters for lattice signatures, namely, high standard deviation, σ. Section 4.2 sets up the theoretical basis of the constant-time Gaussian function with Theorem 1 and discusses the required input precision, with Theorem 2. Finally, the Gaussian function is given explicitly in Algorithm 4 and described throughout the section.

4.1 Timing Attack Resilient, Time-Independent Ziggurat Sampling

A purely constant-time rejection sampler over discrete Gaussians is hard to envisage, apart from one that calculates the probability function at every sample, which is a low memory, low performance extremum. Rather than focus on sample by sample uniformity in the temporal distribution of the sampler, we reduce the number of possible timings of the Ziggurat method from arbitrarily many, depending on how the Gaussian function is called, to two: sampling in the rejection zone in constant time over the integers, or accepting straight away in constant time over the integers.

Apart from the constant-time routine for the Gaussian function, there are a few paths through the Ziggurat which need to be merged before the above can be done. As can be seen in Algorithm 1, the original Ziggurat method will take a unique path when $x = 0$. An attacker with the ability to time the operations of the sampler would, hence, know those samples with value zero, which are also the most frequent. Not all paths through the algorithm are as obviously insecure. For instance, should $x = 0$ be rejected, the attacker still gains information about the state of the underlying PRNG. Either way, information leakage of the kind which gives an attacker a high degree of confidence in the values of variables in the sampler (near certainty, in this case), is required to be mitigated.

Algorithm 2 shows the proposed Ziggurat sampling algorithm. Note that Algorithm 3 is the function which calls $\rho_\sigma(x)$, the Gaussian function of Algorithm 4. For descriptions of the other functions called, see the prose which follows.

Algorithm 2. ZIGGURAT_SAMPLE$(m, s, \lambda, \{\lfloor x_i \rfloor\}_{i=1}^m, \{\bar{y}_i\}_{i=0}^m)$

1: **while** *true* **do**
2:     $r \xleftarrow{\$} \{i\}_{i=1}^m, s \xleftarrow{\$} \{0,1\}, x \xleftarrow{\$} \{i\}_{i=0}^{2^\lambda-1}$
3:     $x = \lfloor x \cdot (x_r + 1) \rfloor$ ▷ $x/2^\lambda \mapsto \mathcal{R}_r$
4:     acc $=$ ct_lte$(x, x_{r-1}) \wedge ($ct_isnonzero$(x) \vee s)$
5:     **if** acc **then**
6:         **break**
7:     **else**
8:         acc $=$ Ziggurat_Sample_y$(x, y_{r-1}, y_r, \sigma, \lambda)$
9:         acc $=$ acc $\wedge$ ct_isnonzero(x)
10:         **if** acc **then**   ▷ $y \leq y'$
11:             **break**
12: **return** $x -$ ct_select$(0, 2x, s)$

Algorithm 3. ZIGGURAT_SAMPLE_Y$(x, \bar{y}_b, \bar{y}_a, \sigma, \lambda)$

1: $y' \xleftarrow{\$} \{i\}_{i=0}^{2^\lambda-1}$
2: $\bar{y} = y' \cdot (\bar{y}_b - \bar{y}_a)$
3: **return** ct_lte$(\bar{y}, \rho_\sigma(x) - \bar{y}_a)$

In Algorithm 2, the table of y values of the rectangles, the $\{\bar{y}_i\}_{i=0}^m$, are p-bit unsigned integers representing numbers in $[0, 1)$. For all cryptographic purposes, p is greater than the length of machine words and requires high precision arithmetic. $\{\lfloor x_i \rfloor\}_{i=1}^m$ are unsigned integers which normally fit within 32 bits. Only when σ is a value higher than those which have so far been proposed, does this change.

Uniform sampling of $\{x_i\}$ to p-bit precision is performed by sampling x to p bits from a cryptographically secure pseudo-random number generator

(CSPRNG). This number is interpreted as an integer representing the numerator of a fixed-point fraction in $[0, 1)$. Thus, by multiplying this uniformly random fraction by the discrete size of the rectangle, as in Algorithm 2 of Algorithm 2, and taking the floor, we get a uniform sample in the rectangle.

The important novelty in this algorithm, with regards to timing, is the pair of accept (acc) conditions. In Algorithm 1, if a non-zero sample was accepted, it was negated with probability $1/2$. If the sample was zero, it was accepted with probability $1/2$. We use this fact in Algorithm 2 to handle these cases in the same computational step. Algorithm 2 gives the logical shortcut to the desired outcome. Before describing this shortcut, a note on constant-time logical operations follows.

All functions beginning `ct_` are constant-time functions which return a 0 or a 1 as an unsigned integer. As an example, `ct_lte(a,b)` returns 1 if $a \le b$ and 0 otherwise. All logical operations in these algorithms are implemented as bitwise operations on values returned from these functions. Hence, the logical binary operations can be synthesised in constant time by bitwise operations restricted to values of 0 and 1.

The particular logic of Algorithm 2 comes from the fact that the same bit is used to determine if the case $x = 0$ is accepted, as is used to determine the sign of non-zero accepted samples. The logic for accepting is thus $(x = 0 \rightarrow s) \wedge x \le x_{i-1}$. As $P \rightarrow Q \equiv \neg P \vee Q$, we get Algorithm 2.

If the accept condition holds, the loop breaks and the sample is returned in Algorithm 2. If it does not hold, the algorithm goes into the rejection phase. The algorithm sends rejected $x = 0$ samples through a redundant rejection phase, to prevent a timing attack revealing such a rejection. Thus, an attacker can know when a sample has been rejected, which is probably unavoidable with a rejection sampler, but not what the sample was. This is crucial for ensuring that the state of the underlying CSPRNG is not compromised.

The loop will continue until it breaks, in which case a sample will be ready to be returned. A constant-time select function, `ct_select(a, b, c)`, returns a if $c = 0$ and b if $c = 1$. Thus, Algorithm 2 converts a sample $x \ne 0$ to a negative if the sign bit is set and leaves it alone if not. This operation will leave an $x = 0$ sample alone and the sampler will have two possible timings for an accepted sample and all rejections traverse the same computational path. If the function $\rho_\sigma(x)$ is made constant-time, the Ziggurat sampler is now significantly more robust against side-channel analysis.

4.2   Constant-Time Gaussian Evaluation

The Ziggurat sampler requires the evaluation of the exponential function to high precision, which must be done in constant time if it is to be suitable for cryptographic purposes. This is the fundamental design specification. The exponential function must also preserve, if not accentuate, many of the advantageous qualities of the Ziggurat sampler. Particularly, the Ziggurat method offers comparable performance to the CDT and Knuth/Yao samplers, but at a fraction of the memory consumption. This quality makes it a desirable candidate for hardware and embedded lattice-based cryptosystems.

Accordingly, the exponential function must have a small memory footprint, require as few hardware features (e.g. floating point arithmetic) as possible and avoid hardware-expensive division. The 8 kB tables of glibc's standard 128-bit exp() function [15], for example, would triple the memory required for a 128-bit Ziggurat sampler with 128 rectangles. The lack of large lookup tables will result in a performance hit. However, there are numerous areas where at least some of this penalty can be diminished.

For example, the use of unsigned integers instead of floating point types and the replacement of divisions with multiplications should soften the penalty incurred. Combining this with the fact that the Ziggurat can be tuned so that calls to exp() will be made only for a small fraction of samples, the performance should remain comparable to that of the competing samplers.

Several challenges arise from the design criteria:

- Generating multi-precision arithmetic operations from the largest unsigned integer types which can be deemed standard (64 bits in this paper).
- Avoiding division for rational approximations, where division is a common component.
- Utilising these operations to mimic the floating point operations often used to approximate real numbers.
- Maintaining the Ziggurat's light-weight memory profile, whilst ensuring that the performance is comparable to other attempts at extending to high σ or λ.

Mathematical Underpinnings. Recall that the Gaussian function is the evaluation of the exponential function over negative reals.

Theorem 1. *The evaluation of the exponential function $f(x') = \exp(x')$, $\forall x' \in \mathbb{R}_0^-$ and $f(x') \in [0, 1)$, can be formulated to output an integer in $\mathbb{Z}_q$, where $q = 2^\lambda$, representing the numerator of the closest fraction, over q, to $f(x')$. The problem is transformed to that of calculating a left shift,*

$$l_{\mathbb{Z}} = \left(\log_2 e \cdot (\lambda \cdot \ln 2 - s \cdot x^2)_{\mathbb{Z}} \right)_{\mathbb{Z}}, \tag{1}$$

and $y_\chi = \exp(\chi)$, for the fractional exponent

$$\chi = \ln 2 \cdot \left(\log_2 e \cdot (\lambda \cdot \ln 2 - s \cdot x^2)_{\mathbb{Z}} \right)_{\mathbb{Q}} + (\lambda \cdot \ln 2 - s \cdot x^2)_{\mathbb{Q}} \tag{2}$$

Proof. The objective is to calculate y' such that

$$\frac{y'}{2^\lambda} \approx y = e^{-x^2/2\sigma^2}, \tag{3}$$

for all $x \in \beta^+$. Changing the denominator of the left hand side to base e and rearranging gives

$$y' = e^{-x^2/2\sigma^2 + \lambda \ln 2}. \tag{4}$$

Let $x' = -x^2/2\sigma^2$ and $k = x' + \lambda \ln 2$, then observe that the range of values input to the exponential function shifts from $-\tau^2/2 \leq x' \leq 0$ to $\lambda \ln 2 - \tau^2/2 \leq k \leq \lambda \ln 2$. For $\lambda = 128$ and $\tau = 13$, for example, the range is from ~ 4.2 to ~ 88.7. Also, $y' \in \mathbb{Z}_{2^\lambda}$, always.

The new exponent k will consist of an integer part, $k_\mathbb{Z}$, and fractional part, $k_\mathbb{Q}$. Thus,

$$e^{k_\mathbb{Z} + k_\mathbb{Q}} = e^{k_\mathbb{Z}} \cdot e^{k_\mathbb{Q}} \tag{5}$$

$$= 2^{k_\mathbb{Z} \log_2 e} \cdot e^{k_\mathbb{Q}}, \tag{6}$$

where a change to base 2 is made to convert the integer exponentiation to a shift on the result of the fractional exponentiation. Before this can be done, the fractional part of $k_\mathbb{Z} \log_2 e$ must be subtracted and added back into the fractional exponentiation.

Let $l = k_\mathbb{Z} \log_2 e$. Hence,

$$2^l = 2^{l_\mathbb{Z}} \cdot 2^{l_\mathbb{Q}} \tag{7}$$

$$= 2^{l_\mathbb{Z}} \cdot e^{l_\mathbb{Q} \cdot \ln 2} \tag{8}$$

and, therefore,

$$e^k = 2^{l_\mathbb{Z}} \cdot e^{l_\mathbb{Q} \cdot \ln 2 + k_\mathbb{Q}}. \tag{9}$$

Hence, the final left shift is $l_\mathbb{Z}$, and the input to the Gaussian Taylor Series is $\chi = l_\mathbb{Q} \cdot \ln 2 + k_\mathbb{Q}$. Here,

$$k = \lambda \cdot \ln 2 - s \cdot x^2 \tag{10}$$

and

$$l = k_\mathbb{Z} \cdot \log_2 e \tag{11}$$

∎

Theorem 1 shows that the Gaussian function can be approximated with an integer, so long as a suitable approximation method is used for y_χ. Algorithm 4 presents the Gaussian function explicitly.

The design criteria which limits the choice of approximation method the most is the absence of division. For example, whereas methods such as continued fractions converge more rapidly, they require division by the input value. As the input values cannot be stored as precomputed fixed-point fractions, the criteria demands that the algorithm does not divide by the input. Hence, the only (immediately obvious) choice for the approximation method is the Taylor series. Theorem 1 is useful because, without converting the integer component of the exponentiation to a shift, the terms of the Taylor series, although converging, would contain x to too high a power to efficiently store and process.

Algorithm 4. $\rho(x, s, \lambda)$

1: **Require**: $\{f_i = \frac{1}{i!}\}_{i=1}^{N}$ $\triangleright$ N s.t. $f_{N+1} < 2^{-\lambda}$
2: $k_{\mathbb{Z}} = (\lambda \cdot \ln 2 - s \cdot x^2)_{\mathbb{Z}}$
3: $k_{\mathbb{Q}} = (\lambda \cdot \ln 2 - s \cdot x^2)_{\mathbb{Q}}$
4: $l_{\mathbb{Z}} = (k_{\mathbb{Z}} \cdot \log_2 e)_{\mathbb{Z}}$
5: $l_{\mathbb{Q}} = (k_{\mathbb{Z}} \cdot \log_2 e)_{\mathbb{Q}}$
6: $\chi = l_{\mathbb{Q}} \cdot \ln 2 + k_{\mathbb{Q}}$
7: $\psi = 1 + \sum_{i=1}^{N} \chi^i \cdot f_i$
8: **return** $\left((\psi \cdot \alpha_e) << l_{\mathbb{Z}}\right)_{\mathbb{Z}}$

The exponential function takes, as its fundamental input, a uniformly sampled $x \in \beta_0^+$ and returns a $y \in [0, 1)$, to λ bits of precision. This y will be represented as a fraction over 2^λ, or more precisely, as a λ-bit extended unsigned integer type with the implied denominator having been accounted for by the operations which act on x. There are three steps: (i) Calculate shift and input to Taylor series, (ii) Evaluate the Taylor series and (iii) apply shift to the result of the Taylor series.

Let f_i be an approximation, to p bits of precision, of $1/i!$. Hence, the fixed-point Taylor series is given by

$$y = \sum_{i=1}^{n} \chi^i \cdot f_i. \tag{12}$$

Because of the propagation of uncertainty through operations on finite representations of numbers in $\mathbb{R}$, the constants (such as $\ln 2$, the inverse factorials, etc.) are required to have greater precision than the output precision, λ.

Theorem 2. *The precision, p, to which χ and the set of f_i must be stored is given by*

$$p = \lambda + \log_2 \left(\sum_{i=1}^{n} |i \cdot \chi^{i-1} \cdot f_i| + |\chi^i| \right). \tag{13}$$

Proof. As $y_\chi = \sum_{i=1}^{n} \chi^i \cdot f_i$, and has λ bits of precision, the input value χ and the factorial constants, f_i, will be required to have p bits of precision such that $\delta \chi = 2^{-(p+1)}$ and $\delta f_i = 2^{-(p+1)}$. From this it is required that

$$\delta \left(\sum_{i=1}^{n} \chi^i \cdot f_i \right) \leq 2^{-(\lambda+1)}. \tag{14}$$

Uncertainty propagates through this expression in the following ways

$$\frac{\delta \chi^i}{|\chi^i|} = |i| \cdot \frac{\delta \chi}{|\chi|}, \quad \frac{\delta(\chi^i \cdot f_i)}{|\chi^i \cdot f_i|} = \frac{\delta \chi^i}{|\chi|} + \frac{\delta f_i}{|f_i|} \tag{15}$$

and, hence,

$$\delta\left(\sum_{i=1}^{n}\chi^i \cdot f_i\right) = \sum_{i=1}^{n}\delta(\chi^i \cdot f_i) \tag{16}$$

$$= \sum_{i=1}^{n}\left(\frac{\delta\chi^i}{|\chi|} + \frac{\delta f_i}{|f_i|}\right) \cdot |\chi^i \cdot f_i| \tag{17}$$

$$= \sum_{i=1}^{n}\left(|i| \cdot \frac{\delta\chi}{|\chi|} + \frac{\delta f_i}{|f_i|}\right) \cdot |\chi^i \cdot f_i| \tag{18}$$

Substituting in the required uncertainties in terms of λ and p and rearranging gives

$$2^{-(\lambda+1)} = 2^{-(p+1)} \cdot \sum_{i=1}^{n}\left(|i \cdot \chi^{i-1} \cdot f_i| + |\chi^i|\right) \tag{19}$$

and

$$p = \lambda + \log_2\left(\sum_{i=1}^{n}|i \cdot \chi^{i-1} \cdot f_i| + |\chi^i|\right). \tag{20}$$

∎

Note that the $i = 0$ term, which goes to 1, contributes nothing to the error and has furtively disappeared from the analysis. Equation (20) gives the precision to which the inverse factorials must be stored and a similar analysis on the constants used before the Taylor Series shows that, in total, 32 extra bits would suffice. The reference implementation uses an extra 64 bits for maintaining simplicity in the arbitrary precision arithmetic, so the algorithm can be further optimised for performance as the Taylor series is the bottleneck of the Gaussian function and sensitive to the size of the input.

The number of terms, n, is small for values close to the point around which a Taylor expansion was taken, $x = 0$ in this case. As this algorithm must exit all iterations as if it were the worst case, n and, hence, χ must not grow large. Equation (20) is monotonically increasing, but grows to only 2 extra bits for χ between 0 and 1, whereas for χ approaching 2, the required extra bits is above 40. This amounts to extra storage required for the inverse factorials and overhead in the most computationally expensive part of the algorithm, in dealing with the non-zero, increasing integer components χ^i.

The potential overflow from converting between base 2 and base e to get Eq. (9) is to be avoided and we choose to allow χ to overflow or underflow, keeping track of this with a selective multiplication by either 1, $1/e$ or e. We propose a constant-time solution to this issue with the final Gaussian function defined in Algorithm 5.

The constant-time underflow and overflow operations adhere to the same logical conventions as described in Sect. 4.1. The function ct_lt is a constant-time $<$ operation and ct_select is the same as before, although it is now used twice in succession to select between 1, e or $1/e$.

Algorithm 5. GAUSS_EXP(x, s, λ)

1: **Require:** $\{f_i = \frac{1}{i!}\}_{i=1}^N$ ▷ N s.t. $f_{N+1} < 2^{-\lambda}$
2: $x'_\mathbb{Z} = (s \cdot x^2)_\mathbb{Z}$
3: $x'_\mathbb{Q} = (s \cdot x^2)_\mathbb{Q}$
4: $l_\mathbb{Z} = \left(\log_2 e \cdot (\lambda \cdot \ln 2 - x'_\mathbb{Z})\right)_\mathbb{Z}$
5: $l_\mathbb{Q} = \left(\log_2 e \cdot (\lambda \cdot \ln 2 - x'_\mathbb{Z})\right)_\mathbb{Q}$
6: $\chi = l_\mathbb{Q} \cdot \ln 2 - x'_\mathbb{Q}$
7: $b_e = 0$ ▷ Let b_e be unsigned.
8: $b_e \mathrel{-}= \mathtt{ct\_underflow}(\chi, l_\mathbb{Q} \cdot \ln 2, x'_\mathbb{Q})$
9: $t = \chi$
10: $\chi \mathrel{+}= (\lambda \cdot \ln 2)_\mathbb{Q}$
11: $b_e \mathrel{+}= \mathtt{ct\_overflow}(\chi, t, (\lambda \cdot \ln 2)_\mathbb{Q})$
12: $\psi = 1 + \sum_{i=1}^N \chi^i f_i$
13: $c_e = \mathtt{ct\_lt}(0, b_e) \wedge \mathtt{ct\_lt}(b_e, 0 - 1)$ ▷ 1 if $b_e = 1$
14: $\alpha_e = \mathtt{ct\_select}(1, e, c_e)$
15: $c_e = \mathtt{ct\_lt}(1, c_e)$
16: $\alpha_e = \mathtt{ct\_select}(\alpha_e, 1/e, c_e)$
17: **return** $\left((\psi \cdot \alpha_e) << l_\mathbb{Z}\right)_\mathbb{Z}$

Listing 1[1] shows the code for the constant-time operations used in the reference implementation of the Ziggurat sampler. The UINT types are the standard unsigned integers prefixed by whichever number of bits they have. The fix_t types are also labelled by their bit precision and represent fixed point fractions composed of a number of UINT64 types. For example, if n is a fix128_t, it will contain two UINT64 types in a struct, called n.a0 and n.a1. The logical functions return a 0 or 1 and the selection functions return the selected value.

```
UINT32 ct_isnonzero_f128(fix128_t x)
{
    return ((x.a0|-x.a0) >> 63) & ((x.a1|-x.a1) >> 63);
}

UINT32 ct_isnonzero_u32(UINT32 x)
{
    return (x|-x)>>31;
}

UINT32 ct_lt_u32(UINT32 x, UINT32 y)
{
    return (x^((x^y)|((x-y)^y)))>>31;
}

UINT32 ct_lt_u64(UINT64 x, UINT64 y)
{
    return (x^((x^y)|((x-y)^y)))>>63;
```

---

[1] These functions are adapted from https://cryptocoding.net/index.php/Coding_rules and have been extended to use multi-precision logic.

```
}

UINT32 ct_lte_u32(UINT32 x, UINT32 y)
{
   return 1 ^ ((y^((y^x)|((y-x)^x)))>>31);
}

UINT32 ct_lte_f128(fix128_t a, fix128_t b)
{
   return ct_lt_u64(a.a1, b.a1) |
          ct_select_64(0, (1^ct_lt_u64(b.a0, a.a0)),
             (1^((a.a1-b.a1)|(b.a1-a.a1))>>63));
}

UINT32 ct_neq_u32(UINT32 x, UINT32 y)
{
    return ((x-y)|(y-x))>>63;
}

UINT32 ct_select_u32 (UINT32 a, UINT32 b, UINT32 bit)
{
   /* -0 = 0, -1 = 0xff....ff */
   UINT32 mask = - bit;
   UINT32 ret = mask & (a^b);
   ret = ret ^ a;
   return ret;
}

fix256_t ct_select_f256 (fix256_t a, fix256_t b, UINT64 bit)
{
   /* -0 = 0, -1 = 0xff....ff */
   UINT64 mask = - bit;
   fix256_t ret;

   ret.a0 = mask & (a.a0 ^ b.a0);
   ret.a1 = mask & (a.a1 ^ b.a1);
   ret.a2 = mask & (a.a2 ^ b.a2);
   ret.a3 = mask & (a.a3 ^ b.a3);

   ret.a0 = ret.a0 ^ a.a0;
   ret.a1 = ret.a1 ^ a.a1;
   ret.a2 = ret.a2 ^ a.a2;
   ret.a3 = ret.a3 ^ a.a3;
   return ret;
}
```

Listing 1: Constant-time operations to the various precisions required for a 128-bit implementation of the Ziggurat sampler.

5 Results

This section discusses the enhancements to the Ziggurat method provided by our algorithm. In particular, the low-level construction of the sampler leads to a significant reduction in the memory footprint, as presented in Sect. 5.1, and, as outlined in Sect. 5.2, the side-channel resilience of our algorithm makes the Ziggurat method, and the range of parameters to which it is suited (i.e. high standard deviation), a more attainable objective for LBC.

5.1 Performance and Validation

The algorithm presented in this paper solves issues involved with sampling from the discrete Gaussian distribution over the integers via the Ziggurat method, with significantly better resilience to side-channel attacks. The sampler retains its efficiency, improves upon use of memory resources and is more suitable for application to low-memory devices and hardware due to the integer arithmetic and lack of division.

Section 5.1 shows the performance and memory profiles of our proposed sampler, as well as the original Ziggurat and the CDT [17] samplers. We refer to our sampler as Ziggurat_O and to the original algorithm, proposed by Buchmann et al. [13], as Ziggurat_B. We notice only a slight decrease in performance, accompanied by improvements of orders of magnitude in memory use, especially when code is taken into account (as can be seen by the sizes of executables). It should be noted, however, that the reference implementation was built with functionality in mind, and there is room for optimising the code, see Sect. 4.1. The results show significant improvements in the memory consumption of the Ziggurat sampler. It should be noted that the CDT algorithm has been optimised for both efficiency and memory, as it is a core component of the *Safecrypto* library [17]. For example, the full table sizes of the cumulative distribution function for $\sigma = 19600$ is a few times the value given here. The table sizes have been decreased using properties of the Kullback-Leibler divergence of the Gaussian distribution [18]. The Ziggurat's memory profile is orders of magnitude better than that of the CDT and its performance is a small factor slower. With algorithmic ideas for increasing performance suggested in Sect. 4.1, alongside low-level optimisations already applied to the CDT sampler (e.g. struct packing), we expect the small factor by which the performance drops can be reduced, possibly to the extent of becoming a performance gain (Table 2).

For qualitative assurance of functionality, see Fig. 3 which shows the frequency distributions for 10^8 samples for Buchmann's sampler and that proposed in this paper. The sampler behaves as expected, producing a discrete Gaussian distribution at high standard deviation.

Table 2. Performance and memory profile of 10^6 samples at $\sigma = 19600$ for our sampler, Ziggurat_O, Buchmann et al.'s sampler, Ziggurat_B, and the CDT sampler [17]. All measurements were made with a single CPU on an Intel(R) Core(TM) i7-6700HQ CPU @ 2.60 GHz. Note, the number of rectangles was 64.

Sampler	Time (ms for 10^6 samples)	Stack and heap allocations (Max) (B)	Size of executable (B)
Ziggurat_O	1,102	1,200	27,376
Ziggurat_B	1,012	123,000	2,036,608
CDT	320	5,961,000	45,576

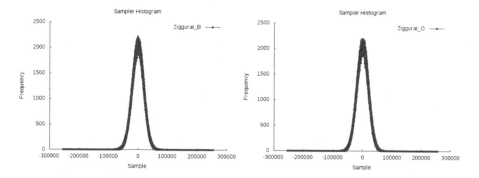

Fig. 3. Histograms obtained from 10^8 samples of the two Ziggurat algorithms.

5.2   Side Channel Security

We referred to a possible attack on the unmodified Ziggurat sampler in Sect. 4.1, where the $x = 0$ sample is readily obtained by the difference in timing of the logic in Algorithm 1 in Algorithm 1 to every other sample. It is seemingly not mentioned elsewhere in the literature. Furthermore, most implementations of the exponential function are not constant-time and will perform the approximation over a given, low valued, domain and raise it to a power dependent on how large the initial exponent was. Large lookup tables are often used to achieve high performance and, should the exponent match a member exactly, the worst-case scenario is direct leakage of samples through any timing method.

Typical side-channel protections to timing attacks involve ensuring that operations which depend on secret data are done in constant time. This is, seemingly, impossible for a rejection sampler. For the Ziggurat sampler, limiting to two possible paths from beginning to accept/reject is, hence, the best that can be done. It is important, however, that all elements of the sample space can be found to have been sampled via both accept paths, which is the case for the enhanced Ziggurat.

Further to the more general timing attacks, the "Flush, Gauss and Reload" attack [3] is a topic of on-going research for which the solutions must be tested on the Ziggurat method. This paper presents an attack on the Gaussian samplers of the BLISS signature scheme [4], but also provides unique countermeasures for each sampling method. Fitting these countermeasures individually and assessing the impact on performance is beyond the scope of this paper, but the authors of the cache attack have discussed how the Ziggurat's countermeasures have significantly less overhead, in theory, than those of the CDT and Knuth/Yao.

The attack can be summarised as follows. Any non-uniformity in the accessing of table elements can lead to cache misses and timing leakage. It requires that the attacker have shared cache space, which is not typical of constrained systems, but also not an impossible situation. The countermeasure for the Ziggurat sampler amounts to ensuring a `load` operation is called on all rectangle points, regardless of whether they are needed. The data is loaded but not used further in most cases.

General solutions also exist to counter this attack. One such solution was proposed by Roy [19], whereby the samples are shuffled and the particular samples for which a timing difference can be made are obscured. An analysis of the shuffling method was carried out by Pessl [20] and improvements were made, but research into the effect of these on the performance and memory profile of samplers is, also, on-going.

Despite the uncertainty surrounding this attack, and the performance penalties induced by the suggested solutions, we expect that the sampler proposed in this paper will not be impacted negatively under the imposed constraints of the "Flush, Gauss and Reload" attack. It is suggested by the authors of the paper that the Knuth/Yao and CDT samplers be implemented in constant time to counter the attack. In contrast, the countermeasures for the Ziggurat sampler amount to two more (blind) load operations with every sample, which is both negligible compared to the operations already being performed and significantly less expensive than implementing the Ziggurat in constant time. We argue, however, that the sampler is required to be secure against attacks from direct timing measurements of operations, before countermeasures against cache attacks can be facilitated.

6   Conclusion

We proposed a discrete Gaussian sampler using the Ziggurat method, which significantly negates its vulnerability to side-channel cryptanalysis. Our research improves the Ziggurat sampler's memory consumption by more than a factor of 100 and maintains its efficiency under the new security constraints. Compared with the CDT sampler, the Ziggurat is nearly 5,000 times less memory-intensive. A significant amount of work has been carried out on making the sampler more portable and lightweight, as well as less reliant on hardware or software features, such as floating-point arithmetic and extended precision integers. The result is a sampler which is notably more suitable for use in industry, for its portability and lack of dependencies, and as a research tool, for its self-contained implementation of the low-level components which make up the entire sampler.

References

1. Peikert, C.: A decade of lattice cryptography. Found. Trends Theor. Comput. Sci. **10**(4), 283–424 (2016). https://doi.org/10.1561/0400000074
2. Micciancio, D., Regev, O.: Worst-case to average-case reductions based on Gaussian measures. In: 45th Annual IEEE Symposium on Foundations of Computer Science, October 2004, pp. 372–381 (2004)
3. Groot Bruinderink, L., Hülsing, A., Lange, T., Yarom, Y.: Flush, gauss, and reload – a cache attack on the BLISS lattice-based signature scheme. In: Gierlichs, B., Poschmann, A.Y. (eds.) CHES 2016. LNCS, vol. 9813, pp. 323–345. Springer, Heidelberg (2016). https://doi.org/10.1007/978-3-662-53140-2_16
4. Ducas, L., Durmus, A., Lepoint, T., Lyubashevsky, V.: Lattice signatures and bimodal Gaussians. In: Canetti, R., Garay, J.A. (eds.) CRYPTO 2013. LNCS, vol. 8042, pp. 40–56. Springer, Heidelberg (2013). https://doi.org/10.1007/978-3-642-40041-4_3
5. Genise, N., Micciancio, D.: Faster Gaussian sampling for trapdoor lattices with arbitrary modulus. Cryptology ePrint Archive, Report 2017/308 (2017). https://eprint.iacr.org/2017/308
6. Chen, L., et al.: Report on post-quantum cryptography. US Department of Commerce, National Institute of Standards and Technology (2016)
7. Hoffstein, J., Pipher, J., Whyte, W., Zhang, Z.: pqNTRUSign: update and recent results (2017). https://2017.pqcrypto.org/conference/slides/recent-results/zhang.pdf
8. Zhang, Z., Chen, C., Hoffstein, J., Whyte, W.: NTRUEncrypt. Technical report, National Institute of Standards and Technology (2017). https://csrc.nist.gov/projects/post-quantum-cryptography/round-1-submissions
9. Le Trieu Phong, T.H., Aono, Y., Moriai, S.: Lotus. Technical report, National Institute of Standards and Technology (2017). https://csrc.nist.gov/projects/post-quantum-cryptography/round-1-submissions
10. Peikert, C.: An efficient and parallel Gaussian sampler for lattices. In: Rabin, T. (ed.) CRYPTO 2010. LNCS, vol. 6223, pp. 80–97. Springer, Heidelberg (2010). https://doi.org/10.1007/978-3-642-14623-7_5
11. Sinha Roy, S., Vercauteren, F., Verbauwhede, I.: High precision discrete gaussian sampling on FPGAs. In: Lange, T., Lauter, K., Lisoněk, P. (eds.) SAC 2013. LNCS, vol. 8282, pp. 383–401. Springer, Heidelberg (2014). https://doi.org/10.1007/978-3-662-43414-7_19
12. Micciancio, D., Walter, M.: Gaussian sampling over the integers: efficient, generic, constant-time. Technical report 259 (2017). https://eprint.iacr.org/2017/259
13. Buchmann, J., Cabarcas, D., Göpfert, F., Hülsing, A., Weiden, P.: Discrete Ziggurat: a time-memory trade-off for sampling from a Gaussian distribution over the integers. In: Lange, T., Lauter, K., Lisoněk, P. (eds.) SAC 2013. LNCS, vol. 8282, pp. 402–417. Springer, Heidelberg (2014). https://doi.org/10.1007/978-3-662-43414-7_20
14. Shoup, V.: Number theory C++ library (NTL) version 10.3.0 (2003). http://www.shoup.net/ntl
15. GNU: glibc-2.7 (2018). https://www.gnu.org/software/libc/
16. Marsaglia, G., Tsang, W.W.: The ziggurat method for generating random variables. J. Stat. Softw. **5**(1), 1–7 (2000). https://www.jstatsoft.org/index.php/jss/article/view/v005i08

17. libsafecrypto: WP6 of the SAFEcrypto project - a suite of lattice-based crypto-graphic schemes, July 2018, original-date: 2017-10-16T14:56:31Z. https://github.com/safecrypto/libsafecrypto

18. Pöppelmann, T., Ducas, L., Güneysu, T.: Enhanced lattice-based signatures on reconfigurable hardware. In: Batina, L., Robshaw, M. (eds.) CHES 2014. LNCS, vol. 8731, pp. 353–370. Springer, Heidelberg (2014). https://doi.org/10.1007/978-3-662-44709-3_20

19. Roy, S.S., Reparaz, O., Vercauteren, F., Verbauwhede, I.: Compact and side channel secure discrete Gaussian sampling. IACR Cryptology ePrint Archive 2014, 591 (2014)

20. Pessl, P.: Analyzing the shuffling side-channel countermeasure for lattice-based signatures. In: Dunkelman, O., Sanadhya, S.K. (eds.) INDOCRYPT 2016. LNCS, vol. 10095, pp. 153–170. Springer, Cham (2016). https://doi.org/10.1007/978-3-319-49890-4_9

Secure Realization of Lightweight Block Cipher: A Case Study Using GIFT

Varsha Satheesh[1](✉) and Dillibabu Shanmugam[2](✉)

[1] Sri Sivasubramaniya Nadar College of Engineering, Chennai, India
varsha98_satheesh@yahoo.co.in
[2] Society for Electronic Transactions and Security, Chennai, India
dillibabu@setsindia.net
http://www.ssn.edu.in/, http://www.setsindia.in

Abstract. Lightweight block ciphers are predominately useful in resource constrained Internet-of-Things(IoT) applications. The security of ciphers is often overthrown by various types of attacks, especially, side-channel attacks. These attacks make it necessary for us to come up with efficient countermeasure techniques that can revert the effect caused by these attacks. PRESENT inspired block cipher, GIFT is taken for analysis and development of countermeasure. In this paper: Firstly, we have implemented the GIFT algorithm in (Un)rolled fashion for vulnerability analysis. Then cipher key is revealed successfully using correlation power analysis. We proposed various protected implementation profiles using Threshold Implementation (TI) and realization techniques carried out on the GIFT algorithm. We believe, the case study widens the choice of level-of-security with trade-off factors for secure realization of the cipher based on application requirement.

Keywords: Lightweight block cipher · Side-channel
Threshold Implementation · Internet of Things (IoT) devices

1 Introduction

In recent decades, there has to be no question of doubt whatsoever about the mass deployment of smart electronic devices in our routine lives. These small devices get connected to each other and are used in a wide variety of applications from small light bulbs, toasters, etc. to heart monitoring implants. These embedded devices require cryptographic algorithms for secure transmission of data. The solution for transmitting data securely has been studied for a long time. Since these devices have limited computational capacity, lightweight cryptography ciphers are the best candidates to ensure secure computation and transmission of data in these type of devices. With the widespread presence of embedded devices, security has become a serious issue. The modern adversary can get close to the device, measure the electromagnetic emanation from the device. In some cases, the adversary has even physical access to the device. This adds the

© Springer Nature Switzerland AG 2018
A. Chattopadhyay et al. (Eds.): SPACE 2018, LNCS 11348, pp. 85–103, 2018.
https://doi.org/10.1007/978-3-030-05072-6_6

whole field of physical attacks, Implementation attacks to the potential attack scenarios.

When a cryptographic algorithm is getting executed, there is information leakage through the side-channels mostly as differences in execution time, power or electromagnetic radiations. Attacking these side-channels to reveal the secret key of the device is referred to as Side-Channel analysis attacks. The most notable ones being Simple, Differential and Correlation Power Analysis. The Differential Power Analysis (DPA) attack, a subset of SCA captures the power output from a microprocessor performing the encryption algorithm and analyzes the information to reveal the secret key [8]. Subsequently, research community explored various possible attack methods, say, [1,4,6]. Over the years, side channel analysis attack description is categorized into four parts, type of leakage (Power or Electromagnetic emanation), target function attack model(Hamming weight, hamming distance), statistical distinguish-er(Difference of means, correlation or entropy), key candidate selection(key rank enumeration).

In general, unprotected implementation of ciphers are vulnerable against these attacks. However, vulnerability analyses help us to identify the weak components of the cipher against side channel attacks, and also minimal attack complexity required for the attack. Furthermore, enable us to come up with different and efficacious countermeasures. On one-hand these countermeasures focus on changing the ephemeral key regularly, thereby limiting the number of power traces required to reveal key from the cryptographic device. On the other-hand they decrease the signal-to-noise ratio to make the correlation invisible. This approach provides provable or high security under some leakage conditions even many number of traces were to be analyzed.

Threshold Implementation (TI) was proposed by Nikova [14,15], arrived based on secret sharing [3,18], threshold cryptography [5] and multi-party computation protocols [21]. This is basically splitting the state, specifically the non-linear component of the block cipher into several shares by using some random variables. This division is done in a way that combining all the shares will recover the original value and combining all except one will not reveal any information. The degree of S-Box, say d, decides the number of secret shares such that $s \geq d + 1$. TI mainly relies on three properties, namely correctness, non-completeness, uniformity of the shared functions. It can be a challenging task to implement TI when nonlinear functions, such as the S-boxes of symmetric key algorithms, are considered. Satisfying all the properties can be imposed by using extra randomness or by increasing the number of shares. Both of these solutions imply an increase of resources required by TI. Efficient way of realizing TI for lightweight cipher and a formula for estimating shared TI S-box were presented in [16,17]. Threshold Implementation of 4-bit S-Boxes is proposed in [9]. The countermeasure is provably secure countermeasure against first order attacks. Later, TI also found to be vulnerable against specific types of attack [11,20].

To an extent circuits can be protected from attacks using various implementation techniques. One such technique called unrolled implementation explored on crypto primitivity by Bhasin et al. [2] acts as a countermeasure(resistant) against side channel attack and hinders the adversary to exploit the leakage even after applying the conventional power models. Later in 2015, [22] showed side channel attack on unrolled implementation of various design constraints provided by Electronic Design Automation tools. In this attack, the author used Welch's t-test to identify the functional moment of target circuit and normalized the timing between intermediate values. In 2016, the author of [13,19] was able to recover the key completely using side channel attack.

Many countermeasures techniques have been developed and explored over the years. However, attacker come-up with different techniques to counteract those countermeasures. Though TI is provably secure, experimental study has to be explored against higher-order side channel attacks. As a result, algorithm designers are forced to consider various aspects while designing a cipher such as implementation vulnerability, trade-off parameters and of-course the security analysis of the cipher.

In this paper, we explored various implementation profiles by combining TI and unrolled implementation on the GIFT cipher to increase the attack complexity. We believe these profiles widens the choice of level-of-security and its trade-off based on the application requirement for constrained, conventional and crypto accelerator devices.

The contributions of this paper is two-fold:

- We first performed the DPA attack on the GIFT encryption algorithm in the round based fashion. Then we implemented the GIFT cipher in an Unrolled manner and performed the DPA attack analysis before applying the Threshold Implementation countermeasure to it.
- The countermeasure is commonly applied to the non linear operation of the algorithm, in this case, it being the S-Box. It was found that applying the countermeasure to the first four and last four rounds of the algorithm could provide sufficient security against malicious attacks. Protected implementation profiles are created based on various combination of implementation techniques such as Rolled, Unrolled and Partially unrolled with TI on the first and last four rounds of the cipher.

Organization of the Paper. We share implementation details of cipher, GIFT in Sect. 2. We explained, how the implementation is vulnerable against DPA in Sect. 3. In Sect. 4, implementation profiles are proposed by combining of TI and unrolled and its security against SCA has been studied. Finally, in Sect. 5, the paper is concluded.

2   Implementation Details of GIFT

GIFT is an substitution-permutation network(SPN) based cipher. Its design is strongly influenced by the cipher PRESENT. It has two versions GIFT-64-128: 28 rounds with a block size of 64-bits and GIFT-128-128: 40 rounds with 128-bit blocks. Both the versions have 128-bit keys. For this work, we focus only on GIFT-64-128 version.

Initialization: The cipher state, S is first initialized from the 64-bit plain-text represented as 16 nibbles of 4-bit represented as $W_{15}, \ldots W_1, W_0$. The 128-bit key is divided into 16-bit words $K_7, K_6, \ldots, K_0$ and is used to initialize the key register K.

Round Function: Each round of the cipher comprises of a Substitution Layer (S-layer) followed by a Permutation Layer (P-Layer) and a XOR with the round-key and predefined constants(AddRoundKey).

S-layer (S): Apply the same S-box to each of the 4-bit nibbles of the state S. The truth-table for the S-Box is shown Table 1.

Table 1. GIFT S-Box

x	0	1	2	3	4	5	6	7	8	9	a	b	c	d	e	f
S(x)	1	a	4	c	6	f	3	9	2	d	b	7	5	0	8	e

P-Layer (P): This operation permutes the bits of the cipher state S from position i to P(i). The permutation Table 2 is shown below.

Table 2. GIFT P-Layer

i	0	1	2	3	4	5	6	7	8	9	10	11	12	13	14	15
P(i)	0	17	34	51	48	1	18	35	32	49	2	19	16	33	50	3
i	16	17	18	19	20	21	22	23	24	25	26	27	28	29	30	31
P(i)	4	21	38	55	52	5	22	39	36	53	6	23	20	37	54	7
i	32	33	34	35	36	37	38	39	40	41	42	43	44	45	46	47
P(i)	8	25	42	59	56	9	26	43	40	57	10	27	24	41	58	11
i	48	49	50	51	52	53	54	55	56	57	58	59	60	61	62	63
P(i)	12	29	46	63	60	13	30	47	44	61	14	31	28	45	62	15

AddRoundKey: A 32-bit round key(RK) and a 7-bit round constant (Rcon) is XORed to a part of the cipher state S in this operation.

GIFT Encryption: A single block is processed by the application of a series of round functions. At each round, S-layer, P-Layer and AddRoundKey operations are performed on the previous cipher state. After 28 such rounds, the state provides the cipher-text.

Implementation Platform and Experimental Set-Up: The ModelSim Quartus Prime Pro was used to verify the functionality of the GIFT encryption algorithm written in verilog using test vector as tabled in 4. The SASEBO-

Table 3. FPGA utilization of round based implementation

FPGA	Slice	LUT	GE	GIFT power (W)	Frequency (MHz)
Virtex-XC2VP7	254	331	2358	1.920	262
Kintex-XC7K16T-1BG676	270	261	2438	1.352	490

G Board with two Xilinx Virtex-II Pro FPGA devices, xc2vp7 and xc2vp30, one of which was used for the cryptographic circuits, while the other was used for the RS-232 serial interface. Also, round based implementation was targeted on the XC7K160T-1BG676 chip. FPGA utilization is given Table 3. Oscilloscope(MS07104b) is used to measure the power consumption with help of BNC and trigger probe during execution of the algorithm. Matlab tool is used to analysis.

Table 4. Test vector of round based implementation

Key	FEDCBA9876543210FEDCBA9876543210	BD91731EB6BC2713A1F9F6FFC75044E7
Plaintext	FEDCBA9876543210	C450C7727A9B8A7D
Ciphertex	C1B71F66160FF587	E3272885FA94BA8B

3   Implementation Vulnerability Analysis

3.1   DPA on (Un)Rolled Based Implementation of GIFT

A DPA attack consists of following five steps [10]:

– Identify an intermediate points of interest of the executed algorithm.
– Capture the power consumption.
– Arrive hypothetical intermediate values.
– Estimate hypothetical power consumption values, (P_{hyp}) from hypothesis intermediate values.
– Statistically correlate the hypothetical power values with the measured power traces.

The five steps are applied to GIFT (Un)rolled implementation to retrieve 128-bit key. The details are as follows:

Step 1: Point of Interest (PoI)
Many ways are there arrive at PoI for GIFT based on the implementation techniques.

In general round and unrolled based implementation are used in practice. In round(rolled) based implementation, PoI is register. Which is updated by each round function output of the cipher as shown in the Fig. 1(a). Attack phases of round based implementation is given Fig. 1(b). In unrolled based implementation, PoI is functional derivatives of the algorithm, computed on-the-fly on

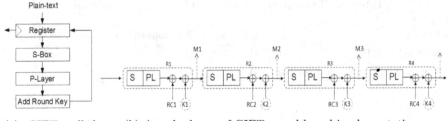

(a) GIFT rolled   (b) Attack phases of GIFT round based implementation
implementation

Fig. 1. GIFT round based implementation and attack details

wires. PoI for GIFT unrolled implementation is analyzed in two cases, linear and nonlinear functions as described below.

Case 1: Attacking linear function. In GIFT, S-box is the nonlinear function, but there are no key bits involved in this operation for the first round. Hence, it would make no sense to attack the S-box layer. Key is XORed with the output of P-Layer function. Therefore from DPA perspective PoI is AddRoundKey. The output of the first round AddRoundKey, POI_1, is influenced by 32 key bits. Hence, 32 bits of key can be retrieved in the first round. The outputs of the AddRoundKey layer has to be attacked four times at first or last four rounds. Thus the GIFT requires four PoI to retrieve 128 bit key completely as shown in Fig. 2.

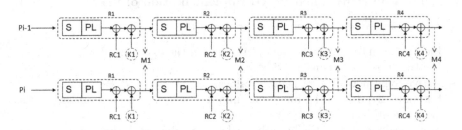

Fig. 2. GIFT linear function attack phases

Case 2: Attacking non-linear function, the S-Box operation: First round S-Box is not influenced by 32 key bits, it is only dissolved from the second round S-Box. Therefore attacking second round S-Box makes sense and provides 2 key bits guess per S-Box. By expanding to 16 chunks of S-Box, 32 key bits can be guessed. Similarly, second, third and fourth round keys are influenced by third, fourth and fifth round S-Box functions respectively. On attacking subsequent rounds of S-box at four different PoI as shown in Fig. 3, we were able to retrieve 128 bit key completely. Thus the GIFT requires four PoI from plain-text or cipher-text side to retrieve 128 key bits for both rolled or unrolled attack as shown in the Figs. 1(a) and 4 respectively. All 128 key bits are retrieved after four rounds of attack.

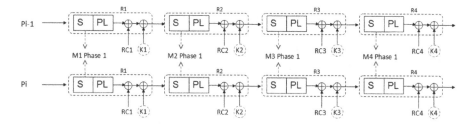

Fig. 3. GIFT non-linear function attack phases

Step 2: Capture power consumption (P_{msd}). Power consumption of both Round and Unrolled based implementation are captured as shown in Fig. 4(a) and (b) respectively. From the Fig. 4(a) round functions are distinguishable whereas for Unrolled implementation power consumption raises abruptly during execution and then comes down as in Fig. 4(b). Voltage points of a power trace are stored in MATLAB matrix format for analysis, $P_{msd}(i,T)$, where 'i' represent i^{th} encryption and 'T' represent total number of points in a power trace.

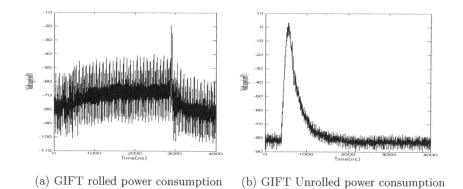

(a) GIFT rolled power consumption   (b) GIFT Unrolled power consumption

Fig. 4. GIFT round based implementation and attack details

Step 3: Calculate hypothetical intermediate values. The divide and conquer approach is used for Correlation Power Analysis(CPA) attack. As long as the chunks are small, their attack complexity also reduces significantly. Therefore, a chunk of 2-bit is taken at a time from POI for analysis. All the possible combination of key values (key search space) for those 2-bit with the corresponding bits of plaintext used for encryption are extracted to generate hypothetical intermediate value at POI. Hypothetical intermediate value for first, $M1_j^i$, second, $M2_j^i$, third, $M3_j^i$ and fourth, $M4_j^i$ POIs are given in the Eqs. (1), (2), (3) and (4) respectively.

$$M1_j^i = PL(S(P_j^i)) \oplus K1_{j,t} \oplus RC1_j \tag{1}$$

$$M2_j^i = PL(S(PL(S(P_j^{i+1})) \oplus K1_{j,t} \oplus RC1_j)) \oplus K2_{j,t} \oplus RC2_j \tag{2}$$

$$M3_j^i = PL(S(PL(S(PL(S(P_j^{i+1})) \oplus K1_{j,t} \oplus RC1_j)) \\ \oplus K2_{j,t} \oplus RC2_j)) \oplus K3_{j,t} \oplus RC3_j \tag{3}$$

$$M4_j^i = PL(S(PL(S(PL(S(PL(S(P_j^{i+1})) \oplus K1_{j,t} \oplus RC1_j)) \\ \oplus K2_{j,t} \oplus RC2_j)) \oplus K3_{j,t} \oplus RC3_j)) \oplus K4_{j,t} \oplus RC4_j \tag{4}$$

where, P_j^i is denoted as plaintext of jth nibble of ith encryption. j ranges from $0 \le j \le 15$, and $K1_{j,t}, K2_{j,t}, K3_{j,t}, K4_{j,t}$, $t =$ ranges from 1 to 2.

Step 4: Compute hypothetical power consumption
In order to arrive at the hypothetical power consumption, the power model should be realistic enough to describe the power consumption between each and every intermediate stages of the algorithm executed in the hardware module. In round based implementation the same register is repeatedly used for storing each round output. This helps to find, how-much power is required for computing a single round function. Conceptually, the number of flip-flop transition between the first and second round on the register reflect power consumption of a single round function. Hamming distance (HD) model suits very well to describe the power consumption of round(rolled) GIFT implementation which is basically the, Hamming distance between two round functions. Normally, HD is calculated between two state values of the register.

In unrolled implementation there is no concept of register to store and update rounds output value and entire algorithm is executed in a single clock cycle. Therefore power consumption of a specific function is calculated by observing variation that happen between the present encryption and previous encryption of the cipher at same instances in the wire. Using HD, hypothetical power consumption is arrived for four PoIs as follows, $P1_{hyp}^i$, $P2_{hyp}^i$, $P3_{hyp}^i$, and $P4_{hyp}^i$, are represented in (5), (6), (7) and (8) respectively.

$$P1_{hyp}^i = HD(M1_j^i \oplus M1_j^{i-1}) \tag{5}$$

$$P2_{hyp}^i = HD(M2_j^i \oplus M2_j^{i-1}) \tag{6}$$

$$P3_{hyp}^i = HD(M2_j^i \oplus M3_j^{i-1}) \tag{7}$$

$$P4_{hyp}^i = HD(M4_j^i \oplus M4_j^{i-1}) \tag{8}$$

P_{hyp}^i denotes the power consumption of ith encryption

Step 5: Correlation between measured (P_{msd}) and hypothetical (P_{hyp}) power consumption. Pearson's Correlation coefficient is used to correlate measured power consumption and hypothetical power consumption. Each column of the P_{msd} is correlated with each column of the P_{hyp} to obtain rank matrix. The rank matrix shows the correct key guess with highest correlation value.

$$r(i,j) = \frac{\sum_{i=1}^{n}(P_{msd,i} - \overline{P_{msd,i}})(P_{hyp} - \overline{P_{hyp}})}{\sqrt{\sum_{i=1}^{n}(P_{msd,i} - \overline{P_{msd}})^2}\sqrt{\sum_{i=1}^{n}(P_{hyp,i} - \overline{P_{hyp}})^2}} \qquad (9)$$

Here, i and j represent i^{th} row and j^{th} column of the corresponding power consumption matrix.

3.2   Attack Description

In this section, the attack is explored in four phases as shown in the Fig. 1. In the first phase attack, the plaintext is correlated with the first round output to decipher the key bit positions[31 to 0] as represented in test vector Table 4.

Phase 1 attack at PoI(M1): After a single round, the intermediate value is updated in the register by overwriting plain-text value. Let us consider an example with MSB four bits of plaintext, [P63, P62, P61, P60]. First, S-box randomly changes the value, say, [S63, S62, S61, S60]. Then permutation is performed, that is, [S63, S62, S61, S60] bits are changed with the corresponding bits [S51, S62, S57, S52].

$$HD = HW[(P63, P62, P61, P60) \oplus (1 \oplus S51, S62, S57 \oplus K31, S52 \oplus K15)] \quad (10)$$

In the Add Round key operation, 1 is XORed with S51, S62 remains as it is, S57 and S52 bits are XORed with key bits K31 and K15 respectively. Finally, these [1 ⊕ S51, S62, S57 ⊕ K31, S52 ⊕ K15] bits replace MSB four bits of plaintext, [P63, P62, P61, P60] in the register as highlighted in yellow color in Fig. 5.
    Therefore, the power consumption for four bits can be computed by calculating Hamming distance(HD) between MSB four bits of plaintext and MSB four bits of first round output, that is, as in Eq. 10, where K31 and K15 bits are unknown, whereas all other bits are known or can be derived from plaintext or ciphertext. By doing hypothesis for the two bits and correlating with captured power traces, the two key bits K31 and K15 would be revealed as shown in Fig. 6. In Fig. 6(a) significant peak shows at index one, hence key value in binary is "00", meaning $K31 = 0$ and $K15 = 0$. Minimum number of power-traces required are 25,000 thousand to reveal key bits as depicted in Fig. 6(b). In a similar way, the remaining 15 chunks of 4-bit data can be correlated to obtain 30 key bits. Hence, the first round attack can fetch 32 key bits. The correlation of the plaintext bits with the first round output bits and the corresponding retrieval of the key bits can be inferred from the hypothetical power model for GIFT that has been derived and given in Appendix A, Table 6.
    In the second phase attack, the first round output is correlated with the second round output to decipher the [63:32] key bit positions using guessed key bits K[31 to 0].

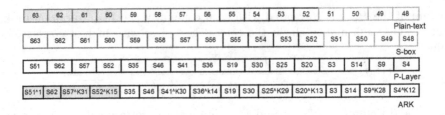

Fig. 5. Round function and its bits position for MSB four bits (Color figure online)

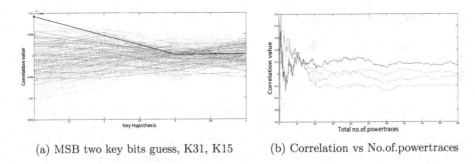

(a) MSB two key bits guess, K31, K15   (b) Correlation vs No.of.powertraces

Fig. 6. Phase 1 attack of GIFT

Phase 2 attack at PoI(M2): A similar approach as described in phase 1, is followed to decipher the 32 key bits so that at the end of two rounds, there would have been 64 bits out of the total 128 key bits retrieved as given in Appendix A, Table 7.

In the third and fourth phase of attack, remaining 64 bits were retrieved as given in Appendix A, Table 8 and 9 respectively.

3.3   Attack Complexity

In generally, attack complexity refers to key-hypothesis required to guess the secret key. In GIFT, 2-bit key hypothesis is required to reveal two bits of the key using correlation. Therefore, the attack complexity to retrieve two bits is 2^2. After the first round correlation, there are 32 bits of the key deciphered. Therefore, the attack complexity for 16 such 2-bit keys would be 64. We mounted a similar attack on the second, third and fourth rounds respectively to reveal the remaining 96 key bits. We found that, to decipher 32 key bits, there is an attack complexity of 64. In order to retrieve all the 128 key bits, the attack complexity would be equal to $4 * 64$ which equals 256. Using described process in Sect. 3.1 attack on unrolled implementation is explored successfully to retrieve the key.

Therefore, the overall Attack Complexity to retrieve all the key bits equals 2^8 as given in Appendix A.

4   Countermeasures: Threshold Implementation for GIFT

We implemented the following profiles by applying TI on first and last four rounds of GIFT with Rolled, Partially Unrolled and Unrolled fashions.

1. Round based implementation with TI on specific rounds
2. Partially unrolled cum TI
3. Partially unrolled cum TI on specific rounds
4. Unrolled cum TI
5. Unrolled cum TI on specific rounds.

The following factors are important to arrive efficient TI implementation of a cipher, namely, properties of TI, algebraic degree of S-box, feasibility of S-box decomposition and number of shares adopted for the implementation. Three basic properties, Correctness, Non-completeness and Uniformity should be satisfied for TI realization. Predominantly, algebraic degree of S-box(d) decides number of shares(S) for the implementation($S \geq d + 1$). In case of GIFT, algebraic degree of S-box(d) is 3, so need 4 shares($4 \geq 3 + 1$). As number of shares increase area utilization also increases, therefore, feasibility study of S-box decomposition is important, which will decompose a cubic functions into two quadratic functions. The realization of a quadratic function can be done using three shares, thereby area will be reduced. The decomposed S-box quadratic functions belongs to quadratic class represented in the paper [7] is taken for our analysis.

1. **Round based implementation with TI on specific rounds**
   From Sect. 3.1 it is clear that, to retrieve 128 keybits attacking vulnerable PoIs at first four rounds or last four rounds is enough. Therefore, applying TI countermeasure solution only on those rounds makes sense. Implementation details are shown in the Fig. 7 with metric Table 5.

Fig. 7. GIFT round based implementation with TI on specific rounds

This will increase attack complexity from 2^2 to 2^6 for every two key bits. Hence, for 128 key bits attack complexity is $2^6 * 64$. Moreover, power consumption of the device will be reduced during the execution of middle rounds. FPGA utilization are shared in the Table 5.

2. **Partially unrolled cum TI**
   First four rounds or last four rounds are vulnerable against side channels. It is evident from [12], that, single countermeasure technique is not enough to thwart the attack. Here the idea is to combine two solutions in an efficient

way, which will increase the attack complexity and also resource trade-off can be achieved based on the security requirement. As four rounds are vulnerable, unrolled implementation with TI is adopted for every four rounds, meaning 28 rounds of the cipher is executed in seven clock cycles. Implementation architecture is shown in the Fig. 8.

1	2	3	4	5	6	7	8	9	10	11	12	13	14	15	16	17	18	19	20	21	22	23	24	25	26	27	28
1	2	3	4	5	6	7	8	9	10	11	12	13	14	15	16	17	18	19	20	21	22	23	24	25	26	27	28
1	2	3	4	5	6	7	8	9	10	11	12	13	14	15	16	17	18	19	20	21	22	23	24	25	26	27	28

1 CC	2 CC	3 CC	4 CC	5 CC	6 CC	7 CC

Fig. 8. GIFT partially unrolled cum TI

Parametric metrics for the implementation are shared in the Table 5. Now the effort to attack the implementation is two fold. Firstly, a large number of power-traces is required to attack the unrolled implementation. Secondly, additional key hypothesis factors have to be considered because of masking. This will definitely increase the complexity.

3. **Partially unrolled cum TI on specific rounds**
   In this profile, first four rounds and last four rounds are implemented in unrolled manner with TI. The profile is sub-classified into three cases based on middle rounds realization as shown in Fig. 9 to understand utilization of various implementation styles as follows:

(a) Rounds 5 to 24 are implemented in rolled fashion.
   Meaning, first and last four rounds are executed in each one cycle, remaining middle 20 rounds are execute in 20 clock cycles. Totally 22 clock cycle are required for the cipher realization.

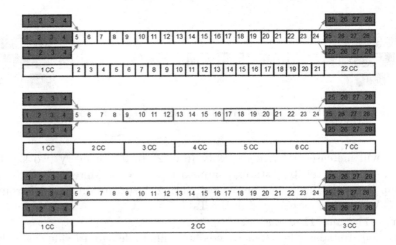

Fig. 9. GIFT partial unrolled cum TI on specific rounds

(b) Rounds 5 to 24 are realized in partially unrolled manner.
   Middle 20 rounds takes 5 clock cycles for realization. Finally, seven clock cycle are required for the cipher execution.

(c) Rounds 5 to 24 are realized in unrolled way.
   So, first and last four rounds are executed in each one cycle, remaining middle 20 rounds are execute in single clock cycle. Totally 3 clock cycle are required for the cipher realization.

This kind of implementation suitable for resource constrained and conventional crypto devices.

4. **Unrolled cum TI**
   Enter cipher is executed in a single cycle with TI protection on all the rounds of the cipher. Though it makes use of more hardware resources, it provides high security and low latency cipher during execution. Implementation details and hardware utilization are given in Fig. 10 and Table 5 respectively.

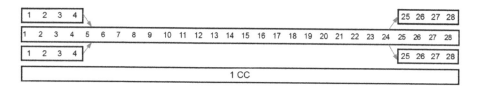

Fig. 10. GIFT unrolled cum TI

5. **Unrolled cum TI on specific rounds**
   In this profile, the enter cipher is executed in a single cycle with TI protection on first and last four rounds of the cipher. Implementation details Fig. 11, architecture Fig. 13 and hardware details are given in the Table 5.

Fig. 11. GIFT unrolled cum TI on specific rounds

We further narrowed down this approach by applying this TI countermeasure to only those equations of the non-linear component that is influenced by the key bits. This will provide the same degree of security as by applying to all the equations.

The profile 4 and 5 are suitable for high end resource constrained devices, conventional devices and to an extent the protection techniques can also be adopted for crypto accelerator devices. In our TI implementation, the intermediate register is not used between G and F functions. As a result, the circuit may be prone to glitches, but the functionality will not affected. Also, it was concluded that employing the TI countermeasures to only those equations of the S-box affected

Table 5. GIFT implementation profiles: performance metrics

Profiles	Slices	4LUT	Slice FF	Frequency (MHz)	Clock cycles
Profile 1	1147	2060	792	155	28
Profile 2	3416	5456	751	55	7
Profile 3.a	2442	4538	789	66	22
Profile 3.b	2416	4456	551	64	7
Profile 3.c	4482	8412	571	34	3
Profile 4	4918	9374	479	22	1
Profile 5	3894	7246	260	20	1
Round	254	331	370	262	28
Unrolled	1638	2969	205	35	1

by the key bits provides the same degree of security as employing it to all the equations of the S-Box. This kind of approach tends to reduce the tediousness and complexity of the experiment. We evaluated side channel leakage against the profile, GIFT Partial Unrolled Cum TI on specific rounds using Test Vector Leakage Assessment(TVLA) as shown in Fig. 12(a) and (b) found secure upto 1 Million traces. Similarly for all the profile resistant were evaluated using TVLA.

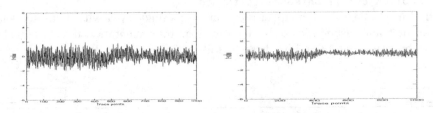

(a) Leakage evaluation at first round output, (b) Leakage evaluation of first round(in/out) 60th bit   on most significant nibble

Fig. 12. TVLA: GIFT partially unrolled cum TI

5   Conclusion

While implementations of cryptographic algorithms in pervasive devices face serious area and power constraints, their resistance against physical attacks has to be taken into account. Unfortunately, nearly all side-channel countermeasures introduce power and area overheads which are proportional to the values of the unprotected implementation. Therefore, this fact prohibits the implementation of a wide range of proposed countermeasures and also limits possible cipher candidates for ubiquitous computing applications. In this paper, we successfully mounted a Correlation Power Analysis attack on two kinds of GIFT implementation, namely Round based and Unrolled manner. We also applied Threshold Implementation as a countermeasure on the first four and last four rounds of the GIFT cipher with rolled, unrolled and partially unrolled implementation techniques. In the future, we plan to explore Orthogonal Direct Sum Masking techniques with these profiles to reduce glitches and fault attacks.

Acknowledgments. I would like to thank the Executive Director of Society for Electronic Transactions and Society (SETS), Dr. N Sarat Chandra Babu for providing the internship opportunity in hardware security research. We would also like to thank Associate Professor, Thomas Peyrin of Nanyang Technological University (NTU) for sharing the Gift cipher test vectors and anonymous reviewers for their useful comments.

A   Appendix

Attack Phases of GIFT.

Table 6. Attack phase 1 of GIFT

Plaintext bits	After AddRoundkey bits	Keybits	Complexity
PT[63,62,61,60]	ARK[51,62,57,52]	K[31],K[15]	4
PT[59,58,57,56]	ARK[35,46,41,36]	K[30],K[14]	4
PT[55,54,53,52]	ARK[19,30,25,20]	K[29],K[13]	4
PT[51,50,49,48]	ARK[3,14,9,4]	K[28],K[12]	4
PT[47,46,45,44]	ARK[55,50,61,56]	K[27],K[11]	4
PT[43,42,41,40]	ARK[39,34,45,40]	K[26],K[10]	4
PT[39,38,37,36]	ARK[23,18,29,24]	K[25],K[9]	4
PT[35,34,33,32]	ARK[7,2,13,8]	K[24],K[8]	4
PT[31,30,29,28]	ARK[59,54,49,60]	K[23],K[7]	4
PT[27,26,25,24]	ARK[43,38,33,44]	K[22],K[6]	4
PT[23,22,21,20]	ARK[27,22,17,28]	K[21],K[5]	4
PT[19,18,17,16]	ARK[11,6,1,2]	K[20],K[4]	4
PT[15,14,13,12]	ARK[53,58,53,48]	K[19],K[3]	4
PT[11,10,9,8]	ARK[47,42,37,32]	K[18],K[2]	4
PT[7,6,5,4]	ARK[31,26,21,16]	K[17],K[1]	4
PT[3,2,1,0]	ARK[15,10,5,0]	K[16],K[0]	4

Hence overall attack complexity is $4 * 64$ is 256.

Architecture of GIFT Unrolled Cum TI on Specific Rounds

Table 7. Attack phase 2 of GIFT

Plaintext bits	AddRoundkey bits	Keybits	Complexity
$PT[51,62,57 \oplus k[31],52 \oplus k[15]]$	$ARK[3,62,41 \oplus k[30] \oplus k[63],20 \oplus k[13] \oplus k[47]]$	K[63],K[47]	4
$PT[35,46,41 \oplus k[30],36 \oplus k[14]]$	$ARK[7,50,45 \oplus k[26] \oplus k[62],24 \oplus k[9] \oplus k[46]]$	K[62],K[46]	4
$PT[19,30,25 \oplus k[29],20 \oplus k[13]]$	$ARK[11,54,33 \oplus k[22] \oplus k[61],28 \oplus k[5] \oplus k[45]]$	K[61],K[45]	4
$PT[3,14,9 \oplus k[28],4 \oplus k[12]]$	$ARK[15,5837 \oplus k[18] \oplus k[60],16 \oplus k[1] \oplus k[44]]$	K[60],K[44]	4
$PT[55,50,61 \oplus k[27],56 \oplus k[11]]$	$ARK[19,14,57 \oplus k[31] \oplus k[59],36 \oplus k[14] \oplus k[43]]$	K[59],K[43]	4
$PT[39,34,45 \oplus k[26],40 \oplus k[10]]$	$ARK[23,2,61 \oplus k[27] \oplus k[58],40 \oplus k[10] \oplus k[42]]$	K[58],K[42]	4
$PT[23,18,29 \oplus k[25],24 \oplus k[9]]$	$ARK[27,6,49 \oplus k[23] \oplus k[57],44 \oplus k[6] \oplus k[41]]$	K[57],K[41]	4
$PT[7,2,13 \oplus k[24],8 \oplus k[8]]$	$ARK[31,10,53 \oplus k[19] \oplus k[56],32 \oplus k[2] \oplus k[40]]$	K[56],K[40]	4
$PT[59,54,49 \oplus k[23],60 \oplus k[7]]$	$ARK[35,30,9 \oplus k[28] \oplus k[55],52 \oplus k[15] \oplus k[39]]$	K[55],K[39]	4
$PT[43,38,33 \oplus k[22],44 \oplus k[6]]$	$ARK[39,18,13 \oplus k[24] \oplus k[54],56 \oplus k[11] \oplus k[38]]$	K[54],K[38]	4
$PT[27,22,17 \oplus k[21],28 \oplus k[5]]$	$ARK[43,22,1 \oplus k[20] \oplus k[53],60 \oplus k[7] \oplus k[37]]$	K[53],K[37]	4
$PT[11,6,1 \oplus k[20],12 \oplus k[4]]$	$ARK[47,26,5 \oplus k[16] \oplus k[52],48 \oplus k[3] \oplus k[36]]$	K[52],K[36]	4
$PT[63,58,53 \oplus k[19],48 \oplus k[3]]$	$ARK[51,46,25 \oplus k[29] \oplus k[51],4 \oplus k[12] \oplus k[35]]$	K[51],K[35]	4
$PT[47,42,37 \oplus k[18],32 \oplus k[2]]$	$ARK[55,34,29 \oplus k[25] \oplus k[50],8 \oplus k[8] \oplus k[34]]$	K[50],K[34]	4
$PT[31,26,21 \oplus k[17],16 \oplus k[1]]$	$ARK[59,38,17 \oplus k[21] \oplus k[49],12 \oplus k[4] \oplus k[33]]$	K[49],K[33]	4
$PT[15,10,5 \oplus k[16],0 \oplus k[0]]$	$ARK[63,42,21 \oplus k[17] \oplus k[48],0 \oplus k[0] \oplus k[32]]$	K[48],K[32]	4

Table 8. Attack phase 3 of GIFT

Plaintext bits	AddRoundkey bits	Keybits	Complexity
$PT[3,62,41 \oplus k[63],20 \oplus k[47]]$	$ARK[15,62,45 \oplus k[62] \oplus k[95],28 \oplus k[45] \oplus k[79]]$	K[95],K[79]	4
$PT[7,50,45 \oplus k[62],24 \oplus k[46]]$	$ARK[31,14,61 \oplus k[58] \oplus k[94],44 \oplus k[41] \oplus k[78]]$	K[94],K[78]	4
$PT[11,54,33 \oplus k[61],28 \oplus k[45]]$	$ARK[47,30,13 \oplus k[54] \oplus k[93],60 \oplus k[37] \oplus k[77]]$	K[93],K[77]	4
$PT[15,58,37 \oplus k[60],16 \oplus k[44]]$	$ARK[63,46,29 \oplus k[50] \oplus k[92],12 \oplus k[33] \oplus k[76]]$	K[92],K[76]	4
$PT[19,14,57 \oplus k[59],36 \oplus k[43]]$	$ARK[11,58,41 \oplus k[63] \oplus k[91],24 \oplus k[46] \oplus k[75]]$	K[91],K[75]	4
$PT[23,2,61 \oplus k[58],40 \oplus k[42]]$	$ARK[27,10,57 \oplus k[59] \oplus k[90],40 \oplus k[42] \oplus k[74]]$	K[90],K[74]	4
$PT[27,6,49 \oplus k[57],44 \oplus k[41]]$	$ARK[43,26,9 \oplus k[55] \oplus k[89],56 \oplus k[38] \oplus k[73]]$	K[89],K[73]	4
$PT[31,10,53 \oplus k[56],32 \oplus k[40]]$	$ARK[59,42,25 \oplus k[51] \oplus k[88],8 \oplus k[34] \oplus k[72]]$	K[88],K[72]	4
$PT[35,30,9 \oplus k[55],52 \oplus k[39]]$	$ARK[7,54,37 \oplus k[60] \oplus k[87],20 \oplus k[47] \oplus k[71]]$	K[87],K[71]	4
$PT[39,18,13 \oplus k[54],56 \oplus k[38]]$	$ARK[23,6,53 \oplus k[56] \oplus k[86],36 \oplus k[43] \oplus k[70]]$	K[86],K[70]	4
$PT[43,22,1 \oplus k[53],60 \oplus k[37]]$	$ARK[39,22,5 \oplus k[52] \oplus k[85],52 \oplus k[39] \oplus k[69]]$	K[85],K[69]	4
$PT[47,26,5 \oplus k[52],48 \oplus k[36]]$	$ARK[55,38,21 \oplus k[48] \oplus k[84],4 \oplus k[35] \oplus k[68]]$	K[84],K[68]	4
$PT[51,46,25 \oplus k[51],4 \oplus k[35]]$	$ARK[3,50,33 \oplus k[61] \oplus k[83],16 \oplus k[44] \oplus k[67]]$	K[83],K[67]	4
$PT[55,34,29 \oplus k[50],8 \oplus k[34]]$	$ARK[19,2,49 \oplus k[57] \oplus k[82],32 \oplus k[40] \oplus k[66]]$	K[82],K[66]	4
$PT[59,38,17 \oplus k[49],12 \oplus k[33]]$	$ARK[35,18,1 \oplus k[53] \oplus k[81],48 \oplus k[36] \oplus k[65]]$	K[81],K[65]	4
$PT[63,42,21 \oplus k[48],0 \oplus k[32]]$	$ARK[51,34,17 \oplus k[49] \oplus k[80],0 \oplus k[32] \oplus k[64]]$	K[80],K[64]	4

Table 9. Phase 4 of GIFT

Plaintext bits	AddRoundkey bits	Keybits	Complexity
$PT[15,62,45 \oplus k[62] \oplus k[95],28 \oplus k[45] \oplus k[79]]$	$ARK[63,62,61 \oplus k[58] \oplus k[94] \oplus k[127],60 \oplus k[37] \oplus k[77] \oplus k[111]]$	K[127],K[111]	4
$PT[31,14,61 \oplus k[58] \oplus k[94],44 \oplus k[41] \oplus k[78]]$	$ARK[59,58,57 \oplus k[59] \oplus k[90] \oplus k[126],56 \oplus k[38] \oplus k[73] \oplus k[110]]$	K[126],K[110]	4
$PT[47,30,13 \oplus k[54] \oplus k[93],60 \oplus k[37] \oplus k[77]]$	$ARK[55,54,53 \oplus k[56] \oplus k[86] \oplus k[125],52 \oplus k[39] \oplus k[69] \oplus k[109]]$	K[125],K[109]	4
$PT[63,46,29 \oplus k[50] \oplus k[92],12 \oplus k[33] \oplus k[76]]$	$ARK[51,50,49 \oplus k[57] \oplus k[82] \oplus k[124],48 \oplus k[36] \oplus k[65] \oplus k[108]]$	K[124],K[108]	4
$PT[11,58,41 \oplus k[63] \oplus k[91],24 \oplus k[46] \oplus k[75]]$	$ARK[47,46,45 \oplus k[62] \oplus k[95] \oplus k[123],44 \oplus k[41] \oplus k[78] \oplus k[107]]$	K[123],K[107]	4
$PT[27,10,57 \oplus k[59] \oplus k[90],40 \oplus k[42] \oplus k[74]]$	$ARK[43,42,41 \oplus k[63] \oplus k[91] \oplus k[122],40 \oplus k[42] \oplus k[74] \oplus k[106]]$	K[122],K[106]	4
$PT[43,26,9 \oplus k[55] \oplus k[89],56 \oplus k[38] \oplus k[73]]$	$ARK[39,38,37 \oplus k[60] \oplus k[87] \oplus k[121],36 \oplus k[43] \oplus k[70] \oplus k[105]]$	K[121],K[105]	4
$PT[59,42,25 \oplus k[51] \oplus k[88],8 \oplus k[34] \oplus k[72]]$	$ARK[35,34,33 \oplus k[61] \oplus k[83] \oplus k[120],32 \oplus k[40] \oplus k[66] \oplus k[104]]$	K[120],K[104]	4
$PT[7,54,37 \oplus k[60] \oplus k[87],20 \oplus k[47] \oplus k[71]]$	$ARK[31,30,29 \oplus k[50] \oplus k[92] \oplus k[119],28 \oplus k[45] \oplus k[79] \oplus k[103]]$	K[119],K[103]	4
$PT[23,6,53 \oplus k[56] \oplus k[86],36 \oplus k[43] \oplus k[70]]$	$ARK[27,26,25 \oplus k[51] \oplus k[88] \oplus k[118],24 \oplus k[46] \oplus k[75] \oplus k[102]]$	K[118],K[102]	4
$PT[39,22,5 \oplus k[52] \oplus k[85],52 \oplus k[39] \oplus k[69]]$	$ARK[23,22,21 \oplus k[48] \oplus k[84] \oplus k[117],20 \oplus k[47] \oplus k[71] \oplus k[101]]$	K[117],K[101]	4
$PT[55,38,21 \oplus k[48] \oplus k[84],4 \oplus k[35] \oplus k[68]]$	$ARK[19,18,17 \oplus k[49] \oplus k[80] \oplus k[116],16 \oplus k[44] \oplus k[67] \oplus k[100]]$	K[116],K[100]	4
$PT[3,50,33 \oplus k[61] \oplus k[83],16 \oplus k[44] \oplus k[67]]$	$ARK[15,14,13 \oplus k[54] \oplus k[93] \oplus k[115],12 \oplus k[33] \oplus k[76] \oplus k[99]]$	K[115],K[99]	4
$PT[19,2,49 \oplus k[57] \oplus k[82],32 \oplus k[40] \oplus k[66]]$	$ARK[11,10,9 \oplus k[55] \oplus k[89] \oplus k[114],8 \oplus k[34] \oplus k[72] \oplus k[98]]$	K[114],K[98]	4
$PT[35,18,1 \oplus k[53] \oplus k[81],48 \oplus k[36] \oplus k[65]]$	$ARK[7,6,5 \oplus k[52] \oplus k[85] \oplus k[113],4 \oplus k[35] \oplus k[68] \oplus k[97]]$	K[113],K[97]	4
$PT[51,34,17 \oplus k[49] \oplus k[80],0 \oplus k[32] \oplus k[64]]$	$ARK[3,2,1 \oplus k[53] \oplus k[81] \oplus k[112],0 \oplus k[32] \oplus k[64] \oplus k[96]]$	K[112],K[96]	4

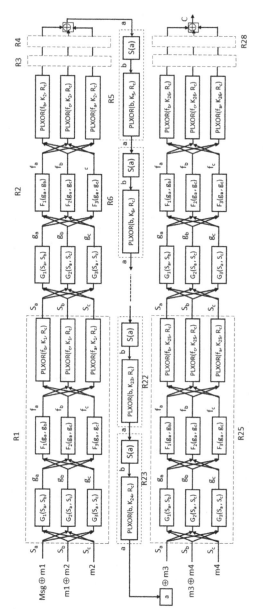

Fig. 13. Architecture of GIFT unrolled cum TI on specific rounds

References

1. Becker, G.C., et al.: Test vector leakage assessment (TVLA) methodology in practice (2013)
2. Bhasin, S., Guilley, S., Sauvage, L., Danger, J.-L.: Unrolling cryptographic circuits: a simple countermeasure against side-channel attacks. In: Pieprzyk, J. (ed.) CT-RSA 2010. LNCS, vol. 5985, pp. 195–207. Springer, Heidelberg (2010). https://doi.org/10.1007/978-3-642-11925-5_14
3. Blakley, G.R., et al.: Safeguarding cryptographic keys. In: Proceedings of the National Computer Conference, vol. 48, pp. 313–317 (1979)
4. Brier, E., Clavier, C., Olivier, F.: Correlation power analysis with a leakage model. In: Joye, M., Quisquater, J.-J. (eds.) CHES 2004. LNCS, vol. 3156, pp. 16–29. Springer, Heidelberg (2004). https://doi.org/10.1007/978-3-540-28632-5_2
5. Desmedt, Y.: Some recent research aspects of threshold cryptography. In: Okamoto, E., Davida, G., Mambo, M. (eds.) ISW 1997. LNCS, vol. 1396, pp. 158–173. Springer, Heidelberg (1998). https://doi.org/10.1007/BFb0030418
6. Gierlichs, B., Batina, L., Tuyls, P., Preneel, B.: Mutual information analysis. In: Oswald, E., Rohatgi, P. (eds.) CHES 2008. LNCS, vol. 5154, pp. 426–442. Springer, Heidelberg (2008). https://doi.org/10.1007/978-3-540-85053-3_27
7. Gupta, N., Jati, A., Chattopadhyay, A., Sanadhya, S.K., Chang, D.: Threshold implementations of gift: a trade-off analysis. Technical report. https://eprint.iacr.org/2017/1040.pdf
8. Kocher, P., Jaffe, J., Jun, B.: Differential power analysis. In: Wiener, M. (ed.) CRYPTO 1999. LNCS, vol. 1666, pp. 388–397. Springer, Heidelberg (1999). https://doi.org/10.1007/3-540-48405-1_25
9. Kutzner, S., Nguyen, P.H., Poschmann, A., Wang, H.: On 3-share threshold implementations for 4-bit S-boxes. In: Prouff, E. (ed.) COSADE 2013. LNCS, vol. 7864, pp. 99–113. Springer, Heidelberg (2013). https://doi.org/10.1007/978-3-642-40026-1_7
10. Mangard, S., Oswald, E., Popp, T.: Power Analysis Attacks - Revealing the Secrets of Smart Cards. Springer, New York (2007). https://doi.org/10.1007/978-0-387-38162-6
11. Moos, T., Moradi, A., Richter, B.: Static power side-channel analysis of a threshold implementation prototype chip. In: Atienza, D., Natale, G.D. (eds.) Design, Automation & Test in Europe Conference & Exhibition, DATE 2017, Lausanne, Switzerland, 27–31 March 2017, pp. 1324–1329. IEEE (2017). https://doi.org/10.23919/DATE.2017.7927198
12. Moos, T., Moradi, A., Richter, B.: Static power side-channel analysis of a threshold implementation prototype chip. In: Proceedings of the Conference on Design, Automation & Test in Europe, pp. 1324–1329. European Design and Automation Association (2017)
13. Moradi, A., Schneider, T.: Side-channel analysis protection and low-latency in action. In: Cheon, J.H., Takagi, T. (eds.) ASIACRYPT 2016. LNCS, vol. 10031, pp. 517–547. Springer, Heidelberg (2016). https://doi.org/10.1007/978-3-662-53887-6_19
14. Nikova, S., Nikov, V.: Secret sharing and error correcting. In: Enhancing Cryptographic Primitives with Techniques from Error Correcting Codes, pp. 28–38 (2009). https://doi.org/10.3233/978-1-60750-002-5-28

15. Nikova, S., Rechberger, C., Rijmen, V.: Threshold implementations against side-channel attacks and glitches. In: Ning, P., Qing, S., Li, N. (eds.) ICICS 2006. LNCS, vol. 4307, pp. 529–545. Springer, Heidelberg (2006). https://doi.org/10.1007/11935308_38

16. Poschmann, A., Moradi, A., Khoo, K., Lim, C., Wang, H., Ling, S.: Side-channel resistant crypto for less than 2, 300 GE. J. Cryptol. **24**(2), 322–345 (2011). https://doi.org/10.1007/s00145-010-9086-6

17. Selvam, R., Shanmugam, D., Annadurai, S., Rangasamy, J.: Decomposed S-boxes and DPA attacks: a quantitative case study using PRINCE. In: Carlet, C., Hasan, M.A., Saraswat, V. (eds.) SPACE 2016. LNCS, vol. 10076, pp. 179–193. Springer, Cham (2016). https://doi.org/10.1007/978-3-319-49445-6_10

18. Shamir, A.: How to share a secret. Commun. ACM **22**(11), 612–613 (1979). http://doi.acm.org/10.1145/359168.359176

19. Shanmugam, D., Selvam, R., Annadurai, S.: IPcore implementation susceptibility: a case study of low latency ciphers. IACR Cryptology ePrint Archive 2017, 248 (2017). http://eprint.iacr.org/2017/248

20. Vaudenay, S.: Side-channel attacks on threshold implementations using a glitch algebra. In: Foresti, S., Persiano, G. (eds.) CANS 2016. LNCS, vol. 10052, pp. 55–70. Springer, Cham (2016). https://doi.org/10.1007/978-3-319-48965-0_4

21. Yao, A.C.: Protocols for secure computations (extended abstract). In: 23rd Annual Symposium on Foundations of Computer Science, Chicago, Illinois, USA, 3–5 November 1982, pp. 160–164. IEEE Computer Society (1982). https://doi.org/10.1109/SFCS.1982.38

22. Yli-Mäyry, V., Homma, N., Aoki, T.: Improved power analysis on unrolled architecture and its application to PRINCE block cipher. In: Güneysu, T., Leander, G., Moradi, A. (eds.) LightSec 2015. LNCS, vol. 9542, pp. 148–163. Springer, Cham (2016). https://doi.org/10.1007/978-3-319-29078-2_9

Exploiting Security Vulnerabilities
in Intermittent Computing

Archanaa S. Krishnan[✉] and Patrick Schaumont[✉]

Virginia Tech, Blacksburg, VA 24060, USA
{archanaa,schaum}@vt.edu

Abstract. Energy harvesters have enabled widespread utilization of ultra-low-power devices that operate solely based on the energy harvested from the environment. Due to the unpredictable nature of harvested energy, these devices experience frequent power outages. They resume execution after a power loss by utilizing intermittent computing techniques and non-volatile memory. In embedded devices, intermittent computing refers to a class of computing that stores a snapshot of the system and application state, as a checkpoint, in non-volatile memory, which is used to restore the system and application state in case of power loss. Although non-volatile memory provides tolerance against power failures, they introduce new vulnerabilities to the data stored in them. Sensitive data, stored in a checkpoint, is available to an attacker after a power loss, and the state-of-the-art intermittent computing techniques fail to consider the security of checkpoints. In this paper, we utilize the vulnerabilities introduced by the intermittent computing techniques to enable various implementation attacks. For this study, we focus on TI's Compute Through Power Loss utility as an example of the state-of-the-art intermittent computing solution. First, we analyze the security, or lack thereof, of checkpoints in the latest intermittent computing techniques. Then, we attack the checkpoints and locate sensitive data in non-volatile memory. Finally, we attack AES using this information to extract the secret key. To the best of our knowledge, this work presents the first systematic analysis of the seriousness of security threats present in the field of intermittent computing.

Keywords: Intermittent computing · Attacking checkpoints
Embedded system security · Non-volatile memory

1 Introduction

Energy harvesters generate electrical energy from ambient energy sources, such as solar [JM17], wind [HHI+17], vibration [YHP09], electromagnetic radiation [CLG17], and radio waves [GC16]. Recent advances in energy-harvesting technologies have provided energy autonomy to ultra-low-power embedded devices. Since the energy is harvested depending on the availability of ambient energy, the harvester does not harvest energy continuously. Based on the

© Springer Nature Switzerland AG 2018
A. Chattopadhyay et al. (Eds.): SPACE 2018, LNCS 11348, pp. 104–124, 2018.
https://doi.org/10.1007/978-3-030-05072-6_7

availability of energy, the device is powered on/off, leading to an intermittent operation.

Classical devices come equipped with volatile memory, such as SRAM [AKSP18] or DRAM [NNM+18], which loses its state on power loss. In recent years, there has been a vast influx of devices with write efficient non-volatile memory, such as FRAM [YCCC07] or MRAM [SVRR13]. Non-volatile memory retains its state even after a power loss and provides instant on/off capabilities to intermittent devices. A majority of these devices contain both volatile and non-volatile memory. Typically, volatile memory is used to store the system and application state as it is relatively faster than non-volatile memory. The system state includes the processor registers, such as the program counter, stack pointer, and other general purpose registers, and settings of all the peripherals in use. The application state includes the stack, heap and any developer defined variables that are needed to resume program execution. And non-volatile memory is used to store the code sections, which is non-rewritable data. In the event of a power loss, volatile memory loses its program state, wiping both the application and system state. Thus, it is difficult to implement long-running applications on intermittent devices with only non-volatile memory to ensure accurate program execution.

Intermittent computing was proposed as a cure-all for the loss of program state and to ensure forward progress of long-running applications. Instead of restarting the device, intermittent computing creates a checkpoint that can be used to restore the device when power is restored. A checkpoint contains all the application and system state information necessary to continue the long-running application. It involves two steps: *checkpoint generation* and *checkpoint restoration*. In the checkpoint generation process, all the necessary information is stored as a checkpoint in non-volatile memory. When the device is powered up again, after a power loss, instead of restarting the application, checkpoint restoration is initiated. In the checkpoint restoration process, the system and application state are restored using the most recently recorded checkpoint, ensuring that the application resumes execution. There is extensive research in the field of intermittent computing, which is discussed further in the paper, that focuses on efficient checkpointing techniques for intermittent devices.

The introduction of non-volatile memory to a device changes the system dynamics by manifesting new vulnerabilities. Although the purpose of non-volatile memory is to retain checkpointed data even after a power loss, the sensitive data present in a checkpoint is vulnerable to an attacker who has access to the device's non-volatile memory. The non-volatile memory may contain passwords, secret keys, and other sensitive information in the form of checkpoints, which are accessible to an attacker through a simple JTAG interface or advanced on-chip probing techniques [HNT+13,SSAQ02]. As a result, non-volatile memory must be secured to prevent unauthorized access to checkpoints.

Recent work in securing non-volatile memory guarantees confidentiality of stored data [MA18]. Sneak -path encryption (SPE) was proposed to secure non-volatile memory using a hardware intrinsic encryption algorithm [KKSK15]. It exploits physical parameters inherent to a memory to encrypt the data stored in non-volatile memory. iNVM, another non-volatile data protection solution, encrypts main memory incrementally [CS11]. These techniques encrypt the non-volatile memory in its entirety and are designed primarily for classical computers with unlimited compute power. We are unaware of any lightweight non-volatile memory encryption technique that can be applied to an embedded system. Consequently, a majority of the intermittent computing solutions do not protect their checkpoints in non-volatile memory [Hic17, JRR14, RSF11]. As far as we know, the state-of-the-art research in the intermittent computing field does not provide a comprehensive analysis of the vulnerabilities enabled by its checkpoints.

In this paper, we focus on the security of checkpoints, particularly that of intermittent devices, when the device is powered off. We study existing intermittent computing solutions and identify the level of security provided in their design. For evaluation purposes, we choose Texas Instruments'(TI) Compute Through Power Loss (CTPL) utility as a representative of the state-of-the-art intermittent computing solutions [Tex17a]. We exploit the vulnerabilities of an unprotected intermittent system to enable different implementation attacks and extract the secret information. Although the exploits will be carried out on CTPL utility, they are generic and can be applied to any intermittent computing solution which stores its checkpoints in an insecure non-volatile memory.

Contribution: We make the following contributions in this paper:

- We are the first to analyze the security of intermittent computing techniques and to identify the vulnerabilities introduced by its checkpoints.
- We implement TI's CTPL utility and attack its checkpoints to locate the sensitive variables of Advanced Encryption Standard (AES) in non-volatile memory.
- We then attack a software implementation of AES using the information identified from unsecured checkpoints.

Outline: Section 2 gives a brief background on existing intermittent computing solutions and their properties, followed by a detailed description of CTPL utility in Sect. 3. Section 4 details our attacker model. Section 5 enumerates the vulnerabilities of an insecure intermittent system, with a focus on CTPL utility. Section 6 exploits these vulnerabilities to attack CTPL's checkpoints to locate sensitive information stored in non-volatile memory. Section 7 utilizes the unsecured checkpoints to attack AES and extract the secret key. We conclude in Sect. 8.

2   Background on Intermittent Computing and Its Security

Traditionally, to generate a checkpoint of a long-running application, the application is paused before the intermittent computing technique can create a checkpoint. The process of saving and restoring the device state consumes extra energy

Table 1. A comparison of the state-of-the-art intermittent computing techniques based on the properties of its checkpoints and the nature of the checkpoint generation calls, such as online checkpoint calls, checkpoint calls placed around idempotent sections of code that do not affect the device state after multiple executions, voltage-aware techniques that dynamically checkpoint based on the input voltage, energy-aware techniques that dynamically generate checkpoints depending on the availability of energy and checkpoint (CKP) security

Intermittent model	Properties						
	Online	Idempotency	Voltage aware	Energy aware	HW	SW	CKP security
DINO [LR15]	–	–	–	–	–	✓	None
Mementos [RSF11]	–	–	–	✓	–	✓	None
QuickRecall [JRR14]	✓	–	✓	–	✓	✓	None
Clank [Hic17]	–	✓	–	–	✓	–	None
Ratchet [WH16]	–	✓	–	–	–	✓	None
Hibernus [BWM+15]	✓	–	–	✓	✓	✓	None
CTPL [Tex17a]	✓	–	✓	–	–	✓	None
Ghodsi et al. [GGK17]	✓	–	–	–	–	✓	Confidentiality

and time over the regular execution of the application, which is treated as the checkpoint overhead. This overhead depends on several factors such as the influx of energy, power loss patterns, progress made by the application, checkpoint size, and frequency of checkpoint generation calls. The latest intermittent computing techniques strive to be efficient, by minimizing the checkpoint overhead in their design. Table 1 compares various state-of-the-art intermittent computing techniques based on their design properties.

In DINO [LR15], Lucia et al. developed a software solution to maintain the volatile and non-volatile data consistency using a task-based programming and task-atomic execution model of an intermittent device. Ransford et al. [RSF11] developed Mementos, a software checkpointing system, which can be used without any hardware modifications. Mementos is an energy-aware checkpointing technique because checkpoint calls are triggered online depending on the availability of energy. At compile time, energy checks are inserted at the control points of the software program. At runtime, these checks trigger the checkpoint call depending on the capacitor voltage.

QuickRecall [JRR14], another online checkpointing technique, is a lightweight in-situ scheme that utilizes FRAM as a unified memory. When FRAM is utilized as a unified memory, it acts as both the conventional RAM and ROM. Now, FRAM contains both the application state from RAM and non-writable code sections from ROM. In the event of power-loss, RAM data remains persistent in FRAM and upon power-up, the program resumes execution without having to restore it. The checkpoint generation call is triggered upon detecting a drop in

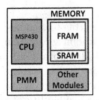

Fig. 1. MSP430FRxxxx architecture, contains the core (CPU), power management module (PMM), volatile memory (SRAM), non-volatile memory (FRAM) and other peripheral modules

Table 2. State of the core (CPU), the power management module (PMM), volatile memory (SRAM) and various clock sources (MCLK, ACLK, SMCLK) that drive various peripheral modules in different operating modes

Mode	CPU	PMM	SRAM	MCLK	ACLK	SMCLK
LPM0	On	On	On	On	On	Optional
LPM1	Off	On	On	Off	On	Optional
LPM2	Off	On	On	Off	On	Optional
LPM3	Off	On	On	Off	On	Off
LPM4	Off	On	On	Off	Off	Off
LPMx.5	Off	Off	Off	Off	Off	Off

the supply voltage. The net overhead incurred for checkpointing is reduced to storing and restoring the volatile registers that contain system state information. Apart from these energy-aware checkpointing techniques, other schemes have been proposed that leverages the natural idempotent properties of a program in their design [Hic17,WH16]. This property aids in identifying idempotent sections of code that can be executed multiple times and generate the same output every time.

None of the above intermittent computing solutions consider the security of its checkpoints, and the vulnerabilities introduced by non-volatile memory are ignored. An attacker with physical access to the device has the potential to read out the sensitive data stored in non-volatile memory. We know of one work which attempts to secure its checkpoints by encryption [GGK17]. Although encryption provides confidentiality, it does not guarantee other security properties, such as authenticity and integrity, without which an intermittent system is not fully secure because of the following reason. In all the latest checkpointing solutions, the device decrypts and restores the stored checkpoint without checking if it is a good or a corrupt checkpoint. If the attacker has the potential to corrupt the encrypted checkpoints, unbeknownst to the device, it will be restored to an attacker-controlled state. We exploit the lack of checkpoint security to mount our attacks in Sect. 7.

In the next section, we focus on TI's CTPL utility as an example of the latest intermittent computing solution.

3   CTPL

TI has introduced several low power microcontrollers in the MSP430 series. The FRAM series of devices, with a component identifier of the form MSP430FRxxxx, has up to 256 kB of on-chip FRAM for long-term data storage [Tex17b]. FRAM is an ideal choice of non-volatile memory for these microcontrollers for its high speed, low power, and endurance properties [KJJL05].

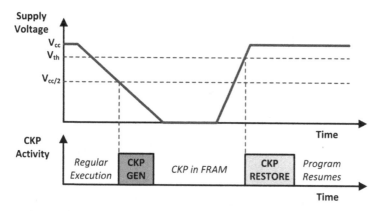

Fig. 2. Principle of operation of CTPL, checkpoint (CKP) generation and restoration based on the supply voltage, V_{cc}, and its set threshold voltage, V_{th}

Figure 1 illustrates the architecture of the FR series of devices. The MSP430 CPU is a 16-bit RISC processor with sixteen general purpose registers (GPR). The power management module (PMM) manages the power supply to CPU, SRAM, FRAM and other modules that are used. Typically, SRAM is the main memory that holds the application and system state. These microcontrollers can be operated in different operating modes ranging from Active Mode (AM) to various low power modes (LPM), listed in Table 2.

In active mode, PMM is enabled, which supplies the power supply to the device. The master clock (MCLK) is active and is used by the CPU. The auxiliary clock (ACLK), which is active, and subsystem master clock (SMCLK), which is either be active or disabled, are software selectable by the individual peripheral modules. For example, if a timer peripheral is used, it can either be sourced by ACLK or SMCLK, depending on the software program.

In low power modes, the microcontroller consumes lesser power compared to the active mode. The amount of power consumed in these modes depends on the type of LPM. Typically, there are five regular low power modes - LPM0 to LPM4; and two advanced low power modes - LPM3.5 and LPM4.5, also known as LPMx.5. As listed in Table 2, in all low power modes, the CPU is disabled as MCLK is not active. Apart from the CPU, other modules are disabled depending on its clock source. For instance, if a timer peripheral is sourced by SMCLK in active mode, this timer will be disabled in LPM3 as SMCLK is not active in this low power mode. But in all the regular low power modes, as PMM is enabled, SRAM remains active, which leaves the system and application state unchanged. Upon wakeup from a regular LPM, the device only needs to reinitialize the peripherals in use and continue with the retained SRAM state.

In LPMx.5, most of the modules are powered down, including PMM, to achieve the lowest power consumption of the device. Since PMM is no longer enabled, SRAM is disabled and the system and application state stored in SRAM are lost. Upon wakeup from LPMx.5, the core is completely reset. The applica-

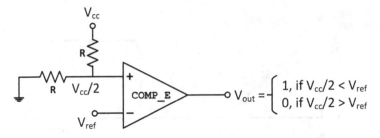

Fig. 3. Voltage monitor using comparator, COMP_E

tion has to reinitialize both the system and application state in SRAM, including the CPU state, required peripheral state, local variables, and global variables. Even though LPMx.5 is designed for ultra-low power consumption, the additional initialization requirement increases the start-up time and complexity of the application. TI introduced CTPL [Tex17a], a checkpointing utility that saves the necessary system and application state depending on the low power mode, to remove the dependency of saving and restoring state from the application.

CTPL utility also provides a checkpoint on-demand solution for intermittent systems, similar to QuickRecall [JRR14]. It defines dedicated linker description files for all its MSP430FRxxxx devices that allocates all the application data sections in FRAM and allocates a storage location to save volatile state information. Figure 2 illustrates the checkpoint generation and restoration process with respect to the supply voltage. A checkpoint is generated upon detecting power loss, which stores the volatile state information in non-volatile memory. Volatile state includes the stack, processor registers, general purpose registers and the state of the peripherals in use. Power loss is detected either using the on-chip analog-to-digital (ADC) converter or with the help of the internal comparator. Even after the device loses the main power supply, it is powered by the decoupling capacitors for a small time. The decoupling capacitors are connected to the power rails, and they provide the device with sufficient grace time to checkpoint the volatile state variables. After the required states are saved in a checkpoint, the device waits for a brownout reset to occur as a result of power loss. A timer is configured to timeout for false power loss cases when the voltage ramps up to the threshold voltage, V_{th}, illustrated in Fig. 2. Checkpoint restoration process is triggered by a timeout, device reset or power on, where the device returns to the last known application state using the stored checkpoint.

Using a Comparator to Detect Power Loss: The voltage monitor in Fig. 3 can be constructed using the comparator peripheral, COMP_E, in conjunction with an external voltage divider, to detect power loss. The input voltage supply, V_{CC}, is fed to an external voltage divider which provides an output equivalent to $V_{CC}/2$. The comparator is configured to trigger an interrupt if the output from the voltage divider falls below the 1.5 V reference voltage, V_{ref}, i.e, an interrupt is triggered if V_{CC} falls below 3 V. V_{ref} is generated by the on-chip reference

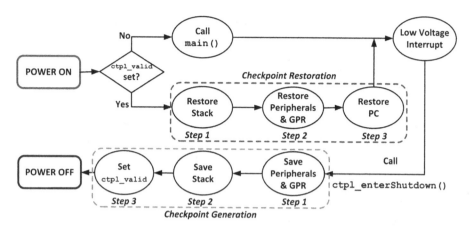

Fig. 4. CTPL checkpoint generation and restoration flowchart

module, REF_A [Tex17b]. The interrupt service routine will disable the voltage monitor and invoke the ctpl_enterShutdown() function, which saves the volatile state information.

Using ADC to Detect Power Loss: MSP430FRxxxx devices are equipped with a 12-bit ADC peripheral, ADC12_B, which can also be used to monitor the input voltage. Similar to the comparator based voltage monitor, the $V_{CC}/2$ signal is constantly compared to a fixed reference voltage to detect power loss. ADC peripheral is configured with the 2 V or 1.5 V reference voltage from the device's reference module, REF_A. $V_{CC}/2$ signal is provided by the internal battery monitor channel. The high side comparator is configured to 3.1 V. ADC monitor is triggered when the device has a stable input voltage of 3.1 V, upon which the device disables the high side trigger, enables the low side triggers, and begins monitoring V_{CC}. Upon detecting power loss the ADC monitor invokes ctpl_enterShutdown() function to save the volatile state information. The rest of the brownout and timeout functionalities are the same for the comparator and ADC based voltage monitor.

Checkpoint Generation: Call to ctpl_enterShutdown() function saves the volatile state in three steps, as shown in the bottom of Fig. 4. In the first step, the volatile peripheral state, such as a timer, comparator, ADC, UART, etc., and general purpose registers (GPRs) are stored in the non-volatile memory. The second and third step are programmed in assembly instructions to prevent mangling the stack when it is copied to the non-volatile memory. In the second step, the watchdog timer module is disabled to prevent unnecessary resets and the stack is saved. Finally, the ctpl_valid flag is set. ctpl_valid flag, which is a part of the checkpoint stored in FRAM, is used to indicate the completion of the checkpoint generation process and is set after the CTPL utility has checkpointed all the volatile state information. Until ctpl_valid is set, the system does not have a complete checkpoint. After the flag is set, the device waits for a brownout reset or timeout. CTPL defines dedicated linker description files for all MSP430FRxxxx devices that places its application data sections in FRAM. Application specific variables, such as local and global variables, are retained in FRAM through power loss without explicitly storing or restoring them.

Checkpoint Restoration: Upon power-up, the start-up sequence checks if the ctpl_valid flag is set, as illustrated in Fig. 4. If the flag is set, then the non-volatile memory contains a valid checkpoint which can be used to restore the device, else the device starts execution from main(). Checkpoint restoration is also carried out in three steps. First, the stack is restored from the checkpoint location using assembly instructions, which resets the program stack. Second, CTPL restores the saved peripherals and general purpose registers before restoring the program counter in the final step. Then, the device jumps to the program counter set in the previous step and resumes execution.

In this complex mesh of checkpoint generation and restoration process of CTPL, checkpoint security is ignored. All the sensitive information from the application that is present in the stack, general purpose registers, local variables and global variables are vulnerable in the non-volatile memory. In the following sections, we describe our attacker model and enumerate various security risks involved in leaving checkpoints unsecured in a non-volatile memory.

4   Attacker Model

To evaluate the security of the current intermittent computing solutions, we focus on the vulnerabilities of the system when it is suspended after a power loss, and assume that the device incorporates integrity and memory protection features when it is powered on. We study two attack scenarios to demonstrate the seriousness of the security threats introduced by the checkpoints of an intermittent system. In the first case, we consider a *knowledgeable attacker* who has sufficient information about CTPL and the target device to attack the target algorithm. In the second case, we consider a *blind attacker* who does not have any information about CTPL or the target device but still possess the objective to attack the target algorithm. In both the cases, the attacker has the following capabilities.

- The attacker has physical access to the device.
- The attacker can access the memory via traditional memory readout ports or employ sophisticated on-chip probing techniques [HNT+13,SSAQ02], to retrieve persistent data. This allows unrestricted reads and writes to the data stored in the device memory, particularly the non-volatile memory, directly providing access to the checkpoints after a power loss. All MSP430 devices have a JTAG interface, which is mainly used for debugging and program development. We use it to access the device memory using development tools, such as TI's Code Composer Studio (CCS) and mspdebug.

- The attacker has sufficient knowledge about the target algorithm to analyze the memory. We assume that each variable of the target algorithm is stored in a contiguous memory location on the device. The feasibility of this assumption is described in Sect. 6 using Fig. 5
- The attacker can also modify the data stored in non-volatile memory without damaging the device. Therefore, the attacker has the ability to corrupt the checkpoints stored in non-volatile memory.

5   Security Vulnerabilities of Unsecured Checkpoints

Based on the above attacker model, we identify the following vulnerabilities, which are introduced by the checkpoints of an intermittent system.

Checkpoint Snooping: An attacker with access to the device's non-volatile memory has direct access to its checkpoints. Any sensitive data included in a checkpoint, such as secret keys, the intermediate state of a cryptographic primitive and other sensitive application variables, is now available to the attacker. Since CTPL is an open-source utility, a knowledgeable attacker can study the utility and easily identify the location of checkpoints, and in turn, extract sensitive information. A blind attacker can also extract sensitive information by detecting patterns that occur in memory. Section 6 provides a detailed description of techniques used in this paper to extract sensitive information. Vulnerable data, which is otherwise private during application execution, is now available for the attacker to use at their convenience. A majority of the intermittent computing techniques, similar to CTPL, do not protect their checkpoints. Although encrypting checkpoints protects the confidentiality of data, as in [GGK17], it is not sufficient to provide overall security to an intermittent system.

Checkpoint Spoofing: With the ability to modify non-volatile memory, the attacker can make unrestricted changes to checkpoints. In CTPL and other intermittent computing solutions, if a checkpoint exists, it is used to restore the device without checking if it is indeed an unmodified checkpoint of the current application setting. Upon power off, both the blind and knowledgeable attacker can locate the sensitive variable in a checkpoint, change it to an attacker-controlled value. As long as the attacker does not reset `ctpl_valid`, the checkpoint remains valid for CTPL. At the next power-up, unknowingly, the device restores this tampered checkpoint. From this point, the device continues execution in an attacker-controlled sequence. Encrypting checkpoints is not sufficient protection against checkpoint spoofing. The attacker can corrupt the encrypted checkpoint at random, and the device will decrypt and restore the corrupted checkpoint. Since the decrypted checkpoint may not necessarily correspond to a valid system or application state, the device may restore to an unstable state, leading to a system crash.

Place variable in FRAM	Variable name	Output of nm main.elf | grep aes
__attribute__ ((persistent)) uint8_t	aes_round_counter[16];	0001036f D aes_round_counter
__attribute__ ((persistent)) uint8_t	aes_key_sched[11][16];	000102bf D aes_key_sched
__attribute__ ((persistent)) uint8_t	aes_state[16];	000102af D aes_state
__attribute__ ((persistent)) uint8_t	aes_key [16];	0001029f D aes_key

Fig. 5. AES variables present in a checkpoint and their contiguous placement in FRAM identified using the Linux command nm. nm lists the symbol value (hexadecimal address), symbol type (D for data section) and the symbol name present in the executable file main.elf.

Checkpoint Replay: An attacker who can snoop into the non-volatile memory can also make copies of all the checkpoints. Since both the blind and knowledgeable attackers are aware of the nature of the software application running on the device, they possess enough information to control the sequence of program execution. Equipped with the knowledge of the history of checkpoints, the attacker can overwrite the current checkpoint with any arbitrary checkpoint from their store of checkpoints. Since ctpl_valid is set in every checkpoint, the device is restored to a stale state from the replayed checkpoint. This gives the attacker capabilities to jump to any point in the software program with just a memory overwrite command. Similar to CTPL, the rest of the intermittent computing techniques also restore replayed checkpoints without checking if it is indeed the latest checkpoint.

6 Exploiting CTPL's Checkpoints

In this section, we provide a brief description of the software application under attack, followed by our experimental setup. We then explain our method to identify the location of checkpoints and sensitive data in FRAM, based on the capabilities of the attacker. We show that checkpoint snooping is sufficient to identify the sensitive data in non-volatile memory.

6.1 Experimental Setup

To mount our attack on CTPL utility, we used TI's MSP430FR5994 LaunchPad development board. The target device is equipped with 256 kB of FRAM which is used to store the checkpoints. We use TI's FRAM utility library to implement CTPL as a utility API [Tex17a]. We implement TI's software AES128 library on MSP430FR5994 as the target application running on the intermittent device. Figure 5 lists a minimum set of variables that must be checkpointed to ensure forward progress of AES. They are declared persistent to ensure that they are placed in FRAM. Figure 5 also lists the location of these variables in FRAM, identified using the Linux nm command. All the AES variables are placed next to each other in FRAM, from 0x1029F to 0x1037E, which satisfies our assumption that the variables of the target algorithm are stored in a contiguous memory

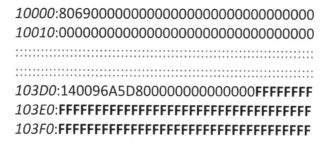

10000:80690000000000000000000000000000
10010:00000000000000000000000000000000
::
::
103D0:140096A5D800000000000000FFFFFFFF
103E0:FFFFFFFFFFFFFFFFFFFFFFFFFFFFFFFF
103F0:FFFFFFFFFFFFFFFFFFFFFFFFFFFFFFFF

Fig. 6. Memory dump of FRAM, where the checkpoint begins from 0x10000 and ends at 0x103DB

location. The executable file, main.elf, was only used to prove the feasibility of this assumption and is not needed to carry out the attack described in this paper.

As CTPL is a voltage-aware checkpointing scheme, the application developer need not place checkpoint generation and restoration calls in the software program. CTPL, which is implemented as a library on top of the software program, automatically saves and restores the checkpoint based on the voltage monitor output. To access the checkpoints, we use mspdebug commands memory dump (md) and memory write (mw) to read from and write to the non-volatile memory, respectively, via the JTAG interface. Other memory probing techniques, [HNT+13, SSAQ02], can also be utilized to deploy our attack on AES when JTAG interface is disabled or unavailable.

6.2   Capabilities of a Knowledgeable Attacker

Armed with the information about CTPL and the target device, a knowledgeable attacker analyzes the 256 kB of FRAM to identify the location and size of checkpoints in non-volatile memory. The following analysis can be performed after CTPL generates at least one checkpoint, which is generated at random, on the target device.

Locate the Checkpoints in Memory: A knowledgeable attacker examines CTPL's linker description file for MSP430FR5994 to identify the exact location of FRAM region in the device's memory that hosts the checkpoints. In the linker description file, FRAM memory region is defined from 0x10000, which is the starting address of .persistent section of memory. CTPL places all application data sections in the .persistent section of the memory. Thus, the application specific variables required for forward progress are stored somewhere between in 0x10000 and 0x4E7FF.

Identifying Checkpoint Size: A knowledgeable attacker has the ability to distinguish the checkpoint storage from regular FRAM memory regions using two

```
diff md_001.txt md_010.txt              diff md_001.txt md_008.txt
43,44c43,44                             43,44c43,44
< :102A2:FF709AE3CC8FDB755E4FA44F2471AA09   < :102A2:FF709AE3CC8FDB755E4FA44F2471AA09
< :102B2:3A0A68F305143A9F01A4CECE20843600   < :102B2:3A0A68F305143A9F01A4CECE20843600
---                                     ---
> :102A2:FF709AE3CC8FDB755E4FA44F2471AA1B   > :102A2:FF709AE3CC8FDB755E4FA44F2471AA64
> :102B2:2A1B515A23F3B8C2995274B82AE25F00   > :102B2:57BDB25EE955979F01A4CECE20843600

diff md_003.txt md_006.txt              diff md_001.txt md_007.txt
43,44c43,44                             43,44c43,44
< :102A2:FF709AE3CC8FDB755E4FA44F2471AA7C   < :102A2:FF709AE3CC8FDB755E4FA44F2471AA09
< :102B2:4F95825EE955979F01A4CECE20843600   < :102B2:3A0A68F305143A9F01A4CECE20843600
---                                     ---
> :102A2:FF709AE3CC8FDB755E4FA44F2471AA63   > :102A2:FF709AE3CC8FDB755E4FA44F2471AA68
> :102B2:50B4BC5EE955979F01A4CECE20843600   > :102B2:5BA9AA5EE955979F01A4CECE20843600
```

Fig. 7. A section of the `diff` output of memory dumps that locates a consistent difference of 16 bytes at the memory location 0x102B0, which pinpoints the location of the intermediate state of AES

properties of the target device. First, any variable stored in FRAM must either be initialized by the program or it will be initialized to zero by default. Second, the target device's memory reset pattern is 0xFFFF. Based on these properties, the attacker determines that the checkpoint region of FRAM will either be initialized to a zero or non-zero value and the unused region of FRAM will retain the reset pattern. The knowledgeable attacker generates a memory dump of the entire FRAM memory region to distinguish the location of checkpoints. In the memory dump, only a small section of the 256 kB of FRAM was initialized, and the majority of the FRAM was filled with 0xFFFF, as shown in Fig. 6. Thus, the checkpoint is stored starting from 0x10000 up to 0x103DB, with a size of 987 bytes. In an application where the length of input and output are fixed, which is the case of our target application, the size of a checkpoint will remain constant. It is sufficient to observe this 987 bytes of memory to monitor the checkpoints.

Thus, a knowledgeable attacker who has access to the device's linker description file and device's properties can pinpoint the exact location of the checkpoint with a single copy of FRAM.

6.3   Capabilities of a Blind Attacker

Unlike knowledgeable attackers, blind attackers do not possess any information about CTPL or the device, but only have unrestricted access to the device memory. They can still analyze the device memory to locate sensitive information stored in it. The set capabilities of a knowledgeable attacker is a superset of the set of capabilities of a blind attacker. Therefore, the following analysis can also be performed by a knowledgeable attacker.

To ensure continuous operation of AES, CTPL stores the intermediate state of AES, state; secret key, key; round counter, round and other application variables in FRAM. These variables are present in every checkpoint and can be identified by looking for a pattern in the memory after a checkpoint is generated. To study the composition of device memory, the blind attacker collects 100 different dumps of the entire memory of the device, where each memory dump is captured after a checkpoint is generated at a random point in AES, irrespective of the location and frequency of checkpoint calls. 100 was chosen as an arbitrary number of memory dumps to survey as a smaller number may not yield conclusive results. And a larger number will affirm the conclusions derived from 100 memory dumps. The blind attacker uses the following technique to locate `state` in the memory.

Locate the Intermediate State of AES: At a given point of time, AES operates on 16 bytes of intermediate state. This intermediate state is passed through 10 rounds of operation before a ciphertext is generated. By design, each round of AES confuses and diffuses its state such that at least half the state bytes are changed after every round. After two rounds of AES, all the 16 bytes of intermediate state are completely different from the initial state [DR02]. Thus, any 16 bytes of contiguous memory location that is different between memory dumps is a possible intermediate state. To identify the intermediate state accurately, the blind attacker stores each of the collected memory dump in an individual text file for post-processing using the Linux `diff` command. `diff` command locates the changes between two files by comparing them line by line. The attacker computes the difference between each of the 100 memory dumps using this command and makes the following observation. On average, seven differences appear between every memory dump. Six of the seven differences correspond to small changes to memory ranging from a single bit to a couple of bytes. Only one difference, located at 0x102A2, corresponds to a changing memory of up to 16 contiguous bytes, as shown in Fig. 7. Based on the design of AES, the attacker concludes that any difference in memory that lines up to a 16 bytes can be inferred as a change in `state`. From the `diff` output highlighted in Fig. 7, the blind attacker accurately identifies `state` to begin from 0x102B0 and end at 0x102BF. It is also reasonable to assume that `state` is stored in the same location in every checkpoint as it appears at 0x102B0 in all memory dumps.

The attacker can also pinpoint the location of the round counter using a similar technique. `round` is a 4-bit value that ranges from 0 to 11 depending on the different rounds of AES. Thus, any difference in memory that spans across 4 contiguous bits, and takes any value from 0 to 11 are ideal candidates for the round counter.

7   Attacking AES with Unsecured Checkpoints

Equipped with the above information on checkpoints and location of sensitive variables in FRAM, we extract the secret key using three different attacks - brute forcing the memory, injecting targeted faults in the memory and replaying checkpoints to enable side channel analysis. We demonstrate that when the attacker can control the location of checkpoint generation call, it is most efficient to extract the secret key using fault injection techniques, and when the attacker has no control over the location of checkpoint call, brute forcing the key from memory yields the best results.

7.1 Brute Forcing the Key from Memory

Since the device must checkpoint all the necessary variables to ensure forward progress, it is forced to checkpoint the secret key used for encryption as well. To extract the key by brute forcing the memory, the attacker needs a checkpoint or a memory dump with a checkpoint, a valid plaintext/ciphertext pair, and AES programmed on an attacker-controlled device who's plaintext and key can be changed by the attacker. The attacker generates all possible keys from the memory, programs the attacker-controlled device with the correct plaintext and different key guesses. The key guess that generates the correct ciphertext output on the attacker-controlled device is the target device's secret key. Based on the assumption that the key stored in FRAM appears in 16 bytes of contiguous memory location, the attacker computes the number of possible keys using the following equation:

$$N_{KeyGuess} = L_{memory} - L_{key} + 1 \tag{1}$$

where, $N_{KeyGuess}$ is the total number of key guesses that can be derived from a memory, L_{memory} is the length of the memory in bytes and L_{key} is the length of key in bytes. The number of key guesses varies depending on the capabilities of the attacker, as detailed below.

Knowledgeable Attack: Knowledgeable attackers begins with a copy of a single checkpoint from FRAM. The 16-byte key is available in FRAM amidst the checkpointed data, which is 987 bytes long. Using Eq. 1, a knowledgeable attacker computes the number of possible key guesses to be 972. Thus, for a knowledgeable attacker, the key search space is reduced from 2^{128} to $2^9 + 460$.

Blind Attack: Since blind attackers do not know the location or size of the checkpoint, they start with a copy of the memory of the device that contains a single checkpoint. MSP430FR5994 has 256 kB of FRAM, which is 256,000 bytes long. Using Eq. 1, the number of key guesses for a blind attacker equals 255,985. For a blind attacker, the search space for the key is reduced to $2^{18} - 6159$

In both the attacker cases, all possible keys are derived by going over the memory 16 contiguous bytes at a time. These key guesses are fed to the attacker-controlled device to compute the ciphertext. The key guess that generates the correct ciphertext is found to be the secret key of AES. Even though a blind attacker generates more key guesses and requires more time, they can still derive the key in less than 2^{18} attempts, which is far less compared to the 2^{128} attempts of a regular brute force attack. The extracted key can be used to decrypt subsequent ciphertexts as long as it remains constant in checkpoints. If none of the key guesses generate the correct ciphertext, then the secret was not checkpointed by CTPL. When the key is not stored in FRAM, it can be extracted using the two attacks described below.

7.2 Injecting Faults in AES via Checkpoints

Fault attacks alter the regular execution of the program such that the faulty behavior discloses information that is otherwise private. Several methods of fault injection have been studied by researchers, such as single bit faults [BBB+10] and single byte faults [ADM+10]. A majority of these methods require dedicated hardware support in the form of laser [ADM+10] or voltage glitcher [BBGH+14] to induce faults in the target device. Even with dedicated hardware, it is not always possible to predict the outcome of a fault injection. In this paper, we focus on injecting precise faults to AES and use existing fault analysis methods to retrieve the secret key.

To inject a fault on the target device, the attacker needs the exact location of the intermediate state in memory and the ability to read and modify the device memory. They also require a correct ciphertext output to analyze the effects of the injected fault. The correct ciphertext output is the value of `state` after the last round of AES, which is obtained from a memory dump of the device that contains a checkpoint that was generated after AES completed all ten rounds of operation. Both the blind and the knowledgeable attacker know the location of `state` in memory and have access to memory. A simple memory write command can change the state and introduce single or multiple bit faults in AES. This type of fault injection induces targeted faults in AES without dedicated hardware support. We describe our method to inject single bit and single byte fault to perform differential fault analysis (DFA) on AES introduced in [Gir05] and [DLV03] respectively.

Inducing Single Bit Faults: To implement the single-bit DFA described in [Gir05], the attacker requires a copy of the memory that contains a checkpoint that was generated just before the final round of AES. This memory contains the intermediate state which is the input to the final round. The attacker reads `state` from 0x102B0, modifies a single-bit at an arbitrary location in `state` and overwrites it with this faulty state to induce a single-bit fault. When the device is powered-up, CTPL restores the tampered checkpoint and AES resumes computation with the faulty state. The attacker then captures the faulty ciphertext output and analyzes it with the correct ciphertext to compute the last round key and subsequently the secret key of AES using the method described in [Gir05]. With the help of the unsecured checkpoints from CTPL, both blind and knowledgeable attackers can inject targeted faults in AES with single bit precision, enabling easy implementation of such powerful attacks.

Inducing Single Byte Faults: To induce a single byte fault and implement the attack described in [DLV03], the attacker requires a copy of the memory that contains a checkpoint that was generated before the Mix Column transformation of the ninth round of AES. Similar to a single bit fault, the attacker overwrites state with a faulty state. The faulty state differs from the original state by a single byte. For example, if state contains 0x0F in the first byte, the attacker can induce a single byte fault by writing 0x00 to 0x102B0. When the device is powered-up again, CTPL restores the faulty checkpoint. AES resumes execution and the single byte fault is propagated across four bytes of the output at the end of the tenth round of AES. The faulty ciphertext differs from the correct ciphertext at memory locations 0x102B0, 0x102B7, 0x102BA and 0x102BD. Using this difference, the attacker derives all possible values for four bytes of the last round key. They induce other single byte faults in state and collect the faulty ciphertexts. They use the DFA technique described in [DLV03] to analyze the faulty ciphertext output and find the 16 bytes of AES key with less than 50 ciphertexts. Thus, the ability to modify checkpoints aids in precise fault injection which can be exploited to break the confidentiality of AES.

7.3   Replaying Checkpoints to Side Channel Analysis

The secret key of AES can also be extracted by using differential power analysis (DPA) [KJJ99]. In DPA, several power traces of AES are needed, where each power trace corresponds to the power required to process a different plaintext using the same secret key. These power traces are then analyzed to find the relation between the device's power consumption and secret bits, to derive the AES key.

Similar to DFA, to extract the secret key using DPA, the attacker needs the correct location of state of AES, which is known by both the blind and knowledgeable attacker. With access to the device memory, the attacker can read and modify state to enable DPA. To perform DPA on the target device, they need a copy of the device memory that contains a checkpoint that was generated just before AES begins computation. The state variable in this checkpoint contains the plaintext input to AES. It is sufficient to replay this checkpoint to restart AES computations multiple times. To obtain useful power traces from each computation, the attacker overwrites state with a different plaintext every time. Upon every power-up, CTPL restores the replayed checkpoint and AES begins computation with a different plaintext each time. The target device now encrypts each of the plaintext using the same key. The power consumption of each computation is recorded and processed to extract the secret bits leaked in the power traces, and consequently, derive the secret key. Even though this attack also requires a copy of memory and modifications to state, it requires other hardware, such as an oscilloscope, to collect and process the power traces to derive the secret key.

7.4   Attack Analysis

If it is feasible to obtain a copy of the memory that contains a checkpoint from a specified round of AES, then extracting the secret key by injecting faults in checkpoints and performing DFA is the most efficient method for two reasons. First, DFA can extract secret key with less than 50 ciphertexts and an existing DFA technique, such as [DLV03, Gir05], but DPA requires thousands of power traces. Second, unlike DPA, DFA does not require hardware resources such as an oscilloscope to extract the secret key. Thus, injecting faults in checkpoints breaks the confidentiality of AES with the least amount of time and resources, compared to replaying checkpoints. If it not possible to determine when the checkpoint was generated, brute forcing the memory to extract the secret key is the only feasible option. All the attacks described in this paper can be carried out without any knowledge of the device or the intermittent computing technique in use. The attacker only needs unrestricted access to the non-volatile memory to extract sensitive data from it.

Apart from AES, the attacks explored in this paper are also effective against other cryptographic algorithms and security features, such as control flow integrity protection [DHP+15] and attestation solutions [EFPT12], that maybe implemented on an intermittent device. Thus, unprotected checkpoints undermine the security of the online protection schemes incorporated in intermittent devices.

8   Conclusions

Intermittent computing is emerging as a widespread computing technique for energy harvested devices. Even though several researchers have proposed efficient intermittent computing techniques, the security of such computing platforms is not a commonly explored problem. In this paper, we study the security trends in the state-of-the-art intermittent computing solutions and investigate the vulnerabilities of the checkpoints of CTPL. Using the unsecured checkpoints, we demonstrate several attacks on AES that was used to retrieve the secret key. This calls for intermittent computing designs that address the security pitfalls introduced in this paper. Since security is not free, resource constrained devices require lightweight protection schemes for their checkpoints. Hence, dedicated research is needed to provide comprehensive, energy efficient security to intermittent computing devices.

Acknowledgements. This work was supported in part by NSF grant 1704176 and SRC GRC Task 2712.019.

References

[ADM+10] Agoyan, M., Dutertre, J.M., Mirbaha, A.P., Naccache, D., Ribotta, A.L., Tria, A.: Single-bit DFA using multiple-byte laser fault injection. In: 2010 IEEE International Conference on Technologies for Homeland Security (HST), pp. 113–119, November 2010

[AKSP18] Afzali-Kusha, H., Shafaei, A., Pedram, M.: A 125mV 2ns-access-time 16Kb SRAM design based on a 6T hybrid TFET-FinFET cell. In: 2018 19th International Symposium on Quality Electronic Design (ISQED), pp. 280–285, March 2018

[BBB+10] Barenghi, A., Bertoni, G.M., Breveglieri, L., Pellicioli, M., Pelosi, G.: Fault attack on AES with single-bit induced faults. In: 2010 Sixth International Conference on Information Assurance and Security, pp. 167–172, August 2010

[BBGH+14] Beringuier-Boher, N., et al.: Voltage glitch attacks on mixed-signal systems. In: 2014 17th Euromicro Conference on Digital System Design, pp. 379-386, August 2014

[BWM+15] Balsamo, D., Weddell, A.S., Merrett, G.V., Al-Hashimi, B.M., Brunelli, D., Benini, L.: Hibernus: sustaining computation during intermittent supply for energy-harvesting systems. IEEE Embed. Syst. Lett. **7**(1), 15–18 (2015)

[CLG17] Chaari, M.Z., Lahiani, M., Ghariani, H.: Energy harvesting from electromagnetic radiation emissions by compact flouresent lamp. In: 2017 Ninth International Conference on Advanced Computational Intelligence (ICACI), pp. 272–275, February 2017

[CS11] Chhabra, S., Solihin, Y.: i-NVMM: a secure non-volatile main memory system with incremental encryption. In: 38th International Symposium on Computer Architecture (ISCA 2011), San Jose, CA, USA, 4–8 June 2011, pp. 177–188 (2011)

[DHP+15] Davi, L., et al.: HAFIX: hardware-assisted flow integrity extension. In: 2015 52nd ACM/EDAC/IEEE Design Automation Conference (DAC), pp. 1–6, June 2015

[DLV03] Dusart, P., Letourneux, G., Vivolo, O.: Differential fault analysis on A.E.S. In: Zhou, J., Yung, M., Han, Y. (eds.) ACNS 2003. LNCS, vol. 2846, pp. 293–306. Springer, Heidelberg (2003). https://doi.org/10.1007/978-3-540-45203-4_23

[DR02] Daemen, J., Rijmen, V.: The Design of Rijndael: AES - The Advanced Encryption Standard. Springer, Heidelberg (2002). https://doi.org/10.1007/978-3-662-04722-4

[EFPT12] El Defrawy, K., Francillon, A., Perito, D., Tsudik, G.: SMART: secure and minimal architecture for (establishing a dynamic) root of trust. In: NDSS: 19th Annual Network and Distributed System Security Symposium, San Diego, USA, 5–8 February 2012 (2012)

[GC16] Ghosh, S., Chakrabarty, A.: Green energy harvesting from ambient RF radiation. In: 2016 International Conference on Microelectronics, Computing and Communications (MicroCom), pp. 1–4, January 2016

[GGK17] Ghodsi, Z., Garg, S., Karri, R.: Optimal checkpointing for secure intermittently-powered IoT devices. In: 2017 IEEE/ACM International Conference on Computer-Aided Design (ICCAD), pp. 376–383, November 2017

[Gir05] Giraud, C.: DFA on AES. In: Dobbertin, H., Rijmen, V., Sowa, A. (eds.) AES 2004. LNCS, vol. 3373, pp. 27–41. Springer, Heidelberg (2005). https://doi.org/10.1007/11506447_4

[HHI+17] Habibzadeh, M., Hassanalieragh, M., Ishikawa, A., Soyata, T., Sharma, G.: Hybrid solar-wind energy harvesting for embedded applications: supercapacitor-based system architectures and design tradeoffs. IEEE Circuits Syst. Mag. **17**(4), 29–63 (2017)

[Hic17] Hicks, M.: Clank: architectural support for intermittent computation. In: Proceedings of the 44th Annual International Symposium on Computer Architecture, ISCA 2017, pp. 228–240. ACM, New York (2017)

[HNT+13] Helfmeier, C., Nedospasov, D., Tarnovsky, C., Krissler, J.S., Boit, C., Seifert, J.-P.: Breaking and entering through the silicon. In: Proceedings of the 2013 ACM SIGSAC Conference on Computer & #38; Communications Security, CCS 2013, pp. 733–744. ACM, New York (2013)

[JM17]   Jokic, P., Magno, M.: Powering smart wearable systems with flexible solar energy harvesting. In: 2017 IEEE International Symposium on Circuits and Systems (ISCAS), pp. 1–4, May 2017

[JRR14]   Jayakumar, H., Raha, A., Raghunathan, V.: QUICKRECALL: a low overhead HW/SW approach for enabling computations across power cycles in transiently powered computers. In: 2014 27th International Conference on VLSI Design and 2014 13th International Conference on Embedded Systems, pp. 330–335, January 2014

[KJJ99]   Kocher, P., Jaffe, J., Jun, B.: Differential power analysis. In: Wiener, M. (ed.) CRYPTO 1999. LNCS, vol. 1666, pp. 388–397. Springer, Heidelberg (1999). https://doi.org/10.1007/3-540-48405-1_25

[KJJL05] Kim, K., Jeong, G., Jeong, H., Lee, S.: Emerging memory technologies. In: Proceedings of the IEEE 2005 Custom Integrated Circuits Conference, pp. 423–426, September 2005

[KKSK15] Kannan, S., Karimi, N., Sinanoglu, O., Karri, R.: Security vulnerabilities of emerging nonvolatile main memories and countermeasures. IEEE Trans. Comput.-Aided Des. Integr. Circuits Syst. **34**(1), 2–15 (2015)

[LR15]   Lucia, B., Ransford, B.: A simpler, safer programming and execution model for intermittent systems. In: Proceedings of the 36th ACM SIGPLAN Conference on Programming Language Design and Implementation, PLDI 2015, pp. 575–585. ACM, New York (2015)

[MA18]   Mittal, S., Alsalibi, A.I.: A survey of techniques for improving security of non-volatile memories. J. Hardw. Syst. Secur. **2**(2), 179–200 (2018)

[NNM+18] Navarro, C., et al.: InGaAs capacitor-less DRAM cells TCAD demonstration. IEEE J. Electron Dev. Soc. **6**, 884–892 (2018)

[RSF11]   Ransford, B., Sorber, J., Kevin, F.: Mementos: system support for long-running computation on RFID-scale devices. SIGARCH Comput. Archit. News **39**(1), 159–170 (2011)

[SSAQ02] Samyde, D., Skorobogatov, S., Anderson, R., Quisquater, J.J.: On a new way to read data from memory. In: Proceedings of First International IEEE Security in Storage Workshop, pp. 65–69, December 2002

[SVRR13] Sharad, M., Venkatesan, R., Raghunathan, A., Roy, K.: Multi-level magnetic RAM using domain wall shift for energy-efficient, high-density caches. In: International Symposium on Low Power Electronics and Design (ISLPED), pp. 64–69, September 2013

[Tex17a] Texas Instruments: MSP MCU FRAM Utilities (2017)

[Tex17b] Texas Instruments: MSP430FR58xx, MSP430FR59xx, MSP430FR68xx, and MSP430FR69xx Family User's Guide (2017)

[WH16]   Van Der Woude, J., Hicks, M.: Intermittent computation without hardware support or programmer intervention. In: 12th USENIX Symposium on Operating Systems Design and Implementation (OSDI 2016), pp. 17–32. USENIX Association, Savannah (2016)

[YCCC07] Yang, C.F., Chen, K.H., Chen, Y.C., Chang, T.C.: Fabrication of one-transistor-capacitor structure of nonvolatile TFT Ferroelectric RAM devices using BA(Zr0.1 Ti0.9)O3 gated oxide film. IEEE Trans. Ultrason. Ferroelectr. Freq. Control **54**(9), 1726–1730 (2007)

[YHP09] Yun, S.-N., Ham, Y.-B., Park, J.H.: Energy harvester using PZT actuator with a cantilver. In: 2009 ICCAS-SICE, pp. 5514–5517, August 2009

EdSIDH: Supersingular Isogeny Diffie-Hellman Key Exchange on Edwards Curves

Reza Azarderakhsh[1], Elena Bakos Lang[2], David Jao[2,3,4], and Brian Koziel[5(✉)]

[1] Department of Computer and Electrical Engineering and Computer Science,
Florida Atlantic University, Boca Raton, FL, USA
[2] Department of Combinatorics and Optimization,
University of Waterloo, Waterloo, ON N2L 3G1, Canada
[3] Centre for Applied Cryptographic Research,
University of Waterloo, Waterloo, ON N2L 3G1, Canada
[4] evolutionQ, Inc., Waterloo, ON, Canada
[5] Texas Instruments, Dallas, TX, USA
kozielbrian@mail.com

Abstract. Problems relating to the computation of isogenies between elliptic curves defined over finite fields have been studied for a long time. Isogenies on supersingular elliptic curves are a candidate for quantum-safe key exchange protocols because the best known classical and quantum algorithms for solving well-formed instances of the isogeny problem are exponential. We propose an implementation of supersingular isogeny Diffie-Hellman (SIDH) key exchange for complete Edwards curves. Our work is motivated by the use of Edwards curves to speed up many cryptographic protocols and improve security. Our work does not actually provide a faster implementation of SIDH, but the use of complete Edwards curves and their complete addition formulae provides security benefits against side-channel attacks. We provide run time complexity analysis and operation counts for the proposed key exchange based on Edwards curves along with comparisons to the Montgomery form.

Keywords: Edwards curves · Isogeny arithmetic
Supersingular isogeny Diffie-Hellman key exchange

1 Introduction

According to our current understanding of the laws of quantum mechanics, quantum computers based on quantum phenomena offer the possibility of solving certain problems much more quickly than is possible on any classical computer. Included among these problems are almost all of the mathematical problems upon which currently deployed public-key cryptosystems are based. NIST has recently announced plans for transitioning to post-quantum cryptographic protocols, and organized a standardization process for developing such cryptosystems [9]. One of the candidates in this process is Jao and De Feo's Supersingular

© Springer Nature Switzerland AG 2018
A. Chattopadhyay et al. (Eds.): SPACE 2018, LNCS 11348, pp. 125–141, 2018.
https://doi.org/10.1007/978-3-030-05072-6_8

Isogeny Diffie-Hellman (SIDH) proposal [14], which is based on the path-finding problem in isogeny graphs of supersingular elliptic curves [8,10]. Isogenies are a special kind of morphism of algebraic curves, which have been studied extensively in pure mathematics but only recently proposed for use in cryptography. We believe isogeny-based cryptosystems offer several advantages compared to other approaches for post-quantum cryptography:

- Their security level is determined by a simple choice of a single public parameter. The temptation in cryptography is always to cut parameter sizes down to the bare minimum security level, for performance reasons. By reducing the number of security-sensitive parameters down to one, it becomes impossible to accidentally choose one parameter too small in relation to the others (which harms security), or too large (which harms performance).
- They achieve the smallest public key size among those post-quantum cryptosystems which were proposed to NIST [30, Table 5.9].
- They are based on number-theoretic complexity assumptions, for which there is already a large base of existing research, activity, and community expertise.
- Implementations can leverage existing widely deployed software libraries to achieve necessary features such as side-channel resilience.

Relative to other post-quantum candidates, the main practical limitation of SIDH currently lies in its performance which requires more attention from cryptographic engineers.

The majority of speed-optimized SIDH implementations (in both hardware and software platforms) use Montgomery curves [1,2,11–14,16,17,22–26,32], which are a popular choice for cryptographic applications due to their fast curve and isogeny arithmetic. Only [27] is an exception as it considers a hybrid Edwards-Montgomery SIDH scheme that still uses isogenies over Montgomery curves. Alternative models for elliptic curves have been studied for fast computation such as Edwards curves, whose complete addition law presents security and speed benefits for the implementation of various cryptographic protocols. Edwards curves and Montgomery curves share many characteristics, as there is a birational equivalence between the two families of curves. Edwards curves remove the overhead of checking for exceptional cases, and twisted Edwards form removes the overhead of checking for invalid inputs. In this paper, we study the possibility of using isogenies of Edwards curves in the SIDH protocol, and study its potential speed and security benefits. Our results indicate that although Montgomery curves are faster for SIDH computations, the completeness of Edwards curves formulae provides additional security benefits against side-channel attacks. Since SIDH is still in its infancy, it is unclear if exceptional cases could be used as the basis for a side-channel attack, but in any case our EdSIDH implementation defends against this possibility.

Our contributions can be summarized as follows:

- We propose EdSIDH: fast formulas for SIDH over Edwards curves.
- We investigate isogeny formulas on projective and completed Edwards forms.
- We propose fast formulas for Edwards curve isogenies of degree 2, 3, and 4.

The rest of the paper is organized as follows: In the rest of this section, we provide preliminaries of Edwards curves and review the SIDH protocol. In Sect. 2, we provide new formulae for a key exchange scheme based on Edwards curves. In Sect. 3, we present fast equations for EdSIDH arithmetic and analyze their running time complexity in terms of operation counts. In Sect. 4, we analyze the complexity of incorporating our Edwards arithmetic in SIDH. Finally, we conclude the paper in Sect. 5.

Independent work on fast isogeny formulas for Edwards curves was done in [19].

1.1   The Edwards Form

In 2007, Edwards introduced a new model for elliptic curves [15] called Edwards curves. Twisted Edwards curves are a generalization of Edwards curves, with each twisted Edwards curve being a quadratic twist of an Edwards curve. Twisted Edwards curves are defined by the equation $E_{a,d} : ax^2 + y^2 = 1 + dx^2y^2$ over a field $\mathbb{K}$, with $d \neq 0, 1; a \neq 0$. When $a = 1$, the curve defined by $E_{a,d}$ is an Edwards curve.

The isomorphism $(x, y) \mapsto \left(\frac{x}{\sqrt{a}}, y\right)$ maps the twisted Edwards curve $E_{a,d}$ to the isomorphic Edwards curve $E_{1,d/a}$, with the inverse map given by $(x, y) \mapsto (\sqrt{a}x, y)$ [4]. Over finite fields, only curves with order divisible by 4 can be expressed in the (twisted) Edwards form.

The group addition law on twisted Edwards curves is defined by:

$$(x_1, y_1) + (x_2, y_2) = \left(\frac{x_1y_2 + x_2y_1}{1 + dx_1x_2y_1y_2}, \frac{y_1y_2 - ax_1x_2}{1 - dx_1x_2y_1y_2} \right), \tag{1}$$

with identity element $(0, 1)$. If $\frac{a}{d}$ is not a square in $\mathbb{K}$, then the twisted Edwards addition law is strongly unified and complete: it can be used for both addition and doubling, and has no exceptional points. Additionally, when this is the case, the curve $E_{a,d}$ has no singular points. These properties of Edwards curves have in the past proved valuable, and have been used for simpler implementations and protection against side channel attacks in various cryptographic protocols [6].

However, if $\frac{a}{d}$ is not a square, then $E_{a,d}$ has only one point of order 2, namely $(0, -1)$ [5, Theorem 3.1]. As we will see later, the SIDH protocol is based on the repeated computation of 2-isogenies (with the private key defined as a point of order 2^k). As such, a unique point of order 2 would compromise the scheme's security, which means we must consider curves where $\frac{a}{d}$ is a square in $\mathbb{K}$. In the next section, we consider the additional points that occur when $\frac{a}{d}$ is a square, and present curve embeddings that allow us to desingularize these points.

In the case where $\frac{a}{d}$ is not a square, it is often useful to consider the dual addition law for Edwards curves:

$$(x_1, y_1) + (x_2, y_2) \mapsto \left(\frac{x_1y_1 + x_2y_2}{y_1y_2 + ax_1x_2}, \frac{x_1y_1 - x_2y_2}{x_1y_2 - y_1x_2} \right). \tag{2}$$

The addition law and dual addition law return the same value if both are defined. Additionally, for any pair of points on a twisted Edwards curve, at least one of the two addition laws will be defined.

1.2 Projective Curves and Completed Twisted Edwards Curves

If $\frac{a}{d}$ is a square in $\mathbb{K}$, then there are points $(x_1, y_1), (x_2, y_2)$ on the curve $E_{a,d}$ for which $(1 - dx_1x_2y_1y_2)(1 + dx_1x_2y_1y_2) = 0$ and the group law is not defined. We can embed the curve into projective space, add new singular points at infinity and generalize the group law to work for the new embedding, as is often done. We consider two representations of points on twisted Edwards curves, namely projective coordinates and completed coordinates.

The projective twisted Edwards curve is defined by $aX^2Z^2 + Y^2Z^2 = Z^4 + dX^2Y^2$. The projective points are given by the affine points, embedded as usual into P^2 by $(x, y) \mapsto (x : y : 1)$, and two extra points at infinity, $(0 : 1 : 0)$ of order 4, and $(1 : 0 : 0)$ of order 2. A projective point $(X : Y : Z)$ corresponds to the affine point $(x, y) = (\frac{X}{Z}, \frac{Y}{Z})$. Adding a generic pair of points takes $10M + 1S + 1A + 1D$ operations, and doubling takes $3M + 4S + 1A$ operations [5].

The completed twisted Edwards curve is defined by the equation:

$$\bar{E}_{a,d} := aX^2T^2 + Y^2Z^2 = Z^2T^2 + dX^2Y^2 \tag{3}$$

The completed points are given by the affine points embedded into $\mathbb{P}^1 \times \mathbb{P}^1$ via $(x, y) \mapsto ((x : 1), (y : 1))$, and up to four extra points at infinity, $((1 : 0), (\pm\sqrt{\frac{a}{d}} : 1))$ and $((1 : \pm\sqrt{d}), (1 : 0))$ [7]. The affine equivalent of a completed point $((X : Z), (Y : T))$ is given by $(x, y) = (\frac{X}{Z}, \frac{Y}{T})$.

If $P_1 = ((X_1 : Z_1), (Y_1 : T_1))$ and $P_2 = ((X_2 : Z_2), (Y_2 : T_2))$, then the group law is defined as follows:

$$
\begin{aligned}
X_3 &= X_1Y_2Z_2T_1 + X_2Y_1Z_1T_2 & X_3' &= X_1Y_1Z_2T_2 + X_2Y_2Z_1T_1, \\
Z_3 &= Z_1Z_2T_1T_2 + dX_1X_2Y_1Y_2 & Z_3' &= aX_1X_2T_1T_2 + Y_1Y_2Z_1Z_2, \\
Y_3 &= Y_1Y_2Z_1Z_2 - aX_1X_2T_1T_2 & Y_3' &= X_1Y_1Z_2T_2 - X_2Y_2Z_1T_1, \\
T_3 &= Z_1Z_2T_1T_2 - dX_1X_2Y_1Y_2 & T_3' &= X_1Y_2Z_2T_1 - X_2Y_1Z_1T_1.
\end{aligned}
$$

Hence we have $X_3Z_3' = X_3'Z_3$ and $Y_3T_3' = Y_3'T_3$, with either $(X_3, Z_3) \neq (0, 0)$ and $(Y_3, T_3) \neq (0, 0)$ or $(X_3', Z_3') \neq (0, 0)$ and $(Y_3', T_3') \neq (0, 0)$. We set $P_1 + P_2 = P_3$, where P_3 is either $((X_3 : Z_3), (Y_3 : T_3))$ or $((X_3' : Z_3'), (Y_3' : T_3'))$, depending on which of the above equations holds. With the identity point $((0 : 1)(1 : 1))$, the above defines a complete set of addition laws for complete twisted Edwards curves. This result formalizes the combination of the affine and dual addition law into a single group law.

The following result from Bernstein and Lange in [7] allows us to categorize pairs of points for which each addition law is defined:

When computing the result of $P + Q$, the original addition law fails exactly when $P - Q = ((1 : \pm\sqrt{d}), (1 : 0))$ or $P - Q = ((1 : 0), (\pm\sqrt{a/d} : 1))$. By the categorization of points of low even order from [5], the original addition law fails when $P - Q$ is a point at infinity of order 2 or 4. In particular, the original addition law is always defined for point doubling, as $P - P = O$, which has order 1.

The dual addition law fails exactly when $P - Q = ((1 : \pm\sqrt{a}), (0 : 1))$ or $P - Q = ((0 : 1), (\pm 1 : 1))$. In particular, the dual addition law fails exactly when $P - Q$ is a point of order $1, 2$ or 4 and is not a point at infinity.

We can use this categorization results to minimize the number of times we need to use the addition law for completed Edwards curves by considering order of the pairs of points involved in each section of the EdSIDH protocol.

1.3 Isogenies and Isogeny Computation

Isogenies are defined as structure preserving maps between elliptic curves. They are given by rational maps between the two curves, but can be equivalently defined by their kernel. If this kernel is generated by a point of order ℓ, then the isogeny is known as an ℓ-isogeny. In [31], Vélu explicitly showed how to find the rational functions defining an isogeny for an elliptic curve in Weierstrass form, given the kernel F.

The computation of isogenies of large degree can be reduced to the computation of smaller isogenies composed together, as described in [14]. For instance, consider computing an isogeny of degree ℓ^e. We reduce it to e computations of degree ℓ isogenies by considering a point $R \in E$ of degree ℓ^e that generates the kernel. We start with $E_0 := E, R_0 := R$ and iteratively compute $E_{i+1} = E_i / \langle \ell^{e-i-1} R_i \rangle$, $\phi_i \colon E_i \to E_{i+1}$, $R_{i+1} = \phi_i(R_i)$, using Vélu's formulas to compute the ℓ-isogeny at each iteration.

1.4 A review of Isogeny-Based Key-Exchange

Fix two small prime numbers ℓ_A and ℓ_B and an integer cofactor f, and let p be a large prime of the form $p = \ell_A^{e_A} \ell_B^{e_B} f \pm 1$ for some integers e_A, e_B. Let E be a supersingular elliptic curve defined over $\mathbb{F}_{p^2}$ which has group order $(\ell_A^{e_A} \ell_B^{e_B} f)^2$. All known implementations to date choose $\ell_A = 2, \ell_B = 3$ and $f = 1$, although other choices of ℓ_A, ℓ_B are possible. Public parameters consist of the supersingular elliptic curve E, and bases $\{P_A, Q_A\}$ and $\{P_B, Q_B\}$ of $E[\ell_A^{e_A}]$ and $E[\ell_B^{e_B}]$ respectively. During one round of key-exchange, Alice chooses two secret, random elements $m_A, n_A \in \mathbb{Z}/\ell_A^{e_A}\mathbb{Z}$, not both divisible by ℓ_A, and computes an isogeny $\phi_A \colon E \to E_A$ with kernel $K_A := \langle [m_A]P_A, [n_A]Q_A \rangle$. She also computes the image $\phi_A(P_B), \phi_A(Q_B)$ of the basis $\{P_B, Q_B\}$. Similarly, Bob selects random elements $m_B, n_B \in \mathbb{Z}/l_B^{e_B}\mathbb{Z}$, and computes an isogeny $\phi_B \colon E \to E_B$ with kernel $K_B := \langle [m_B]P_B, [n_B]Q_B \rangle$, along with the points $\phi_B(P_A), \phi_B(Q_A)$. After receiving $E_B, \phi_B(P_A), \phi_B(Q_A)$, Alice computes an isogeny $\phi_A' \colon E_B \to E_{AB}$ with kernel $\langle [m_A]\phi_B(P_A), [n_A]\phi_B(Q_A) \rangle$. Bob proceeds similarly to obtain a curve E_{BA} that is isomorphic to E_{AB}. Alice and Bob then use as their shared secret the j-invariant common to E_{BA} and E_{AB}. For more about the key exchange based on isogenies, please refer to [14].

2   EdSIDH

In this section, we provide even and odd isogenies over Edwards curves and propose a new formulation for SIDH, which we call EdSIDH moving forward. Here, we use M, S, C to refer to the cost of a multiplication, squaring, and multiplication by a curve constant in $\mathbb{F}_{p^2}$. We will also use R to refer to the cost of a square root, and I to the cost of an inversion. As is usually done, we ignore the cost of addition and subtraction as the cost is significantly smaller than the cost of multiplication and inversion.

2.1   Odd Isogenies in Edwards Form

In [29], Moody and Shumow presented ℓ-isogeny formulas for odd ℓ on Edwards curves. Let the subgroup $F = \langle(\alpha, \beta)\rangle = \{(0, 1), (\pm\alpha_1, \beta_1), \ldots, (\pm\alpha_s, \beta_s)\}$ be the kernel of the desired ℓ-isogeny, with $\ell = 2s + 1$ and (α, β) a point of order ℓ on the curve E_d that generates F. Then

$$\psi(P) = \left(\prod_{Q \in F} \frac{x_{P+Q}}{y_Q}, \prod_{Q \in F} \frac{y_{P+Q}}{y_Q} \right) \tag{4}$$

maps E_d to $E_{d'}$, where $d' = B^8 d^\ell$ and $B = \prod_{i=1}^{s} \beta_i$.

If d is not a square in $\mathbb{K}$, the affine addition law is defined everywhere. Note that any odd isogeny from a curve with d not square maps to a curve with d' not square, as for an odd ℓ $d' = B^8 d^\ell$ is a square if and only if d is a square. This implies that if we chain odd isogenies starting with the curve E_d with d not a square in $\mathbb{K}$, then the affine addition law will be defined for any pair of points on any Edwards curve in the chain as they will all have a non-square coefficient.

The next proposition shows that the affine addition law is defined for all pairs of points in an odd isogeny computation even if d is not a square in $\mathbb{K}$.

Proposition 1. *The affine addition law is defined for all point additions in the EdSIDH protocol.*

Proof. During the EdSIDH protocol, we need to evaluate each 3-isogeny three times: on the current kernel point of order 3^k for some $k \leq e_A$, and on Alice's public points P_A, Q_A of order 2^{ℓ_A}. When evaluating $\psi(P)$, we must compute $P + Q$ for all $Q \in F$ (note that all such Q's have odd order). These are the only additions we need to do in order to compute an ℓ-isogeny. We now consider a few cases that cover these additions.

If P and Q both have odd order, then $-Q$ also has odd order, and $P - Q$ must have odd order as the order divides $lcm(ord(P), ord(Q))$. Therefore, it cannot be equal to a point at infinity as they have order either 2 or 4. Thus, by the categorization of exceptional points for the group law in Sect. 1.2, we can compute $P + Q$ using the affine addition law.

Similarly, if P has even order 2^{ℓ_A}, we note that $gcd(ord(P), ord(-Q)) = 1$ for all Q in the kernel of the 3 isogeny. Hence, we have that $ord(P - Q) = $

$lcm(ord(P), ord(-Q)) = lcm(ord(P), ord(Q))$. As $ord(Q)$ is odd, this implies $P - Q$ is not a point of order 2 or 4 (if $ord(Q) = 1 \implies Q = O$, then the affine addition law is always defined for $P + Q$).

Thus, in all cases, we can use the original addition law to compute and evaluate a 3-isogeny.

We can use the affine addition law to derive explicit coordinate maps for a ℓ-isogeny with kernel F (where $\ell = 2s + 1$):

$$\psi(x, y) = \left(\frac{x}{B^2} \prod_{i=1}^{s} \frac{\beta_i^2 x^2 - \alpha_i^2 y^2}{1 - d^2 \alpha_i^2 \beta_i^2 x^2 y^2}, \frac{y}{B^2} \prod_{i=1}^{s} \frac{\beta_i^2 y^2 - \alpha_i^2 x^2}{1 - d^2 \alpha_i^2 \beta_i^2 x^2 y^2} \right)$$

Moody and Shumow also presented an ℓ-isogeny formula for twisted Edwards curves. However, since each twisted Edwards curve is isomorphic to an Edwards curve, and the even isogeny formulas presented later output Edwards curves (with $a = 1$), one can use the isogeny formulas for Edwards curves (which are slightly faster to compute).

2.2   Even Isogenies in Edwards Form

In [29], Moody and Shumow presented Edwards curves isogenies formulas for isogenies with kernel $\{(0, 1), (0, -1)\}$. We generalize their work in two ways. First, we extend their formulas to work for 2-isogenies on completed twisted Edwards curves with arbitrary kernels. Then we show how to calculate 4-isogenies on Edwards curves. Finally, we consider methods for decreasing the computation cost for even isogenies in EdSIDH.

Suppose we want to compute an isogeny with kernel $\langle P_2 \rangle$, where P_2 is a point of order 2 on $E_{a,d}$. We follow an approach similar to that given in [14]. Since we already know how to calculate 2-isogenies with kernel $\{(0, 1), (0, -1)\}$, we find an isomorphism that maps P_2 to $(0, -1)$ and then use one of Moody's [29] isogeny formulas.

Proposition 2. *There exists an isomorphism between complete twisted Edwards curves that maps a point P_2 of order 2 to the point $(0, -1)$.*

Proof. We construct the desired isomorphism as follows. An isomorphism between the complete Edwards curve $\bar{E}_{a,d}$ and the Montgomery curve $E_{A,B}$: $By^2 = x^3 + Ax^2 + x$ (in projective coordinates) is given in [7] by:

$$\phi \colon ((X : Z), (Y : T)) \mapsto \begin{cases} (0 : 0 : 1) \text{ if } ((X : Z), (Y : T)) = ((0 : 1), (-1 : 1)) \\ ((T + Y)X : (T + Y)Z : (T - Y)X) \text{ otherwise} \end{cases}$$

$$\phi^{-1} \colon (U : V : W) \mapsto \begin{cases} ((0 : 1), (1 : 1)) & (U : V : W) = (0 : 1 : 0) \\ ((0 : 1), (-1 : 1)) & (U : V : W) = (0 : 0 : 1) \\ ((U : V), (U - W : U + W)) & \text{otherwise} \end{cases}$$

where $A = \frac{2(a+d)}{(a-d)}, B = \frac{4}{(a-d)}$ (and $a = \frac{A+2}{B}, d = \frac{A-2}{B}$). This isomorphism maps the point $(0, -1)$ to $(0, 0)$, and vice versa.

An isomorphism between Montgomery curves mapping any point (x_2, y_2) of order 2 to $(0, 0)$ and a point (x_4, y_4) doubling to it to the point $(1, \ldots)$ is presented in [14, Eq. (15)]:

$$\phi_2 \colon (x, y) \mapsto \left(\frac{x - x_2}{x_4 - x_2}, \frac{y}{x_4 - x_2} \right) \qquad (5)$$

The new curve has equation $E' \colon \frac{B}{x_4 - x_2} y^2 = x^3 + \frac{3x_2 + A}{x_4 - x_2} x^2 + x$.

Since ϕ, ϕ^{-1}, and ϕ_2 are isomorphisms, $\phi^{-1} \cdot \phi_2 \cdot \phi$ is also an isomorphism. Thus, we get an isomorphism mapping any point of order 2 to $((0 : 1)(-1 : 1))$ on $\bar{E}_{a,d}$.

The resulting curve has coefficients

$$a' = \frac{[x_2 + 2x_4](a - d) + 2(a + d)}{4} \qquad d' = \frac{[5x_2 - 2x_4](a - d) + 2(a + d)}{4},$$

where x_2 and x_4 are the x-coordinates of the point of order 2 and 4 on the Montgomery curve. These coordinates can be retained from the isogeny computation, and thus can be used here at no cost. The map $(x, y) \mapsto (\frac{x}{2}, y)$ maps the curve $E_{a',d'}$ to the curve $E_{4a',4d'}$, thus removing the inversion. The curve coefficients can thus be calculated in $2M$.

By using projective coordinates, we can calculate this isomorphism in $14M$ operations. Mapping a completed point to the Montgomery curve takes $3M$ operations, and $2M$ operations if we only need the X, Z coordinates (as is the case for the points of order 2 and 4), for a total of $7M$ to map all points to the Montgomery curves. The isomorphism ϕ_2 then takes $7M$ operations in projective coordinates, and the isomorphism back to an Edwards curve does not involve any addition. Thus, the total operations needed (ignoring addition and subtraction as is usually done) is $14M$ operations.

To calculate an arbitrary 2-isogeny of Edwards curves, we can first use the isomorphism presented above, and then apply one of the three Edwards curve 2-isogenies presented in [29].

2-isogenies on Edwards Curves. All 2-isogeny equations given by Moody and Shumow [29] require the computation of a square root, which makes them ill-suited to the SIDH framework, as many of them need to be calculated. However, when we know a point P_8 of order 8 such that $4P_8 = (0, -1)$, we can find a square root-free 2-isogeny formula for Edwards curves.

Consider a twisted Edwards curve $E_{a,d} \colon ax^2 + y^2 = 1 + dx^2 y^2$. A birational transformation sending $E_{a,d}$ to the curve $E \colon y^2 = x^3 + 2(a + d)x^2 + (a - d)^2 x$ is given by:

$$\phi_1 \colon (x, y) \mapsto \left((a - d)\frac{1 + y}{1 - y}, (a - d)\frac{2(1 + y)}{x(1 - y)} \right)$$

By Vélu's formulas [31], a 2-isogeny on this curve with kernel $\{(0,0), \infty\}$ is given by:

$$\phi_2 \colon (x, y) \mapsto \left(\frac{x^2 + (a - d)^2}{x}, y \frac{x^2 - (a - d)^2}{x^2} \right)$$

The equation for the resulting curve is

$$E' : y^2 = x^3 + 2(a + d)x^2 - 4(a - d)^2 x - 8(a + d)(a - d)^2$$

Using one of the points of order 2 on this curve, we can map it to a curve of the form $y^2 = x^3 + ax^2 + x$. For instance, the point $(2(a - d), 0)$ has order 2, and the transformation $(x, y) \mapsto (x - 2(a - d), 0)$ maps the curve E' to the curve

$$E'' : y^2 = x^3 - 4(d - 2a)x^2 + 16(a - d)x$$

Now, if we have a point of order 4 (r_1, s_1), the map $\phi_3 \colon (x, y) \mapsto \left(\frac{s_1 x}{r_1 y}, \frac{x - r_1}{x + r_1} \right)$ maps to the curve $x^2 + y^2 = 1 + d'x^2 y^2$, where $d' = 1 - \frac{4r_1^3}{s_1^2}$.

If we evaluate the point P_8 of order 8 through the first three maps, we obtain a point of order 4 on the curve E'', since the 2-isogeny brings $4P_8 = (0, 0)$ to the identity point. Doing so, we can obtain explicit equations for a 2-isogeny.

Consider a point $P_8 = (\alpha, \beta)$ of order 8 on the curve $E_{a,d}$ (Note that P_8 can be written in affine form, as all singular points have order 2 or 4). Then we have that

$$(\alpha_1, \beta_1) = \left((-4\frac{\beta^2(a - d)}{\beta^2 - 1}, 8\frac{\beta(a - d)}{\alpha(1 - \beta^2)} \right)$$

is a point of order 4 on the curve $y^2 = x^3 - 4(d - 2a)x^2 + 16(a - d)x$. We obtain $d' = 1 + 4\frac{\beta^4 \alpha^2 (a - d)}{\beta^2 - 1}$. Thus, a 2-isogeny mapping the curve $E_{a,d}$ to the curve $E_{1,d'}$ is given by:

$$(x, y) \mapsto \left(\frac{xy}{\alpha\beta}, \frac{x(\beta^2 - 1) + 4\beta^2(a - d)}{x(\beta^2 - 1) - 4\beta^2(a - d)} \right)$$

In the SIDH key-exchange calculations, a point of order 8 will be known for all but the last two isogeny calculations, as we are calculating an isogeny with kernel generated by a point of order 2^{e_A}, with e_A large.

Recall that in the SIDH protocol, Alice selects an element $R_A = [m_A]P_A + [n_A]Q_A$ of the elliptic curve E of order 2^e_A, which generates the kernel of the isogeny ϕ_A. She computes the isogeny iteratively, one 2 or 4 isogeny at a time. Consider one step in this process:

Suppose R'_A is a point of order $2^{e_A - k}$ on the curve E', a k-isogeny of the original curve E. For the next step in the iteration, Alice computes the points $R''_A = 2^{e_A - k - 3}R_A$ and $4R''_A = 2^{e_A - k - 1}R_A$. We have that $4R''_A$ is a point of order 2 on the curve E', with R''_A a point of order 8 above it. Thus, we can use these points to calculate a 2-isogeny with kernel $4R''_A$, as described above.

4-isogenies on Edwards Curves. Let us assume we are given a twisted Edwards curve $E_{a,d}$ and a point P_4 on the curve of order 4. We want to calculate a 4-isogeny on the curve with kernel generated by P_4, without knowing a point of order 8 that doubles to P_4. We can do so as follows: Use the isomorphism presented earlier to map P_4 and $2P_4$ to $((1 : \sqrt{a'}), (0 : 1)), ((0 : 1), (-1 : 1))$ respectively, on some isomorphic curve $E_{a',d'}$. Then use the isomorphism $(x, y) \mapsto (\frac{x}{\sqrt{a'}}, y)$ to map the curve to $E_{1, \frac{d'}{a'}}$. Finally, compose the following two 2-isogeny formulas of Moody and Shumow [29] to calculate the 4-isogeny:

$$\phi_1(x, y) \mapsto \left((\gamma \pm 1)xy, \frac{(\gamma \mp 1)y^2 \pm 1}{(\gamma \pm 1)y^2 \mp 1} \right)$$

$$\phi_2(x, y) \mapsto \left(i(\rho \mp 1)\frac{x}{y}\frac{1 - d'y^2}{1 - d'}, \frac{d' \mp \rho\,\rho y^2 \pm 1}{d' \pm \rho\,\rho y^2 \mp 1} \right)$$

that map $E_{1,d}$ to $E_{1,d'}$ with $d' = (\frac{\gamma \pm 1}{\gamma \mp 1})^2$ and $E_{1,d'}$ to $E_{1,\hat{d}}$ with $\hat{d} = (\frac{\rho \pm 1}{\rho \mp 1})^2$, where $\gamma^2 = 1 - d$ and $\rho^2 = d', i^2 = -1$ in $\mathbb{K}$. Note that d' is, by definition, a square in $\mathbb{K}$ and so the curve $E_{1,d'}$ will have singular points and exceptions to the group law.

Both isogenies have kernel $\{((0 : 1), (-1 : 1)), ((0 : 1), (1 : 1))\}$ and the first isogeny maps $((1 : \sqrt{a'}), (0 : 1))$ to $((0 : 1), (-1 : 1))$, so the composition is well defined as a 4-isogeny with kernel generated by $((1 : \sqrt{a'}), (0 : 1))$. Composing the two equations for the curve coefficient, we get:

$$\hat{d} = \left(\frac{\rho \pm 1}{\rho \mp 1} \right)^2 = \left(\frac{(\frac{\gamma \pm 1}{\gamma \mp 1}) \pm 1}{(\frac{\gamma \pm 1}{\gamma \mp 1}) \mp 1} \right)^2 = \left(\frac{(\gamma \pm 1) \pm (\gamma \mp 1)}{(\gamma \pm 1) \mp (\gamma \mp 1)} \right)^2$$

which costs one square root and one inversion. The value of $i = \sqrt{-1}$ in $\mathbb{K}$ can be computed and stored ahead of time to evaluate 4-isogenies.

3   EdSIDH Arithmetic

Here we describe our explicit formulas for fast isogenies of degree 2, 3, and 4 for Edwards curves.

3.1   Point Multiplication by ℓ

Let P be a point on our curve and ℓ an integer, and suppose we want to compute ℓP. By [5], we know that the affine group law is always defined for point doublings (even when d is a square in the field K). To compute this, we can use a ladder algorithm, which takes n steps (where n is the number of bits of ℓ), each consisting of a doubling and a point addition.

On a projective curve, we know from [6] that we can double a point by $3M + 4S$, and adding arbitrary points takes $10M + 1S + 1C$. On complete curves, doubling takes $5M + 4S + 1C$, and addition takes $29M$ operations.

3.2 Computing 3-isogenies

In the case where $a = 1$ and d is not a square in K, Moody and Shumow [29] presented a way to calculate a 3-isogeny in projective form with kernel $\{(0,0), (\pm A, B, 1)\}$ at a cost of $6M + 4S + 3C$. Generalizing to the case where $P_3 = (\alpha, \beta, \zeta)$ is a point of order 3 (with $A = \alpha/\zeta, B = \beta/\zeta$), and we want to evaluate the 3-isogeny with kernel $\langle P_3 \rangle$ on a generic projective point (x, y, z), we get the following equations for the evaluation of the 3-isogeny:

$$\psi(x, y, z) = (xz\gamma^4(\beta^2 x^2 - \alpha^2 y^2), yz\gamma^4(\beta^2 y^2 - \alpha^2 x^2), \beta^2(\gamma^4 z^4 - d^2 x^2 y^2 \alpha^2 \beta^2)))$$

It takes $13M + 9S$ operations to compute $\psi(x, y, z)$. If we are evaluating the isogeny at multiple points, we don't need to recompute $\alpha^2, \beta^2, \gamma^2, \gamma^4, d^2$, thus bringing the cost to $13M + 4S$ for each additional point evaluation.

We can compute the curve coefficient $d' = \beta^8 d^3$ by computing $\beta^8 = ((\beta^2)^2)^2$ and $d^3 = d^2 d$ for a total cost of $3S + 2M$, or $4S + 2M$ if we didn't evaluate the isogeny ahead of time.

3.3 Computing 2-isogenies

Let us consider the 2-isogeny equation presented in Sect. 2.2, where (α, β) is a point of order 8 on the curve $E_{a,d}$.

$$(x, y) \mapsto \left(\frac{xy}{\alpha\beta}, \frac{x(\beta^2 - 1) + 4\beta^2(a - d)}{x(\beta^2 - 1) - 4\beta^2(a - d)} \right)$$

We can compute it using $2I + 7M + 1S$ or $I + 10M + 1S$ with a simultaneous inversion. Alternatively, we can define an equivalent version for completed coordinates by representing $x = \frac{X}{Z}, y = \frac{Y}{T}, \alpha = \frac{A}{Z_P}, \beta = \frac{B}{T_P}$:

$$((X : Y), (Z : T)) \mapsto ((XYZ_PT_P : ABZT),$$
$$(X(B^2 - T_P^2) + 4B^2(a - d)Z : X(B^2 - T_P^2) - 4B^2(a - d)Z))$$

Precomputing shared subexpressions allows us to compute this in $9M + 2S$ operations. Combined with the $14M$ operations for the isomorphism bringing any point of order 2 to $(0, -1)$, we get a total of $23M + 2S$ operations.

We could also compute this isogeny using projective coordinates, where $x = \frac{X}{Z}, y = Y, Z, \alpha = \frac{A}{Z_0}, \beta = \frac{B}{Z_0}$:

$$(X : Y : Z) \mapsto (XYZ_0^2, X(B^2 - Z_0^2) + 4B^2Z(a - d),$$
$$Z^2 A^2 B^2(X(B^2 - Z_0^2) - 4B^2Z(a - d)))$$

which can be computed in $7M + 3S$ operations. Combining this with the $14M$ operations for the isomorphism bringing any point of order 2 to $((0:1), (-1:1))$ and the map $((X:Z), (Y:T)) \mapsto (XT, YZ, TZ)$ $(3M)$ that embeds a completed point into a projective curve, we get a total cost of $24M + 3S$ (which is more expensive than using completed coordinates).

The curve coefficient is given by $d' = 1 + 4\frac{\beta^4 \alpha^2 (a-d)}{\beta^2 - 1}$. This can be computed in $5M + 1I$ operations. Combining this with the $2M$ operations used to compute the curve coefficients from the isomorphism, we get a total of $7M + 1I$ operations.

3.4   Computing 4-isogenies

Recall the 4-isogeny formulas presented in the Sect. 2.2

$$\phi_1(x,y) \mapsto \left((\gamma \pm 1)xy, \frac{(\gamma \mp 1)y^2 \pm 1}{(\gamma \pm 1)y^2 \mp 1}\right)$$

that maps $E_{1,d}$ to $E_{1,d'}$ with $d' = (\frac{\gamma \pm 1}{\gamma \mp 1})^2$ where $\gamma^2 = 1 - d$, and

$$\phi_2(x,y) \mapsto \left(i(\rho \mp 1)\frac{x}{y}\frac{1 - d'y^2}{1 - d'}, \frac{d' \mp \rho}{d' \pm \rho}\frac{\rho y^2 \pm 1}{\rho y^2 \mp 1}\right)$$

that maps $E_{1,d'}$ to $E_{1,\hat{d}}$ with $\hat{d} = (\frac{\rho \pm 1}{\rho \mp 1})^2$, where $\rho^2 = d'$, $i^2 = -1$ in $\mathbb{K}$. We can rewrite these in $\mathbb{P}_1 \times \mathbb{P}_1$, writing $x = \frac{X}{Z}, y = \frac{Y}{T}$ as follows:

$$\phi_1((X,Z), (Y,T)) \mapsto (((\gamma \pm 1)XY, ZT), ((\gamma \mp 1)Y^2 \pm T^2, (\gamma \pm 1)Y^2 \mp T^2))$$

and

$$\phi_2((X,Z), (Y,T)) \mapsto (((i(\rho \mp 1)XT(T^2 - dY^2), YZT^2(1-d)),$$
$$((d \mp \rho)(\rho Y^2 \pm T^2), (d \pm \rho)(\rho Y^2 \mp T^2)))$$

We can compute ϕ_1 in $7M$ operations, and ϕ_2 in $13M$ operations. Adding the cost of the isomorphism that brings our point of order 4 to $((1 : \sqrt{a'}), (0 : 1))$, we get a total cost of $34M$ to evaluate a 4-isogeny.

Due to the complete lack of symmetry between the x and y coordinates in both the ϕ_1 and ϕ_2 maps, using projective coordinates takes even more operations than using completed coordinates (for instance evaluating ϕ_1 in projective coordinates would take $7M + 2S$ to compute). Hence, the fastest way to evaluate a 4-isogeny with points on projective coordinates would be to embed them in the complete curve (no cost), evaluate the isogeny, and map them back to a projective curve via the map $((X:Z), (Y:T)) \mapsto (XT, YZ, TZ)$ which takes $3M$ operations. The total cost is thus $37M$ operations.

Calculating the curve coefficient, given by $(\frac{(\gamma \pm 1) \pm (\gamma \mp 1)}{(\gamma \pm 1) \mp (\gamma \mp 1)})^2$ with $\gamma = \sqrt{1 - d}$ additionally requires $1R + 1I + 1S$.

Since computing 4-isogenies is significantly more expensive than computing 2-isogenies due to the need to compute a square root, we propose using 2-isogenies whenever a suitable point of order 8 is known. In practice, this means we will only compute one 4-isogeny, at the very last iteration of isogeny computations.

4 EdSIDH Computation Cost

Here, we analyze the full complexity to use Edwards curves for SIDH. Notably, we look at the cost of the large-degree isogeny computations, based on the operation costs presented in Sect. 3.

4.1 Secret Kernel Generation

In SIDH, the secret kernel is generated from the double-point multiplication $R = nP + mQ$. However, as noted by [14], we can choose any such generator formula, including $R = P + mQ$. This formulation for a double-point multiplication greatly reduces the total cost of the double-point multiplication. In particular, [14] describes a 3-point Montgomery differential ladder that can be used with Montgomery coordinates, at the cost of two differential point additions and one point doubling per step. Faz-Hernández et al. [16] recently proposed a right-to-left variant of the 3-point ladder that only requires a single differential point addition and a single point doubling per step.

Table 1. SIDH secret kernel generation cost per bit

Scheme	Cost per bit
Kummer Montgomery [14]	$9M + 6S$
Kummer Montgomery [16]	$6M + 4S$
Edwards with Montgomery ladder	
Projective Edwards	$13M + 5S + 1C$
Complete Edwards	$34M + 4S + 1C$
Edwards with window method $(k = 4)$	
Projective Edwards	$5.5M + 4.25S + 0.25C$
Complete Edwards	$12.25M + 4S + 1C$

For EdSIDH, a 3-point ladder is not necessary to perform $R = P + mQ$. We can first perform the mQ computation and then simply finish with a point addition with P. Two options to compute the mQ computation are the standard Montgomery powering ladder [28] or the window approach [6]. The Montgomery ladder is a constant set of an addition and doubling for each step, whereas the window approach with a k-bit window performs k point doublings and then an addition. In Table 1, we compare the relative costs per bit in the secret key for this double-point multiplication. Note that this cost per bit does not include the final point addition for $P + mQ$ as this operation is a constant cost.

Thus, as we can see, there is a slight speed advantage with using projective Edwards curves with the Window method. We note that there are some security implications when using the window method instead of the Montgomery ladder, which we do not discuss here.

4.2 Secret Isogeny Computation

The second part of the SIDH protocol involves a secret isogeny walk based on the secret kernel. In this computation we chain isogenies of degree ℓ with kernel points $\ell^{e-i-1}R_i$. To efficiently calculate these kernel representations, we used the combinatorics strategy from [14]. By using pivot points to traverse a one-way acyclic graph, we can create an optimal strategy that represents the least cost to compute the large-degree isogeny.

To evaluate our EdSIDH formulas against the known Montgomery formulas, we computed the costs of our point multiplication by ℓ and isogeny evaluation by ℓ. Based on the relative cost, we computed an optimal strategy based on the algorithm from [14]. We used this to calculate the total cost of a large-degree isogeny for our Edwards isogeny formulas as well as the Montgomery formulas from previous works. Table 2 compares the cost of various isogeny and elliptic curve operations and Table 3 represents the full and normalized cost of a large-degree isogeny for the primes listed. We chose the primes $p_{503} = 2^{250}3^{159} - 1$ and $p_{751} = 2^{372}3^{239} - 1$ which have a quantum security of 83 and 124 bits, respectively.

As these tables show, Edwards arithmetic is a fair bit slower than Montgomery arithmetic. Large-degree isogenies with base degree 2 or 3 appear to be 2–3 times slower and base degree 4 isogenies are about 10 times slower when comparing Edwards to Montgomery. Interestingly, isogenies of degree 3 appear to be more efficient than isogenies of degree 2 for Edwards curves.

Table 2. Affine isogeny formulas vs. projective isogenies formulas. For the first column, the isogeny computations follow the form: $2P$ for point doubling, 2coef for finding a new isogenous curve of degree 2, and 2pt for pushing an point through an isogeny of degree 2. For this work's columns, the first column is for projective Edwards coordinates and the second column is for completed Edwards coordinates.

Iso. Comp.	Affine Mont. [14]	Proj. Mont. [12]	Affine Ed. (this work)	
			Proj.	Complete
$2P$	$3M + 2S$	-	$3M + 4S$	$5M + 4S + C$
2coef	$I + 4M + S + C$	-	$I + 7M$	$I + 7M$
2pt	$2M + 1S$	-	$24M + 3S$	$23M + 2S$
$3P$	$7M + 4S$	$7M + 5S$	$13M + 5S + C$	-
3coef	$I + 4M + S + C$	$2M + 3S$	$2M + 4S$	-
3pt	$4M + 2S$	$4M + 2S$	$13M + 9S$	-
$4P$	$6M + 4S$	$8M + 4S$	$6M + 8S$	$10M + 8S + 2C$
4coef	$I + 2M + C$	$4S$	$R + I + S$	$R + I + S$
4pt	$6M + S$	$6M + 2S$	-	$34M$

Table 3. Normalized complexities for a large-degree isogeny computation for different coordinate schemes. We found the total cost of a large-degree isogeny for the formulas in Table 2 over isogenies with base 2, 3, and 4. We then converted these costs from quadratic extension field arithmetic to the number of multiplications in the base prime field for easy comparison. Notably, we assumed that SIDH arithmetic is in $\mathbb{F}_{p^2}$ with irreducible modulus $x^2 + 1$ (as is the case in known implementations) for efficient computations. These are the total number of $\mathbb{F}_p$ multiplications ($\tilde{M}$), where $\mathbb{F}_{p^2}$ operations are converted as follows: $R = 22\lceil \log_2 p \rceil \tilde{M}$, $I = 10\tilde{M}$, $M = 3\tilde{M}$, $S = 2\tilde{M}$, and $C = 2\tilde{M}$. We assumed an inversion was performed with extended Euclidean algorithm and the square root required two large exponentiations.

Large-degree isogeny	Affine Mont. [14]	Proj. Mont. [12]	Affine Ed. (this work)	
			Proj.	Complete
2^{250}	$27102\tilde{M}$	-	$87685\tilde{M}$	$97841\tilde{M}$
3^{159}	$29686\tilde{M}$	$28452\tilde{M}$	$65355\tilde{M}$	-
4^{125}	$22617\tilde{M}$	$24126\tilde{M}$	$181582\tilde{M}$	$191278\tilde{M}$
2^{372}	$42516\tilde{M}$	-	$140454\tilde{M}$	$155450\tilde{M}$
3^{239}	$47650\tilde{M}$	$45864\tilde{M}$	$105469\tilde{M}$	-
4^{186}	$36118\tilde{M}$	$38842\tilde{M}$	$385756\tilde{M}$	$384732\tilde{M}$

5 Conclusions and Future Work

In this paper, we investigated employing Edwards curve for the supersingular isogeny Diffie-Hellman key exchange protocol and provided the required arithmetic and complexity analyses. Edward curves are attractive in the sense that they provide extra security benefits by having complete and unified addition formulae, which are not offered by Weierstrass and Montgomery forms.

Furthermore, we have seen that there are simple and elegant odd isogenies for Edwards curves. We note that an EdSIDH protocol with two odd primes would preserve a non-square curve coefficient and the completeness of the (simple) curve E_d for every isogeny computation. Because of this and the simple and fast formulas for odd isogenies presented, we suggest that Edwards curves would be a good choice for an odd-primes only implementation of SIDH.

Moving forward, we encourage cryptographic implementers to further investigate the performance of EdSIDH proposed in this paper for a fair and proper comparison to their counterparts. Integration of these formulas into SIKE [18] and static-static SIDH-like schemes [3] could also be interesting. Lastly, we will be following advances in side-channel attacks on isogeny-based schemes, such as those proposed in [20,21], to see if our scheme will provide additional defense against such methods.

Acknowledgement. The authors would like to thank the reviewers for their comments. This work is supported in parts by awards NIST 60NANB16D246, NIST 60NANB17D184, and NSF CNS-1801341. Also, this research was undertaken thanks in part to funding from the Canada First Research Excellence Fund, Natural Sciences and Engineering Research Council of Canada, CryptoWorks21, Public Works and Government Services Canada, and the Royal Bank of Canada.

References

1. Azarderakhsh, R., Fishbein, D., Jao, D.: Efficient implementations of a quantum-resistant key-exchange protocol on embedded systems. Technical report (2014)
2. Azarderakhsh, R., Jao, D., Kalach, K., Koziel, B., Leonardi, C.: Key compression for isogeny-based cryptosystems. In: Proceedings of the 3rd ACM International Workshop on ASIA Public-Key Cryptography, AsiaPKC 2016, pp. 1–10. ACM, New York (2016)
3. Azarderakhsh, R., Jao, D., Leonardi, C.: Post-quantum static-static key agreement using multiple protocol instances. In: Adams, C., Camenisch, J. (eds.) SAC 2017. LNCS, vol. 10719, pp. 45–63. Springer, Cham (2018). https://doi.org/10.1007/978-3-319-72565-9_3
4. Bernstein, D.J., Birkner, P., Joye, M., Lange, T., Peters, C.: Twisted Edwards curves. In: Vaudenay, S. (ed.) AFRICACRYPT 2008. LNCS, vol. 5023, pp. 389–405. Springer, Heidelberg (2008). https://doi.org/10.1007/978-3-540-68164-9_26
5. Bernstein, D.J., Birkner, P., Lange, T., Peters, C.: ECM using Edwards curves. Math. Comp. **82**(282), 1139–1179 (2013)
6. Bernstein, D.J., Lange, T.: Faster addition and doubling on elliptic curves. In: Kurosawa, K. (ed.) ASIACRYPT 2007. LNCS, vol. 4833, pp. 29–50. Springer, Heidelberg (2007). https://doi.org/10.1007/978-3-540-76900-2_3
7. Bernstein, D.J., Lange, T.: A complete set of addition laws for incomplete Edwards curves. J. Number Theory **131**(5), 858–872 (2011). Elliptic Curve Cryptography
8. Charles, D., Lauter, K., Goren, E.: Cryptographic hash functions from expander graphs. J. Cryptol. **22**(1), 93–113 (2009)
9. Chen, L., et al.: Report on post-quantum cryptography. Technical report, National Institute of Standards and Technology (NIST) (2016)
10. Costache, A., Feigon, B., Lauter, K., Massierer, M., Puskas, A.: Ramanujan graphs in cryptography. Cryptology ePrint Archive, Report 2018/593 (2018)
11. Costello, C., Longa, P., Naehrig, M.: Efficient algorithms for supersingular isogeny Diffie-Hellman. In: Robshaw, M., Katz, J. (eds.) CRYPTO 2016. LNCS, vol. 9814, pp. 572–601. Springer, Heidelberg (2016). https://doi.org/10.1007/978-3-662-53018-4_21
12. Costello, C., Hisil, H.: A simple and compact algorithm for SIDH with arbitrary degree isogenies. In: Takagi, T., Peyrin, T. (eds.) ASIACRYPT 2017. LNCS, vol. 10625, pp. 303–329. Springer, Cham (2017). https://doi.org/10.1007/978-3-319-70697-9_11
13. Costello, C., Jao, D., Longa, P., Naehrig, M., Renes, J., Urbanik, D.: Efficient compression of SIDH public keys. In: Coron, J.-S., Nielsen, J.B. (eds.) EUROCRYPT 2017. LNCS, vol. 10210, pp. 679–706. Springer, Cham (2017). https://doi.org/10.1007/978-3-319-56620-7_24
14. De Feo, L., Jao, D., Plût, J.: Towards quantum-resistant cryptosystems from supersingular elliptic curve isogenies. J. Math. Cryptol. **8**(3), 209–247 (2014)
15. Edwards, H.M.: A normal form for elliptic curves. In: Bulletin of the American Mathematical Society, pp. 393–422 (2007)
16. Faz-Hernández, A., López, J., Ochoa-Jiménez, E., Rodríguez-Henríquez, F.: A faster software implementation of the supersingular isogeny Diffie-Hellman key exchange protocol. IEEE Trans. Comput. (2018, to appear)

17. Jalali, A., Azarderakhsh, R., Mozaffari-Kermani, M., Jao, D.: Supersingular isogeny Diffie-Hellman key exchange on 64-bit ARM. IEEE Trans. Dependable Secur. Comput. I: Regul. Pap. (2017)
18. Jao, D., et al.: Supersingular isogeny key encapsulation. Submission to the NIST Post-Quantum Standardization Project (2017)
19. Kim, S., Yoon, K., Kwon, J., Hong, S., Park, Y.-H.: Efficient isogeny computations on twisted Edwards curves. Secur. Commun. Netw. (2018)
20. Koziel, B., Azarderakhsh, R., Jao, D.: An exposure model for supersingular isogeny Diffie-Hellman key exchange. In: Smart, N.P. (ed.) CT-RSA 2018. LNCS, vol. 10808, pp. 452–469. Springer, Cham (2018). https://doi.org/10.1007/978-3-319-76953-0_24
21. Koziel, B., Azarderakhsh, R., Jao, D.: Side-channel attacks on quantum-resistant supersingular isogeny Diffie-Hellman. In: Adams, C., Camenisch, J. (eds.) SAC 2017. LNCS, vol. 10719, pp. 64–81. Springer, Cham (2018). https://doi.org/10.1007/978-3-319-72565-9_4
22. Koziel, B., Azarderakhsh, R., Jao, D., Mozaffari-Kermani, M.: On fast calculation of addition chains for isogeny-based cryptography. In: Chen, K., Lin, D., Yung, M. (eds.) Inscrypt 2016. LNCS, vol. 10143, pp. 323–342. Springer, Cham (2017). https://doi.org/10.1007/978-3-319-54705-3_20
23. Koziel, B., Azarderakhsh, R., Mozaffari-Kermani, M.: Fast hardware architectures for supersingular isogeny Diffie-Hellman key exchange on FPGA. In: Dunkelman, O., Sanadhya, S.K. (eds.) INDOCRYPT 2016. LNCS, vol. 10095, pp. 191–206. Springer, Cham (2016). https://doi.org/10.1007/978-3-319-49890-4_11
24. Koziel, B., Azarderakhsh, R., Mozaffari-Kermani, M.: A high-performance and scalable hardware architecture for isogeny-based cryptography. IEEE Trans. Comput. **PP**(99), 1 (2018)
25. Koziel, B., Azarderakhsh, R., Mozaffari-Kermani, M., Jao, D.: Post-quantum cryptography on FPGA based on isogenies on elliptic curves. IEEE Trans. Circ. Syst. I: Regul. Pap. **64**, 86–99 (2017)
26. Koziel, B., Jalali, A., Azarderakhsh, R., Jao, D., Mozaffari-Kermani, M.: NEON-SIDH: efficient implementation of supersingular isogeny Diffie-Hellman key exchange protocol on ARM. In: Foresti, S., Persiano, G. (eds.) CANS 2016. LNCS, vol. 10052, pp. 88–103. Springer, Cham (2016). https://doi.org/10.1007/978-3-319-48965-0_6
27. Meyer, M., Reith, S., Campos, F.: On hybrid SIDH schemes using Edwards and Montgomery curve arithmetic. Cryptology ePrint Archive, Report 2017/1213 (2017)
28. Montgomery, P.L.: Speeding the Pollard and elliptic curve methods of factorization. Math. Comput. **48**, 243–264 (1987)
29. Moody, D., Shumow, D.: Analogues of Vélu's formulas for isogenies on alternate models of elliptic curves. Math. Comp. **85**(300), 1929–1951 (2016)
30. Valyukh, V.: Performance and comparison of post-quantum cryptographic algorithms. Master's thesis, Linkoping University (2017)
31. Vélu, J.: Isogénies entre courbes elliptiques. C. R. Acad. Sci. Paris Sér. A-B **273**, A238–A241 (1971)
32. Yoo, Y., Azarderakhsh, R., Jalali, A., Jao, D., Soukharev, V.: A post-quantum digital signature scheme based on supersingular isogenies. In: Kiayias, A. (ed.) FC 2017. LNCS, vol. 10322, pp. 163–181. Springer, Cham (2017). https://doi.org/10.1007/978-3-319-70972-7_9

Correlation Power Analysis on KASUMI: Attack and Countermeasure

Devansh Gupta[1]($\boxtimes$), Somanath Tripathy[1], and Bodhisatwa Mazumdar[2]

[1] Indian Institute of Technology Patna, Patna 801106, India
devanshguptaa@gmail.com, som@iitp.ac.in
[2] Indian Institute of Technology Indore, Indore, India
bodhisatwa@iiti.ac.in

Abstract. The KASUMI block cipher imparts confidentiality and integrity to the 3G mobile communication systems. In this paper we present power analysis attack on KASUMI as a two-pronged attack: first the FL function is targeted, and subsequently the recovered output of FL function is used to mount attack on 7×7 and 9×9 S-boxes embedded in the FO function of the cipher. Our attack recovers all 128 bits of the secret key of KASUMI. Further, we present a countermeasure for this attack which requires lesser resource footprint as compared to existing countermeasures, rendering such implementations practically feasible for resource-constrained applications, such as IoT and RFID devices.

Keywords: Side channel attack · Power analysis attack
Correlation power analysis · KASUMI block cipher

1 Introduction

Mobile Phones are very popular nowadays and have become a crucial part of our everyday life. In some applications, they complement traditional computing devices, such as laptops. Due to this massive popularity of mobile devices, security in mobile communication is very important. In this respect, the 3rd generation partnership project (3GPP) based technologies have been constantly evolving through generations of commercial cellular or mobile systems. Since the completion of long-term evolution (LTE), 3GPP has become focal point for mobile systems beyond 3G. To ensure data confidentiality and data integrity of the users in 3GPP technology [25] a 64-bit block cipher called KASUMI [15] is used. Therefore, security of a 3GPP based mobile network depends on the security of the underlying KASUMI block cipher. Further, security of GSM (Global System for Mobile Communications) and the second generation (2G) mobile cellular system relies on A5/3, which is also based on KASUMI block cipher.

In existing literature, the modes of operation in KASUMI are provably secure if KASUMI is a pseudorandom permutation (PRP) and it is also secured in differential-based related key attacks [10]. Meanwhile, an impossible differential attack [13] and a related key differential attack was performed on a 6-round

© Springer Nature Switzerland AG 2018
A. Chattopadhyay et al. (Eds.): SPACE 2018, LNCS 11348, pp. 142–156, 2018.
https://doi.org/10.1007/978-3-030-05072-6_9

version of KASUMI [5]. Also, a related key rectangle attack on an entire 8-round version of KASUMI is demonstrated in [3]. The attack required $2^{54.6}$ chosen plaintexts encrypted with four related keys, and has time complexity of $2^{76.1}$ encryptions. Further, a related key boomerang distinguisher was also presented. This result showed that the strength of KASUMI against classical cryptanalysis attacks is crucial to the security of the mobile data transfer between the mobile device and the base station that may render attacks such as channel hijack attacks. All these attacks comprise classical cryptanalysis where the attackers perform a theoretical security analysis of the underlying cryptographic primitive.

A cryptographic system is assumed to be a perfect black box; an attacker gains no extra information apart from the plaintext and ciphertext during a cryptographic operation. However, whenever a cryptographic algorithm is implemented in hardware, information about the embedded secret key of the device is leaked through physical side-channels. A side-channel may be in terms of power consumption of the device, temperature variance or time taken to run the algorithm. If this information is related to the secret key then it can be exploited to perform attack on the algorithm.

Power Analysis attack [12] is a form of side channel attack [26] introduced by Kocher, Jaffe and Jun. It relies on the fact that different operations incur different power consumption depending on the data on which the operation is being performed. The power analysis attack assumes that the power consumed by a device is related to the intermediate values in the algorithm. Hence if the intermediate values have a relation to the secret key then this fact can be exploited to obtain the secret key. Another power analysis attack model was introduced named Correlation Power Analysis attack [6] in which a power consumption model is created for the encryption process and then the predicted power is correlated to the actual power and the highest peak of correlation plot gives the correct key. Correlation power analysis (CPA) attack works in the following way:

- For a uniformly random set of plaintexts or ciphertexts, obtain the corresponding power traces.
- Select the intermediate value (the intermediate value is a function of the secret key embedded in the device and input plaintext or round input) of the algorithm's output to attack.
- Guess a subkey and find the intermediate value according to the subkey.
- Model the power consumption for the subkey depending on the intermediate value of a round, and compute the correlation of the power consumption from the model with that of the original trace.
- The subkey yielding the highest correlation value is the correct subkey.

The existing literature is populated with countermeasures [7,8,16,20] against power analysis attacks. However, most of them focused on AES depicting that its software and hardware implementations are vulnerable against power analysis attacks. Subsequently, multiple countermeasures were proposed against these attacks, and later broken.

This paper aims to perform the CPA attack on KASUMI block cipher. To the best of our knowledge, security vulnerabilities of implementation of KASUMI based on power analysis attacks, has been scarcely examined, and that too on idealized hardware model without noise, thereby leading to ideal power traces [14]. Such a noise-independent hardware implementation are very expensive to meet in practice. Our proposed attack can recover the complete key by exploiting a weakness in the key scheduling algorithm of KASUMI. Further, we propose an efficient countermeasure technique to mitigate such attacks using minimal additional hardware resources.

The rest of the work is organized as follows. Next section discusses precisely the existing work. The block cipher KASUMI is briefly discussed in Sect. 4. Section 5 discusses the proposed attack technique and we present the mitigation technique in Sect. 6. Section 7 discusses the effectiveness of the proposed attack and mitigation approach. Finally, the conclusion is drawn in Sect. 8.

2   Related Works

In literature, lightweight hardware implementations of KASUMI block cipher exist that apply to standard architectures such as 3GPP [22]. The KASUMI block cipher has been analyzed with respect to classical cryptanalysis attacks such as related key attacks [17]. In A5/3 algorithm, the KASUMI block cipher employs a 64-bit session key, wherein multiple related key attacks that failed for larger versions of KASUMI block cipher, are found effective in yielding information about the round keys. Further, impossible differential attacks were mounted on the last 7 rounds of KASUMI for 128-bit session key [11]. Moreover, higher order differential attacks on KASUMI has also been examined [23] that employs linearizing attack on a reduced 5-round KASUMI block cipher.

In existing literature, Differential fault analysis attack (DFA) [25] has been proposed on KASUMI. The DFA attack [25] states that only one 16-bit word fault is enough for a successful key recovery attack. However, there are limited analysis of resilience of KASUMI against power analysis attacks. The power analysis attack has so long been emphasized on Advanced Encryption Standard (AES), and many countermeasures [7,8,16,20] have been proposed for power analysis attacks on this cipher. All proposed countermeasures attempt to mitigate the relation between the key and power consumed. Such countermeasures can be applied to KASUMI as well. Masking is one of the most commonly used countermeasure against power analysis attack.

Masking [4] involves hiding the intermediate value with some other random value. It is of two types: boolean and arithmetic. In boolean masking the intermediate value is XORed with the random mask whereas in arithmetic masking the random value is modulo added or multiplied to the intermediate value. In this way the intermediate value appears independent of the data and power traces cannot be correlated to the secret key.

In **first order countermeasure** a randomized mask value can prevent the information leakage of the secret key in the power traces. The mask can randomize the intermediate data values on algorithmic level [1,7], at gate implementation level [9,24], or a combination of circuit implementation approaches [19].

When implemented, masking is a very slow operation. Some commonly used masking schemes are S-box masking and High Order Masking. S-box masking involves hiding the S-box operations. Masking S-box is difficult due to its high nonlinearity and all masked values must eventually be unmasked to restore the correct ciphertext. It is also a very slow operation reducing the speed of the system by at least half. Rotating S-box masking [16] is one of the methods of S-box masking. This scheme [16] uses Rotating Masked S-boxes. Fixed numbers of precomputed constant masks are used and customized S-Boxes are used which get a masked input. The S-Box unmasks the input and then performs the sub-bytes operation and re-masks the output with another constant for the next round. But the S-boxes are stored in RAM/ROM to prevent information leakage in logic gates. High order masking [21] involves using higher number of masks per key-dependent variable. This prevents higher order DPA which extracts the information of the intermediate values by comparing the intermediate values that share the same mask. But due to a large number of masks the complexity of using high order masking is very high.

3   Power Analysis Attack

3.1   Differential Power Analysis Attack

Differential power analysis attack [18] (DPA) uses statistical analysis to guess the secret key. The steps of DPA attack are as follows:

- Selection function $D(C, b, K_s)$ computes value of target bit b, given ciphertext C and subkey guess K_s. It depends on the function that computes the targeted intermediate value.
- m power traces are collected of k samples each namely $T_{1:m}[1 : k]$ along with the corresponding ciphertext values $C_{1:m}$.
- The power traces are then sorted into two groups corresponding to the value of $D(C, b, K_s)$ is 0 or 1.
- The average of the two sets are taken namely $P(1)$ and $P(0)$.
- The difference between $P(0)$ and $P(1)$ is taken and let it be called as ΔD.
- If the key guess was correct then ΔD shall contain spikes in the region where the correct operation is performed, else the trace of ΔD shall have no spikes with amplitude values close to zero.

3.2   Correlation Power Analysis Attack

Correlation power analysis attack [20] is an extension of DPA attack, in which, a model of power consumption is created in the analysis phase. Then power consumption is predicted using the model created. The correlation is found between the observed power trace and predicted trace. The highest peak of the correlation plot gives the correct key hypothesis. In AES, CPA is performed for each of the 16 bytes of the key. The models for power consumption can be one of the following:

- *Hamming Weight Model*: This model assumes that the power consumed is proportional to the number of bits that are logic 1 during the operation.
- *Hamming Distance Model*: It assumes that the power consumption is due to the logic transition of bits. Precisely, if a bit is 0 or 1 during the whole operation, it does not contribute to the power, but if the bit changes from 0 to 1 or from 1 to 0, it consumes the same power.

The steps of CPA are as follows:

- Power traces are collected for the encryption along with the corresponding plaintexts or ciphertexts.
- A power consumption model is assumed.
- A key byte is guessed and the intermediate value to be attacked is calculated using the guessed key.
- Hamming weight of the intermediate value is calculated and power is predicted.
- Correlation is calculated for the predicted power and actual power consumed.
- The highest correlation peak gives the correct key.

The correlation factor is calculated using the below formula:

$$\rho_{WH}(R) = \frac{N \sum W_i H_{i,R} - \sum W_i \sum H_{i,R}}{\sqrt{N \sum W_i^2 - (\sum W_i)^2}\sqrt{N \sum H_{i,R}^2 - (\sum H_{i,R})^2}}$$

In the formula, N is the number of power traces, W_i is the power consumed at time i and $H_{i,R}$ is the predicted Hamming Distance at time i.

4   KASUMI Block Cipher

KASUMI is an eight round block cipher with 128 bit key; the input and output comprise 64 bits each. The complete structure of KASUMI is shown in Fig. 1. Each round uses eight 16-bit sub keys derived from original key using key scheduling algorithm. Also, each round has two functions, namely, FL and FO. In even numbered rounds FO precedes FL, while FL precedes FO in odd numbered rounds. FL and FO both take a 32-bit input and provide the corresponding 32-bit output.

This work uses the following notations. L and R are 32-bit inputs (each) to the first round. XL is the input to FL function. KL is the key used in FL function. The input to FO is denoted as XO. $XO_{i,l}$ and $XO_{i,r}$ ($1 \leq i \leq 8$) represent the left and right 16 bits of XO in round i, respectively. KO denotes the key used in FO function. $XI_{i,j}$ denotes the input to the FI function in j^{th} subround of FO function, which is present in the ith round of KASUMI. KI denotes the key used in FI function. S_9 and S_7 denotes the 9×9 and 7×7 S-boxes, respectively.

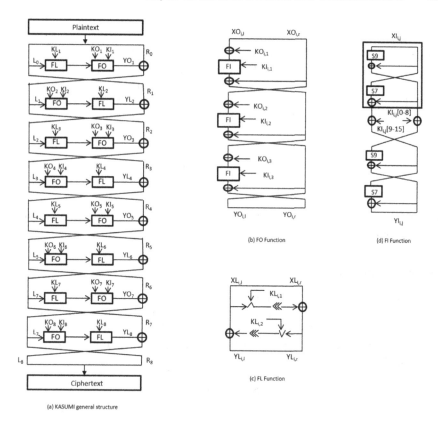

(a) KASUMI general structure

Fig. 1. KASUMI structure; the odd numbered rounds comprise FL function followed by FO function, while the even numbered rounds comprise FO function followed by FL function. In functions FL, FO, and FI, the indices i and j in round keys $KL_{i,j}$, $KO_{i,j}$, and $KI_{i,j}$ indicate the round number and subround number, respectively.

4.1 Function FL

Figure 1(c) shows the FL function which takes a 32 bit input XL that is divided into two 16 bit halves, $XL_{i,l}$ and $XL_{i,r}$. Subscript i denotes the ith round, i.e., $(1 \leq i \leq 8)$. The output of FL function is $YL_{i,l}$ and $YL_{i,r}$. $YL_{i,l}$ and $YL_{i,r}$ are derived as follows:

$$YL_{i,r} = ((XL_{i,l} \wedge KL_{i,1}) \lll 1) \oplus XL_{i,r}.$$
$$YL_{i,l} = ((YL_{i,r} \vee KL_{i,2}) \lll 1) \oplus XL_{i,l}.$$

where, $\wedge$ denotes bitwise AND and $\vee$ denotes bitwise OR. Also $a \lll b$ denoted a rotated left by b bits. Now the output YL from FL function goes as input to the FO function.

4.2 Function FO

The structure of the FO function is shown in Fig. 1(b). FO comprises 3 rounds, each round has an FI function. FO takes a 32 bit input, XO. The input is divided into two 16-bit halves, $XO_{i,l}$ and $XO_{i,r}$. The subscript i denotes the ith round. Let l_j and r_j denote the left and right output to the jth round of FO function. These outputs of FO are calculated as follows:

$$l_0 = XO_{i,l}, r_0 = XO_{i,r}$$
$$r_j = FI(KI_{i,j}, l_{j-1} \oplus KO_{i,j}) \oplus r_{j-1}$$
$$l_j = r_{j-1}$$

The output of the FO function is denoted by YO. $YO = l_3 \parallel r_3$, where $\parallel$ denotes concatenation.

4.3 Function FI

Figure 1(d) shows the function FI. The input comprises 32-bit, $XI_{i,j}$. The FI function performs two S-box operations, which comprises a 9×9 S-box, $S9$, and a 7×7 S-box, $S7$. Let the input to FI function be denoted as l_0 and r_0. l_0 represents the most significant 9 bits of $XI_{i,j}$ and r_0 represents the least significant 7 bits of $XI_{i,j}$. The next r_1 and l_1 are calculated as follows:

$$r_1 = S9(l_0) \oplus (00 \parallel r_0)$$
$$l_1 = S7(l_0) \oplus r_1[6:0]$$

where, $r_1[6:0]$ indicates seven least significant bits of r_1. Subsequently, r_1 and l_1 are XORed with KI to get the values of l_2 and r_2, which will be further input to S-boxes.

$$l_2 = r_1 \oplus KI_{i,j}^{0-8}$$
$$r_2 = l_1 \oplus KI_{i,j}^{9-15}$$

Finally the final output l_3 and r_3 are computed as follows:

$$r_3 = S9(l_2) \oplus (00 \parallel l_2)$$
$$l_3 = S7(l_2) \oplus r_3[6:0]$$

where $r_3[6:0]$ denotes seven least significant bits of r_3. The final output $YI_{i,j}$ is $l_3 \parallel r_3$.

4.4 Key Scheduling

KASUMI uses 128 bit key denoted by K, which is subdivided into eight 16-bit subkeys K_i. Another key is used in KASUMI known as K', which is derived by $K \oplus 0x0123456789ABCDEFFEDCBA9876543210$. Each round has 8 round

Table 1. KASUMI key scheduling

Round	$KL_{i,1}$	$KL_{i,2}$	$KO_{i,1}$	$KO_{i,2}$	$KO_{i,3}$	$KI_{i,1}$	$KI_{i,3}$	$KI_{i,3}$
1	$k_1 \lll 1$	k'_3	$k_2 \lll 5$	$k_6 \lll 8$	$k_7 \lll 13$	k'_5	k'_4	k'_8
2	$k_2 \lll 1$	k'_4	$k_3 \lll 5$	$k_7 \lll 8$	$k_8 \lll 13$	k'_6	k'_5	k'_1
3	$k_3 \lll 1$	k'_5	$k_4 \lll 5$	$k_8 \lll 8$	$k_1 \lll 13$	k'_7	k'_6	k'_2
4	$k_4 \lll 1$	k'_6	$k_5 \lll 5$	$k_1 \lll 8$	$k_2 \lll 13$	k'_8	k'_7	k'_3
5	$k_5 \lll 1$	k'_7	$k_6 \lll 5$	$k_2 \lll 8$	$k_3 \lll 13$	k'_1	k'_8	k'_4
6	$k_6 \lll 1$	k'_8	$k_7 \lll 5$	$k_3 \lll 8$	$k_4 \lll 13$	k'_2	k'_1	k'_5
7	$k_7 \lll 1$	k'_1	$k_8 \lll 5$	$k_4 \lll 8$	$k_5 \lll 13$	k'_3	k'_2	k'_6
8	$k_8 \lll 1$	k'_2	$k_1 \lll 5$	$k_5 \lll 8$	$k_6 \lll 13$	k'_4	k'_3	k'_7

keys. The round keys are labeled as $KL_{i,1}$, $KL_{i,2}$, $KO_{i,1}$, $KO_{i,2}$, $KO_{i,3}$, $KI_{i,1}$, $KI_{i,2}$ and $KI_{i,3}$. The round keys are derived using key scheduling algorithm as shown in Table 1. k_i denotes the ith 16-bit subkey derived from K, and k'_i denotes the ith 16-bit subkey derived from K'. In this notation, $a \lll b$ denotes a rotated left by b bits and $a \oplus b$ denotes bitwise XOR operation between a and b.

5   Proposed Power Analysis Attack on KASUMI

In this section, we present the proposed attack against KASUMI to recover the round keys, which can be subsequently used to obtain the secret key due to the weak key scheduling of KASUMI.

5.1   Overview of the Attack

The main goal of this attack is to obtain all the 8 subkeys, by exploiting the S-box operation of KASUMI in FO function, i.e., the key values of $KI_{i,j}$ and $KO_{i,j}$, that are derived from $k_1, \ldots, k_8$, and $k'_1, \ldots, k'_8$ in Table 1. However, k'_i, $1 \leq i \leq 8$, can be obtained from k_i from the following set of equations:

$$k'_1 = k_1 \oplus 0x0123$$
$$k'_2 = k_2 \oplus 0x4567$$
$$k'_3 = k_3 \oplus 0x89AB$$
$$k'_4 = k_4 \oplus 0xCDEF$$
$$k'_5 = k_5 \oplus 0xFEDC$$
$$k'_6 = k_6 \oplus 0xBA98$$
$$k'_7 = k_7 \oplus 0x7654$$
$$k'_8 = k_8 \oplus 0x3210$$

So, a power-based side-channel adversary targets the key bytes, k_1, k_2, ..., k_8, only. We observe that one can obtain these key bytes by attacking the first round FO function. However, mounting power analysis attack on the first round FO function requires the input to the FO function. From Fig. 1, the input to the first round FO function is the output of the first round FL function. The side-channel adversary can select the plaintext as input to the first round FL function. By recovering KL_1, he can obtain the output of the FL function. Further, he can use this output to attack the corresponding FO function and get the above-mentioned subkeys. Therefore, our proposed attack executes as follows:

Step 1: Sub keys k_1 and k_3 are first obtained by attacking the FO function in the last round of KASUMI. The input to the FO function in last round is the least significant 32 bits of ciphertext.

Step 2: KL for the first round is calculated using the subkeys k_1 and k_3 obtained in Step 1.

Step 3: Since L is known (as it is the plaintext), and from the value of KL calculated in the previous step, the output of FL function is computed. The output of FL function is XO.

Step 4: Now the XO from the previous step is used to mount an attack the FO function in the first round to obtain all the remaining subkeys.

Step 5: Finally, all the extracted subkeys are combined to obtain the secret key.

5.2   Extracting Subkeys of First Round FL

We know that the input to the first round FL function is the plaintext. Now the key used in the first round FL function is KL_1. KL_1 is derived from k_1 and k_3. So we need to somehow obtain the subkeys k_1 and k_3. If we successfully get the keys we can get the output of the FL function and mount an attack on the first round FO function.

Again from the KASUMI structure, we can observe that the last round FO function involves the subkeys k_1 and k_3, which are precisely the subkeys that we want to recover. As mentioned earlier, we can attack the S-box in the FO function to obtain the corresponding subkeys. Hence we need to attack the last round FO function to obtain the subkeys k_1 and k_3 to perform the attack mentioned in Subsect. 3.2.1 and obtain all the other subkeys.

5.3   Attacking the Last Round FO Function

The input to the last round FO function is the ciphertext. Using this input we will perform the power analysis attack on the last round FO function as mentioned below to obtain the subkeys k_1 and k_3.

The following are the steps to mount an attack on FO function in the last round. The input to the last round FO function (XO_8) is least significant 32 bits of ciphertext. The following steps are adopted to mount attack on any FO function.

Step 1: The 16-bit left part of XO is computed and denoted as $XO_{8,l}$.

Step 2: All 2^9 combinations are guessed for the first 9 bits of $KO_{8,1}$. Each of the 9-bit key value is XORed with the first 9 bits of $XO_{8,l}$. The output after XOR is denoted as XI_{l9} (In this notation, 9 in $l9$ denotes the first 9 bits of XI_l). Subsequently, the output of S_9 for each XI_{l9} is computed, and the Hamming weight model based correlation power analysis attack is computed on this output. The 9-bit key value which gives the highest correlation is considered to be the correct first 9 bits of $KO_{8,1}$. This step is again repeated for the last 7 bits of $XO_{8,l}$ to get the last 7 bits of $KO_{8,1}$.

Step 3: After obtaining the correct value of $KO_{8,1}$ from the previous attack, the correct value of $XI_{8,1}$ is computed. From this value of $XI_{8,1}$, step 2 is repeated to mount an attack on the second S_9 and S_7 of the FI function to get the correct key bits of $KI_{8,1}$.

Step 4: Steps 2 and 3 are repeated to get the correct key bit values of $KO_{8,2}$, $KI_{8,2}$, $KO_{8,3}$ and $KI_{8,3}$.

5.4   Simulation

We used *OpenSCA* simulator for mounting the power analysis attack [18]. The code of KASUMI was taken from GitHub [2]. We implemented the attack in MATLAB using the steps mentioned in the previous subsection. Subsequently, we used the simulator for mounting the correlation power analysis attack using our algorithm. We simulated our attack 100 times. In each attack, a random key was generated and 50 random plaintexts were encrypted with the session key. We obtained the entire 128 bits of the key on all the mounted attacks.

From Fig. 2, the peak of the correlation trace can be observed at around 220 time units with correlation value of 1.0. This shows that $KI_{1,3}^{9-15}$ is being used at around 220 time units. But after applying proposed countermeasure we can observe in Fig. 4 that for the same correct subkey, at around the same time when

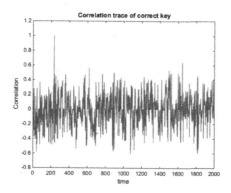

Fig. 2. Correlation trace of correct subkey ($KI_{1,3}^{9-15}$) guessed without any countermeasure

$KI_{1,3}^{9-15}$ is being actually used (at approximately 220 time units) the correlation value is around 0.4 that is masked by several higher ghost peaks at subsequent time instances. Due to this occurrence of multiple peaks, the attack cannot guess the correct subkey after applying the proposed countermeasure.

6   Proposed Countermeasure

We present an approach to counter the power analysis attack on KASUMI. The countermeasure hides the power consumption information in the S-box operation and masks the relation between the power consumption in S-box operation and the involved sub key. For this purpose we propose that a new S-box be created before the encryption and decryption operation. As shown in Fig. 3, let S' denote the new S-box, which is generated with random values.

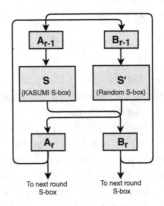

Fig. 3. Random S-box S' as a countermeasure against CPA attack.

There will be two new randomly generated S-boxes for each encryption operation, one will be a 9×18 S-box and the other is a 7×14 S-box. Let the input to the S-box be stored in register A. We use one more register (register B) which stores a dummy value. Henceforth, the following two S-box operations will be performed simultaneously (in parallel) to hide the power consumption information. The content of register B will be given as input to S' and the content of register A will be given as input to original S-box S. The output of S is stored in B, whereas the output of S' is stored in A. Contents of A and B will be interchanged later to allow the normal flow of the algorithm. In this way the power consumed is not correlated to the operation of S-box S and the intermediate data processed by S. Also the new S-Box S' is generated for each new plaintext or ciphertext. Hence, the power consumption and the embedded key are not linearly correlated anymore due to the randomness of S' for each encryption or decryption, which mitigates the attack efficiency.

6.1 Simulation

To simulate the parallel execution of the S-box operation as proposed in our scheme, we used new S-boxes with same input width but double output width. The 9 × 9 S-box was changed to 9 × 18 bit S-box where the most significant 9 bits were the 9 bits of the original S-box and the least significant 9 bits are the randomly generated 9 bits for each encryption or decryption. Similarly the 7 × 7 S-box was transformed into a 7 × 14 S-box, which follows the same scheme as the 9 × 18 S-box, i.e., the most significant 7 bits were the 7 bits of the original S_7 S-box and the least significant 7 bits were randomly generated 7 bits for each encryption or decryption. The input to the new S_9 is 9 bit and the output is of 18 bits. The most significant 9 bits are then stored in another variable, which will be used later for all other operations of KASUMI. Similarly the input to the new S_7 S-box is of 7 bits and the output has 14 bits. The most significant 7 bits are then stored in some other variable of 7 bits which will be used to perform remaining steps of KASUMI. We implemented the proposed countermeasure and simulated the correlation power analysis attack 100 times. In each attack, a random key was generated and 100 random plaintexts were encrypted with the session key. We could not recover any of the sub-key correctly. Hence the proposed countermeasure was successful in mitigating the power analysis attack.

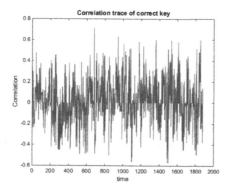

Fig. 4. Correlation trace of correct subkey $(KI_{1,3}^{9-15})$ guessed with proposed countermeasure

7 Discussion

On performing the attack on KASUMI we extracted all 128 bits of the key. The result of the correlation trace for correct $KI_{1,3}^{9-15}$ is shown in Fig. 2. As can be observed from Fig. 2, the maximum correlation is 1.000 for 7 × 7 S-box. This shows that the correct key can be easily recovered by performing CPA on unmasked KASUMI (Fig. 5).

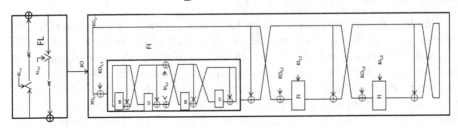

Fig. 5. Odd round of KASUMI

After implementing our proposed scheme, the correlation trace of $KI_{1,3}^{9-15}$ is shown in Fig. 4. This shows that the correct sub-keys cannot be identified for the countermeasure, and the correlation based power analysis attack cannot succeed against our proposed scheme.

7.1 Comparison with Masking Techniques

S-box Masking: Our proposed mitigation approach uses only two new S-boxes (a 9×18 S-box and a 7×14 S-box) for each encryption whereas if we apply the concept of rotating S-box masking then we will need a new S-box for each mask used. With increase in number of masks, the memory used in rotating S-box masking is larger as compared to the number of S-boxes used by our scheme. Hence our algorithm is more memory efficient as compared to rotating S-box masking.

High Order Masking: Due to high number of masks used in higher order masking the approach is very costly. Whereas the proposed mitigation technique needs to generate only two new random S-boxes for each encryption or decryption. Also the operation is only performed once before the start of the encryption or decryption process. Hence our scheme is cost effective as compared to higher order masking.

8 Conclusion

This paper proposes an efficient method to apply correlation power analysis attack on KASUMI. The attack successfully recovers 128-bit secret key by exploiting the simple key scheduling of KASUMI. In addition, we proposed a simple but efficient countermeasure to mitigate the correlation power analysis attack on KASUMI that yields performance improvement of many orders in resource constrained applications, such as IoTs, as compared to conventional protection techniques, such as masking and higher order masking techniques.

References

1. Akkar, M.-L., Giraud, C.: An implementation of DES and AES, secure against some attacks. In: Koç, Ç.K., Naccache, D., Paar, C. (eds.) CHES 2001. LNCS, vol. 2162, pp. 309–318. Springer, Heidelberg (2001). https://doi.org/10.1007/3-540-44709-1_26
2. ApS, N.: unabto (2015). https://github.com/nabto/unabto/blob/master/3rdparty/libtomcrypt/src/ciphers/kasumi.c
3. Biham, E., Dunkelman, O., Keller, N.: A related-key rectangle attack on the full KASUMI. In: Roy, B. (ed.) ASIACRYPT 2005. LNCS, vol. 3788, pp. 443–461. Springer, Heidelberg (2005). https://doi.org/10.1007/11593447_24
4. Blömer, J., Guajardo, J., Krummel, V.: Provably secure masking of AES. In: Handschuh, H., Hasan, M.A. (eds.) SAC 2004. LNCS, vol. 3357, pp. 69–83. Springer, Heidelberg (2004). https://doi.org/10.1007/978-3-540-30564-4_5
5. Blunden, M., Escott, A.: Related key attacks on reduced round KASUMI. In: Matsui, M. (ed.) FSE 2001. LNCS, vol. 2355, pp. 277–285. Springer, Heidelberg (2002). https://doi.org/10.1007/3-540-45473-X_23
6. Brier, E., Clavier, C., Olivier, F.: Correlation power analysis with a leakage model. In: Joye, M., Quisquater, J.-J. (eds.) CHES 2004. LNCS, vol. 3156, pp. 16–29. Springer, Heidelberg (2004). https://doi.org/10.1007/978-3-540-28632-5_2
7. Chari, S., Jutla, C.S., Rao, J.R., Rohatgi, P.: Towards sound approaches to counteract power-analysis attacks. In: Wiener, M. (ed.) CRYPTO 1999. LNCS, vol. 1666, pp. 398–412. Springer, Heidelberg (1999). https://doi.org/10.1007/3-540-48405-1_26
8. Chen, Z., Zhou, Y.: Dual-rail random switching logic: a countermeasure to reduce side channel leakage. In: Goubin, L., Matsui, M. (eds.) CHES 2006. LNCS, vol. 4249, pp. 242–254. Springer, Heidelberg (2006). https://doi.org/10.1007/11894063_20
9. Ishai, Y., Sahai, A., Wagner, D.: Private circuits: securing hardware against probing attacks. In: Boneh, D. (ed.) CRYPTO 2003. LNCS, vol. 2729, pp. 463–481. Springer, Heidelberg (2003). https://doi.org/10.1007/978-3-540-45146-4_27
10. Iwata, T., Kohno, T.: New security proofs for the 3GPP confidentiality and integrity algorithms. In: Roy, B., Meier, W. (eds.) FSE 2004. LNCS, vol. 3017, pp. 427–445. Springer, Heidelberg (2004). https://doi.org/10.1007/978-3-540-25937-4_27
11. Jia, K., Li, L., Rechberger, C., Chen, J., Wang, X.: Improved cryptanalysis of the block cipher KASUMI. In: Knudsen, L.R., Wu, H. (eds.) SAC 2012. LNCS, vol. 7707, pp. 222–233. Springer, Heidelberg (2013). https://doi.org/10.1007/978-3-642-35999-6_15
12. Kocher, P., Jaffe, J., Jun, B.: Differential power analysis. In: Wiener, M. (ed.) CRYPTO 1999. LNCS, vol. 1666, pp. 388–397. Springer, Heidelberg (1999). https://doi.org/10.1007/3-540-48405-1_25
13. Kühn, U.: Cryptanalysis of reduced-round MISTY. In: Pfitzmann, B. (ed.) EUROCRYPT 2001. LNCS, vol. 2045, pp. 325–339. Springer, Heidelberg (2001). https://doi.org/10.1007/3-540-44987-6_20
14. Masoumi, M., Moghadam, S.S.: A simulation-based correlation power analysis attack to FPGA implementation of KASUMI block cipher. Int. J. Internet Technol. Secur. Trans. **7**(2), 175–191 (2017)
15. Matsui, M., Tokita, T.: MISTY, KASUMI and camellia cipher algorithm development. Mitsibishi Electr. Adv. (Mitsibishi Electr. Corp.) **100**, 2–8 (2001)

16. Nassar, M., Souissi, Y., Guilley, S., Danger, J.L.: RSM: a small and fast counter-measure for AES, secure against 1st and 2nd-order zero-offset SCAs. In: Design, Automation & Test in Europe Conference & Exhibition (DATE), pp. 1173–1178. IEEE (2012)

17. Nguyen, P.H., Robshaw, M.J.B., Wang, H.: On related-key attacks and KASUMI: the case of A5/3. In: Bernstein, D.J., Chatterjee, S. (eds.) INDOCRYPT 2011. LNCS, vol. 7107, pp. 146–159. Springer, Heidelberg (2011). https://doi.org/10.1007/978-3-642-25578-6_12

18. Oswald, E., et al.: OpenSCA, an open source toolbox for MATLAB (2008)

19. Popp, T., Mangard, S.: Masked dual-rail pre-charge logic: DPA-resistance without routing constraints. In: Rao, J.R., Sunar, B. (eds.) CHES 2005. LNCS, vol. 3659, pp. 172–186. Springer, Heidelberg (2005). https://doi.org/10.1007/11545262_13

20. Popp, T., Mangard, S., Oswald, E.: Power analysis attacks and countermeasures. IEEE Des. Test Comput. **24**(6) (2007)

21. Rivain, M., Prouff, E.: Provably secure higher-order masking of AES. In: Mangard, S., Standaert, F.-X. (eds.) CHES 2010. LNCS, vol. 6225, pp. 413–427. Springer, Heidelberg (2010). https://doi.org/10.1007/978-3-642-15031-9_28

22. Satoh, A., Morioka, S.: Small and high-speed hardware architectures for the 3GPP standard cipher KASUMI. In: Chan, A.H., Gligor, V. (eds.) ISC 2002. LNCS, vol. 2433, pp. 48–62. Springer, Heidelberg (2002). https://doi.org/10.1007/3-540-45811-5_4

23. Sugio, N., Aono, H., Hongo, S., Kaneko, T.: A study on higher order differential attack of KASUMI. IEICE Trans. Fundam. Electron., Commun. Comput. Sci. **90**(1), 14–21 (2007)

24. Trichina, E., Korkishko, T., Lee, K.H.: Small size, low power, side channel-immune AES coprocessor: design and synthesis results. In: Dobbertin, H., Rijmen, V., Sowa, A. (eds.) AES 2004. LNCS, vol. 3373, pp. 113–127. Springer, Heidelberg (2005). https://doi.org/10.1007/11506447_10

25. Wang, Z., Dong, X., Jia, K., Zhao, J.: Differential fault attack on KASUMI cipher used in GSM telephony. Math. Prob. Eng. **2014**, 1–7 (2014)

26. Zhou, Y., Feng, D.: Side-channel attacks: ten years after its publication and the impacts on cryptographic module security testing. IACR Cryptology ePrint Archive 2005/388 (2005)

On the Performance of Convolutional Neural Networks for Side-Channel Analysis

Stjepan Picek[1], Ioannis Petros Samiotis[1], Jaehun Kim[1], Annelie Heuser[2], Shivam Bhasin[3(⊠)], and Axel Legay[4]

[1] Delft University of Technology, Mekelweg 2, Delft, The Netherlands
[2] CNRS, IRISA, Rennes, France
[3] Physical Analysis and Cryptographic Engineering, Temasek Laboratories, Nanyang Technological University, Singapore, Singapore
sbhasin@ntu.edu.sg
[4] Inria, IRISA, Rennes, France

Abstract. In this work, we ask a question whether Convolutional Neural Networks are more suitable for side-channel attacks than some other machine learning techniques and if yes, in what situations. Our results point that Convolutional Neural Networks indeed outperform machine learning in several scenarios when considering accuracy. Still, often there is no compelling reason to use such a complex technique. In fact, if comparing techniques without extra steps like preprocessing, we see an obvious advantage for Convolutional Neural Networks when the level of noise is small, and the number of measurements and features is high. The other tested settings show that simpler machine learning techniques, for a significantly lower computational cost, perform similarly or sometimes even better. The experiments with guessing entropy indicate that methods like Random Forest or XGBoost could perform better than Convolutional Neural Networks for the datasets we investigated.

Keywords: Side-channel analysis · Machine learning · Deep learning Convolutional Neural Networks

1 Introduction

Side-channel analysis (SCA) is a process exploiting physical leakages in order to extract sensitive information from a cryptographic device. The ability to protect devices against SCA represents a paramount requirement for the industry. One especially attractive target for physical attacks is the Internet of Things (IoT) [1] since (1) the devices to be attacked are widespread and in the proximity of an attacker and (2) the available resources to implement countermeasures on devices are scarce. Consequently, we want a setting where the countermeasures are simple (i.e., cheap) and yet being able to protect from the most powerful

© Springer Nature Switzerland AG 2018
A. Chattopadhyay et al. (Eds.): SPACE 2018, LNCS 11348, pp. 157–176, 2018.
https://doi.org/10.1007/978-3-030-05072-6_10

attacks. At the same time, many products have transaction counters which set a limit for the number of side-channel measurements one is able to collect.

The profiled side-channel analysis defines the worst case security assessment by conducting the most powerful attacks. In this scenario, the attacker has access to a clone device, which can be profiled for any chosen or known key. Afterward, he is able to use the obtained knowledge to extract the secret key from a different device. Profiled attacks are conducted in two distinctive phases where the first phase is known as the profiling (or sometimes learning/training) phase, while the second phase is called the attack (test) phase. A well-known example of such an attack is template attack (TA) [2], a technique that is the best (optimal) from an information theoretic point of view if the attacker has an unbounded number of traces [3,4]. Soon after the template attack, the stochastic attack that uses linear regression in the profiling phase was developed [5]. In coming years, researchers recognized certain weaknesses in template attack and they tried to modify it in order to better account for different (usually, more difficult) attack scenarios. One example of such an approach is the pooled template attack where only one pooled covariance matrix is used in order to cope with statistical difficulties [6].

Alongside such techniques, the SCA community recognized that the same general profiled approach is actually used in supervised machine learning. Machine learning (ML) is a term encompassing a number of methods that can be used for tasks like classification, clustering, feature selection, and regression [7]. Consequently, the SCA community started to experiment with different ML techniques and to evaluate whether they are useful in the SCA context, see e.g., [4,8–18]. Although considering different scenarios and often different machine learning techniques (with some algorithms used in a prevailing number of works like Support Vector Machines and Random Forest), all those works have in common that they establish numerous scenarios where ML techniques can outperform template attack and are the best choice for profiled SCA.

More recently, deep learning techniques started to capture the attention of the SCA community. In 2016, Maghrebi et al. conducted the first analysis of deep learning techniques for profiled SCA as well as a comparison against a number of ML techniques [19]. The results were very encouraging with deep learning surpassing other, simpler machine learning techniques and TA. Less than one year later, a paper focusing on Convolutional Neural Networks (CNNs) showed impressive results: this technique was better performing than TA but was also successful against device protected with different countermeasures [20]. This, coupled with a fact that the authors were able to propose several clever data augmentation techniques, boosted even further the confidence in deep learning for SCA.

In this work, we take a step back and investigate a number of profiled SCA scenarios. We compare one deep learning technique that got the most attention in SCA community up to now – CNNs against several, well-known machine learning techniques. Our goal is to examine the strengths of CNNs when compared with different machine learning techniques and to recognize what are the most suitable scenarios (considering complexity, explainability, ease of use, etc.) to use deep learning. We emphasize that the aim of this paper is not to doubt CNNs as a good approach but to doubt it as the best approach for any profiled SCA setting. The main contributions of this work are:

1. We conduct a detailed comparison between several machine learning techniques in an effort to recognize situations where convolutional neural networks offer clear advantages. We especially note XGBoost algorithm, which is well-known as an extremely powerful technique but has never before been used in SCA. We show results for both accuracy and guessing entropy in an effort to better estimate the behavior of tested algorithms.
2. We design a convolutional neural network architecture that is able to reach high accuracies and compete with ML techniques as well as with the other deep learning architecture designed in [19].
3. We conduct an experiment showing that the topology of measurements does not seem to be the key property for CNNs' good performance.
4. We discuss scenarios where convolutional neural networks could be the preferred choice when compared with other, simpler machine learning techniques.

2   Background

2.1   Profiled Side-Channel Analysis

Let calligraphic letters ($\mathcal{X}$) denote sets, capital letters (X) denote random variables taking values in these sets, and the corresponding lowercase letters (x) denote their realizations. Let k^* be the fixed secret cryptographic key (byte), k any possible key hypothesis, and the random variable T the plaintext or ciphertext of the cryptographic algorithm, which is uniformly chosen. We denote the measured leakage as X and consider multivariate leakage $\boldsymbol{X} = X_1, \ldots, X_D$, with D being the number of time samples or points-of-interest (i.e., features as called in ML domain). To guess the secret key, the attacker first needs to choose a model $Y(T, k)$ depending on the key guess k and on some known text T, which relates to the deterministic part of the leakage. When there is no ambiguity, we write Y instead of $Y(T, k)$.

We consider a scenario where a powerful attacker has a device with knowledge about the secret key implemented and is able to obtain a set of N profiling traces $\boldsymbol{X}_1, \ldots, \boldsymbol{X}_N$ in order to estimate the leakage model. Once this phase is done, the attacker measures additional traces $\boldsymbol{X}_1, \ldots, \boldsymbol{X}_Q$ from the device under attack in order to break the unknown secret key k^*. Although it is usually considered that the attacker has an unlimited number of traces available during the profiling phase, this is of course always bounded.

2.2   Machine Learning Techniques

We select several machine learning techniques to be tested against CNN approach. More precisely, we select one algorithm based on Bayes theorem (Naive Bayes), one tree-based method based on boosting (Extreme Gradient Boosting), one tree-based method based on bagging (Random Forest), and finally, one neural network algorithm (Multilayer perceptron). We do not use Support Vector Machines (SVM) in our experiments despite their good performance as reported in a number of related works. This is because SVM is computationally expensive (especially when using radial kernel) and our experiments showed problems when dealing with imbalanced data (as occurs here since we consider the Hamming weight model) and large amounts of noise. For all ML techniques, we use scikit-learn library in Python 3.6 while for CNNs we use Keras with TensorFlow backend [21, 22].

We follow that line of investigation since the "No Free Lunch Theorem" for supervised machine learning proves there exists no single model that works best for every problem [23]. To find the best model for a specific given problem, numerous algorithms and parameter combinations should be tested. Naturally, not even then one can be sure that the best model is obtained but at least some estimate about trade-offs between the speed, accuracy, and complexity of the obtained models is possible. Besides the "No Free Lunch Theorem" we briefly discuss two more relevant machine learning notions. The first one is connected with the curse of dimensionality [24] and the Hughes effect [25], which states that with a fixed number of training samples, the predictive power reduces as the dimensionality increases. This indicates that for scenarios with a large number of features, we need to use more training examples, which is a natural scenario for deep learning. Finally, the Universal Approximation theorem states that neural network is a universal functional approximator, more precisely, even a feed-forward neural network with a single hidden layer that consists of a finite number of neurons can approximate many continuous functions [26]. Consequently, by adding hidden layers and neurons, neural networks gain more approximation power.

Naive Bayes – NB. The Naive Bayes classifier is a method based on the Bayesian rule. It works under the simplifying assumption that the predictor attributes (measurements) are mutually independent among the features given the target class [27]. The existence of highly correlated attributes in a dataset can thus influence the learning process and reduce the number of successful predictions. NB assumes a normal distribution for predictor attributes and outputs posterior probabilities.

Multilayer Perceptron – MLP. The Multilayer perceptron is a feed-forward neural network that maps sets of inputs onto sets of appropriate outputs. MLP consists of multiple layers of nodes in a directed graph, where each layer is fully connected to the next one. To train the network, the backpropagation algorithm is used, which is a generalization of the least mean squares algorithm in the linear perceptron. An MLP consists of three or more layers (since input and output represent two layers) of nonlinearly-activating nodes [28]. Note, if there is more than one hidden layer, we can already talk about deep learning.

Extreme Gradient Boost – XGBoost. The XGBoost is a scalable implementation of gradient boosting decision tree algorithm [29]. Chen and Guestrin designed this algorithm where they use a sparsity aware algorithm for handling sparse data and a theoretically justified weighted quantile sketch for approximate learning [30]. As the name suggests, its core part is gradient boosting (since it uses a gradient descent algorithm to minimize the loss when adding new models). Here, boosting is an ensemble technique where new models are added to correct the errors made by existing models. Models are added sequentially until no further improvements can be made. Today, XGBoost is due to his execution speed and model performance one of the top performing algorithms in the ML domain. Since this algorithm is based on decision trees, it has additional advantages as being robust in noisy scenarios.

Random Forest – RF. The Random Forest algorithm is a well-known ensemble decision tree learner [31]. Decision trees choose their splitting attributes from a random subset of k attributes at each internal node. The best split is taken among these randomly chosen attributes and the trees are built without pruning, RF is a parametric algorithm with respect to the number of trees in the forest. RF is a stochastic algorithm because of its two sources of randomness: bootstrap sampling and attribute selection at node splitting.

2.3 Convolutional Neural Networks – CNNs

CNNs are a specific type of neural networks which were first designed for 2-dimensional convolutions as it was inspired by the biological processes of animals' visual cortex [32]. They are primarily used for image classification but lately, they have proven to be powerful classifiers for time series data such as music and speech [33]. Their usage in side-channel analysis has been encouraged by [19,20]. As we explain in Sect. 3.2, in order to find the most optimized model for the available datasets, we use random search for hyperparameter tuning. This enabled us to study how different architectures behaved on the datasets and compare the results to determine the best candidate model for our experimental setup. As this work is not attempting to propose a new optimal architecture for side-channel data classification, we used the most optimized network found through the Random Search for our benchmarks. The final architecture was chosen after creating hyperparameter constraints based on the literature and tests we conducted, followed by an optimization of their values through a random search. The hyperparameters that are modeled and optimized are number of convolutional/pooling/fully connected layers, number of activation maps, learning rate, dropout magnitude, convolutional activation functions, convolutional/pooling kernel size, and stride and number of neurons on fully connected layers.

During the training, we use early stopping to further avoid overfitting by monitoring the loss on the validation set [34]. Thus, every training session is interrupted before reaching high accuracy on the training dataset. To help the network increase its accuracy on the validation set, we use a learning rate scheduler to decrease the learning rate depending on the loss from the validation set. We initialize the weights to small random values and we use "adam" optimizer [35].

In this work, we ran the experiment with computation nodes equipped with 32 NVIDIA GTX 1080 Ti graphics processing units (GPUs). Each of it has 11 Gigabytes of GPU memory and 3 584 GPU cores. We implement the experiments with the Tensorflow [22] computing framework and Keras deep learning framework [21] to leverage the GPU computation.

2.4   Performance Analysis

To assess the performance of the classifiers (and consequently the attacker) we use accuracy: $ACC = \frac{TP+TN}{TP+FP+FN+TN}$. TP refers to true positive (correctly classified positive), TN to true negative (correctly classified negative), FP to false positive (falsely classified positive), and FN to false negative (falsely classified negative) instances. TP, TN, FP, and FN are well-defined for hypothesis testing and binary classification problems. When dealing with the multiclass classification, they are defined in one class–vs–all other classes manner and are calculated from the confusion matrix. The confusion matrix is a table layout where each row represents the instances in an actual class, while each column represents the instances of a predicted class.

Besides accuracy, we use also Success rate (SR) and Guessing entropy (GE) [36]. Given a certain amount of traces, SR is defined as the estimated average probability of success of an attack. In other words, what is the probability on average that the attack predicts the correct secret key given a certain amount of traces. Given a ranking of secret key candidates (i.e., from probabilities or scores) of an attack, the guessing entropy is the average position of the correct secret key in the ranking.

3   Experimental Setting

3.1   Datasets

In our experiments, we use three datasets: one representing an easy target to attack due to a low level of noise, one more difficult target due to a high level of noise, and finally, one with the random delay countermeasure.

DPAcontest v4 Dataset [37]. This dataset (denoted DPAv4) gives measurements of a masked AES software implementation but since the mask is known, one can easily transform it into an unprotected scenario. Since it is a software implementation, the most leaking operation is not the register writing but the processing of the S-box operation and we attack the first round:

$$Y(k^*) = \text{Sbox}[P_{b_1} \oplus k^*] \oplus \underbrace{M}_{\text{known mask}} , \tag{1}$$

where P_{b_1} is a plaintext byte and we choose $b_1 = 1$. We consider here a setting with 9 classes corresponding to the Hamming weight of the output of an S-box. The SNR for this dataset lies between 0.1188 and 5.8577. For our experiments, we start with a preselected window of 3 000 features (around the S-box part of the algorithm execution) from the original trace. Note that we maintain the lexicographical ordering (topology) of features after the feature selection (by lexicographical ordering we mean keeping the features in the order they appear in measurements and not, for instance, sorting them in accordance to their relevance).

DPAcontest v2 Dataset [38]. DPAcontest v2 (denoted DPAv2) provides measurements of an AES hardware implementation. Previous works showed that the most suitable leakage model (when attacking the last round of an unprotected hardware implementation) is the register writing in the last round:

$$Y(k^*) = \underbrace{\mathsf{Sbox}^{-1}[C_{b_1} \oplus k^*]}_{\text{previous register value}} \oplus \underbrace{C_{b_2}}_{\text{ciphertext byte}} . \tag{2}$$

Here, C_{b_1} and C_{b_2} are two ciphertext bytes and the relation between b_1 and b_2 is given through the inverse ShiftRows operation of AES. We select $b_1 = 12$ resulting in $b_2 = 8$ since it is one of the easiest bytes to attack [38]. In Eq. (2), $Y(k^*)$ consists of 256 values but we apply the Hamming weight (HW) on those values resulting in 9 classes. These measurements are relatively noisy and the resulting model-based signal-to-noise ratio $SNR = \frac{var(signal)}{var(noise)} = \frac{var(y(t,k^*))}{var(x-y(t,k^*))}$, lies between 0.0069 and 0.0096. There are several available datasets under the DPAcontest v2 name and we use the traces from the "template" set. This dataset has 3 253 features.

Random Delay Countermeasure Dataset. As our last use case, we use a protected (i.e., with a countermeasure) software implementation of AES. The target smartcard is an 8-bit Atmel AVR microcontroller. The protection uses random delay countermeasure as described by Coron and Kizhvatov [39]. Adding random delays to the normal operation of a cryptographic algorithm has as an effect on the misalignment of important features, which in turns makes the attack more difficult to conduct. As a result, the overall SNR is reduced (the SNR has a maximum value of 0.0556). We mounted our attacks in the Hamming weight power consumption model against the first AES key byte, targeting the first S-box operation. This dataset has 50 000 traces with 3 500 features each. This countermeasure has been shown to be prone to deep learning based side-channel [20]. The random delay is quite often used countermeasure in commercial products, while not modifying the leakage order (like masking). The dataset is publicly available at https://github.com/ikizhvatov/randomdelays-traces.

3.2   Data Preparation and Parameter Tuning

We denote the training set size as Tr, validation set size as V, and testing set size as Te. Here, $Tr + V + Te$ equals to the total set size S. We experiment with four dataset sizes $S - [1\,000, 10\,000, 50\,000, 100\,000]$. For the Random delay dataset, we use the first three sizes since it has only 50 000 measurements. The ratios for Tr, V, and Te equal 50% : 25% : 25%. All features are normalized into $[0, 1]$ range. When using ML techniques, instead of validation, we use 5-fold cross-validation. In the 5-fold cross-validation, the original sample is first randomly partitioned into 5 equal sized subsets. Then, a single subsample is selected to validate the data while the remaining 4 subsets are used for training. The cross-validation process is repeated 5 times where each of the 5 subsamples is used once for validation. The obtained results are then averaged to produce an estimation. We select to conduct 5-fold cross-validation on the basis of the number of measurements belonging to the least populated class for the smallest dataset we use. Since the number of features is too large for ML techniques, we conduct feature selection where we select the 50 most important features while we keep the lexicographical ordering of selected features. We use 50 features for ML techniques since the datasets are large and the number of features is one of two factors (the second one is the number of measurements) comprising the time complexity for ML algorithms. Additionally, 50 features is a common choice in the literature [12,14]. To select those features, we use the correlation coefficient where we calculate it for the target class variables HW, which consists of categorical values that are interpreted as numerical values [40]:

$$Pearson(x, y) = \frac{\sum_{i=1}^{N}((x_i - \bar{x})(y_i - \bar{y}))}{\sqrt{\sum_{i=1}^{N}(x_i - \bar{x})^2}\sqrt{\sum_{i=1}^{N}(y_i - \bar{y})^2}}. \tag{3}$$

Despite the fact it is not the best practice to use such selected features with the CNNs, we also include the experiment using CNNs with the selected features as an input for the purpose of the comparison and completeness. For CNNs, we do not conduct cross-validation since it is too computationally expensive but rather we additionally use the validation set, that serves as an indicator of early stopping to avoid overfitting.

In order to find the best hyperparameters, we tune the algorithms with respect to their most important parameters as described below:

1. The Naive Bayes has no parameters to tune.
2. For MLP, we tune the solver parameter that can be either *adam*, *lbfgs*, or *sgd*. Next, we tune activation function that can be either *ReLU* or *Tanh*, and the number and structure of hidden layers in MLP. The number of hidden layers is tuned in the range $[2, 3, 4, 5, 6]$ and the number of neurons per layer in the range $[10, 20, 30, 40, 50]$.
3. For XGBoost, we tune the learning rate and the number of estimators. For learning rate, we experiment with values $[0.001, 0.01, 0.1, 1]$ and for the number of estimators with values of $[100, 200, 400]$.
4. For RF, we tune the number of trees in the range $[10, 50, 100, 200, 500]$, with no limit to the tree size.

When dealing with CNNs, in order to find the best fitting model, we optimized 13 hyperparameters: convolutional kernel size, pooling size, stride on convolutional layer, initial number of filters and neurons, learning rate, the number of convolutional/pooling/fully connected layers, type of activation function, optimization algorithm, and dropout on convolutional and fully connected layers.

The hyperparameter optimization was implemented through a random search, where the details on possible parameter ranges are given in Table 1). We tune our CNN architecture for the DPAcontest v4 dataset.

Table 1. Hyperparameters and their value ranges.

Hyperparameter	Value range	Constraints
Convolutional kernel	$k_{conv} \in [3, 20]$	-
Pooling kernel	$k_{pool} \in [3, 20]$	$k_{pool} \leq k_{conv}$
Stride	$s \in [1, 5]$	In pooling layers, $s = k_{pool} - 1$
# of convolutional layers	$layers_{conv} \in [2, 6]$	-
# of pooling layers	$layers_{pool} \in [1, 5]$	$layers_{pool} \leq layers_{conv}$
# of fully-connected layers	$layers_{fc} \in [0, 2]$	-
Initial # of activation maps	$a \in [8, 32]$	Follows geometric progression with ratio r = 2, for the # of $layers_{conv}$
Initial # of neurons	$n \in [128, 1024]$	Follows geometric progression with ratio $r = 2$, for the # of $layers_{fc}$
Convolutional layer dropout	$drop_{conv} \in [0.05, 0.10]$	-
Fully-connected layer dropout	$drop_{fc} \in [0.10, 0.20]$	-
Learning rate	$l \in [0.001, 0.012]$	A learning rate scheduler was applied
Activation function	ReLU, ELU, SELU, LeakyReLU, PReLU	The same for all layers except the last which uses Softmax
Optimization algorithm	Adam, Adamax, NAdam, Adadelta, Adagrad, SGD, RMSProp	-

We use the Softmax activation function in the classification layer combined with the Categorical Cross Entropy loss function. For regularization, we use dropout on convolutional and fully connected layers while on the classification layer we use an activity L2 regularization. These regularization techniques help to avoid overfitting on the training set, which in turn help lower the bias of the model. The number of activation maps increases per layer, following a geometric progression with an initial value $a = 16$ and a ratio $r = 2$ (16, 32, 64, 128). The number of activation maps is optimized for GPU training. The network is composed of 4 convolutional layers and 4 pooling layers in between, followed by the classification layer. All convolutional layers use kernel size of 6 and stride 2 creating a number of activation maps for each layer. For pooling we use Average Pooling on the first pooling layer and Max Pooling on the rest, using the kernel of size 4 and stride of 3. The convolutional layers use "Scaled Exponential Linear

Unit" (SELU) activation function, an activation function which induces self-normalizing properties [41]. We depict our architecture in Fig. 1 and give details about it in Table 2.

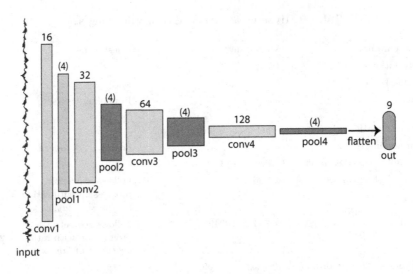

Fig. 1. The developed CNN architecture. The simplified figure illustrates the applied architecture. The yellow rectangular blocks indicate 1-dimensional convolution layer, and the blue blocks indicate pooling layers. The first light blue block indicates average pooling, which is different from the other max pooling blocks. After the flattening of every trailing spatial dimension into a single feature dimension, we apply a fully-connected layer for classification. (Color figure online)

Table 2. Developed CNN architecture.

Layer	Output shape	Weight shape	Sub-sampling	Activation
conv (1)	$1\,624 \times 16$	$1 \times 16 \times 6$	2	SELU
average-pool(1)	542×16	-	(4), 3	-
conv (2)	271×32	$1 \times 32 \times 6$	2	SELU
max-pool (2)	91×32	-	(4), 3	-
conv (3)	46×64	$1 \times 64 \times 6$	2	SELU
max-pool (3)	16×64	-	(4), 3	-
conv (4)	8×128	$1 \times 128 \times 6$	2	SELU
max-pool (4)	3×128	-	(4), 3	-
fc-output	9	384×9	-	Softmax

4   Results

It has been already established that accuracy is often not sufficient performance metric in SCA context but something like the key enumeration should be used to really assess the performance of classifiers [13, 20]. The problem with accuracy is most pronounced in imbalanced scenarios since high accuracy can just mean that the classifier classified all measurements into the dominant class (i.e., the one with the most measurements). This phenomenon is well-known in the machine learning community. Since we consider in our experiments the Hamming weight model, we have imbalanced data where HW class 4 (all S-box outputs with the Hamming weight equal to 4) is the most represented one. In fact, on average HW4 is 70 times more represented than HW0 or HW8. Consequently, a classifier assigning all measurements into HW4 will have a relatively good accuracy $(70/256 \approx 27.3\%)$ but will not be useful in SCA context. To denote such cases, we depict the corresponding accuracies in cells with the gray background color.

First, we briefly address the fact that we do not use template attack. The decision for this is based on previous works as listed in Sect. 1 where it is shown that machine learning and deep learning can outperform TA. Consequently, we keep our focus here only on techniques coming from the machine learning domain.

4.1   Accuracy

In Table 3, we give results for DPAcontest v4 dataset when considering 50 most important features. First, we can observe that none of the techniques have problems with obtaining high accuracy values. In fact, we notice a steady increase in the accuracy values as we add more measurements to the training/testing process. By comparing the methods simply by the accuracy score, we see that XGBoost reaches the highest performance, followed closely by Random Forest. When considering CNN, we see that only Naive Bayes is resulting in smaller accuracies. Interestingly, when considering 1 000 measurements scenario, we see that CNN actually has by far the best accuracy. We believe this to be due to a combination of a small number of measurements and a small number of features. For a larger number of measurements, CNN also needs more features in order to train a strong model.

Table 3. Testing results, DPAcontest v4, 50 features

Dataset size	NB	MLP	XGBoost	RF	CNN
1 000	37.6	44.8	52.0	49.2	60.4
10 000	65.2	81.3	79.7	82.4	77.2
50 000	64.1	86.8	88.8	87.9	81.4
100 000	66.5	91	92.1	90.3	84.5

In Table 4, we present results for DPAcontest v2 with 50 features. As observed in related work (e.g., [13, 19, 20]) DPAcontest v2 is a difficult dataset for profiled attacks. Indeed, CNN here always assigns all the measurements into the class HW4. Additionally, although MLP does not assign all the measurements into HW4, by examining confusion matrices we observed that the prevailing number of measurements is actually in that class, with only a few ones belonging to HW3 and HW 5. Finally, we see that the best performing technique is XGBoost. The confusion matrix for XGBoost results reveals that even when the accuracy for XGBoost is similar as assigning all measurements into HW4, the algorithm is actually able to correctly classify examples of several classes. Since for this dataset we have the same imbalanced scenario as for DPAcontest v4, we can assume that the combination of high noise and imbalancedness represents the problem for CNNs. Additionally, our experiments indicate that with this dataset, the more complex the architecture, the easier is to assign all the measurements into HW4. Consequently, simpler architectures work better as there is not enough expressive power in the network to learn perfectly the training set. For this reason, the CNN architecture used in [19] works better for DPAcontest v2 since it is much simpler than the CNN architecture we use here.

Table 4. Testing results, DPAcontest v2, 50 features

Dataset size	NB	MLP	XGBoost	RF	CNN
1 000	14.4	28.8	28.8	25.6	28.8
10 000	10.6	28.3	27.3	25.8	28.2
50 000	12	26.6	26.6	25.3	26.7
100 000	11.7	27.1	27.1	25.8	27.1

Finally, in Table 5, we give results for the Random delay dataset with 50 features. We can observe that the accuracies are similar to the case of DPAcontest v2 but here we do not have such pronounced problems with assigning all measurements into HW4. In fact, that behavior occurs in only one case – CNN with 50 000 measurements.

Table 5. Testing results, Random delay, 50 features

Dataset size	NB	MLP	XGBoost	RF	CNN
1 000	20	22	27.32	26.8	21.2
10 000	22	26.7	24.9	27	28.2
50 000	25.6	27.6	26.3	26.9	27.1

One could ask why setting the limit to only 50 features? For many machine learning techniques, the complexity increases drastically with the increase in the number of features. Combining that fact with a large number of measurements and we soon arrive into a situation where machine learning is simply to slow for practical evaluations. This is especially pronounced since only a few algorithms have optimized versions (e.g., supporting multi-core and/or GPU computation). For CNNs we do not have such limiting factors. In fact, modern implementations of deep learning architectures like CNNs enable us to work with thousands of features and millions of measurements. Consequently, in Table 6, we depict the results for CNNs for all three considered datasets when using all available features. For DPAcontest v4, we see improvements in accuracy in all cases, where for cases with more measurements we see drastic improvements. It is especially interesting to consider cases with 50 000 and 100 000 measurements where we reach more than 95% accuracy. These results confirm our intuition that CNNs need many features (and not only many measurements) to reach high accuracies. For DPAcontest v2, we see no difference when using 50 features or all the features. Although disappointing, this is expected: if our architecture was already too complex when using only 50 features, adding more features does not help. Finally, when considering the Random delay dataset, we see that the accuracies for two smaller dataset sizes decrease while the accuracy for 50 000 measurements increases where we do not see that all measurements are assigned to HW4 class. Again, this is a clear sign that when working with more complex datasets, having more features helps but only if it is accompanied by the increase in the number of measurements.

Table 6. Testing results for CNN, all features

Dataset size	DPAcontest v4	DPAcontest v2	Random delay
1 000	60.8	28.8	20.3
10 000	92.7	22.6	20.2
50 000	97.4	22.3	28
100 000	96.2	27.1	–

Naturally, a question can be made whether it is really necessary to use deep learning for such a small increase in accuracy when compared with computationally simpler techniques given in Tables 3, 4, and 5. Still, we need to note that while for CNNs having 100 000 measurements is not considered as a large dataset, for many other machine learning techniques this would be already a huge dataset. To conclude, based on the presented results, we clearly see cases where CNNs offer advantages over other machine learning techniques but we note there are cases where the opposite is true.

4.2 Success Rate and Guessing Entropy

Figures 2a until f give guessing entropy and success rate for all three datasets when using 50 000 traces in total. One can see from Figs. 2a and b that the correct secret key is found for nearly all methods already using less than 10 traces when considering DPAcontest v4. Interestingly, we see that the CNN architecture that uses all the features is less successful than the one using only 50 features, which is opposite from the results on the basis of accuracy. The most efficient techniques are MLP and XGBoost, but in this scenario, we see that even a simple method like Naive Bayes is more than enough.

For DPAcontest v2, we see that NB is significantly outperforming all the other methods. This could be due to a fact that other methods are more prone to classify most of the measurements into HW4 and thus do not contribute significant information to recover the secret key. For the Random delay dataset, we observe that NB, XGBoost, and RF are the most efficient methods when considering guessing entropy. On the basis of the success rate, Naive Bayes and Random Forest are the best. To conclude, we can see that all machine learning techniques display consistent behavior for both metrics. This means that those algorithms have stable behavior in ranking not only the best key candidate but also the other key candidates.

5   Discussion and Future Work

We start this section with a small experiment where we consider DPAcontest v4 and Random delay datasets with all features. We do not give results for DPA-contest v2 since even when using all features, all the measurements are classified into HW4 class. One reason why CNNs are so successful in domains like image classification is that they are able to maintain the topology, i.e., shuffling features in an image would result in a wrong classification. We do exactly that: we shuffle the features uniformly at random. Since the results indicate that the topological information in the trace signal used in experiments is not as important as expected, we tried to investigate such observation in depth by testing the CNN model with the extreme case. Expectedly, running our CNN architecture on such datasets results in decreased accuracy, but one that is still quite high as given in Table 7. When comparing Tables 6 and 7, we see that for DPAcontest v4, accuracy drops 10–15%. For Random delay and 10 000 measurements, the result is even slightly better after shuffling. In Figs. 3a and b, we give results for guessing entropy when using shuffled features. Interestingly, we see that shuffling the features did not significantly decrease the results for guessing entropy.

Table 7. Testing results for CNN, features shuffled

Dataset size	DPAcontest v4	Random delay
10 000	77.88	21.44
50 000	84.83	27.3
100 000	84.17	–

The results imply that the topological information between features of the trace is not more useful than the other characteristics of the signal. Thus, we

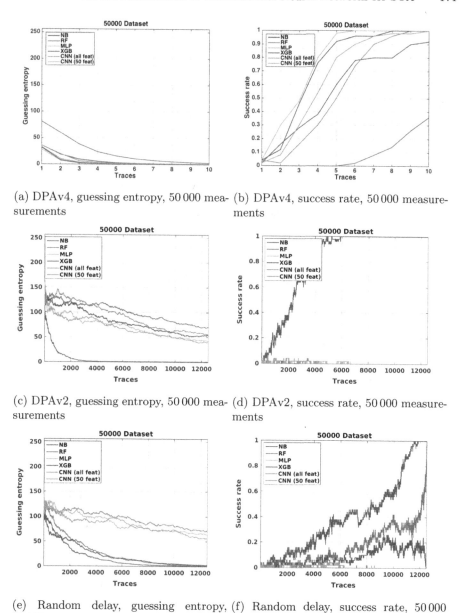

(a) DPAv4, guessing entropy, 50 000 measurements

(b) DPAv4, success rate, 50 000 measurements

(c) DPAv2, guessing entropy, 50 000 measurements

(d) DPAv2, success rate, 50 000 measurements

(e) Random delay, guessing entropy,
50 000 measurements

(f) Random delay, success rate, 50 000
measurements

Fig. 2. Guessing entropy and success rate results

hypothesize that a specific local topology or a certain feature can be a more
important factor than global topology, which is coherent to the fact that the
independently selected subset of features shows a decent performance in previous

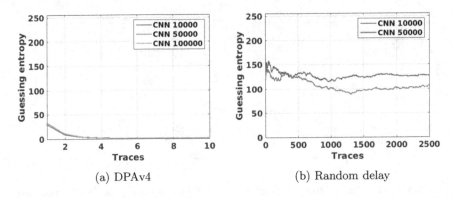

(a) DPAv4   (b) Random delay

Fig. 3. Shuffled features, guessing entropy

experiments. To verify such a hypothesis, we investigated the feature importance which is derived from the Random Forest classifier that is trained on all the features, which is illustrated in Fig. 4. Note that it is reported that the importance analysis is not reliable when it is applied on the features where they are inter-correlated such as the trace signals, compared to the features that are composed of independent variables [42]. To relax such problem, we applied the bootstrap without replacement, which is suggested in [42].

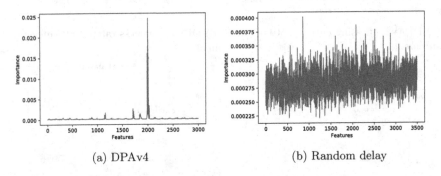

(a) DPAv4   (b) Random delay

Fig. 4. The feature importance derived from the Random Forest classifier trained on DPAcontest v4 dataset. Higher value indicates corresponding feature dimension is relatively more important than others. The values are normalized such that the sum of all the importance is equal to 1.

Figure 4a suggests the features near 2 000th dimension are treated as substantially more important to the RF model than the others. It partially explains the behavior of the CNN, whose main advantage is the ability to capture meaningful information in topology, which seems a less crucial factor in the DPAcontest v4 dataset. Differing from that, Fig. 4b shows there is no such region for the Random delay dataset that stands out when compared to other areas. Consequently, this implies the random delay applied in the dataset make the positional importance less influential.

Naturally, CNNs also have the implicit feature selection part. It is possible that current good results on SCA stem from that, which would mean we could use separate feature selection and classification to the same goal.

When considering deep learning architectures, and more specifically their sizes, a valid question is whether the architectures currently used in SCA are really deep. For instance, Cagli et al. mention their architecture as being "quite deep CNN architecture" but if we compare that with the state-of-the-art CNNs architectures used today, we see a striking difference. The current "best" architecture for image classification called ResNet has 152 hidden layers [43]. Our architectures look very shallow compared to that. Naturally, the question is if we even need such deep architectures, and if the answer is no, then maybe computationally simpler machine learning techniques could be a good alternative.

We do not need to investigate only the deep learning part. As Cagli et al. showed, using smart preprocessing (e.g., data augmentation) can bring a more striking increase in the performance than by changing the network architecture [20]. Machine learning domain is extensively using various data augmentation techniques for years and there is no reason why some of those, more general methods could not be used in SCA. Additionally, we must mention that data augmentation is not limited to deep learning and it would be interesting to see what would happen if SCA-specific data augmentation would be used with other, simpler machine learning techniques. Finally, in this work, we do not consider masked implementations, which could be the case where convolutional neural networks outperform other techniques. Still, when considering the related work it is not so clear whether this is a trait of CNNs or simply deep architectures [20,44].

When discussing the results on a more general level, we can observe some trends.

1. The number of measurements and the number of features are connected and simply increasing one quantity without the other does not guarantee an improvement in performance.
2. The level of noise in conjunction with the highly imbalanced data seem to affect CNNs more than some simpler machine learning techniques. Naturally, to reduce the level of noise, it is possible to use various forms of preprocessing and to reduce the imbalancedness, a simple solution is to undersample the most represented classes. This could be problematic in scenarios where we require a large number of measurements (but are limited in the amount we can acquire) since undersampling will drastically reduce the number of measurements we have at our disposal.
3. As a measure of performance in all algorithms, we use accuracy. When comparing the performance on the basis of accuracy vs guessing entropy, we can see there are differences and cases when accuracy cannot be used as a definitive measure of performance. Still, our results do not indicate that any of the tested algorithms are less sensitive to this problem.
4. CNNs are more computationally expensive to train and have more parameters than some other (simpler) machine learning techniques. This makes it

a challenging decision whether it is beneficial to invest more resources into tuning for a probably small improvement in the performance.

5. We see that one trained CNN architecture for a specific dataset is suboptimal on some other datasets. This indicates that the obtained models are not easily transferable across scenarios, which even more raises the concern about the computational costs vs. potential performance gains.

6   Conclusions

In this paper, we consider a number of scenarios for profiled SCA and we compare the performance of several machine learning algorithms. Recently, very good results obtained with convolutional neural networks suggested them to be a method of choice when conducting profiled SCA. Our results show that CNNs are able to perform very well but the same could be said for other machine learning techniques. We see a direct advantage for CNN architectures over machine learning techniques for cases where the level of noise is low, the number of measurements is large, and the number of features is high. In other cases, our findings suggest that other machine learning techniques are able to perform on a similar level (with much smaller computational cost) or even surpass CNNs. Of course, stating that CNNs perform well when the level of noise is low does not mean that some other machine learning technique we considered here is very good when the level of noise is high. Rather, when the level of noise is (very) high, we conclude that both CNNs and machine learning techniques have similar difficulties in classifying. When considering the guessing entropy metric, the results favor methods like Random Forest and XGBoost, which is a clear indication more experiments are needed to properly assess the strengths of convolutional neural networks. As discussed in previous sections, there are many possible research directions one could follow, which will, in the end, bring more cohesion to the area and more confidence in the obtained results.

References

1. Ronen, E., Shamir, A., Weingarten, A., O'Flynn, C.: IoT goes nuclear: creating a ZigBee chain reaction. In: IEEE Symposium on Security and Privacy, SP 2017, San Jose, CA, USA, 22–26 May 2017, pp. 195–212. IEEE Computer Society (2017)
2. Chari, S., Rao, J.R., Rohatgi, P.: Template attacks. In: Kaliski, B.S., Koç, K., Paar, C. (eds.) CHES 2002. LNCS, vol. 2523, pp. 13–28. Springer, Heidelberg (2003). https://doi.org/10.1007/3-540-36400-5_3
3. Heuser, A., Rioul, O., Guilley, S.: Good is not good enough. In: Batina, L., Robshaw, M. (eds.) CHES 2014. LNCS, vol. 8731, pp. 55–74. Springer, Heidelberg (2014). https://doi.org/10.1007/978-3-662-44709-3_4
4. Lerman, L., Poussier, R., Bontempi, G., Markowitch, O., Standaert, F.-X.: Template attacks vs. machine learning revisited (and the curse of dimensionality in side-channel analysis). In: Mangard, S., Poschmann, A.Y. (eds.) COSADE 2014. LNCS, vol. 9064, pp. 20–33. Springer, Cham (2015). https://doi.org/10.1007/978-3-319-21476-4_2

5. Schindler, W., Lemke, K., Paar, C.: A stochastic model for differential side channel cryptanalysis. In: Rao, J.R., Sunar, B. (eds.) CHES 2005. LNCS, vol. 3659, pp. 30–46. Springer, Heidelberg (2005). https://doi.org/10.1007/11545262_3
6. Choudary, O., Kuhn, M.G.: Efficient template attacks. In: Francillon, A., Rohatgi, P. (eds.) CARDIS 2013. LNCS, vol. 8419, pp. 253–270. Springer, Cham (2014). https://doi.org/10.1007/978-3-319-08302-5_17
7. Mitchell, T.M.: Machine Learning, 1st edn. McGraw-Hill Inc., New York (1997)
8. Heuser, A., Zohner, M.: Intelligent machine homicide. In: Schindler, W., Huss, S.A. (eds.) COSADE 2012. LNCS, vol. 7275, pp. 249–264. Springer, Heidelberg (2012). https://doi.org/10.1007/978-3-642-29912-4_18
9. Hospodar, G., Gierlichs, B., De Mulder, E., Verbauwhede, I., Vandewalle, J.: Machine learning in side-channel analysis: a first study. J. Cryptogr. Eng. 1, 293–302 (2011). https://doi.org/10.1007/s13389-011-0023-x
10. Lerman, L., Bontempi, G., Markowitch, O.: Power analysis attack: an approach based on machine learning. Int. J. Appl. Cryptol. 3(2), 97–115 (2014)
11. Lerman, L., Bontempi, G., Markowitch, O.: A machine learning approach against a masked AES: reaching the limit of side-channel attacks with a learning model. J. Cryptogr. Eng. 5(2), 123–139 (2015)
12. Lerman, L., Medeiros, S.F., Bontempi, G., Markowitch, O.: A machine learning approach against a masked AES. In: Francillon, A., Rohatgi, P. (eds.) CARDIS 2013. LNCS, vol. 8419, pp. 61–75. Springer, Cham (2014). https://doi.org/10.1007/978-3-319-08302-5_5
13. Picek, S., Heuser, A., Guilley, S.: Template attack versus Bayes classifier. J. Cryptogr. Eng. 7(4), 343–351 (2017)
14. Gilmore, R., Hanley, N., O'Neill, M.: Neural network based attack on a masked implementation of AES. In: 2015 IEEE International Symposium on Hardware Oriented Security and Trust (HOST), pp. 106–111, May 2015
15. Heuser, A., Picek, S., Guilley, S., Mentens, N.: Lightweight ciphers and their side-channel resilience. IEEE Trans. Comput. PP(99), 1 (2017)
16. Heuser, A., Picek, S., Guilley, S., Mentens, N.: Side-channel analysis of lightweight ciphers: does lightweight equal easy? In: Hancke, G.P., Markantonakis, K. (eds.) RFIDSec 2016. LNCS, vol. 10155, pp. 91–104. Springer, Cham (2017). https://doi.org/10.1007/978-3-319-62024-4_7
17. Picek, S., et al.: Side-channel analysis and machine learning: a practical perspective. In: 2017 International Joint Conference on Neural Networks, IJCNN 2017, Anchorage, AK, USA, 14–19 May 2017, pp. 4095–4102 (2017)
18. Picek, S., Heuser, A., Jovic, A., Legay, A.: Climbing down the hierarchy: hierarchical classification for machine learning side-channel attacks. In: Joye, M., Nitaj, A. (eds.) AFRICACRYPT 2017. LNCS, vol. 10239, pp. 61–78. Springer, Cham (2017). https://doi.org/10.1007/978-3-319-57339-7_4
19. Maghrebi, H., Portigliatti, T., Prouff, E.: Breaking cryptographic implementations using deep learning techniques. In: Carlet, C., Hasan, M.A., Saraswat, V. (eds.) SPACE 2016. LNCS, vol. 10076, pp. 3–26. Springer, Cham (2016). https://doi.org/10.1007/978-3-319-49445-6_1
20. Cagli, E., Dumas, C., Prouff, E.: Convolutional neural networks with data augmentation against jitter-based countermeasures. In: Fischer, W., Homma, N. (eds.) CHES 2017. LNCS, vol. 10529, pp. 45–68. Springer, Cham (2017). https://doi.org/10.1007/978-3-319-66787-4_3
21. Chollet, F., et al.: Keras (2015). https://github.com/fchollet/keras
22. Abadi, M., et al.: TensorFlow: large-scale machine learning on heterogeneous systems (2015). Software available from tensorflow.org

23. Wolpert, D.H.: The lack of a priori distinctions between learning algorithms. Neural Comput. **8**(7), 1341–1390 (1996)
24. Bellman, R.E.: Dynamic Programming. Dover Publications, Incorporated, Mineola (2003)
25. Hughes, G.: On the mean accuracy of statistical pattern recognizers. IEEE Trans. Inf. Theory **14**(1), 55–63 (1968)
26. Hornik, K.: Approximation capabilities of multilayer feedforward networks. Neural Netw. **4**(2), 251–257 (1991)
27. Friedman, N., Geiger, D., Goldszmidt, M.: Bayesian network classifiers. Mach. Learn. **29**(2), 131–163 (1997)
28. Collobert, R., Bengio, S.: Links between perceptrons, MLPs and SVMs. In: Proceedings of the Twenty-First International Conference on Machine Learning, ICML 2004, p. 23. ACM, New York (2004)
29. Friedman, J.H.: Greedy function approximation: a gradient boosting machine. Ann. Stat. **29**, 1189–1232 (2000)
30. Chen, T., Guestrin, C.: XGBoost: a scalable tree boosting system. CoRR abs/1603.02754 (2016)
31. Breiman, L.: Random forests. Mach. Learn. **45**(1), 5–32 (2001)
32. LeCun, Y., Bengio, Y., et al.: Convolutional networks for images, speech, and time series. In: The Handbook of Brain Theory and Neural Networks, vol. 3361, no. 10 (1995)
33. Van Den Oord, A., et al.: WaveNet: a generative model for raw audio. arXiv preprint arXiv:1609.03499 (2016)
34. Demuth, H.B., Beale, M.H., De Jess, O., Hagan, M.T.: Neural Network Design. Martin Hagan (2014)
35. Kingma, D.P., Ba, J.: Adam: a method for stochastic optimization. CoRR abs/1412.6980 (2014)
36. Standaert, F.-X., Malkin, T.G., Yung, M.: A unified framework for the analysis of side-channel key recovery attacks. In: Joux, A. (ed.) EUROCRYPT 2009. LNCS, vol. 5479, pp. 443–461. Springer, Heidelberg (2009). https://doi.org/10.1007/978-3-642-01001-9_26
37. TELECOM ParisTech SEN research group: DPA Contest, 4th edn (2013–2014). http://www.DPAcontest.org/v4/
38. TELECOM ParisTech SEN research group: DPA Contest, 2nd edn (2009–2010). http://www.DPAcontest.org/v2/
39. Coron, J.-S., Kizhvatov, I.: An efficient method for random delay generation in embedded software. In: Clavier, C., Gaj, K. (eds.) CHES 2009. LNCS, vol. 5747, pp. 156–170. Springer, Heidelberg (2009). https://doi.org/10.1007/978-3-642-04138-9_12
40. James, G., Witten, D., Hastie, T., Tibshirani, R.: An Introduction to Statistical Learning. STS, vol. 103. Springer, New York (2013). https://doi.org/10.1007/978-1-4614-7138-7
41. Klambauer, G., Unterthiner, T., Mayr, A., Hochreiter, S.: Self-normalizing neural networks. arXiv preprint arXiv:1706.02515 (2017)
42. Strobl, C., Boulesteix, A.L., Zeileis, A., Hothorn, T.: Bias in random forest variable importance measures: illustrations, sources and a solution. BMC Bioinform. **8**(1), 25 (2007)
43. He, K., Zhang, X., Ren, S., Sun, J.: Deep residual learning for image recognition. CoRR abs/1512.03385 (2015)
44. Timon, B.: Non-profiled deep learning-based side-channel attacks. Cryptology ePrint Archive, Report 2018/196 (2018). https://eprint.iacr.org/2018/196

Differential Fault Attack on SKINNY Block Cipher

Navid Vafaei[1], Nasour Bagheri[1,2($\boxtimes$)], Sayandeep Saha[3],
and Debdeep Mukhopadhyay[3]

[1] Electrical Engineering Department, Shahid Rajaee Teacher Training University,
Tehran, Iran
navid.vafaee@gmail.com, NBagheri@sru.ac.ir
[2] School of Computer Science, Institute for Research in Fundamental Sciences (IPM),
Tehran, Iran
[3] Department of Computer Science and Engineering, Indian Institute of Technology
Kharagpur, Kharagpur, India
sahasayandeep@cse.iitkgp.ernet.in, debdeep@iitkgp.ac.in

Abstract. SKINNY is a family of tweakable lightweight block ciphers,
proposed in CRYPTO 2016. The proposal of SKINNY describes two
block size variants of 64 and 128 bits as well as three options for
tweakey. In this paper, we present differential fault analysis (DFA) of
four SKINNY variants – SKINNY 64-64, SKINNY 128-128, SKINNY 64-
128 and SKINNY 128-256. The attack model of tweakable block ciphers
allow the access and full control of the tweak by the attacker. Respecting
this attack model, we assume a fixed tweak for the attack window. With
this assumption, extraction of the master key of SKINNY requires about
10 nibble fault injections on average for 64-bit versions of the cipher,
whereas the 128-bit versions require roughly 21 byte fault injections.
The attacks were validated through extensive simulation. To the best of
authors' knowledge, this is the first DFA attack on SKINNY tweakable
block cipher family and, in fact, any practical realization of tweakable
block ciphers.

Keywords: Block cipher · Differential fault attack · SKINNY

1 Introduction

Fault analysis attacks are one of the potent practical threats to modern cryptographic implementations. Originally proposed by Boneh et al. [8] in September 1996 in the context of the RSA algorithm, fault attacks were readily extended for symmetric key cryptosystems by Biham and Shamir [6] as Differential Fault Analysis (DFA). The main idea of DFA is to analyze the XOR differential between the correct and the corresponding faulty ciphertexts to extract the secret key. So far DFAs are the most fundamental classes of fault attacks for symmetric key primitives and has been applied on several block ciphers like

© Springer Nature Switzerland AG 2018
A. Chattopadhyay et al. (Eds.): SPACE 2018, LNCS 11348, pp. 177–197, 2018.
https://doi.org/10.1007/978-3-030-05072-6_11

AES, PRESENT, PRINCE, SIMON and Hash algorithms like SHA3 and Grøstl [1,3,4,7,9,10,17,23–25,29]. Even with the discovery of certain other sophisticated classes of fault attacks such as Blind Fault Attack (BFA) [16], Fault sensitivity analysis (FSA) [18], Statistical Fault Attack (SFA) [11], Differential Fault Intensity Analysis (DFIA) [12] attacks, DFA still remains as a prime tool for cipher analysis mainly due to its low fault complexity and extremely relaxed fault model assumptions compared to the aforementioned attacks.

SKINNY [5] is a new lightweight tweakable block cipher which was presented to compete with the NSA recent design, SIMON. The *tweakable block cipher* is a relatively new concept for block cipher design, originally proposed by Liskov, Rivest and Wagner in [19]. Unlike conventional block ciphers, which take a secret key and a public message as inputs, a tweakable block cipher expects another public input known as *tweak*. Each fixed setting of the tweak is supposed to give rise to a different, apparently independent, family of block cipher encryption operators. Informally, the security requirement of a tweakable block cipher demands the cipher to remain secure even if the adversary can observe and control the tweak. Also, from a practical point of view, changing the tweak should be more efficient than altering the secret key. Tweaks have been efficiently utilized in past to provide resistance against certain side-channel attacks [13,21]. Apart from that, tweakable block ciphers may find its use for low latency implementations of several applications like memory and disk encryption [5].

SKINNY adopts the concept of tweakable block ciphers in the context of lightweight cryptography. In order to provide the tweak feature, a generalized version of the *STK* construction (also known as the *TWEAKEY* construction) [15] was utilized. On the other hand, the design of SKINNY guarantees high security against conventional differential and linear cryptanalysis. The serialized implementation on ASIC has a very small footprint. Furthermore, the SKINNY family is engineered to be highly customizable. The Substitution-Permutation-Network (SPN) construction of this cipher supports two different block sizes of 64 and 128 bits. The key (termed as *tweakey* in SKINNY specification) size can vary up to 512 bits. The original specification describes the parameterized variants as SKINNY n-n, SKINNY n-$2n$ and SKINNY n-$3n$, where n denotes the block size of the cipher, and n, $2n$ and $3n$ denoting the tweakey size. As recommended by the authors of SKINNY, the tweak material is processed within the same framework as of the key material following the TWEAKEY philosophy [15].

So far, impossible differential attack for reduced-round of all variants of SKINNY was presented [2,14,20,22,27]. However, no implemented-based attack was ever reported on SKINNY, to the best of the authors' knowledge. In this context, it is worth mentioning that, evaluation against implementation-based attacks is crucial for lightweight block ciphers for which the deployment of area and power-hungry countermeasures are not economic. Also, most of the lightweight ciphers are supposed to be deployed on in-field devices (e.g. RFID tags, sensor nodes) which are physically accessible by the adversaries. Consequently, implementation-based attacks like side-channel and fault injection become highly practical for lightweight block ciphers.

In this paper we perform differential fault analysis attacks on four SKINNY variants described as SKINNY n-n, SKINNY n-$2n$ (for $n = 64$ and 128). However, the attacks are easily extendable to the other variants. We consider the tweak may remain fixed during the attack and is known to the attacker. It is found that, *roughly 10 random nibble/byte fault injections at 4 different nibble/byte locations at the beginning of the $R-4$-th round of SKINNY (having total R iterative rounds) is sufficient to extract the master key for variants SKINNY n-n, SKINNY n-$2n$ (while tweak is enabled)*. The theoretical analysis is also validated by extensive simulation experiments on software implementations of SKINNY.

The rest of this paper is organized as follows. In Sect. 2, we present the specification of the SKINNY cipher family. The DFA attacks on SKINNY are described in Sect. 3. Complexity analysis and simulation results to validate the attacks is elaborated in Sect. 4, followed by a discussion in Sect. 5, which sheds some light on the possibility of extending the attacks for other versions of SKINNY. Finally, we conclude in Sect. 6.

2   Specification of SKINNY

In this section, we briefly describe the SKINNY specification. First, an overview of the input-output and key formats are provided. Next, we provide short summaries for the cipher sub-operations which are relevant in the context of DFA attacks. For a detailed description of each sub-operation one may refer to [5]. A summary of important notations, used throughout this paper, is given in Table 1.

2.1   General Description

SKINNY follows an SPN structure supporting two block sizes of 64 and 128 bits, respectively. For convenience, in this paper the block size is denoted as a parameter n. The input plaintext is denoted as $\boldsymbol{m} = m_1||m_2|| \cdots ||m_{15}||m_{16}$, with each m_i denoting an s-bit cell with $s = \frac{n}{16}$ (a cell is a nibble for 64-bit block size or a byte for 128-bit block size). Following the standard convention for representing SPN ciphers, the input as well as the internal states (IS) are arranged as 4×4 matrix of cells. The representation of IS is described in Eq. (1). For the sake of explanation, all the indices start from 1 (i.e. $i \in \{1, 2, 3, \cdots, 15, 16\}$)[1]. Also, the indexing of the state is row-wise.

$$IS = \begin{bmatrix} x_1 & x_2 & x_3 & x_4 \\ x_5 & x_6 & x_7 & x_8 \\ x_9 & x_{10} & x_{11} & x_{12} \\ x_{13} & x_{14} & x_{15} & x_{16} \end{bmatrix} \tag{1}$$

Following the *TWEAKEY* framework of [15], in SKINNY the tweak and the key material are handled in a unified way. The cipher receives a tweakey input

---

[1] Throughout this paper, the array/state indices start from 1.

Table 1. Frequently used notations

Notation	Explanation
n	Block size
s	Width of each cell in bits ($s = \frac{n}{16}$)
R	Total number of rounds
t	Total length of the tweakey
z	$\frac{t}{n}$
TK_l	The l-th tweakey array ($l \in \{1,2,3\}$)
$\mathcal{L}_2$	The LFSR corresponding to the tweakey array TK_2
$\mathcal{L}_3$	The LFSR corresponding to the tweakey array TK_3
IS	Internal state
IS^r	The internal state at round r
$TK_{l,i}^r$	The i-th key-cell of the t-th tweakey array at the r-th round
X_i^r	The i-th cell at the input state of Subcells at round r
Y_i^r	The i-th cell at the input state of AddConstants at round r
Z_i^r	The i-th cell at the input state of AddRoundTweakey at round r
U_i^r	The i-th cell at the input state of ShiftRows at round r
V_i^r	The i-th cell at the input state of MixColumns at round r
$Rcon_i^r$	The i-th cell of the round constant at round r
ΔA_i^r	The i-th cell of the differential of correct and faulty computation at some internal state A at round r
C_i	The i-th cell of the correct ciphertext
C_i^*	The i-th cell of the faulty ciphertext

of length t as $\boldsymbol{tk} = tk_1 \| tk_2 \| \cdots \| tk_{16z}$. Here, tk_i is an s-bit cell and $z = \frac{t}{n}$. In general, three tweakey lengths of $t = n$-bit, $t = 2n$-bit and $t = 3n$-bit are supported. The tweakey state is arranged into three 4×4 matrices for different values of z[2]. Precisely, for $1 \leq i \leq 16$, $TK_1 = tk_i$ when $z = 1$, $TK_1 = tk_i$, $TK_2 = tk_{16+i}$ when $z = 2$, and $TK_1 = tk_i$, $TK_2 = tk_{16+i}$, $TK_3 = tk_{32+i}$ when $z = 3$. Just like the internal state, the tweakey states are also arranged row-wise in the matrices TK_1, TK_2 and TK_3[3].

At this point, it is worth mentioning that the *TWEAKEY* framework of SKINNY provides a very flexible mean of switching between the tweak-enabled and tweak-free version of the cipher. In the classical tweak-free setting all three matrices TK_1, TK_2 and TK_3 can be loaded with key-material. On the other hand, it is recommended that the tweak-enabled version should only use the TK_1

---

[2] The terms tweakey and key have been used interchangeably throughout this paper, whereas to indicate the public material we use the term tweak.

[3] Tweakey/key states and tweakey/key arrays have been used interchangeably with the same meaning in this work.

matrix to handle the tweak material. This flexible unified way of processing the key and the tweaks, however, somewhat simplifies the DFA attacks, as we shall show later in this paper. In the next subsection, we provide necessary details of different sub-operations of SKINNY.

Table 2. Number of rounds of SKINNY for different input and tweakey sizes

Block size (n)/tweakey size (z)	1	2	3
64 bits	32 rounds	36 rounds	40 rounds
128 bits	40 rounds	48 rounds	56 rounds

2.2 Specification of Sub-operations

The specification of SKINNY describes iterative rounds consisting total 5 sub-operations – SubCells (SC), AddConstants (AC), AddRoundTweaks (ART), ShiftRows (SR), and MixColumns (MC). The number of rounds depends on input and tweakey sizes (see Table 2). Figure 1 presents a schematic representation of the SKINNY round function [5].

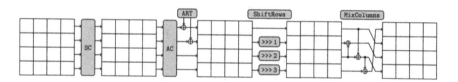

Fig. 1. The SKINNY round function

SubCells(SC): The S-Box sub-operation of SKINNY applies a non-linear bijective transformation on each cell of the internal state (IS). Following the notational conventions of this paper, the S-Box transformation can be represented as

$$Y_i^r = S(X_i^r), \text{with } 1 \le i \le 16, 1 \le r \le R \qquad (2)$$

where X_i^r and Y_i^r present input and output cells of the r-th round S-Box sub-operation. SKINNY utilizes $s \times s$ S-Boxes depending on the block size n. The S-Box for $s = 4$ is shown in Table 3, which is constructed using a simple bit-level non-linear transform followed by bit rotations. We do not show the S-Box for $s = 8$ which is constructed using a similar philosophy. Further details on the S-Boxes can be found in [5].

Table 3. The 4-bit S-box used in SKINNY-64 in hexadecimal form.

x	0	1	2	3	4	5	6	7	8	9	A	B	C	D	E	F
$S_4[x]$	C	6	9	0	1	A	2	B	3	8	5	D	4	E	7	F

`AddConstants`(AC): This sub-operation of SKINNY adds the round constants ($Rcon$) with the internal state. Mathematically, $Z_i^r = Y_i^r \oplus Rcon_i^r$, with $1 \leq i \leq 16, 1 \leq r \leq R$. The constants are generated using a 6-bit affine Linear Feedback Shift Register (LFSR).

`AddRoundTweakey`(ART): The ART sub-operation of SKINNY applies key-whitening to the two first rows of the IS. The tweak-key array TK_1 (also TK_2 and TK_3 whenever applicable) is maintained as 4×4 states of s-bit cells, just like the IS. The first two rows of TK_l ($l \in \{1, 2, 3\}$) are extracted and bitwise XOR-ed with IS, respecting the array positioning. In other words,

$$U_i^r = Z_i^r \oplus TK_{1,i}^r, \text{for } z = 1 \tag{3}$$
$$U_i^r = Z_i^r \oplus TK_{1,i}^r \oplus TK_{2,i}^r, \text{for } z = 2 \tag{4}$$
$$U_i^r = Z_i^r \oplus TK_{1,i}^r \oplus TK_{2,i}^r \oplus TK_{3,i}^r, \text{for } z = 3 \tag{5}$$

where, $1 \leq i \leq 8$, and $1 \leq r \leq R$.

As it is shown in Fig. 2, the tweakey arrays are updated using 2 linear functions. First, a cell-wise permutation PT is applied on each cell, which is followed by the application of a cell-wise LFSR only for the cells of the first two rows of the 4×4 key states. Equation (6) shows the permutation PT, whereas, Eq. (7) presents the LFSRs corresponding to TK_2 and TK_3 (for different cell sizes). For convenience, we represent the LFSR for TK_2 as $\mathcal{L}_2$ and that for TK_3 as $\mathcal{L}_3$, respectively. It is worth mentioning that, no LFSR is applied on TK_1.

$$PT = [9, 15, 8, 13, 10, 14, 12, 11, 0, 1, 2, 3, 4, 5, 6, 7] \tag{6}$$

$$(x_4||x_3||x_2||x_1) \rightarrow (x_3||x_2||x_1||x_4 \oplus x_3), \text{for } TK_2 \text{ and } s = 4 \tag{7}$$
$$(x_8||x_7||x_6||x_5||x_4||x_3||x_2||x_1) \rightarrow (x_7||x_6||x_5||x_4||x_3||x_2||x_1||x_8 \oplus x_6), \text{for } TK_2 \text{ and } s = 8$$
$$(x_4||x_3||x_2||x_1) \rightarrow (x_1 \oplus x_4||x_4||x_3||x_2), \text{for } TK_3 \text{ and } s = 4$$
$$(x_8||x_7||x_6||x_5||x_4||x_3||x_2||x_1) \rightarrow (x_1 \oplus x_7||x_8||x_7||x_6||x_5||x_4||x_3||x_2), \text{for } TK_2 \text{ and } s = 8$$

`ShiftRows`(SR): The SR sub-operation performs a cell-wise right-rotation of 0, 1, 2 and 3 cells for the first, second, third and fourth row of IS. According to the notations used in this paper, it is written as,

$$V_i^r = U_{P[i]}^r, \text{with } 1 \leq i \leq 16, 1 \leq r \leq R \tag{8}$$

where, P is given as,

$$P = [0, 1, 2, 3, 7, 4, 5, 6, 10, 11, 8, 9, 13, 14, 15, 12] \tag{9}$$

`MixColumns`(MC): The final sub-operation of SKINNY multiplies the IS with a 4×4 matrix $\mathbf{M}$. More precisely, we have $X^{r+1} = \mathbf{M} \times V^r$, with $\mathbf{M}$ given as,

$$\mathbf{M} = \begin{bmatrix} 1 & 0 & 1 & 1 \\ 1 & 0 & 0 & 0 \\ 0 & 1 & 1 & 0 \\ 1 & 0 & 1 & 0 \end{bmatrix} \tag{10}$$

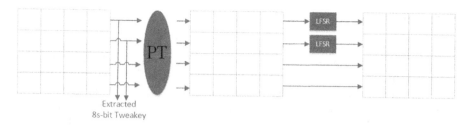

Fig. 2. The tweakey schedule

From the next section onwards, we shall describe the DFA attacks on SKINNY n-n and SKINNY n-$2n$.

3   Differential Fault Analysis of SKINNY

The main concept behind DFA attacks is to a inject localized fault in the computation and then to analyze the XOR difference between the correct and the corrupted computation, starting from the correct and the corresponding faulty ciphertexts. Following this basic approach, in this section, we present key recovery attacks on two SKINNY variants – SKINNY n-n and SKINNY n-$2n$. For the first variant, we assume that no tweak is present, whereas, in the second variant it is assumed that TK_1 carries the tweak material and TK_2 carries key material. In the following subsection, we present the attack model. The attacks will be presented in subsequent subsections.

3.1   Attack Model

The attacks in the paper are based on the following assumptions:

- The attacker can observe the tweak (if exists) but and can fix it to a certain known value. Although, it is a relatively strong assumption, the security model of tweakable block ciphers allow the control of the tweak material. Any breach of security following this attack model can be considered as a potential threat.
- The attacker can inject random byte (or nibble faults if $n = 64$) faults in the datapath of SKINNY. The injected faults can be controlled to corrupt the data in a specific round. In the context of DFA attacks, it is practical and, in fact, the minimal assumption. Further, we assume that the attacker does not know the location of the corrupted byte/nibble. This is also a fairly reasonable and relaxed assumption in the context of fault attacks.

Throughout this paper, the attacks will be described on parameterized versions of the cipher. In the next subsection we describe the basic attack on SKINNY n-n.

3.2   DFA on SKINNY n-n

Let us assume that an s-bit fault (nibble fault for 64 bit versions and byte fault for 128 bit versions), f is injected at the first cell of the SKINNY state at the beginning of round $R-4$ (in other words, the fault corrupts X_1^{R-4}). The propagation of the fault differential is shown in Fig. 3. Referring to Fig. 3, we introduce new variables $(f, F, G, H$ etc.) while the fault differential propagates through a non-linear (S-Box) operation. This is because the differential

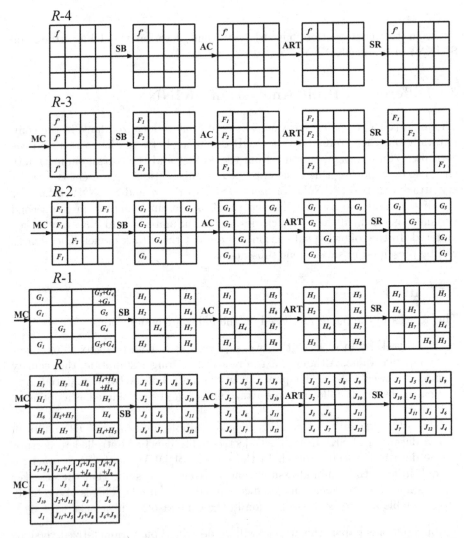

Fig. 3. The fault propagation pattern in SKINNY with the fault induced at the 1st cell in the beginning of round $(R-4)$. Each variable represents a non-zero fault differential and each empty cell specify a zero differential.

propagation through an S-Box is not a bijective mapping. On the other hand, fault propagation through linear diffusion layers is fully bijective. Also, the diffusion layer, especially the MixColumns sub-operation is responsible for the spread (fault diffusion) of the fault throughout the state.

Discovering the Injection Location: Figure 4 describes all the fault diffusion patterns for 16 possible fault injection locations at round $R-4$. The patterns are computed up to the penultimate MixColumns operation (that is up to the end of $R - 1$th round.). However, the patterns remain the same up to the input of the MC operation at round R. It is interesting to observe that all these fault patterns are distinct (except the 4 where the fault is injected at cells from the third row). The distinctness of the fault patterns can be observed by the attacker if she just applies inverse MixColumns on the differential ΔC of the correct ciphertext C and faulty ciphertext C^*. *Due to this correspondence between the injection locations and the fault patterns, the attacker can uniquely deduce the injection location of the fault.* The only exception happens for injections in the third row. The attacker, in this case, can run the attacks assuming all 4 possible positions, one at a time. The attack complexity will increase 4 times for these cases which is reasonable.

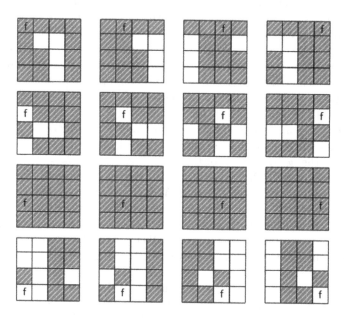

Fig. 4. The fault propagation pattern for each fault location at round $R - 4$. Here f indicates the fault injection location and it the colored pattern presents the fault diffusion pattern upto the MixColumns of the penultimate round (that is at the output of round $R - 1$).

3.3 Key Recovery Attack

Most of the DFA attacks on block ciphers exploit difference equations constructed across the non-linear layers (e.g. S-Boxes) to recover the secret keys. More formally, we are interested in the solutions for x in the equations $SC(x \oplus \Delta_{ip}) \oplus SC(x) = \Delta_o$, where Δ_{ip} and Δ_o denote the input and output differentials of the non-linear layers, respectively and SC denotes the non-linear sub-operation (S-Box for most of the modern block ciphers). The equations are the same for inverse operations and expressed as $SC^{-1}(x \oplus \Delta_o) \oplus SC^{-1}(x) = \Delta_{ip}$.

In the context of DFAs, the quantity x indicates a part of the unknown key. In most of the cases, we are interested in the inverse S-Box equations. From now onwards we shall denote them as *fault difference equations*[4]. One can write several such equations corresponding to each S-Box under consideration. The main idea is to solve this system of equations for keys, with the output differentials Δ_o known. The input differentials Δ_{ip} may not be fully known to the adversary. However, at least some partial knowledge of Δ_{ip} must be there, so that the correct key candidates can be distinguished from the wrong key candidates. For example, in [28], it was shown that for AES, the input differentials for 4 S-Boxes are linearly related. Such linear relations on the input differentials reduced the key space of AES from 2^{128} to 2^8.

A critical factor at this point is the number of solutions for keys of the aforementioned difference equations. The S-Boxes typically behave as non-bijective mappings while given a differential as input (this leads to Differential Distribution Tables (DDTs)). As a result, for the same input-output differential one may obtain multiple solutions for x, as well as, 0 solutions for some input-output differentials which are known as *impossible differentials*. To handle multiple solutions, in DFA, the average number of solutions for one difference equation over the complete DDT is considered for calculation. If both the Δ_{ip} and Δ_o are known exactly, no impossible differential can happen (as otherwise, there will be no solution for the key which is a contradiction). In such cases, the average is to be taken over the non-zero part of the DDT [26].

In the case of SKINNY, the key extraction is somewhat simpler as the attacker can observe both the Δ_{ip} and Δ_o for several cases. The cause for this will be elaborated soon in the subsequent paragraphs. For the time being, we are interested in calculating the *average number of non-zero solutions for the fault difference equations*. Table 4, presents the DDT for the 4×4 S-Box of SKINNY. The average number of non-zero solutions for this S-Box is 2.63.

We elaborate the fault propagation in SKINNY through Fig. 3, which presents a fault propagation pattern for the fault injected at cell 1, at the beginning of round $R - 4$. The last grid in Fig. 3 denotes the ciphertext differential ΔC. One can apply the inverse of MC and SR to reach the output of the ART sub-operation, which, according to the nomenclature of this paper is denoted as U^R. At this point, one needs to guess the keys for the two upper rows of the

---

[4] Note that in this paper we have used both the term difference and differential. Both have the same meaning in the context of this paper.

Table 4. Differential input-output of SubCells of SKINNY 64

Input/output	0	1	2	3	4	5	6	7	8	9	A	B	C	D	E	F
0	16	0	0	0	0	0	0	0	0	0	0	0	0	0	0	0
1	0	0	0	0	0	0	0	0	4	4	4	4	0	0	0	0
2	0	4	0	4	0	4	4	0	0	0	0	0	0	0	0	0
3	0	0	0	0	0	0	0	0	2	2	2	2	2	4	2	2
4	0	0	4	0	0	0	2	2	0	0	0	4	2	2	0	0
5	0	0	4	0	0	0	2	2	0	0	4	0	4	2	0	0
6	0	2	0	2	2	0	0	2	2	0	2	0	0	2	2	0
7	0	2	0	2	2	0	0	2	0	2	0	2	2	0	0	2
8	0	0	0	0	4	4	0	0	0	0	0	0	2	2	2	2
9	0	0	0	0	4	4	0	0	0	0	0	0	2	2	2	2
A	0	0	0	0	0	4	4	0	2	2	2	2	0	0	0	0
B	0	4	0	4	0	0	0	0	0	0	0	0	2	2	2	2
C	0	0	4	0	0	0	2	2	4	0	0	0	0	0	2	2
D	0	0	4	0	0	0	2	2	0	4	0	0	0	0	2	2
E	0	2	0	2	2	0	0	2	0	2	0	2	0	2	2	0
F	0	2	0	2	2	0	0	2	2	0	4	0	2	0	0	2

state in order to invert the ART sub-operation. However, the two lower rows do not require any key addition and they can be easily inverted up to the input of the SC sub-operation. Mathematically, thus we have,

$$\Delta X_i^R = SC^{-1}(Y_i^R) \oplus SC^{-1}(Y_i^{*R})$$
$$= SC^{-1}(AC^{-1}(ART^{-1}(SR^{-1}(MC^{-1}(C)_i)))) \oplus SC^{-1}(AC^{-1}(ART^{-1}(SR^{-1}(MC^{-1}(C^*)_i))))$$

$$(11)$$

which is valid for $i \in \{9, 10 \cdots, 16\}$. On the other hand, for $i \in \{1, 2, \cdots, 8\}$ we have,

$$\Delta X_i^R = SC^{-1}(Y_i^R) \oplus SC^{-1}(Y_i^{*R})$$
$$= SC^{-1}(AC^{-1}(ART^{-1}(SR^{-1}(MC^{-1}(C)_i) \oplus TK_{1,i}^R))) \oplus$$
$$SC^{-1}(AC^{-1}(ART^{-1}(SR^{-1}(MC^{-1}(C^*)_i) \oplus TK_{1,i}^R)))$$

$$(12)$$

In both the Eqs. (11) and (12), $MC^{-1}(C)_i$ and $MC^{-1}(C^*)_i$ denote ith cell of the input of the MixColumns sub-operation. The basic difference between Eqs. (11) and (12) is that for the former X_i^R can be uniquely determined from the correct and the faulty ciphertexts, whereas for the later X_i^R is unknown and depends on the guessed value of $TK_{1,i}^R$. The set equations represented by Eq. (12) actually provides the fault difference equations as follows,

$$\Delta X_i^R = SC^{-1}(Y_i^R) \oplus SC^{-1}(Y_i^{*R})$$
$$= SC^{-1}(U_i^R \oplus TK_{1,i}^R) \oplus SC^{-1}(U_i^R \oplus \Delta U_i^R \oplus TK_{1,i}^R) \tag{13}$$

where $\Delta U_i^R = U_i^R \oplus U_i^{*R}$. Note that $i \in \{1, 2, \cdots 8\}$.

Referring to the Fig. 3, ΔX_i^R indicates the fault differentials at the beginning of the R-th round (in other words, the differentials at the output of $R-1$-th round MC.). Interesting linear patterns can be observed at this stage of computation between ΔX_i^Rs for different values of i. For example, let us consider ΔX_1^R, ΔX_5^R and ΔX_{13}^R. From Fig. 3 we have,

$$\Delta X_1^R = \Delta X_5^R = \Delta X_{13}^R = H_1. \tag{14}$$

Now, according to the previous analysis, ΔX_{13}^R is uniquely known to the adversary. Utilizing this fact, we can solve Eq. (13) for $i = 1$ and $i = 5$. *As in this case both the input and output differences are known and we can expect 2.63 solutions on average for* $TK_{1,1}^R$ *and* $TK_{1,5}^R$. *In general, another one or two injections at the same fault location returns the unique key for this cell.* Similarly, from Fig. 3 we have, $\Delta X_2^R = \Delta X_{14}^R = H_7$, which eventually returns 2.63 solutions for $TK_{1,2}^R$, which can further be reduced to an unique solution with another fault (or 2 more faults in some rare cases).

In the case of ΔX_{12}^R, ΔX_{16}^R we have $\Delta X_{12}^R = H_4$ and $\Delta X_{16}^R = H_4 \oplus H_5$. Using these two, the unique value of H_5 can be computed which is equal to ΔX_8^R. Consequently, unique solution for $TK_{1,8}^R$ can be obtained. *Overall, we can extract 4 key cells* $TK_{1,1}^R$, $TK_{1,2}^R$, $TK_{1,5}^R$, *and* $TK_{1,8}^R$ *uniquely with 2-3 faults injected at the 1-th cell at the beginning of round* $R - 4$ *on average.*

It is worth mentioning that, the rest of the 4 key cells cannot be extracted with the fault location set at the first cell of round $R - 4$. The reason is twofold. Firstly, one should observe that ΔX_6^R, ΔX_7^R, ΔX_{11}^R and ΔX_{15}^R are always 0, due to incomplete diffusion of the fault. No key extraction is possible for these cases, as the fault difference equation returns only one trivial solution 0, while both the input and output differentials are 0. The second situation takes place for ΔX_3^R and ΔX_4^R. For the sake of explanation, let us first consider ΔX_4^R which assumes value $H_3 + H_4 + H_5$. Although, $H_4 + H_5$ is known, the value of H_3 is unknown. As a result, ΔX_4^R will assume all possible 2^s values (2^8 for $n = 128$, and 2^4 for $n = 4$)[5]. For a similar reason, no key can be extracted with ΔX_3^R.

Extraction of the Remaining Rth Round Keys: For the extraction of $TK_{1,3}^R$, $TK_{1,4}^R$, $TK_{1,6}^R$, and $TK_{1,7}^R$ another fault injection is essential. It is apparent that there is no gain if the fault location is kept unaltered. So, the next injection should happen at a different fault location. Choice of the fault location is crucial in this case as according to Fig. 4, different fault location enables

---

[5] Actually this claim is not entirely true. In fact, depending on the value of the output differential, only a certain set of input differentials will satisfy the fault difference equation for this case, whose count is expected to be $< 2^s$. However, to exploit this observation a lot of fault injections will be required. As we shall show, that we can perform the attack with much less number of faults.

extraction of different key cells. Further, the sets of extracted key cells corresponding to two different fault locations may have intersections. In other words, two fault locations may lead to the extraction of same key cells twice, while some of the key cells may still remain unexplored. The solution to this issue is to select two fault locations for which the resulting fault patterns are non-overlapping. As a concrete example, we present the fault pattern for the fault injected at the 3rd cell at the beginning of round $R - 4$ (see Fig. 5). For this fault pattern we can extract $TK_{1,3}^R, TK_{1,4}^R, TK_{1,6}^R$, and $TK_{1,7}^R$. This completes the extraction of the complete round key of the round R (the last round). The *fault complexity* of the attack is $2 \times 2.6 = 5.2$ faults on average. However, it is worth noting that depending on the value of the plaintext and the injected faults, the number of faults may vary. The reason behind this fact is that during the analysis, we consider the average case for which 2.6 solution is expected from the difference equations. However, from the differential distribution table of the 4×4 SKINNY S-Box in Table 4, it can be seen that for a known input-output difference pair, either 2 or 4 solutions are possible for most of the cases. Although this count should get averaged out while different equations are considered together, in practice we may require more or fewer faults in some cases. However, the number of extra injections (or fewer injections) are consistent, in general, with the theoretical estimate and do not influence the efficiency or the attack strategy.

Extraction of the Master Key: The SKINNY key schedule uses only half of the entire key material in each round. Figure 6 describes the two consecutive stages of the SKINNY tweakey schedule. As we are considering SKINNY n-n versions, TK_1 is the only tweakey state involved, which just permutes the tweakey cells using the permutation PT. *It can be observed that completely independent tweakey cells are used in two consecutive rounds.* Consequently, the last round key exposes only half of the tweakey state and in order to obtain the master key, the penultimate round key should also be extracted.

The goal now is to extract two consecutive round keys with minimum number of fault injections. The straightforward way of minimizing the fault injections is to reuse the fault propagation patterns we obtained to extract the last round key. Once the last round keys are extracted, the last round can be inverted. Now the fault difference equations, corresponding to the fault pattern of Fig. 3, can be constructed for round $R - 1$ as follows,

$$\Delta X_i^{R-1} = SC^{-1}(Y_i^{R-1}) \oplus SC^{-1}(Y_i^{*R-1})$$
$$= SC^{-1}(AC^{-1}(ART^{-1}(SR^{-1}(MC^{-1}(X^R)_i)))) \oplus SC^{-1}(AC^{-1}(ART^{-1}(SR^{-1}(MC^{-1}(X^{*R})_i))))$$
(15)

Here, $i \in \{9, 10, \cdots, 16\}$. For the rest of the cells we have,

$$\Delta X_i^{R-1} = SC^{-1}(Y_i^{R-1}) \oplus SC^{-1}(Y_i^{*R-1})$$
$$= SC^{-1}(AC^{-1}(ART^{-1}(SR^{-1}(MC^{-1}(X^R)_i) \oplus TK_{1,i}^{R-1}))) \oplus$$
$$SC^{-1}(AC^{-1}(ART^{-1}(SR^{-1}(MC^{-1}(X^{*R})_i) \oplus TK_{1,i}^{R-1})))$$
(16)

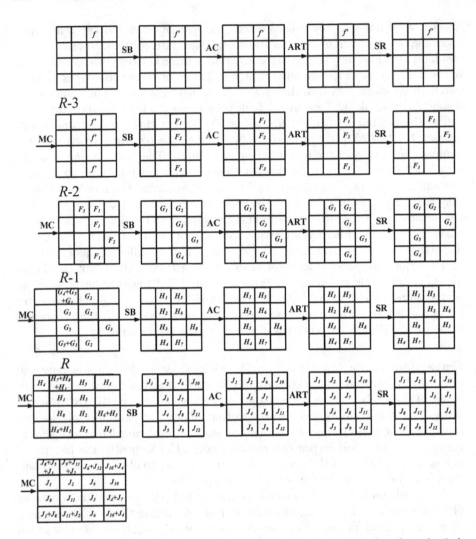

Fig. 5. The fault propagation pattern in SKINNY with the fault induced at the 3rd cell in the beginning of round $(R-4)$ (at cell number 3). Each variable represents a non-zero fault differential and each empty cell specify a zero differential.

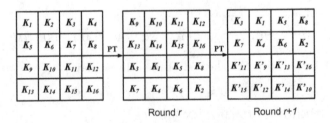

Fig. 6. The usage of the key material in SKINNY for tweakey array TK_1.

In both the equations $MC^{-1}(X^R)_i$ and $MC^{-1}(X^{*R})_i$ denote the i-th cells of the inverse MixColumns sub-operation corresponding to the correct and the faulty ciphertexts, respectively.

It follows from Fig. 3 that only 3 key cells ($TK_{1,1}^{R-1}$, $TK_{1,5}^{R-1}$ and $TK_{1,8}^{R-1}$) can be extracted uniquely with this fault pattern. None of the rest can, however, be extracted. Considering the other pattern from Fig. 5, we can extract total 6 key cells ($TK_{1,1}^{R-1}$, $TK_{1,5}^{R-1}$, $TK_{1,8}^{R-1}$, $TK_{1,3}^{R-1}$, $TK_{1,6}^{R-1}$ and $TK_{1,7}^{R-1}$). To extract rest of the key cells we need to inject more faults. Unfortunately, none of the two remaining fault patterns in the first row is able to extract the rest of the two key cells (i.e. $TK_{1,2}^{R-1}$ and $TK_{1,4}^{R-1}$) alone. As a result we need to inject two more faults (each twice) at cell 2 and cell 4 at the beginning of round $R-4$. *In summary, total $4 \times 2.63 = 10.55$ injections are required to uniquely determine the complete key state TK_1 of SKINNY. Once the full key state is recovered, the initial master key can be recovered trivially.*

Exploring Other Fault Locations: One interesting observation for SKINNY is that the fault patterns are quite diverse for different fault locations. For example, if a cell from the third row is corrupted at round $R-4$, the fault diffusion is complete within the penultimate round (see Fig. 4). Another distinct case happens for an injection in the second row, for which one can extract 5 key cells at the last round. It may seem that the second or third row is a better place for injecting faults. However, this is not entirely true because of the fact that we need to extract keys from two consecutive rounds. *In fact, we observe that at least 4 distinct fault locations are always required to extract these key cells (multiple injections at each location are required).* Alternatively, one may consider injections at the round $R-3$. However, the required number of injections is more for this case since the fault diffusion can not be complete at the penultimate round.

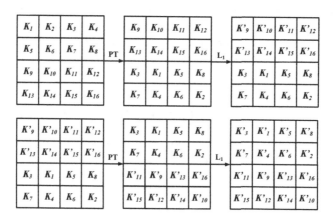

Fig. 7. The usage of the key material in SKINNY in tweakey array TK_2.

3.4 DFA on SKINNY n-$2n$

The attack described in the last two subsections only targets the case, while only TK_1 is used (that is for $z = 3$). However, the SKINNY specification allows two other cases for $z = 2$ and $z = 3$. Most importantly, the tweaks can be allowed. As already pointed out in Sect. 2.2, the TK_1 is recommended for processing the public tweak material. In this section, we shall extend the basic attack on SKINNY, for one of the cases where the tweak can be incorporated. More specifically, we consider the cases where TK_1 is used for the tweak and TK_2 is used for original key material.

Figure 7, describes the tweakey schedule of SKINNY for TK_2. Also, we have already depicted the tweakey schedule for TK_1 in Fig. 6. The first thing to observe in both the cases is that the complete tweakey state is divided into two consecutive rounds. So, just like the previous attack, we have to extract the key materials for two consecutive cases. However, unlike the previous case, where we obtained some permutation $\mathcal{L}_1^m$ of TK_1, here we obtain $\mathcal{L}_1^m(TK_1) \oplus \mathcal{L}_2^m(TK_2)$, where $\mathcal{L}_1$ and $\mathcal{L}_2$ denote the linear operations on TK_1 and TK_2, respectively. The $\mathcal{L}_1$ in this case simply denote the permutation PT whereas $\mathcal{L}_2$ represents the combined effect of the PT and the LFSR on TK_2. The index m is added here just to indicate the repeated use of these linear operations.

In order to extract the master key we need to extract TK_1 and TK_2 separately from $\mathcal{L}_1^m(TK_1) \oplus \mathcal{L}_2^m(TK_2)$. However, it is fairly straightforward in this case as the tweak TK_1 is public. The attacker can simply compute $\mathcal{L}_1^m(TK_1)$ and extract $\mathcal{L}_2^m(TK_2)$. Once the $\mathcal{L}_2^m(TK_2)$ is obtained, the TK_2 can be determined by simply inverting the LFSR and the Permutation round by round.

Although, the attack is fairly simple the consequence is important. It clearly indicates that *the tweaks in SKINNY do not provide any extra protection against fault attack if kept fixed even for a couple of invocations of the cipher*. Although the safest alternative is to change it in every invocation, it might not be easy for resource-constraint devices for which lightweight ciphers are actually meant for. Another obvious alternative is to keep the tweak secret. However, the attacker can still obtain the whole information regarding $\mathcal{L}_1^m(TK_1) \oplus \mathcal{L}_2^m(TK_2)$, which can provide significant entropy reduction for both TK_1 and TK_2 if not exposes them completely.

4 Fault Attack Complexity and Simulation Results

In this section, we summarize the complexity analysis of the attack. Further, we provide experimental support for the attacks described. The experiments were performed on an Intel Core-i5 machine with 8-GM RAM and 1-TB main memory. The simulation platform was MATLAB-2013b.

4.1 Fault Attack Complexity in SKINNY

The attack complexities were already mentioned at different places during describing the attacks. Here we summarize them, just for the sake of clarity. With the faults injected at the granularity of cells (that is 4-bit faults for SKINNY 64-64 and SKINNY 64-128 and 8 bit faults for SKINNY 128-128 and SKINNY 128-256) at the beginning of the $R - 4$th round, we require total 4 fault injection locations on average to extract the keys from last two rounds, which gives the complete key state. Further, taking the average number of non-zero solutions for each S-Box into consideration, the number of solutions for a single key cell of interest becomes 2.63. Among these 2.63 solutions, only one is the correct one. So, with roughly 2–3 more injections at the same location, a unique key can be recovered. Overall, for the 4×4 S-Boxes, we thus require total $4 \times 2.63 = 10.55$ injections.

4.2   Simulation Results

In order to validate the theoretical analysis, we performed extensive experiments through simulation. Here we present the results for SKINNY-64, for which we inject nibble faults. In order to get the general picture, faults were randomly injected at different locations of the internal state (we carefully avoided repetitions in one attack campaign, i.e. for each complete attack only 4 distinct random fault locations were considered.) at the beginning of round $R - 4$. Simulations were performed for 10000 random plaintext-key samples. Further, for each plaintext-key pair, 256 random(consists different location of faults with various value) injections were considered in order to consider the effect of different fault values and the average is taken.

Figure 8, presents the histograms for the number of faults required. Here we only present the results for SKINNY 64-64 and SKINNY 128-128 as the other configurations show similar trends. It can be observed that the average number of injections for SKINNY 64-64 is 10.6, which almost perfectly matches with the theoretically obtained average of 10.55. However, the theoretical average number of faults for the 8×8 S-Box of SKINNY 128-128 is about 21. In simulation, however, we obtain an average around 17. The discrepancy of the simulation and theoretical result in this case can be attributed to the fact that in most of the cases of the 8×8 S-Box, one obtain 2 or 4 solutions, and for a relatively less number of cases obtains 8 solutions (it is a purely statistical observation from the experiments). Due to this bias, the experimental average tends to remain near 17, whereas the theoretical average, which assigns uniform weight to all 2, 4, 6 and 8 solution cases, results in an overestimation. Further, one should also observe the tails of the histograms towards higher fault counts. One important feature of SKINNY attacks is that not every fault location returns an equal number of keys. Also, not every sequence of locations is equally effective. The large fault counts indicate some of these ill-conditioned fault sequences, which may also have a large number of solutions corresponding to each of their fault difference equations.

The execution time for the attacks is another important parameter. Figure 9, presents the execution time for the attacks from simulation. Note that, some of the practical issues like the probability of a successful fault injection, or acquisition time for faulty ciphertexts are ignored in this simulation-based experiments.

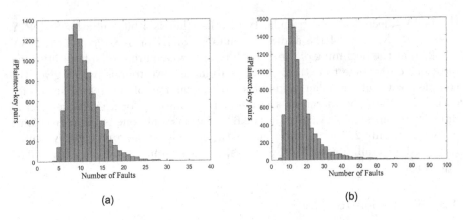

Fig. 8. Histogram showing the number of faults required for different random plaintext-key pairs.

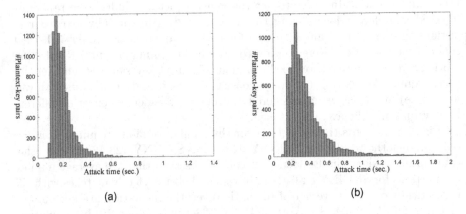

Fig. 9. Histogram showing the attack timing for different random plaintext-key pairs. An attack is considered complete while all the targeted key cells are uniquely discovered.

Here each fault is injected with 100% success probability. It can be observed that the average attack time ranges from 0.28 s (for SKINNY 64-64) to 0.38 s (for SKINNY 128-128). All the average counts have been summarized in Table 5.

Table 5. Average number of faults required to specify round keys

Version	Avg. number of faults	Avg. time for key recover
SKINNY 64	10.6	0.28
SKINNY 128	16.7	0.38

5   Discussion

It is worth mentioning that, the existence of tweaks do not influence the complexity of the attacks, until it is kept fixed. It directly follows from the theoretical analysis we presented in Sect. 3.4. Also, the basic attack for key extraction described in this paper works for other versions of SKINNY (e.g. SKINNY n-$3n$ and derivatives of them). However, extraction of the master keys will change. For example, considering the attacks on SKINNY n-$3n$, with TK_1 used for tweak, one need to extract both TK_2 and TK_3. Future extension of this work will describe attacks for these cases.

6   Conclusion

In this paper, we presented DFA attacks on SKINNY n-n and SKINNY n-$2n$. It has been observed that key extraction of SKINNY requires faults to be injected at different locations of the state, that too multiple times. We also presented supporting experimental validation of the theoretical analysis presented. One very crucial observation was that the public tweak does not provide any added security against fault injection attacks if kept fixed for only a couple of invocations of the cipher. In future, the attacks can be extended for other SKINNY versions. A very important extension could be to extend the attacks for variable tweaks. Another potential direction for future work would be to design suitable lightweight fault attack countermeasures for SKINNY.

References

1. Ali, S.S., Mukhopadhyay, D.: A differential fault analysis on AES key schedule using single fault. In: 2011 Workshop on Fault Diagnosis and Tolerance in Cryptography (FDTC), pp. 35–42. IEEE (2011)
2. Ankele, R., et al.: Related-key impossible-differential attack on reduced-round SKINNY. Technical report, Cryptology ePrint Archive, Report 2016/1127 (2016). http://eprint.iacr.org/2016/1127, 2017
3. Bagheri, N., Ebrahimpour, R., Ghaedi, N.: New differential fault analysis on present. EURASIP J. Adv. Sig. Process. **2013**(1), 145 (2013)
4. Bagheri, N., Ghaedi, N., Sanadhya, S.K.: Differential fault analysis of SHA-3. In: Biryukov, A., Goyal, V. (eds.) INDOCRYPT 2015. LNCS, vol. 9462, pp. 253–269. Springer, Cham (2015). https://doi.org/10.1007/978-3-319-26617-6_14
5. Beierle, C., et al.: The SKINNY family of block ciphers and its low-latency variant MANTIS. In: Robshaw, M., Katz, J. (eds.) CRYPTO 2016. LNCS, vol. 9815, pp. 123–153. Springer, Heidelberg (2016). https://doi.org/10.1007/978-3-662-53008-5_5
6. Biham, E., Shamir, A.: Differential fault analysis of secret key cryptosystems. In: Kaliski, B.S. (ed.) CRYPTO 1997. LNCS, vol. 1294, pp. 513–525. Springer, Heidelberg (1997). https://doi.org/10.1007/BFb0052259
7. Blömer, J., Seifert, J.-P.: Fault based cryptanalysis of the advanced encryption standard (AES). In: Wright, R.N. (ed.) FC 2003. LNCS, vol. 2742, pp. 162–181. Springer, Heidelberg (2003). https://doi.org/10.1007/978-3-540-45126-6_12

8. Boneh, D., DeMillo, R.A., Lipton, R.J.: On the importance of checking cryptographic protocols for faults. In: Fumy, W. (ed.) EUROCRYPT 1997. LNCS, vol. 1233, pp. 37–51. Springer, Heidelberg (1997). https://doi.org/10.1007/3-540-69053-0_4

9. Chen, H., Feng, J., Rijmen, V., Liu, Y., Fan, L., Li, W.: Improved fault analysis on SIMON block cipher family. In: 2016 Workshop on Fault Diagnosis and Tolerance in Cryptography (FDTC), pp. 16–24. IEEE (2016)

10. De Santis, F., Guillen, O.M., Sakic, E., Sigl, G.: Ciphertext-only fault attacks on PRESENT. In: Eisenbarth, T., Öztürk, E. (eds.) LightSec 2014. LNCS, vol. 8898, pp. 85–108. Springer, Cham (2015). https://doi.org/10.1007/978-3-319-16363-5_6

11. Dobraunig, C., Eichlseder, M., Korak, T., Lomné, V., Mendel, F.: Statistical fault attacks on nonce-based authenticated encryption schemes. In: Cheon, J.H., Takagi, T. (eds.) ASIACRYPT 2016, Part I. LNCS, vol. 10031, pp. 369–395. Springer, Heidelberg (2016). https://doi.org/10.1007/978-3-662-53887-6_14

12. Ghalaty, N.F., Yuce, B., Taha, M., Schaumont, P.: Differential fault intensity analysis. In: 2014 Workshop on Fault Diagnosis and Tolerance in Cryptography (FDTC), pp. 49–58. IEEE (2014)

13. Hajra, S., et al.: DRECON: DPA resistant encryption by construction. In: Pointcheval, David, Vergnaud, Damien (eds.) AFRICACRYPT 2014. LNCS, vol. 8469, pp. 420–439. Springer, Cham (2014). https://doi.org/10.1007/978-3-319-06734-6_25

14. Jean, J., Moradi, A., Peyrin, T., Sasdrich, P.: Bit-sliding: a generic technique for bit-serial implementations of SPN-based primitives - applications to AES, PRESENT and SKINNY. Cryptology ePrint Archive, Report 2017/600 (2017)

15. Jean, J., Nikolić, I., Peyrin, T.: Tweaks and keys for block ciphers: the TWEAKEY framework. In: Sarkar, P., Iwata, T. (eds.) ASIACRYPT 2014. LNCS, vol. 8874, pp. 274–288. Springer, Heidelberg (2014). https://doi.org/10.1007/978-3-662-45608-8_15

16. Korkikian, R., Pelissier, S., Naccache, D.: Blind fault attack against SPN ciphers. In: 2014 Workshop on Fault Diagnosis and Tolerance in Cryptography (FDTC), pp. 94–103. IEEE (2014)

17. Kumar, R., Jovanovic, P., Burleson, W., Polian, I.: Parametric Trojans for fault-injection attacks on cryptographic hardware. In: 2014 Workshop on Fault Diagnosis and Tolerance in Cryptography (FDTC), pp. 18–28. IEEE (2014)

18. Li, Y., Sakiyama, K., Gomisawa, S., Fukunaga, T., Takahashi, J., Ohta, K.: Fault sensitivity analysis. In: Mangard, S., Standaert, F.-X. (eds.) CHES 2010. LNCS, vol. 6225, pp. 320–334. Springer, Heidelberg (2010). https://doi.org/10.1007/978-3-642-15031-9_22

19. Liskov, M., Rivest, R.L., Wagner, D.: Tweakable block ciphers. In: Yung, M. (ed.) CRYPTO 2002. LNCS, vol. 2442, pp. 31–46. Springer, Heidelberg (2002). https://doi.org/10.1007/3-540-45708-9_3

20. Liu, G., Ghosh, M., Ling, S.: Security analysis of SKINNY under related-tweakey settings. Technical report, Cryptology ePrint Archive, Report 2016/1108 (2016). http://eprint.iacr.org/2016/1108

21. Patranabis, S., Roy, D.B., Mukhopadhyay, D.: Using tweaks to design fault resistant ciphers. In: 2016 29th International Conference on VLSI Design and 2016 15th International Conference on Embedded Systems (VLSID), pp. 585–586. IEEE (2016)

22. Sadeghi, S., Mohammadi, T., Bagheri, N.: Cryptanalysis of reduced round SKINNY block cipher. Technical report, Cryptology ePrint Archive, Report 2016/1120 (2016)

23. Saha, D., Chowdhury, D.R.: Diagonal fault analysis of Gr∅stl in dedicated MAC mode. In: IEEE International Symposium on Hardware Oriented Security and Trust, HOST 2015, Washington, DC, USA, 5–7 May 2015, pp. 100–105 (2015)
24. Saha, D., Mukhopadhyay, D., Chowdhury, D.R.: A diagonal fault attack on the advanced encryption standard. IACR Cryptology ePrint Archive 2009(581) (2009)
25. Song, L., Hu, L.: Differential fault attack on the PRINCE block cipher. In: Avoine, G., Kara, O. (eds.) LightSec 2013. LNCS, vol. 8162, pp. 43–54. Springer, Heidelberg (2013). https://doi.org/10.1007/978-3-642-40392-7_4
26. Takahashi, J., Fukunaga, T.: Improved differential fault analysis on CLEFIA. In: 5th Workshop on Fault Diagnosis and Tolerance in Cryptography, FDTC 2008, pp. 25–34. IEEE (2008)
27. Tolba, M., Abdelkhalek, A., Youssef, A.M.: Impossible differential cryptanalysis of SKINNY. Technical report, Cryptology ePrint Archive, Report 2016/1115 (2016). http://eprint.iacr.org/2016/1115
28. Tunstall, M., Mukhopadhyay, D., Ali, S.: Differential fault analysis of the advanced encryption standard using a single fault. In: Ardagna, C.A., Zhou, J. (eds.) WISTP 2011. LNCS, vol. 6633, pp. 224–233. Springer, Heidelberg (2011). https://doi.org/10.1007/978-3-642-21040-2_15
29. Tupsamudre, H., Bisht, S., Mukhopadhyay, D.: Differential fault analysis on the families of Simon and speck ciphers. In: 2014 Workshop on Fault Diagnosis and Tolerance in Cryptography (FDTC), pp. 40–48. IEEE (2014)

d-MUL: Optimizing and Implementing a Multidimensional Scalar Multiplication Algorithm over Elliptic Curves

Huseyin Hisil[1], Aaron Hutchinson[2], and Koray Karabina[2(✉)]

[1] Yasar University, İzmir, Turkey
[2] Florida Atlantic University, Boca Raton, USA
kkarabina@fau.edu

Abstract. This paper aims to answer whether *d*-MUL, the multidimensional scalar point multiplication algorithm, can be implemented efficiently. *d*-MUL is known to access costly matrix operations and requires memory access frequently. In the first part of the paper, we derive several theoretical results on the structure and the construction of the addition chains in *d*-MUL. These results are interesting on their own right. In the second part of the paper, we exploit our theoretical results, and propose an optimized variant of *d*-MUL. Our implementation results show that *d*-MUL can be very practical for small *d*, and it remains as an interesting algorithm to further explore for parallel implementation and cryptographic applications.

Keywords: *d*-MUL · Elliptic curve scalar multiplication
Differential addition chain · Isochronous implementation

1 Introduction

Let G be an abelian group of order $|G| = N$. A *single point multiplication algorithm* in G takes as input $a \in [1, N)$ and $P \in G$ and outputs the point aP. More generally, a *d-dimensional point multiplication algorithm* in G takes $a_1, \ldots, a_d \in [1, N)$ and points $P_1, \ldots, P_d \in G$ and produces the point $a_1 P_1 + \cdots + a_d P_d$. Secure and efficient point multiplication algorithms are critical in cryptography and have received much attention over the years. Some of these algorithms are specialized for certain tasks or only work in specific settings, such as when the P_i are fixed versus variable, or when the scalars a_i are public versus secret. See [1,3–5,7,8,10] for examples of such algorithms. In some cases, a linear combination $a_1 P_1 + \cdots + a_d P_d$ must be computed for a_i chosen uniformly at random.

In particular, the *d*-MUL algorithm in [4,7] is a multidimensional point multiplication algorithm which offers uniform operations in its execution, differential additions with each point addition, and has potential for an isochronous implementation. The *d*-MUL paper [7] notes that fixing the dimension parameter *d*

© Springer Nature Switzerland AG 2018
A. Chattopadhyay et al. (Eds.): SPACE 2018, LNCS 11348, pp. 198–217, 2018.
https://doi.org/10.1007/978-3-030-05072-6_12

as 1 yields the Montgomery chain [9], while taking $d = 2$ yields the chain given by Bernstein in [2]. *d*-MUL takes advantage of state matrices in its underlying structure.

Definition 1. *A* $(d + 1) \times d$ **state matrix** *A has non-negative entries and satisfies:*

1. *each row* A_i *has* $(i - 1)$ *odd entries.*
2. *for* $1 \leq i \leq d$, *we have* $A_{i+1} - A_i \in \{e_j, -e_j\}$ *for some* $1 \leq j \leq d$, *where* e_j *is the row matrix having* 1 *in the* j*th column and* 0*'s elsewhere.*

We define the **magnitude** *of A to be* $|A| = \max\{|A_{ij}| : 1 \leq i \leq d+1, 1 \leq j \leq d\}$.

At a high level, on input $a_1, \ldots, a_d \in \mathbb{Z}$ and $P_1, \ldots, P_d \in G$ the *d*-MUL algorithm, as described in [7], consists of three stages:

(1) construct a $(d+1) \times d$ state matrix A having a row consisting of the scalars $a_1, \ldots, a_d$,
(2) construct a sequence $\{A^{(i)}\}_{i=1}^{\ell}$ of state matrices such that $A^{(\ell)} = A$, the entries of $A^{(1)}$ are in the set $\{0, 1, -1\}$, and every row of $A^{(i+1)}$ is the sum of exactly two (possibly not distinct) rows from $A^{(i)}$,
(3) Compute the linear combinations Q_i of the $P_1, \ldots, P_d$ corresponding to the rows of $A^{(1)}$, and then use the row relations among the consecutive $A^{(j)}$ to add pairs of Q_i's together until reaching the final matrix $A^{(\ell)}$.

Suppose that one wishes to compute a random linear combination of $P_1, \ldots, P_d$ such that the coefficients of the combination are scalars having ℓ bits or less. One approach is to choose d many scalars a_i from the interval $[0, 2^{\ell})$ and run the *d*-MUL algorithm with input $a_1, \ldots, a_d$ and $P_1, \ldots, P_d$. This method has some concerning drawbacks:

– A large amount of integer matrix computation is necessary in item (2) above before any point additions can be performed.
– A large amount of storage space is necessary to store the matrices $A^{(i)}$, which each consist of $d(d + 1)$ many i bit integers.

In an effort to avoid these drawbacks, one might instead consider a variant of *d*-MUL which starts with a state matrix $A^{(1)}$ having entries in $\{0, 1, -1\}$ and builds a random sequence $\{A^{(i)}\}_{i=1}^{\ell}$ as in (2) above. In this setting, point additions can begin immediately alongside the generation of the matrices, which also reduces the storage space on the matrix sequence to that of just a single $(d+1) \times d$ state matrix. This new procedure still comes with some concerns, such as how to build such a random sequence of state matrices, and how to ensure that the final output point isn't biased in any way. This idea is the primary focus of this paper.

Contributions: Our contributions can be summarized as follows:

- We present a variant of d-MUL, the multidimensional differential addition chain algorithm described in [7]. The algorithm takes as input points $P_1, \ldots, P_d$, a $(d \cdot \ell)$-bit string r, a permutation $\sigma \in S_d$, and a binary vector v of length d, and it produces a point P from the set $S = \{a_1 P_1 + \cdots + a_d P_d : 0 \le a_i < 2^\ell\}$.
- The algorithm is performed as d-MUL, except that the scalar coefficients are not chosen in advance, and no matrix arithmetic is required prior to point addition; instead, the row additions are chosen through r. Moreover, the scalars a_i for the output point $P = a_1 P_1 + \cdots + a_d P_d$ can be determined through matrix arithmetic either before or after the point P is computed. In particular, our algorithm maintains the uniform pattern of

$$1 \text{ doubling}, d \text{ additions}, 1 \text{ doubling}, d \text{ additions}, \ldots$$

  that d-MUL features.
- We prove that there is a uniform correspondence between the input parameters (r, σ, v), and the scalars $a_1, \ldots, a_d$ determining P. More precisely, if r, σ, and v are chosen uniformly at random, then the point P will be uniformly distributed in S.
- We make some observations to modify and speed up the original algorithm, resulting in a constant-time friendly description. In particular, our algorithm can still benefit from parallelization, and we reduce the storage requirements for the scalar computation algorithm from $O(d^2)$ (the cost of storing a state matrix) to $O(1)$ (a single scalar).
- We report on results from implementations of our algorithm. Initial constant-time implementations of the algorithm gave run times nearing $500\,000$ cycle counts; with the modifications mentioned in the previous bullet this was reduced to $97\,300$ for $d = 2$, $109\,800$ for $d = 3$, and $123\,300$ for $d = 4$ with constant-time operations and differential additions used in each case (combined cost of computing P and $(a_1, \ldots, a_d)$ in each case).

The rest of this paper is organized as follows. Section 2 provides new theoretical results and builds the foundation of the scalar multiplication algorithm. Section 3 details the scalar multiplication algorithm which produces a random linear combination of points. Section 4 shows implementation oriented optimization alternatives on the proposed algorithms. Section 5 reports on the results of these optimizations in an implementation. We derive our conclusions in Sect. 6.

2   Theoretical Results

This section is devoted to developing theoretical results that culminate in our scalar multiplication algorithm. The outline of this section is as follows. Let A and B be state matrices such that every row in A is the sum of two rows from B.

1. We prove Theorem 1: for a fixed A, the matrix B is unique.

2. We prove Lemma 6: for a fixed B, there are exactly 2^d distinct matrices A.
3. In proving Lemma 6 we gain insight on how to construct all such matrices A from a given B: the matrices A are in one-to-one correspondence with binary strings r of length d. We formalize the construction of A from a given B and binary string r.
4. In Theorem 4 we show that iterating the construction of A from B with a bitstring r chosen randomly at each iteration will produce a uniformly random integer row vector $\begin{bmatrix} a_1 & \cdots & a_d \end{bmatrix}$ with $0 \le a_i < 2^\ell$ for $0 \le i \le d$. This results in a version of d-MUL which produces a random output with negligible precomputation.

Throughout this section, row and column indices of all matrices start at 1.

2.1   Uniqueness

In this section, we aim to show that the output of Algorithm 2 in [7] is unique in the following sense: if A and B are $(d+1) \times d$ state matrices (defined below) such that every row in A is the sum of two rows from B, then B is the output of Algorithm 2 in [7] when ran with input A. The proof will be by induction on d, but we first prove several lemmas and corollaries which are required in the main proof. Proofs of some of these lemmas and corollaries, when they are rather mechanical, are omitted due to space restrictions. The results of this section will be used in Sect. 3 to attain an algorithm for generating a uniformly random linear combination of group elements.

Throughout this paper, we will be working with the notion of a state matrix as in Definition 1. This is the same definition used in [7], but we restrict to state matrices with non-negative entries. A simple consequence of Definition 1 is that each index j in property (2) above is obtained from a unique i.

Lemma 1. *Let A be a state matrix. If $A_{m+1} - A_m = c_i e_i$, and $A_{n+1} - A_n = c_j e_j$ with $m \ne n$, then $i \ne j$. As a consequence, each column of A has the form*

$$\begin{bmatrix} 2x & \cdots & 2x & 2x + (-1)^k & \cdots & 2x + (-1)^k \end{bmatrix}^T$$

for some k and some x, where the index at which $2x$ changes to $2x + (-1)^k$ is different for each column.

Remark 1. Since every column of a state matrix A has the form stated in Lemma 1, $|A|$ can be computed by only looking at the rows A_1 and A_{d+1}.

Definition 2. *Let A be a $(d+1) \times d$ state matrix. The **column sequence** for A is the function $\sigma_A : \{2, \ldots, d+1\} \to \{1, \ldots, d\}$, where $\sigma_A(i)$ is the position in which the row matrix $A_i - A_{i-1}$ is nonzero. When A is clear from the context, we will sometimes write σ instead of σ_A. By Lemma 1, σ_A is a bijection.*

Definition 3. *Let A be a $(d+1) \times d$ state matrix. The **difference vector** for A is the vector $c^A := A_{d+1} - A_1$. When A is clear from the context, we will sometimes write c instead of c^A.*

With these definitions, we have $A_k - A_{k-1} = c^A_{\sigma_A(k)} e_{\sigma_A(k)}$ for $2 \leq k \leq d+1$. Next, we formulate results on the number of odd entries in the sum and difference of two rows from a state matrix.

Lemma 2. *If B is a $(d+1) \times d$ state matrix, then $B_m + B_n$ has $|m-n|$ odd entries.*

The following simple corollary will be used extensively throughout the rest of the paper.

Corollary 1. *Let A and B be state matrices such that every row in A is the sum of two rows from B. Then for each k, there is some m such that $A_k = B_m + B_{m+k-1}$.*

Proof. Write $A_k = B_m + B_n$, with $m \leq n$. Property (2) of state matrices says that A_k has $k-1$ odds. By Lemma 2, $B_m + B_n$ has $n-m$ odds. So $k-1 = n-m$ and $n = m + k - 1$.

Corollary 2. *Let A and B be state matrices such that every row in A is the sum of two rows from B. Let h be the number of odds in the integer row matrix $\frac{1}{2}A_1$. Then $2B_{h+1} = A_1$.*

Proof. By Corollary 1 we have $A_1 = 2B_m$ for some index m. By assumption, B_m has h odd entries. By the definition of a state matrix, B_m has $m-1$ odd entries. So $m = h+1$ and $A_1 = 2B_{h+1}$.

Lemma 3. *If B is a $(d+1) \times d$ state matrix, then $B_m - B_n$ has*

(1) $|m-n|$ odd entries, all of which are either 1 or -1,
(2) $d - |m-n|$ even entries, all of which are 0.

We now show that we can write c^B as a function of c^A when every row in A is the sum of two rows from B.

Lemma 4. *Let A and B be state matrices such that every row in A is the sum of two rows from B. Write $A_1 = [2\alpha_1 \cdots 2\alpha_d]$. Then*

$$c^B_j = \begin{cases} c^A_j & \text{if } \alpha_j \text{ is even} \\ -c^A_j & \text{if } \alpha_j \text{ is odd} \end{cases}$$

We can also relate σ_A and σ_B. An explicit formula for σ_A in terms of σ_B can be found, but for our purposes only knowing $\sigma_A(2)$ suffices. The following lemma will be one of the keys to proving Theorem 1 to follow.

Lemma 5. *Let A and B be state matrices such that every row in A is the sum of two rows from B. Write $A_1 = [2\alpha_1 \cdots 2\alpha_d]$ and let h be the number of α_i which are odd. Then*

$$\sigma_A(2) = \begin{cases} \sigma_B(h+1) & \text{if } \alpha_{\sigma_A(2)} \text{ is odd} \\ \sigma_B(h+2) & \text{if } \alpha_{\sigma_A(2)} \text{ is even} \end{cases}$$

We now have all the tools required to prove the main result of this subsection.

Theorem 1. *Let A be any state matrix of size $(d + 1) \times d$. Then there is a unique state matrix B such that every row in A is the sum of two rows from B. In particular, Algorithm 2 in [7] gives a construction for B.*

Proof. We use induction on d. Let $d = 1$ and suppose B is such a matrix. Then B has only two rows, one of which is determined uniquely by Corollary 2. By Corollary 1, we have $A_2 = B_1 + B_2$; two of the three row matrices in this equation are determined already, and so the third is determined as well.

Assume the theorem holds for matrices of size $d \times (d - 1)$. Let A be a $(d + 1) \times d$ state matrix and suppose B and C satisfy the condition stated in the theorem. Write $A_1 = \begin{bmatrix} 2\alpha_1 & \cdots & 2\alpha_d \end{bmatrix}$ and let h be the number of α_i which are odd. Throughout the rest of the proof, for any matrix X we will let ${}^i[X]^j$ denote the matrix obtained by deleting the ith row and jth column of X. Let $A' = {}^1[A]^{\sigma_A(2)}$. That A' is a state matrix follows from A being a state matrix and that the only odd in A_2 occurs in column $\sigma_A(2)$.

1. Suppose $\alpha_{\sigma_A(2)}$ is odd. By Lemma 5, we have $\sigma_B(h+1) = \sigma_C(h+1) = \sigma_A(2)$. Let $B' = {}^{h+1}[B]^{\sigma_B(h+1)}$ and $C' = {}^{h+1}[C]^{\sigma_C(h+1)}$.

    We'll now show that B' is a state matrix. For $2 \leq i \leq h$, we have

$$B'_i - B'_{i-1} = [B]_i^{\sigma_B(h+1)} - [B]_{i-1}^{\sigma_B(h+1)} = [B_i - B_{i-1}]^{\sigma_B(h+1)} = [c^B_{\sigma_B(i)} e_{\sigma_B(i)}]^{\sigma_B(h+1)}$$

which is still a unit basis row matrix since $\sigma_B(h + 1) \neq \sigma_B(i)$. Similarly, for $h + 2 \leq i \leq d + 1$ we have

$$B'_i - B'_{i-1} = [B]_{i+1}^{\sigma_B(h+1)} - [B]_i^{\sigma_B(h+1)} = [B_{i+1} - B_i]^{\sigma_B(h+1)} = [c^B_{\sigma_B(i+1)} e_{\sigma_B(i+1)}]^{\sigma_B(h+1)}$$

(the row index increases by one to account for the deleted row $h + 1$) which is still a unit basis row matrix since $\sigma_B(h+1) \neq \sigma_B(i+1)$. Looking at $i = h+1$, we have

$$\begin{aligned}
B'_{h+1} - B'_h &= [B]_{h+2}^{\sigma_B(h+1)} - [B]_h^{\sigma_B(h+1)} \\
&= [B_{h+2}]^{\sigma_B(h+1)} - [B_h]^{\sigma_B(h+1)} \\
&= [B_h + c^B_{\sigma_B(h+2)} e_{\sigma_B(h+2)} + c^B_{\sigma_B(h+1)} e_{\sigma_B(h+1)}]^{\sigma_B(h+1)} - [B_h]^{\sigma_B(h+1)} \\
&= [c^B_{\sigma_B(h+2)} e_{\sigma_B(h+2)}]^{\sigma_B(h+1)} + [c^B_{\sigma_B(h+1)} e_{\sigma_B(h+1)}]^{\sigma_B(h+1)} \\
&= [c^B_{\sigma_B(h+2)} e_{\sigma_B(h+2)}]^{\sigma_B(h+1)} + 0.
\end{aligned}$$

So B' satisfies the second requirement of being a state matrix. For the first requirement involving parities, we note that $B_{i,\sigma_B(h+1)} = \alpha_{\sigma_B(h+1)} + c^A_{\sigma_B(h+1)}$ (which is even) for $1 \leq i \leq h + 1$ and $B_{i,\sigma_B(h+1)} = \alpha_{\sigma_B(h+1)}$ (which is odd) for $h + 2 \leq i \leq d + 1$. So for $1 \leq i \leq h + 1$, $[B]_i^{\sigma_B(h+1)}$ is obtained from B_i by deleting an even entry, and so the number of odds isn't affected. Similarly, for $h + 1 \leq i \leq d$, $[B]_i^{\sigma_B(h+1)}$ is obtained from B_{i+1} by deleting an odd entry, and so has $i - 1$ odds. This shows B' is a $d \times (d - 1)$ state matrix.

We now show that every row in A' is the sum of two rows from B'. We have

$$A'_i = [A]_{i+1}^{\sigma_A(2)} = [A_{i+1}]^{\sigma_A(2)} = [B_j + B_{j+i}]^{\sigma_B(h+1)} = [B]_j^{\sigma_B(h+1)} + [B]_{j+i}^{\sigma_B(h+1)}$$

for some index j. If neither j or $j+i$ are $h+1$, then both the above row matrices correspond to rows of B'. If one is $h+1$, we just see that

$$[B]_{h+1}^{\sigma_B(h+1)} = [B_h + c_{\sigma_B(h+1)}^B e_{\sigma_B(h+1)}]^{\sigma_B(h+1)} = [B_h]^{\sigma_B(h+1)} = B'_h.$$

Thus B' is a $d \times (d-1)$ state matrix such that every row in A' is the sum of two rows from B'.

An entirely identical argument shows C' is a $d \times (d-1)$ state matrix such that every row from A' is the sum of two rows from C'. Our inductive hypothesis gives that $B' = C'$. We already have $B_{h+1} = \frac{1}{2}A_1 = C_{h+1}$ from Corollary 2. Since $B_{h+1,\sigma_B(h+1)} = C_{h+1,\sigma_C(h+1)}$ and $\sigma_B(h+1) = \sigma_C(h+1)$, we have that column $\sigma_B(h+1)$ is identical in both matrices by Lemma 1. Thus $B = C$.

2. Suppose $\alpha_{\sigma_A(2)}$ is even. The proof is mostly identical to case 1. We get $\sigma_B(h+2) = \sigma_C(h+2) = \sigma_A(2)$ by Lemma 5 and take $B' = {}^{h+2}[B]^{\sigma_B(h+2)}$ and $C' = {}^{h+2}[C]^{\sigma_C(h+2)}$.

To wrap up this section, we prove one additional corollary which will be needed later on.

Corollary 3. *Let A and B be state matrices such that every row in A is the sum of two rows from B. If $A_k = B_m + B_{m+k-1}$ and also $A_k = B_n + B_{n+k-1}$, then $m = n$.*

2.2 Generating Randomness

The task of generating random group elements has many applications in cryptography, most notably in the first round of the Diffie-Hellman key agreement protocol. We will now make use of the results in Subsect. 2.1 to tackle the problem of choosing and computing an element from the set $\{a_1 P_1 + \cdots + a_d P_d : 0 \le a_i < 2^\ell\}$ uniformly at random for a fixed set of points P_i in an abelian group G and for a fixed parameter ℓ. We of course would like to be as efficient and uniform with our intermediate computations as possible.

Many solutions to this problem exist already. One such solution is to choose $a_i \in [0, 2^\ell)$ uniformly at random for $1 \le i \le d$, and then run the d-MUL algorithm of [7] with the input $(a_1, \ldots, a_d)$. This method has the advantage of being uniform with all group operations (see Remark 5.1 in [7]), but comes with the overhead of first computing a sequence $\{A^{(i)}\}_{i=1}^\ell$ of $(d+1) \times d$ matrices before any group addition is done. Once the sequence has been computed the remaining computations within G are relatively efficient, requiring ℓ point doublings and $\ell \cdot d$ point additions.

We propose an alternative solution to the problem by considering a "reversed" version of d-MUL which bypasses the computation of this sequence of matrices. Instead of choosing d many $a_i \in [0, 2^\ell)$, we choose a single $r \in [0, 2^{\ell d})$ uniformly at random, which will be used to construct a unique sequence $\{A^{(i)}\}_{i=1}^\ell$ which we will utilize in the same way as above to perform the group computations. Taking all such sequences $\{A^{(i)}\}_{i=1}^\ell$ corresponding to every $r \in [0, 2^{\ell d})$, the distribution of all integer d-tuples corresponding to all rows in the final matrices $A^{(\ell)}$ are *not* uniform; however by only considering the final rows $A_{d+1}^{(\ell)}$ we find an output which is uniform over all odd integer d-tuples, which we state as a main result in Theorem 3. By subtracting a binary vector from the output, we find a uniformly random d tuple.

In this subsection, we define the tools used to explore the problem and prove many results, culminating in Theorem 4 which gives a method for producing uniformly random output. These results will be used in Sect. 3 to give an algorithm for computing a uniformly random linear combination of group elements.

We now find interest in sequences of state matrices having special properties, as described in the following definition.

Definition 4. A **state matrix chain** is a sequence $\left(A^{(i)}\right)_{i=1}^\ell$ of state matrices $A^{(i)}$ with d columns such that

1. each row of $A^{(i+1)}$ is the sum of two rows from $A^{(i)}$ for $1 \leq i < \ell$,
2. $\{|A^{(i)}|\}_{i=1}^\ell$ is a strictly increasing sequence,
3. $|A^{(1)}| = 1$.

We say ℓ is the length of the chain $\left(A^{(i)}\right)_{i=1}^\ell$.

The sequence of matrices produced by Algorithm 3 in [7] is a state matrix chain. Note that a sequence $\left(A^{(i)}\right)_{i=1}^\ell$ satisfying (1) and (3) may be "trivially extended" to have an arbitrarily greater number of matrices by defining

$$B^{(i)} = \begin{cases} A^{(1)} & i \leq n \\ A^{(i-n)} & i > n \end{cases}$$

which is a sequence containing $\left(A^{(i)}\right)_{i=1}^\ell$ and still satisfying (1) and (3) of the above definition. We therefore attain some degree of uniqueness in excluding such trivial extensions from the current discussion by requiring (2). Note that by Theorem 1, a state matrix chain $\left(A^{(i)}\right)_{i=1}^\ell$ is uniquely determined by $A^{(\ell)}$.

Definition 5. An **augmented** state matrix chain is a pair $\left(\left(A^{(i)}\right)_{i=1}^\ell, h\right)$, where $\left(A^{(i)}\right)_{i=1}^\ell$ is a state matrix chain with matrices having d columns and $1 \leq h \leq d+1$. h is called the output row for the augmented chain. Let SMC_d denote the set of all augmented state matrix chains (of varying length) with matrices having d columns. We define a function

$$\text{OUTPUT} : SMC_d \longrightarrow \mathbb{Z}^{1 \times d}$$

$$\left(\left(A^{(i)}\right)_{i=1}^\ell, h\right) \longmapsto A_h^{(\ell)}.$$

The function OUTPUT (as with any function) naturally gives equivalence classes on its domain defined by the preimage of elements in the codomain; specifically, say augmented chains (C, h) and (C', h') are equivalent if and only if $\text{OUTPUT}(C, h) = \text{OUTPUT}(C', h')$. Since $\text{OUTPUT}(C, h) = A_h$ for some state matrix A, we have that $h - 1$ is the number of odd entries in the row matrix A_h; likewise, $h' - 1$ is the number of odd entries in the row matrix $A'_{h'}$, and since $A_h = A'_{h'}$ we have $h = h'$. That is, the output row is constant over all augmented state matrix chains in the equivalence class $[(C, h)]$. The length of the chains in $[(C, h)]$ is, in general, not constant.

Theorem 2. *For $s \in \mathbb{Z}^{1 \times d}$ having h odd entries, we have*

$$|\text{OUTPUT}^{-1}(s)| = 2^d (d - h)! h!$$

That is, there are $2^d (d - h)! h!$ many state matrix chains which give s as an output.

Proof. By Theorem 1 the number of chains giving s as an output is equal to the number of state matrices containing s as a row. We count all such matrices.

Row $h + 1$ must be s. For rows 1 through h, an odd entry must be selected to change to an even entry by either adding or subtracting 1, giving a total of $\prod_{i=1}^{h} 2i$ possibilities. Similarly, in choosing rows $h + 2$ through $d + 1$ an even entry must be changed to an odd entry by either adding or subtracting 1, giving a total of $\prod_{i=1}^{d-h} 2i$ possibilities. All together, we have

$$\left(\prod_{i=1}^{h} 2i \right) \cdot \left(\prod_{i=1}^{d-h} 2i \right) = 2^d (d - h)! h!$$

many possible matrices.

Note that for a fixed s the number of chains producing s as an output is independent of the bit size of the entries of s.

Lemma 6. *Let B be a $(d+1) \times d$ state matrix. Then there are exactly 2^d pairwise distinct state matrices A such that every row in A is the sum of two rows from B.*

Proof. Fix $0 \le h \le d$ and consider all matrices A such that $A_1 = 2B_{h+1}$ (every A has such a unique h by Corollary 2). By Corollary 3, for every k there are unique x_k and y_k such that $A_k = B_{x_k} + B_{y_k}$ with $x_k \le y_k$. This defines a sequence of pairs $a_k = (x_k, y_k)$ such that $a_1 = (h + 1, h + 1)$ and $a_{d+1} = (1, d + 1)$. By Corollary 3 and Algorithm 2 in [7], we have either $a_{k+1} = (x_k - 1, y_k)$ or $a_{k+1} = (x_k, y_k + 1)$ for each k, and either choice for each k defines a valid and unique state matrix satisfying the conditions stated in the lemma. Since the x_k's must decrease to 1, we have h possible indices k to choose where to place the -1's in the first coordinates of a_{k+1}, and so $\binom{d}{h}$ sequences are possible. Summing over all h, we have $\sum_{h=0}^{d} \binom{d}{h} = 2^d$ total matrices.

The above proof gives insight into the method used in the algorithms to come. There is a one-to-one correspondence between the integers in the interval $[0, 2^d - 1]$ and the possible matrices A stated in the theorem. The number of 1's in the binary expansion of a chosen integer will determine h, and the placement of the 1's determines the positions to place the -1's in the sequence a_k defined in the proof. In particular, choosing an integer in the interval $[0, 2^d - 1]$ uniformly at random corresponds to choosing a matrix A uniformly at random out of all matrices satisfying the conditions in Lemma 6, and defines how to construct the chosen matrix A. We make this formal below.

Definition 6. *Let A and B be $(d + 1) \times d$ state matrices such that every row in A is the sum of two rows from B. The **addition sequence** $\{a_k\}_{k=1}^{d+1}$ for A corresponding to B is defined by $a_k = (x_k, y_k)$, where x_k and y_k are the unique row indices such that $A_k = B_{x_k} + B_{y_k}$.*

Remark 2. Uniqueness follows from Corollary 3.

Definition 7. *Let B be a $(d+1) \times d$ state matrix and r a binary string of length d. Let h be the number of 1's in r. Define a recursive sequence $a_k = (x_k, y_k)$ of ordered pairs by $x_1 = y_1 = h + 1$ and*

$$a_k = \begin{cases} (x_{k-1}, y_{k-1} + 1) & \text{if } r_{k-1} = 0 \\ (x_{k-1} - 1, y_{k-1}) & \text{if } r_{k-1} = 1 \end{cases}$$

*for $2 \leq k \leq d+1$. We define the **extension matrix** of B corresponding to r as the $(d + 1) \times d$ state matrix A having the addition sequence a_k with respect to the matrix B.*

By choosing ℓ many binary strings of length d, we may iterate Definition 7 to produce a sequence of matrices.

Definition 8. *Let B be a $(d+1) \times d$ state matrix and r a binary string of length $\ell \cdot d$. Let $r_1, \ldots, r_\ell$ be the partition of r into ℓ blocks of length d, with r_i being the sequence whose terms are bits $(i - 1) \cdot d + 1$ through $i \cdot d$ of r. We define the **extension sequence with base B** corresponding to r as the sequence of $\ell + 1$ many $(d + 1) \times d$ state matrices $\left(A^{(i)}\right)_{i=1}^{\ell+1}$ defined recursively as $A^{(1)} = B$ and $A^{(i+1)}$ is the extension matrix of $A^{(i)}$ corresponding to r_i.*

By the definition of an extension matrix, every row in $A^{(i)}$ is the sum of two rows from $A^{(i-1)}$ for each i. Note however that not all extension sequences are state matrix chains since $|B| = 1$ is not required, and even if this condition were satisfied many sequences would have B repeated many times (such as when r is the zero string) and so $|A^{(i)}|$ is not strictly increasing in such cases.

Corollary 4. *Fix a $(d + 1) \times d$ state matrix B. Every sequence of $(d + 1) \times d$ state matrices $\left(A^{(i)}\right)_{i=1}^{\ell+1}$ satisfying*

1. $A^{(1)} = B$,
2. For $1 < i \leq \ell + 1$, every row in $A^{(i)}$ is the sum of two rows from $A^{(i-1)}$

is an extension sequence with base B corresponding to some binary sequence r.

Proof. For each i, there is an addition sequence for $A^{(i)}$ corresponding to $A^{(i-1)}$. Concatenating these sequences yields the sequence r.

Since there are $2^{\ell d}$ binary strings of length ℓd, there are $2^{\ell d}$ extension sequences of a fixed matrix B. We now arrive at the primary result of this section.

Theorem 3. *Let* $\mathcal{B} = \{B \in \mathbb{Z}^{(d+1) \times d} : |B| = 1, B$ *a state matrix*$\}$. *Let*

$$S = \left\{ \left(A^{(i)}\right)_{i=1}^{\ell+1} : \left(A^{(i)}\right)_{i=1}^{\ell+1} \text{ is an extension of some } B \in \mathcal{B} \right\}$$

Then the map OUTPUT $\left(\left(A^{(i)}\right)_{i=1}^{\ell+1}\right) = A_{d+1}^{(\ell+1)}$ *defines a* $2^d d!$*-to-1 correspondence from* S *to the set of row matrices of length* d *consisting of positive odd* ℓ*-bit or less integers.*

Proof. Let s be such a row matrix. By Theorem 2, there are $2^d d!$ distinct state matrix chains which give s as an output. Let $\left(A^{(i)}\right)_{i=1}^{n}$ be one such a state matrix chain. Then Theorem 4.3 in [7] and Theorem 1 above give $n \leq \ell + 1$, and since $|A^{(1)}| = 1$ the chain may be uniquely extended into a sequence in S while still having output s by defining

$$B^{(i)} = \begin{cases} A^{(i-\ell-1+n)} & \text{if } \ell + 1 - n < i \leq \ell + 1 \\ A^{(1)} & \text{if } 1 \leq i \leq \ell + 1 - n \end{cases}$$

This essentially says to repeat matrix $A^{(1)}$ sufficiently many times to get a sequence of length $\ell + 1$. This produces a valid extension since it corresponds to choosing the addition sequence on $A^{(1)}$ corresponding to the zero bitstring (in other words, doubling the first row of all 0's produces the same matrix since $|A^{(1)}| = 1$). This is possible for each chain $\left(A^{(i)}\right)_{i=1}^{n}$, and so each fixed s yields $2^d d!$ many distinct extension sequences in S. There are $2^{(\ell-1)d}$ such row matrices s, and each gives $2^d d!$ extensions in S (different choices of s give disjoint sets of extensions since the last row in the last matrix of each extension is s) for a total of $2^{\ell d} d!$ extensions. Since there are $d!$ state matrices B satisfying $|B| = 1$ and $2^{\ell d}$ extensions for each B, this is exactly the size of S.

The implication of the above theorem is that choosing both a matrix B satisfying $|B| = 1$ and an integer in $[0, 2^{\ell d} - 1]$ uniformly at random defines a unique extension sequence of B, which in turn yields a row matrix s chosen uniformly at random from the set of row matrices consisting of ℓ-bit or less odd entries, which is given by the last row in the last matrix of the extension sequence. An arbitrary ℓ-bit row matrix may be obtained by choosing a binary vector uniformly at random and subtracting it from the output row s.

Theorem 4. *Choose the following parameters uniformly at random from their respective sets:*

1. *r a binary string of length ℓd,*
2. *B a $(d+1) \times d$ state matrix satisfying $|B| = 1$,*
3. *v a binary row matrix of length d.*

Let $\left(A^{(i)}\right)_{i=1}^{\ell+1}$ be the extension sequence with base B corresponding to r, and define $s = A_{d+1}^{(\ell+1)}$. Then $s - v$ is an element chosen uniformly at random from the set of row matrices of length d having entries in $[0, 2^\ell - 1]$.

Proof. By Theorem 3, s is chosen uniformly at random from the set of row matrices of length d consisting of odd ℓ-bit or less integers. For each s, define $T_s = \{s - v : v \text{ is a binary vector}\}$. Then $\{T_s : s \text{ has odd } \ell\text{-bit or less integers}\}$ is a partition of the set of row matrices of length d having entries in $[0, 2^\ell - 1]$. Choosing r and B together specify a T_s, and v further specifies an arbitrary vector.

It's worth noting that Theorem 3 (and so also Theorem 4) will not hold true when instead choosing $h = i$ for $i \neq d + 1$ (i.e., $s = A_i^{(\ell+1)}$ for $i \neq d + 1$ in the above). If s contains an entry which is 0 or 2^ℓ, many of the state matrices containing s as a row counted in Theorem 2 will necessarily contain the entry -1 (which we don't allow) or $2^\ell + 1$, and so the conditions of Theorem 4.3 in [7] will not be satisfied. In turn, producing such s containing $2^\ell + 1$ would take one additional iteration of Algorithm 3 in [7] and so yields an extension sequence of length $\ell + 2$. This results in sequences of varying lengths, which we wish to avoid.

3   Algorithms

Given Theorem 4, our scalar multiplication algorithm is now simple. Let $P = [P_1 \ldots P_d]$ be a row matrix of points and choose r, B, and v as in Theorem 4. B can be constructed by applying a random permutation to the columns of a lower triangular matrix whose lower triangle consists of all 1's. We then construct the extension sequence with base B corresponding to the bitstring r. The scalars in the linear combination of the output are given by subtracting v from the last row of the last matrix. These rules are reflected in Algorithm 1.

We perform the scalar multiplication by using the same addition and doubling rules specified by the binary string r on the point column matrix $B \cdot P^T$. Upon arriving at the final point column matrix, we subtract $v \cdot P^T$ from the last entry and return this point as an output. We remark that this process only yields a point; the coefficients of the resulting linear combination are computed through Theorem 4 using Algorithm 1. These rules for point multiplication are reflected in Algorithm 2.

The scalars in Algorithm 1 and the points in Algorithm 2 can be merged in order to scan r only a single time. Alternatively, the two algorithms can

---

Algorithm 1. d-MUL scalars

Input: bitsize parameter ℓ; bitstring r of length ℓd; τ a bijection on
$\qquad \{0, 1, \ldots, d-1\}$; v a bitstring of length d
Output: a row matrix $\begin{bmatrix} a_1 \cdots a_d \end{bmatrix}$

```
1  B[0] ← [0 ··· 0]
2  for i = 0 to d − 1 do
3  |   B[i + 1] ← B[i] + e[τ[i]]                        // Initial state matrix
4  end
5  for i = 0 to ℓ − 1 do
6  |   h, x, y ← r[i · d] + ··· + r[(i + 1)d − 1]
7  |   A[0] ← 2B[h]
8  |   for j = 0 to d − 1 do
9  |   |   if r[i · d + j] = 1 then
10 |   |   |   x ← x − 1
11 |   |   else
12 |   |   |   y ← y + 1
13 |   |   end
14 |   |   A[j + 1] ← B[x] + B[y]
15 |   end
16 |   B ← A
17 end
18 a ← B[d] − v
19 return a                                              // Scalars
```

---

be computed independent of each other. We prefer the latter case because the column vectors of B in Algorithm 1 constitutes a redundant representation. We eliminate this redundancy in Sect. 4.

We take a moment to point out some special cases. As in the original d-MUL algorithm of [7], when taking $d = 1$ here we get a scalar multiplication algorithm reminiscent of the Montgomery chain [9]. To compute aP the Montgomery chain tracks two variables Q_1 and Q_2; each iteration adds these variables together and doubles one of them to get the next pair $[Q_1, Q_2]$. If the point to double is chosen uniformly at random in the Montgomery chain, one gets an algorithm identical to Algorithm 2.

Similarly, when $d = 2$ Algorithm 2 resembles a variant of the "new binary chain" of [2]. To compute $a_1 P_1 + a_2 P_2$ this chain tracks a triple of points (Q_1, Q_2, Q_3) which are linear combinations of P_1 and P_2 for which the scalars of each combination correspond to pairs from the set $S = \{(s, t), (s + 1, t), (s, t + 1), (s + 1, t + 1)\}$ for some (s, t). The missing pair from the set always contains exactly one odd entry. Suppose that Q_1 corresponds to the (even,even) tuple, Q_2 corresponds to the (odd,odd) tuple, and Q_3 is the mixed parity tuple. Then the triple (Q_1', Q_2', Q_3') for the next iteration satisfies $Q_1' = 2Q_i$ for some i, $Q_2' = Q_1 + Q_2$, and either $Q_3' = Q_1 + Q_3$ or $Q_3' = Q_2 + Q_3$ such that the resulting scalars from each linear combination are still of the form given by S for a new pair (s', y'). This leaves $4 = 2^2$ options for (Q_1', Q_2', Q_3') from a fixed triple

(Q_1, Q_2, Q_3), and so choosing an option at random is equivalent to Algorithm 2 when $d = 3$. See [2] for more details on the new binary chain.

Algorithm 2. Simplified d-MUL

Input: bitsize parameter ℓ; $P = \begin{bmatrix} P_1 & \cdots & P_d \end{bmatrix}$ points on curve E; bitstring r of
      length ℓd; τ a bijection on $\{0, 1, \ldots, d-1\}$; v a bitstring of length d
Output: Q satisfying $Q = a_1 P[1] + \cdots + a_d P[d]$ for $0 \le a_i < 2^\ell$ chosen
      uniformly at random; the row matrix $\begin{bmatrix} a_1 & \cdots & a_d \end{bmatrix}$

```
 1  Q[0] ← id(E)
 2  for i = 0 to d − 1 do
 3  |    Q[i + 1] ← Q[i] + P[τ[i]]                    // Initial state matrix
 4  end
 5  for i = 0 to ℓ − 1 do
 6  |    h, x, y ← r[i · d] + · · · + r[(i + 1)d − 1]
 7  |    R[0] ← 2Q[h]
 8  |    for j = 0 to d do
 9  |    |    if r[i · d + j] = 1 then
10  |    |    |    x ← x − 1
11  |    |    else
12  |    |    |    y ← y + 1
13  |    |    end
14  |    |    R[j + 1] ← Q[x] + Q[y]
15  |    end
16  |    Q ← R
17  end
18  T ← Q[d] − v[0] · P[0] − · · · − v[d − 1] · P[d − 1]
19  a ← d-MUL-Scalars(ℓ, r, τ, v)
20  return a, T                                       // Scalars and output point
```

The point addition $R[j + 1] \leftarrow Q[x] + Q[y]$ at line 14 of Algorithm 2 can be implemented using a differential addition $Q[x] \oplus Q[y]$ if $Q[x] \ominus Q[y]$ is known in advance. Algorithm 3 computes a difference vector Δ which satisfies:

$$Q[x] \ominus Q[y] = \Delta[0] \cdot P[0] \oplus \ldots \oplus \Delta[d-1] \cdot P[d-1].$$

Using Δ it's possible to arrange a look-up function for difference points TBL from which the difference point is extracted TBL(Δ). We provide explicit construction of TBL for $d = 2, 3, 4$ in Sect. 4.

Algorithms 1, 2, and 3 use an implementation oriented notation where arrays are used in the place of vectors and the index of an array always starts from zero.

Algorithm 3. Simplified d-MUL with differential additions

Input: bitsize parameter ℓ; $P = [P_1 \cdots P_d]$ points on curve E; bitstring r of
length ℓd; τ a bijection on $\{0, 1, \ldots, d-1\}$; v a bitstring of length d;
TBL a look-up function for difference points

Output: Q satisfying $Q = a_1 P[1] + \cdots + a_d P[d]$ for $0 \le a_i < 2^\ell$ chosen
uniformly at random; the row matrix $[a_1 \cdots a_d]$

```
1  Q[0] ← id(E)
2  for i = 0 to d − 1 do
3  |   Q[i + 1] ← Q[i] + P[τ[i]]                          // Initial state matrix
4  end
5  κ^col ← τ
6  κ^row ← [1 : i ∈ [0, ..., d − 1]]
7  for i = 0 to ℓ − 1 do
8  |   h, x, y ← r[i · d] + · · · + r[(i + 1)d − 1]
9  |   κ^row', κ^col', Δ ← [0 : i ∈ [0, ..., d − 1]]
10 |   R[0] ← 2Q[h]
11 |   for j = 0 to d do
12 |   |   if r[i · d + j] = 1 then
13 |   |   |   x ← x − 1
14 |   |   |   κ^row'[κ^col[x]] ← −κ^row[κ^col[x]]
15 |   |   |   κ^col'[j] ← κ^col[x]
16 |   |   else
17 |   |   |   κ^row'[κ^col[y]] ← κ^row[κ^col[y]]
18 |   |   |   κ^col'[j] ← κ^col[y]
19 |   |   |   y ← y + 1
20 |   |   end
21 |   |   Δ[κ^col'[j]] ← κ^row[κ^col'[j]]
22 |   |   R[j + 1] ← Q[x] ⊕ Q[y]                          // Q[x] ⊖ Q[y] = TBL(Δ)
23 |   end
24 |   κ^row ← κ^row'
25 |   κ^col ← κ^col'
26 |   Q ← R
27 end
28 T ← Q[d] − v[0] · P[0] − · · · − v[d − 1] · P[d − 1]
29 a ← d-MUL-Scalars(ℓ,r, τ, v)
30 return a, T                                             // Scalars and output point
```

---

4 Optimizations

Let A be the extension matrix of B corresponding to the bitstring r. Our first
optimization involves simplifying the computation of A. We notice that the ith
column of A is a function of only the ith column of B and the bitstring r and
is independent of the other columns of B. This means that when computing
an extension sequence $\left(A^{(i)}\right)_{i=1}^{\ell+1}$, the columns of $A^{(\ell+1)}$ can be computed one
at a time, reducing storage costs to only a single column of a state matrix.

Furthermore, the columns of state matrices have a very strict form. Specifically, a column of a state matrix A looks like

$$\left[2x \cdots 2x\; 2x + (-1)^k \cdots 2x + (-1)^k\right]^T,$$

for some integer k. The representation of this column can take the much simpler form $\{2x, (-1)^k, i\}$, where i is the highest index for which the entry of the column is $2x$. This simple representation reduces storage costs further to only storing one large integer $2x$, one bit sign information $(-1)^k$, and one small integer i. In this direction, Algorithm 4 provides an optimized version of Algorithm 1.

We point out that by taking $k = d+1$ in Corollary 1 we always have $A_{d+1}^{(\ell+1)} = A_1^{(\ell)} + A_{d+1}^{(\ell)}$, and by the uniqueness in Corollary 3 this is always the case for any extension sequence. One might consider skipping the computation of $A^{(\ell+1)}$ and simply outputting $A_1^{(\ell)} + A_{d+1}^{(\ell)}$ instead of $A_{d+1}^{(\ell+1)}$ (and likewise with the point additions in Algorithm 2). In our implementation with differential additions we found it difficult to retrieve the point corresponding to the difference $A_1^{(\ell)} + A_{d+1}^{(\ell)}$ in a secure fashion. This approach is viable in an implementation which doesn't take advantage of differential additions. Furthermore, this means the final d bits of the bitstring r are unused. These bits may be used in place of the binary vector v if desired.

Algorithm 4. d-MUL scalars (Optimized)

Input: bitstring r of length ℓd, τ a bijection on $\{0, 1, \ldots, d-1\}$
Output: Array of scalars k corresponding to r and τ

```
1  for i = 0 to d − 1 do
2      k[i] ← 0,  δ ← 1,  index ← i
3      for j = 0 to d(ℓ − 2) by d do
4          h ← r[j] + ... + r[j + d − 1]
5          z ← BoolToInt(h > index)
6          k[i] ← 2(k[i] + δ)
7          δ ← (1 − 2z) · δ
8          q ← index + 1 − h,  a ← 0,  index ← −1,
9          q ← Select(q, −q, BoolToInt(q > 0)) + z
10         for t = 0 to d − 1 do
11             a ← a + Xnor(z, r[j + t])
12             index ← Select(t, index, BoolToInt((a == q) ∧ (index == −1)))
13         end
14     end
15     k[τ[i]] ← 2k[i] + δ − r[(ℓ − 1) · d + τ[i] − 1]
16 end
17 return k                                    // Array of scalars
```

Algorithm 4 uses two auxiliary functions: BoolToInt sends true to 1 and false to 0. The Select function sends the inputs to the first input or to the second input if the third input is false or true, respectively.

Algorithm 2 inputs an array of points which is denoted by P for simplicity. Algorithm 2 also inputs the same ordering v and the random bitstring r as Algorithm 4, and outputs k as the d scalars corresponding to v and r. Algorithm 2 also outputs the point $T = k[0] \cdot P[0] + \cdots + k[d] \cdot P[d]$. In Algorithm 2, the if statement (also given below on the left) can be eliminated as given below on the right. This latter notation sacrifices readability but it helps in simplifying the implementation.

if $r[i \cdot d + j] = 1$ **then**
 | $x \leftarrow x - 1$
else
 $\lfloor \; y \leftarrow y + 1$

$x \leftarrow x - r[i \cdot d + t]$
$y \leftarrow y - r[i \cdot d + t] + 1$

4.1 Constant Time

Algorithm 2 can be implemented to give a constant-time implementation regardless of whether regular additions or differential additions are used. For this purpose, both d and ℓ are fixed. The following additional modifications are also mandatory.

– A table look-up on P that depends on the secret information $\tau[i-1]$ is performed in Line 3 of Algorithm 2. This look-up is implemented with constant-time scanning method. We note that this scanning does not cause a performance bottleneck for small values of d since it is not a part of the main loop (lines 5–13).
– Additional secret dependent table look-ups are performed at Line 7 and Line 10 of Algorithm 2. These look-ups are also implemented with constant-time scanning method. However, this time, the scanning constitute a performance bottleneck. To minimize the performance penalty, the actual implementation in Sect. 5, further optimizes Algorithm 2 by removing the assignment $Q \leftarrow R$ in line 12 and letting the intermediate point array to oscillate between the arrays Q and R. The indexes that can occur for Q and R are given by the sequences $[0 \cdots (d - i)]$ and $[i \cdots d]$, respectively. These indexes are perfectly suitable for constant-time scanning method since they are linearly sequential.
– The table look-ups $Q[0]$ at Line 1, $Q[i], Q[i-1]$ at Line 3, and $Q[0], Q[d], P[0]$, $\ldots, P[d-1], r[d(\ell-1)], \ldots, r[d(\ell-1)+d-1]$ at Line 14 of Algorithm 2 do not depend on the secret information. Therefore, these lines can be implemented in the way they are written. On the other hand, each of $r[d(\ell - 1)] \cdot P[i]$ is equal to either the identity element or $P[i]$. This intermediate values must be selected in constant item with Select. The Select function processes secret data in Algorithm 1 and therefore Select is implemented to run in constant-time.
– Line 15 of Algorithm 1 also requires a secret dependent assignment. The left hand side $k[\tau[i]]$ also requires constant-time scanning.

4.2   Differential Addition

The number of distinct values of Δ in Algorithm 3 increases exponentially with d. Nevertheless, TBL is manageable for small d. We investigate the fixed cases $d = 2, 3, 4$, separately, and the explicit table entries for $d = 2, 3$ (the case $d = 4$ is omitted due to space restrictions) are as follows:

– *Case d = 2:* The table size is 4. The first iteration selects out of the 2 points $[P_0, P_1]$; and the second iteration selects out of the 2 points $[P_0 - P_1, P_0 + P_1]$
– *Case d = 3:* The table size is 13. The first iteration selects out of the 3 points $[P_0, P_1, P_2]$; the second iteration selects out of the 6 points $[P_1 - P_2, P_1 + P_2, P_0 - P_1, P_0 - P_2, P_0 + P_2, P_0 + P_1]$; and the third iteration selects out of the 4 points $[P_0 - P_1 - P_2, P_0 - P_1 + P_2, P_0 + P_1 - P_2, P_0 + P_1 + P_2]$.

Computing Δ with the help of variables κ^{col}, κ^{row}, $\kappa^{\mathrm{row}'}$, $\kappa^{\mathrm{col}'}$ is considerably inefficient. In order to emulate Δ, we derived dedicated boolean functions for each of the cases $d = 2, 3, 4$. We refer to the implementation for these expressions. Our experience is that simplification of computing Δ is open to further investigation.

Since the iterations selects through sequential indexes, the look-ups can be implemented with constant-time scanning method in a subsequence of TBL. The overhead of constant-time scanning is not a bottleneck for $d = 2, 3$ but starts becoming one for $d > 3$.

5   Implementation Results

Sections 2 and 3 provided simplifications on d-MUL by eliminating all of the redundancies and Sect. 4 put d-MUL into an optimized format with low-level expressions. Our main aim in this section is to show that optimized d-MUL can be implemented to give fast implementations. We implemented the optimized d-MUL algorithm for $d = 2, 3, 4$ with point addition method being (i) differential; (ii) regular (i.e. non-differential). In all experiments, we used $\mathbb{F}_p^2 = \mathbb{F}(i)$ where $p = 2^{127} - 1$ and $i^2 = -1$. We did not exploit any endomorphism. We used Montgomery differential addition formulas [9] for (i) and twisted Edwards ($a = -1$) unified addition formulas in extended coordinates [6] for (ii). Since d-MUL is a generic multidimensional scalar point multiplication algorithm, one can switch to other possibly faster fields.

We used a single core of an i7-6500U Skylake processor, where the other cores are turned-off and turbo-boost disabled. GNU-gcc version 5.4.0 with flags -m64 -O2 -fomit-frame-pointer was used to compile the code. The code can be executed on any amd64 or x64 processor since we use the generic 64 × 64 bit integer multiplier. In all of 12 implementations, we used the constant-time method for the scalar generation since the elimination of the branches lead to a slightly faster implementation. Table 1 provides cycle counts for our non-constant time implementation.

As dimension increases, so does the memory access due to look-ups from Q and TBL. On the other hand, the number of additions decreases as d increases.

Table 1. Non-constant time implementation of optimized d-Dmul.

Implementation	Scalars	Point	Total
Regular, $d = 2$	9 100	135 900	145 000
Regular, $d = 3$	12 900	127 600	140 500
Regular, $d = 4$	10 700	125 200	135 900
Differential, $d = 4$	10 700	88 200	98 900
Differential, $d = 3$	12 900	84 600	97 500
Differential, $d = 2$	9 100	86 600	95 700

Therefore, there is a trade-off between the number of memory accesses and the number of point additions, depending on d. In case (i), the fastest dimension turns out to be $d = 2$ for overall computation. Profiling the code we see that the number of memory accesses is dominated by the selection of difference points from TBL for higher dimensions. In case (ii), the fastest dimension turns out to be $d = 4$ since no look-up occurs from TBL.

The variation between the cycle counts in the scalars column of Table 1 is easy to explain. In (i), each scalar is represented by 2 limbs when $d = 2$; 1 limb when $d = 4$. In both cases, almost all available bits are used and the adder circuit is utilized. The case $d = 2$ is slightly faster than $d = 4$ since less effort is spent on scanning r. The $d = 3$ is slower because 84-bit scalars are represented by 2 limbs and more effort is spent on scanning r.

Table 2 provides the cycle counts when all input-dependent computations and input-dependent table look-ups are emulated with arithmetic operations. These implementations run in constant time for all inputs.

Table 2. Constant time implementation of optimized d-Dmul.

Dimension	Scalars	Point	Total
Regular, $d = 2$	9 100	143 500	152 600
Regular, $d = 3$	12 900	135 300	148 200
Regular, $d = 4$	10 700	131 200	141 900
Differential, $d = 4$	10 700	112 600	123 300
Differential, $d = 3$	12 900	96 900	109 800
Differential, $d = 2$	9 100	88 200	97 300

We immediately see that the ranking does not change and switching to the constant-time setting does not constitute a big speed penalty.

6   Concluding Remarks

We presented several theoretical results on the structure and the construction of the addition chains in *d*-MUL. Using our theoretical results, which are interesting on their own right, we proposed an optimized version of *d*-MUL. Our implementation results show that the optimized *d*-MUL gains some significant speed ups. In particular, we were able to reduce the cycle counts of our initial isochronous implementation of the original *d*-MUL algorithm from nearly 500 000 to under 125 000 cycles.

Acknowledgements. The authors would like to thank reviewers for their comments and corrections. Research reported in this paper was supported by the Army Research Office under the award number W911NF-17-1-0311. The content is solely the responsibility of the authors and does not necessarily represent the official views of the Army Research Office.

References

1. Azarderakhsh, R., Karabina, K.: Efficient algorithms and architectures for double point multiplication on elliptic curves. In: Proceedings of the Third Workshop on Cryptography and Security in Computing Systems, CS2 2016 (2016)
2. Bernstein, D.: Differential addition chains. Technical report (2006). http://cr.yp.to/ecdh/diffchain-20060219.pdf
3. Bos, J.W., Costello, C., Hisil, H., Lauter, K.: High-performance scalar multiplication using 8-dimensional GLV/GLS decomposition. In: Bertoni, G., Coron, J.-S. (eds.) CHES 2013. LNCS, vol. 8086, pp. 331–348. Springer, Heidelberg (2013). https://doi.org/10.1007/978-3-642-40349-1_19
4. Brown, D.: Multi-dimensional montgomery ladders for elliptic curves. ePrint Archive: Report 2006/220. http://eprint.iacr.org/2006/220
5. Costello, C., Longa, P.: FourQ: four-dimensional decompositions on a Q-curve over the mersenne prime. In: Iwata, T., Cheon, J.H. (eds.) ASIACRYPT 2015. LNCS, vol. 9452, pp. 214–235. Springer, Heidelberg (2015). https://doi.org/10.1007/978-3-662-48797-6_10
6. Hisil, H., Wong, K.K.-H., Carter, G., Dawson, E.: Twisted Edwards curves revisited. In: Pieprzyk, J. (ed.) ASIACRYPT 2008. LNCS, vol. 5350, pp. 326–343. Springer, Heidelberg (2008). https://doi.org/10.1007/978-3-540-89255-7_20
7. Hutchinson, A., Karabina, K.: Constructing multidimensional differential addition chains and their applications. J. Cryptogr. Eng. 1–19 (2017). https://doi.org/10.1007/s13389-017-0177-2
8. Joye, M., Tunstall, M.: Exponent recoding and regular exponentiation algorithms. In: Preneel, B. (ed.) AFRICACRYPT 2009. LNCS, vol. 5580, pp. 334–349. Springer, Heidelberg (2009). https://doi.org/10.1007/978-3-642-02384-2_21
9. Montgomery, P.: Speeding the Pollard and elliptic curve methods of factorization. Math. Comput. **48**, 243–264 (1987)
10. Subramanya Rao, S.R.: Three dimensional montgomery ladder, differential point tripling on montgomery curves and point quintupling on Weierstrass' and Edwards curves. In: Pointcheval, D., Nitaj, A., Rachidi, T. (eds.) AFRICACRYPT 2016. LNCS, vol. 9646, pp. 84–106. Springer, Cham (2016). https://doi.org/10.1007/978-3-319-31517-1_5

Author Index

Printed in the United States
By Bookmasters